W9-BET-677

GRADES 2–3

2006–2007 YEARBOOK

The Education Center, Inc.
Greensboro, North Carolina

The Mailbox® 2006–2007 Grades 2–3 Yearbook

Editorial Team: Becky S. Andrews, Kimberley Bruck, Diane Badden, Debra Liverman, Karen A. Brudnak, Sharon Murphy, Hope Rodgers, Dorothy C. McKinney

Production Team: Lori Z. Henry, Margaret Freed (COVER ARTIST), Pam Crane, Rebecca Saunders, Chris Curry, Sarah Foreman, Theresa Lewis Goode, Greg D. Rieves, Eliseo De Jesus Santos II, Barry Slate, Donna K. Teal, Zane Williard, Kitty Campbell, Tazmen Carlisle, Kathy Coop, Marsha Heim, Lynette Dickerson, Mark Rainey

ISBN10 1-56234-815-9
ISBN13 978-156234-815-1
ISSN 1088-5544

Printed in the United States of America.

The Education Center, Inc.
P.O. Box 9753
Greensboro, NC 27429-0753

Contents

Departments

Features

Arts & Crafts

Fridge Frames

Post messages where they can't be missed with this eye-catching magnet!

Colleen Dabney
Williamsburg, VA

Materials for each student:
small tissue-box top (about 4" square)
2 pieces of magnetic tape
favorite student photo
tempera paint
paintbrush
assorted craft materials such as ribbon, glitter, stickers, and sequins
tape
glue

Steps:

1. Remove any plastic from the middle of the tissue-box top.
2. Paint the frame as desired.
3. After the paint has dried, use assorted craft materials to add details to your design.
4. Affix the two pieces of magnetic tape to the back of the frame, one in each top corner.
5. Tape a favorite photo to the back of the frame, cutting it to fit if necessary.

Seasonal Stained Glass

Materials for each child:
copy of a seasonal picture
piece of $8\frac{1}{2}$" x 11" cardboard
plastic wrap
aluminum foil
permanent markers in a variety of colors
tape

Directions:

1. Tape the seasonal picture onto the cardboard. Tightly stretch the plastic wrap over it and secure it with tape.
2. Trace and color the picture with the permanent markers.
3. Remove the plastic wrap from the cardboard.
4. Cover the cardboard with aluminum foil. Place the picture atop the foil and secure it with tape.

Misty Koeppen, Kuna, ID

A School of Spoon Fish

These colorful fish are easy to make! Give each child a 6" x 9" sheet of white construction paper and a plastic spoon. The student traces the spoon on his paper. Then he designs fins and a tail to create a fish. He cuts the fish out and turns it over. He personalizes his fish as desired and adds his name. Display the fish on a bulletin board titled "A School of Spoon Fish," or use the fish as labels for student desks or cubbies.

Lydia Hess, Chambersburg, PA

Owl Art

These owls are unbe-'leaf'-ably creative and provide super seasonal decorations for your classroom!

Patricia Wisniewski, Haine Elementary, Cranberry Township, PA

Materials for each child:

supply of brown leaves
6" oaktag circle (head)
8" oaktag circle (body)
construction paper scraps

Steps:

1. Slightly overlap the two circles and glue them together forming a body as shown.
2. Glue brown leaves on the circle, completely covering the owl's body.
3. Add construction paper eyes and a beak.
4. Glue two leaves (ears) to the back of the owl.

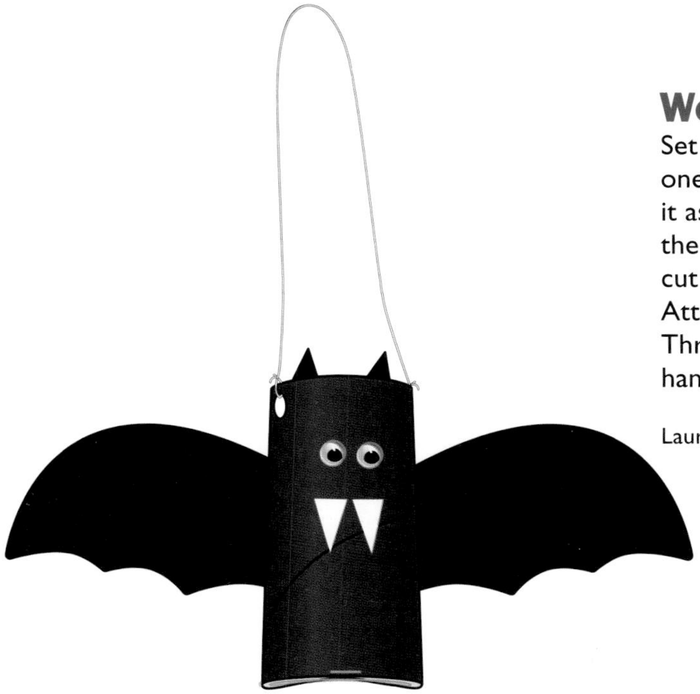

We're Batty!

Set a spooky scene with this winged wonder! Staple shut one end of a toilet paper tube. Paint the tube black and set it aside to dry. Use a white crayon to trace the wings from the pattern on page 32 onto black construction paper. Then cut out the wings and glue them to the tube's back as shown. Attach construction paper fangs and ears and two wiggle eyes. Thread a length of fishing line through two punched holes for hanging.

Laura LaPerna, Tedder Elementary, Pompano Beach, FL

Leaf Magnets

Post important papers with these easy-to-make magnets!

Amy Barsanti, Pines Elementary, Plymouth, NC

Materials for each child:

small ball of air-dry or wet-set clay
small leaf
plastic knife
red, orange, yellow, or brown tempera paint
paintbrush
small magnet
craft glue

Steps:

1. Press the ball of clay to ⅛" thickness. Gently press the leaf into the middle of the clay, making sure to get the full imprint of the leaf, including the veins.
2. Cut around the leaf with the plastic knife. Gently peel the leaf off the clay.
3. Slightly curl the edges of the leaf and set it aside to dry (or immerse it in water if using wet-set clay).
4. Paint the leaf in a desired color.
5. Use craft glue to affix the magnet to the leaf's back.

Arts & Crafts

A Taste of the Holidays

Treat students to these easy-to-make peppermint projects! Then post the projects around the room as individual candies or string them together for a festive garland.

Darla Sanders, Allen Academy, Bryan, TX

Materials for each student:
two 6" white paper plates
ruler
red paint
plastic wrap
yarn

Steps:
1. Draw a small dot in the center of each plate's back. Use the dot as a guide to divide each plate into eight equal parts.
2. Paint alternating sections on both plates red. Allow drying time.
3. When the paint is dry, line up the matching sections and staple the two plates together to make a peppermint.
4. Place the peppermint on a piece of plastic wrap, allowing the wrap to extend past the peppermint on both sides.
5. Place another piece of plastic wrap atop the peppermint. Twist the two pieces together on each side and secure each with a piece of yarn. Then fan out the plastic wrap.

Soft and Fluffy

No matter what the weather is like, this snowman is sure to please! To make the snowman's head and body, glue two clumps of pillow batting to a sheet of blue construction paper as shown. Add more batting across the bottom of the paper. Then use construction paper scraps to glue facial details to the snowman's head and use leftover gift wrap or tissue paper to fashion a scarf. Finally, sprinkle glitter over the snowman. If desired, use the snowman as a story starter for a narrative or descriptive paragraph.

Christine Themeles, Louise Davy Trahan School, Tewksbury, MA

Sweet Treat

To prepare this mouthwatering project, trace several holiday-themed cookie-cutter shapes onto paper. Enlarge the shapes on tagboard and cut them out. Next, have each student choose a cookie shape and trace it onto manila cardstock. She covers the inside of the shape with a half-and-half mixture of glue and shaving cream. Then she decorates her shape with sprinkles or glitter. After allowing the project to dry overnight, she cuts it out. If desired, have each student write on a recipe card a poem about the holiday represented by the shape. Post each poem near its matching project.

Laura Johnson, South Decatur Elementary
Greensburg, IN

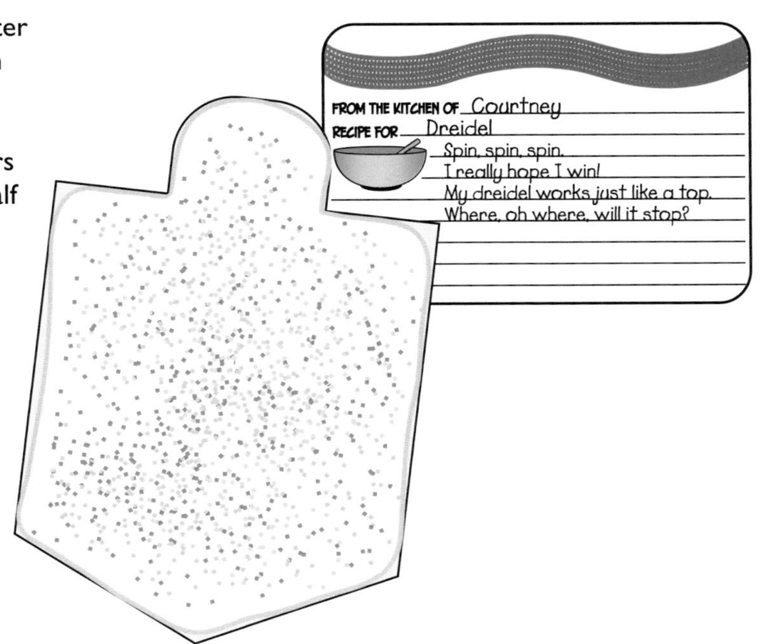

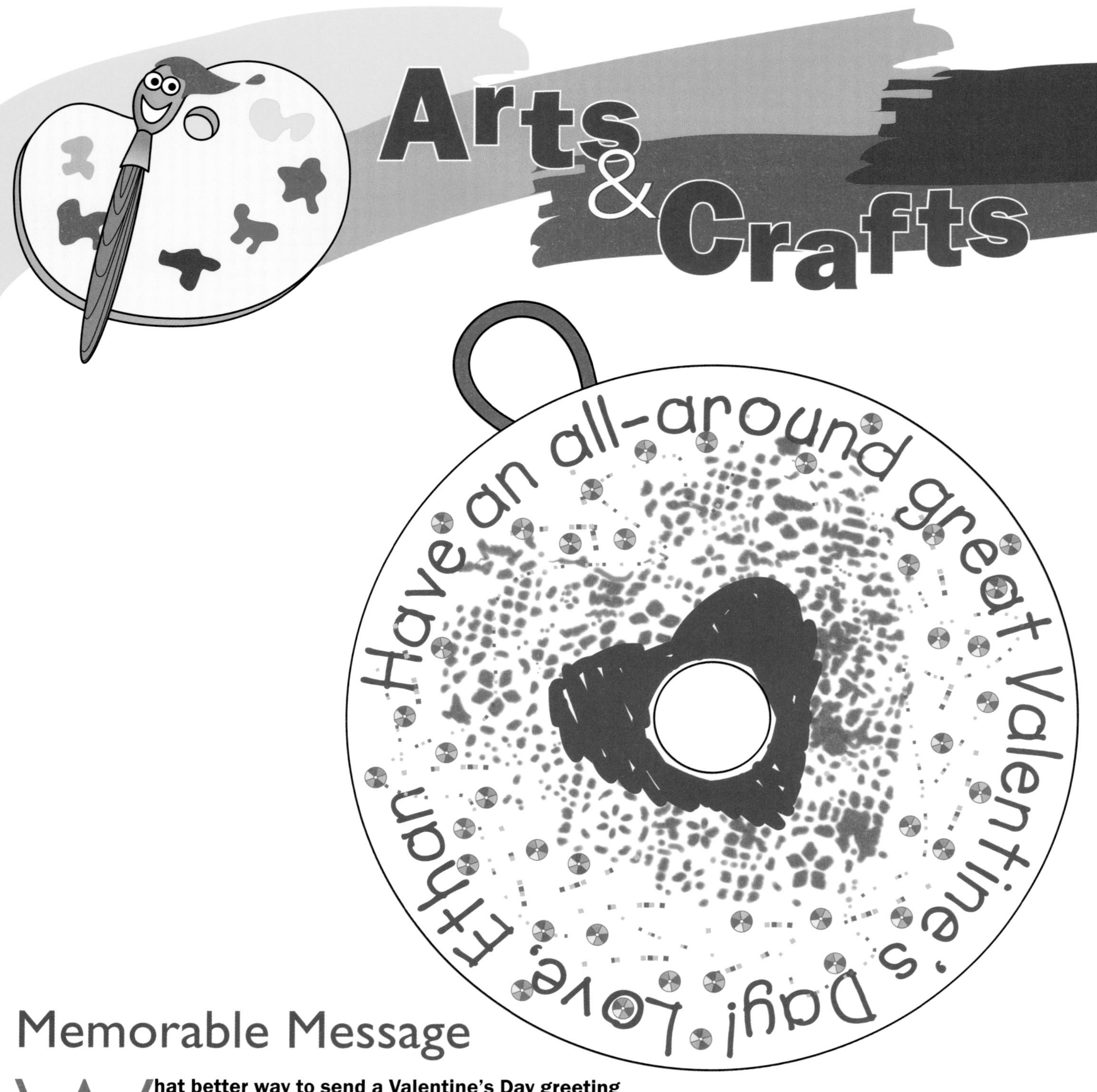

Memorable Message

What better way to send a Valentine's Day greeting to a loved one than with this special gift! Paint one side of an unwanted CD white. While the paint is drying, cut a four-inch doily into a heart shape. Place the heart atop the CD and sponge-paint over the doily with red, pink, or purple paint. Carefully remove the doily and allow time for the paint to dry. Then use a permanent marker to write a message like the one shown. Add desired details with glitter and sequins. To complete the craft, glue on a ribbon hanger.

Deb Dailey, Garfield School, Ottawa, Kansas

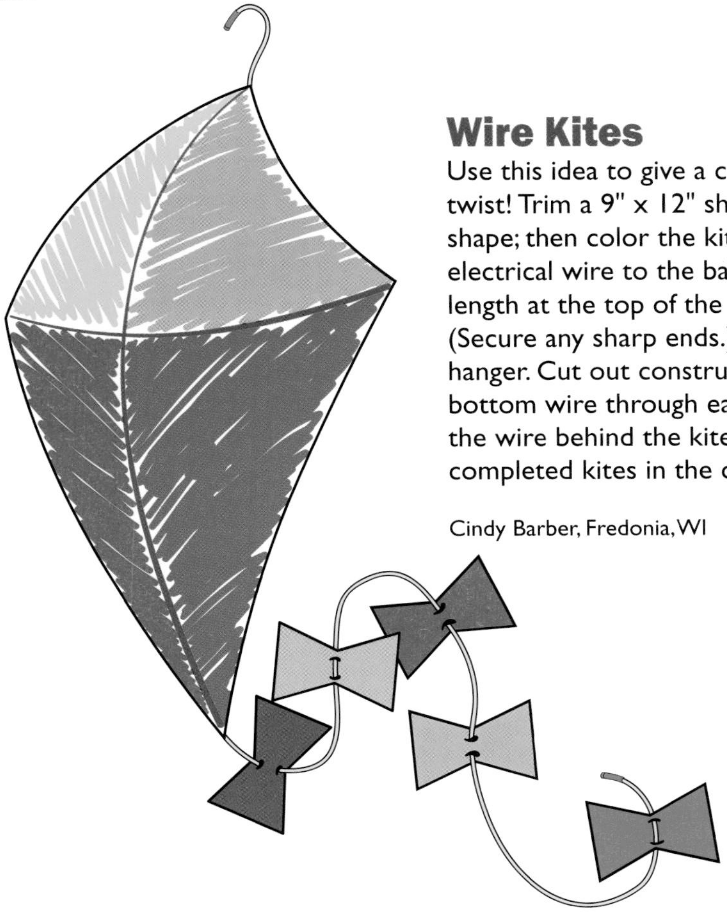

Wire Kites

Use this idea to give a construction paper kite cutout a unique twist! Trim a 9" x 12" sheet of construction paper into a kite shape; then color the kite as desired. Tape a length of colorful electrical wire to the back of the kite, leaving a four-inch length at the top of the kite and a longer length at the bottom. (Secure any sharp ends.) Bend the top of the wire to form a hanger. Cut out construction paper bow shapes; then poke the bottom wire through each bow to resemble a kite tail. Bend the wire behind the kite to add a 3-D effect. Suspend the completed kites in the classroom for a high-flying display!

Cindy Barber, Fredonia, WI

Simple Shamrocks

This textured mosaic is sure to bring good luck! Trace a tagboard shamrock cutout several times on a sheet of white construction paper. Place a textured item such as sandpaper, a flyswatter, or the bottom of a shoe under the paper. Then rub the side of an unwrapped green crayon over the paper to color a shamrock. Use items of different textures and crayons of different shades of green to rub over the remaining shamrocks. To complete the project, make similar rubbings in a mosaic fashion until the entire paper is covered. If desired, display the finished projects along with the title "A Field of Good Luck."

Mary Ann Gildroy, Roundup, MT

Arts & Crafts

Poppy Pins

This wearable craft doubles as a way to honor fallen soldiers on Memorial Day. To make a pin, fold a piece of red tissue paper in half three times. Next, draw a simple heart shape on the top layer and, cutting through all layers, cut along the outline. Place one of the resulting hearts on the work space and apply glue to one half. Lay the opposite half of another heart atop the glued section so that the points of the two hearts meet. Apply glue to the remaining half of the second heart and continue in this manner until the poppy shape is complete. Then use craft glue to secure a plastic button to the middle of the poppy shape. Allow a few minutes of drying time; then use craft glue to attach a clasp pin to the back. If desired, have each student write a paragraph naming other ways he could honor a fallen soldier on Memorial Day or provide time for students to research the tradition behind wearing a poppy on Memorial Day.

Cursive Critter

Combine handwriting practice with symmetry, and a unique springtime bug appears. To make one, fold a piece of 9" x 12" paper in half lengthwise; then unfold the paper. Sign your name along the fold with a dark crayon, exaggerating the final stroke. To make a mirror image of the writing, refold the paper and press firmly over the surface using an open palm or scissor handles. Then unfold the paper and use a crayon to darken the impression. Rotate the paper so the last letter of the name forms the bug's antennae at the top of the page. Color the bug so symmetry is maintained; then cut around the shape and glue it to a paper leaf or two.

Libby Sluder, Taylor Hicks School, Prescott, AZ

Flower Power

Honor moms with an arrangement of flowers that will last! To start, wrap a piece of green construction paper around a plastic cylinder, such as a chip or grated cheese container. Glue the paper to the cylinder and fringe-cut the excess paper at the top so that it resembles grass blades. To make a flower, cut two tissue paper circles and lay one on top of the other. Pinch the middle of the circles and fan out the paper. Then twist a green pipe cleaner stem around the pinched section and wrap tissue paper leaves around the stem. Place the flower in the cylinder and, if desired, tie a decorative ribbon around the cylinder. Include a handmade Mother's Day card and the gift is ready to go!

Kristie Ellis, Rand Road Elementary, Raleigh, NC

Symbol of Freedom

Honor an American symbol with this unique plaque.

Materials for each student:
- **copy of an eagle pattern from page 18**
- **dried black beans (feathers and eye)**
- **dried navy beans (head and tail)**
- **dried yellow split peas or orange lentils (talons and beak)**
- **dried green split peas (branch)**
- **4" x 6" piece of heavy tagboard**
- **length of ribbon**
- **hole puncher**
- **scissors**
- **glue**

Steps:
1. **Punch two holes through the tagboard as shown.**
2. **Cut out the eagle pattern and glue it on the tagboard.**
3. **Apply glue to the pattern one small area at a time. Arrange the appropriate dried food in each area.**
4. **When the project is dry, feed the ribbon through the holes and tie the ends together.**

Laura Edge, Washtenaw Christian Academy, Saline, MI

smart
handy
fun
athletic
Dad
strong
playful
interesting
handsome

What do you know?
It's a special tic-tac-toe,
Not for any average joe,
But for you, the best daddy-o!

Happy Father's Day!

Love,
Camille

Fun and Games

This Father's Day card takes the shape of a tic-tac-toe board. To begin, a child folds a piece of 6" x 12" construction paper in half to make a card. Next, she draws a grid of two-inch squares on the front of the card as shown. She illustrates and labels in the center square a picture of her dad or another important male figure. Then she writes a word or phrase that describes him in each remaining square. Finally, she copies on the inside of the card the poem shown and adds a personalized message.

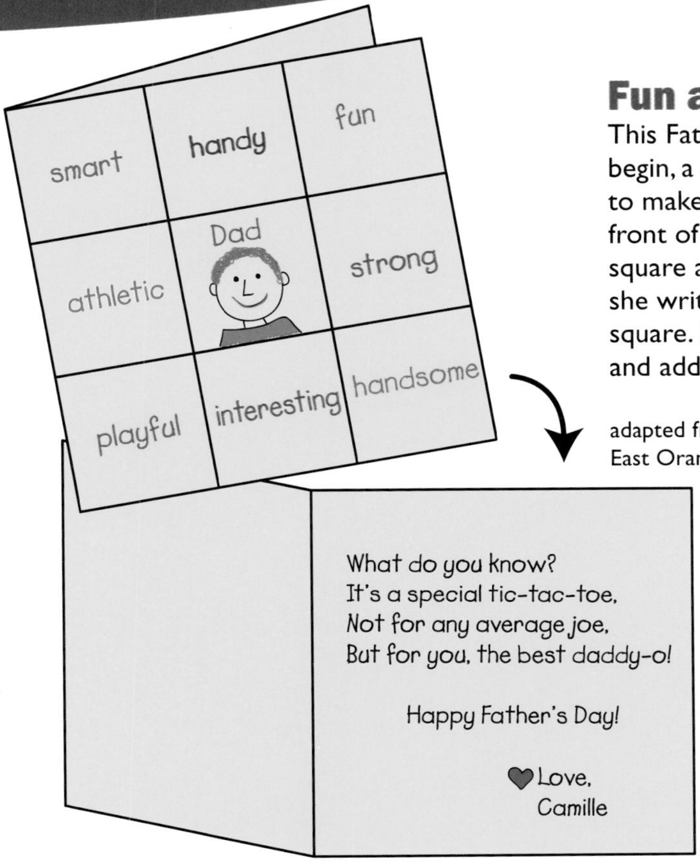

adapted from an idea by Anna Walsh, Mildred Barry Garvin Microsociety School
East Orange, NJ

Soak Up the Sun

To make this colorful suncatcher, tape a piece of plastic wrap to a file folder or piece of cardboard. Brush glue on the plastic wrap; then place one-inch squares of tissue paper on top. Apply another thin coat of glue atop the tissue paper. When dry, cut out a desired animal shape, glue on wiggle eyes, and punch a hole through the top. Feed a piece of yarn through the hole and tie the ends together in a knot. Hang the completed crafts near a window.

Eagle Patterns

Use with "Symbol of Freedom" on page 16.

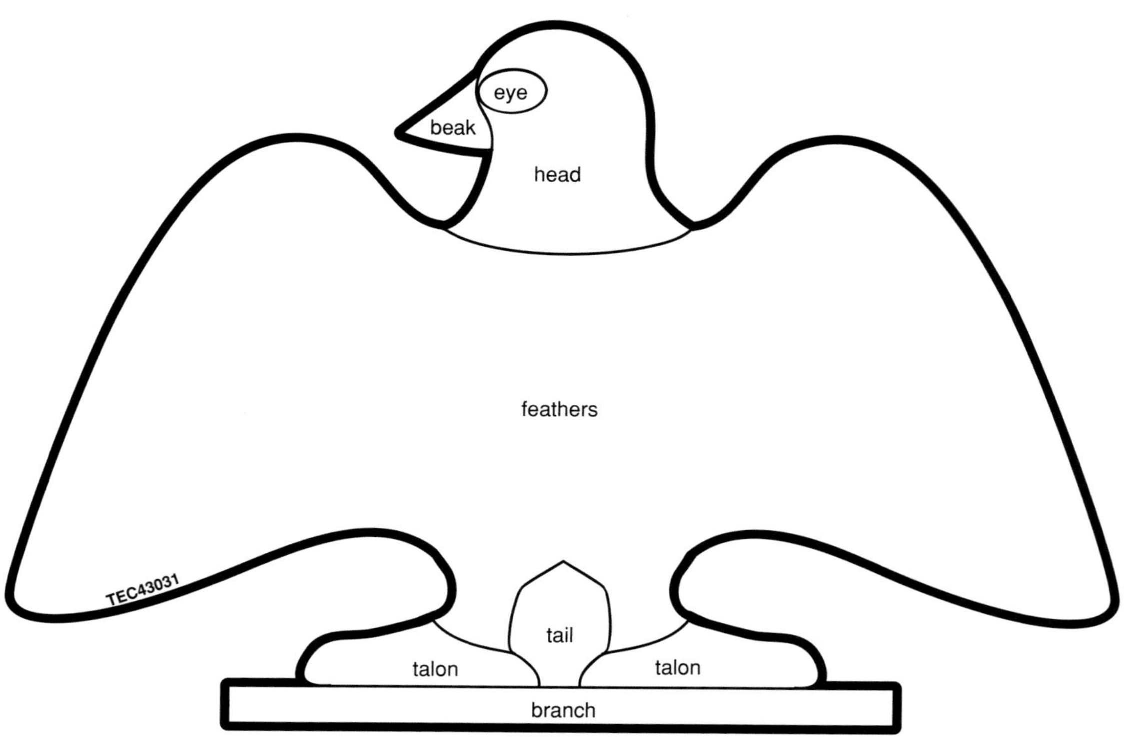

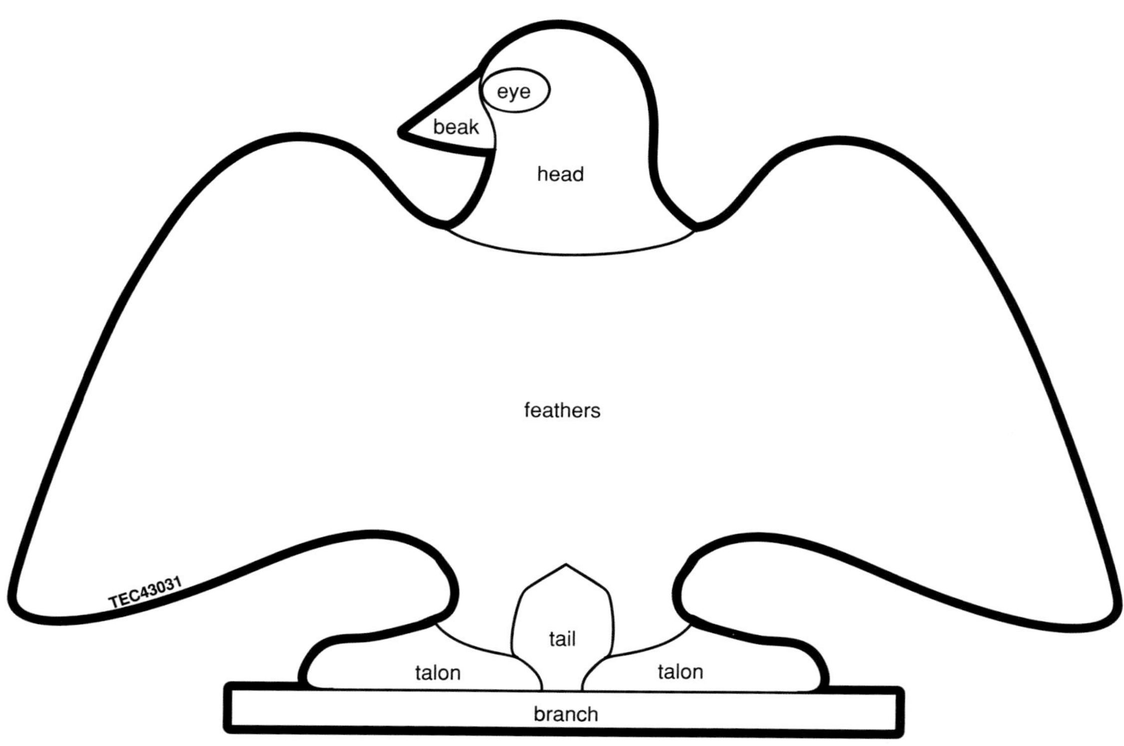

Classroom Displays

CLASSROOM

This simple display gives students a chance to tell about their summer! In advance, post on a bulletin board a sun cutout labeled as shown. Begin by giving each child a yellow or an orange sentence strip. Have him write a strong, descriptive sentence about something he did over the summer. Display the sentences as rays around the sun. As a follow-up, have students identify which classmate wrote each sentence.

Laura Hess
Providence School
Greencastle, PA

Ring in a new school year and welcome students at the same time! In advance, make a class supply of the cell phone pattern on page 31 on colored construction paper. Label each phone's screen with a child's name. Post the phones on a bulletin board around a character with the caption shown.

Jo Ann Stambaugh
Astoria Elementary
Astoria, IL

Reinforce parts of speech with this interactive display! In advance, make a supply of the apple patterns on page 31 on construction paper. Cut the apples out; then label each with a noun or a verb and program its back for self-checking. Also post on a wall a large tree with branches that are accessible to students. Use Velcro fasteners to attach the apples to the tree's branches. Then place two baskets below, one labeled "Nouns" and the other labeled "Verbs." A child visits the display and picks the apples off the tree, placing them in the matching basket. After all of the apples are sorted, he turns them over to check his work. Then he reattaches the apples to the tree for the next student.

Judi Lesnansky
New Hope Academy
Youngstown, OH

CLASSROOM

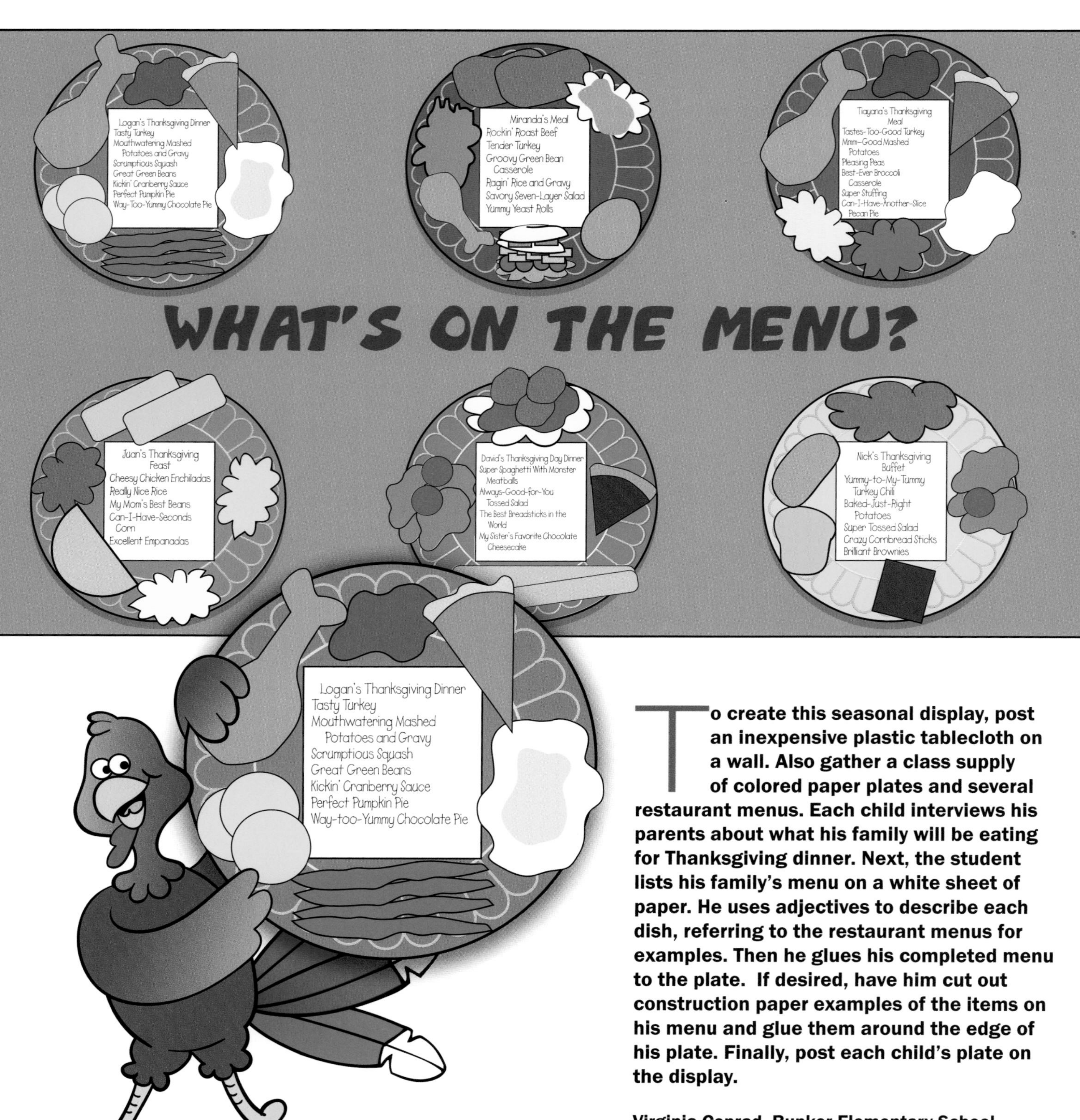

To create this seasonal display, post an inexpensive plastic tablecloth on a wall. Also gather a class supply of colored paper plates and several restaurant menus. Each child interviews his parents about what his family will be eating for Thanksgiving dinner. Next, the student lists his family's menu on a white sheet of paper. He uses adjectives to describe each dish, referring to the restaurant menus for examples. Then he glues his completed menu to the plate. If desired, have him cut out construction paper examples of the items on his menu and glue them around the edge of his plate. Finally, post each child's plate on the display.

Virginia Conrad, Bunker Elementary School, Bunker, MO

DISPLAYS

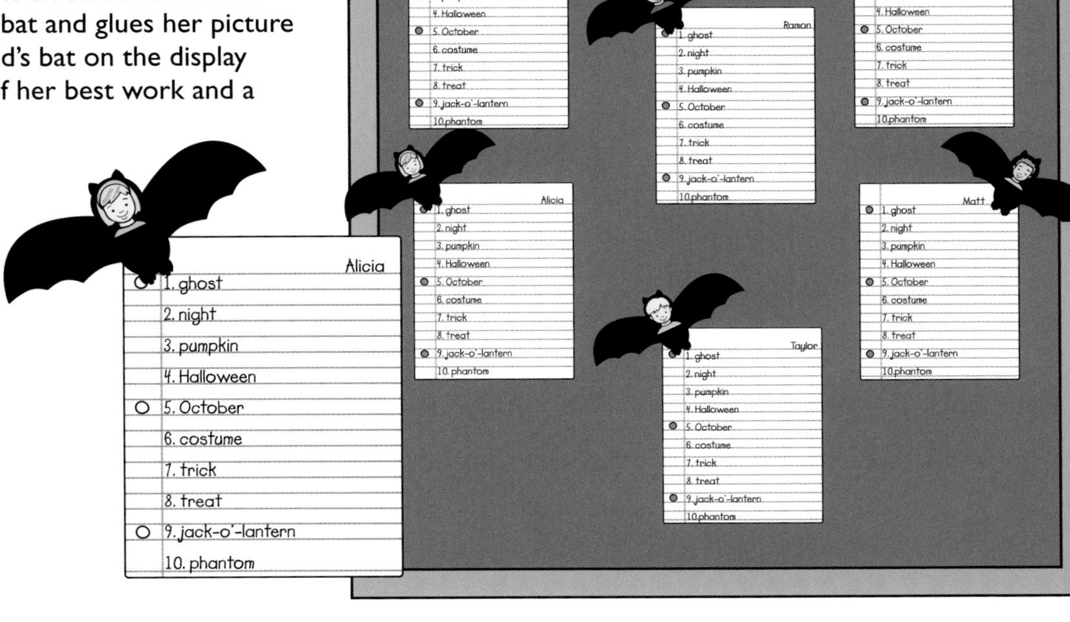

Showcase super student work! Make a class supply of the bat pattern on page 32. Also have each child bring in a favorite close up and have her cut out her head from the photo. The student cuts out the pattern and uses a white crayon to trace it on black construction paper. Then she cuts out the bat and glues her picture to it as shown. Post each child's bat on the display along with a recent sample of her best work and a title like the one shown.

LeeAnn Brantley
Beggs Elementary
Beggs, OK

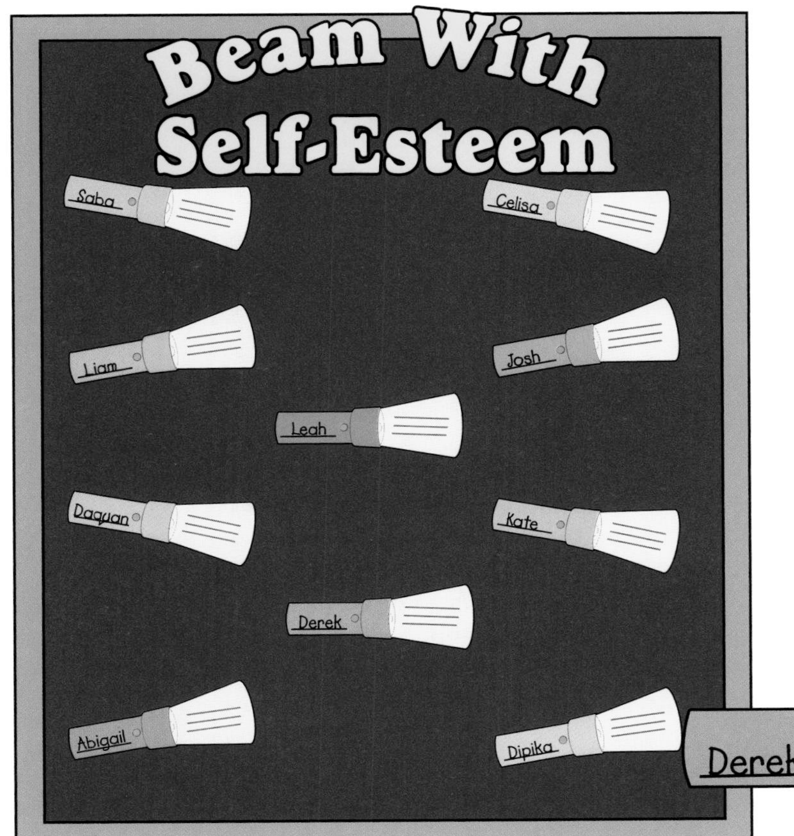

Shine a light on students' strengths! Make a class supply of the flashlight pattern on page 32. Each child writes his name on the handle and lists in the beam something that makes him feel good about himself, such as an accomplishment or helping someone. Then he lightly colors his flashlight and posts it on a board with the title shown.

Lori Henson, Wichita, KS

TRIM THE TREE

Review basic facts with this interactive display! Post a paper evergreen tree. Copy a supply of the ornaments on page 33 on colored paper. Write a sum on each ornament's top and a matching fact on its bottom. Cut apart the ornaments as shown and affix a small piece of Velcro fastener on the back side of each bottom piece. Mount each ornament's top on the tree and attach a piece of Velcro fastener below it. Then invite each child to visit the display and match each ornament bottom to its top.

Sebastian Niz and Gwen Rusher, Houston, TX

DISPLAYS

'Tis the season to share student wishes! Take a photograph of each child pretending to sleep. Next, give each student a sheet of white construction paper and have him fold down the top third of the paper. He glues his photograph to the paper's bottom section. Then he sketches a picture of something he wishes for on the folded section and draws a dream-cloud shape around it. Finally, he lifts the flap and writes a description of the wish underneath. If desired, have him cut out a fabric or gift wrap rectangle and glue it below the paper as a blanket. Post students' wishes on a board with the title shown.

Janice Ferguson, Longfellow Elementary, Idaho Falls, ID

Bring back memories of the year with this rousing display! Make a class supply of the noisemaker pattern on page 33 and give one to each student. Have her write three sentences on the cutout: one telling about a happy event from the past year, one event from the past year that she would like to change, and one thing she would like to experience in the coming year. Then have her cut out the pattern and outline it with crayon, marker, or colored glitter glue. Post the completed noisemakers with streamers and ribbons.

Cindy Barber, Fredonia, WI

Sweet Similes

Chocolate is...

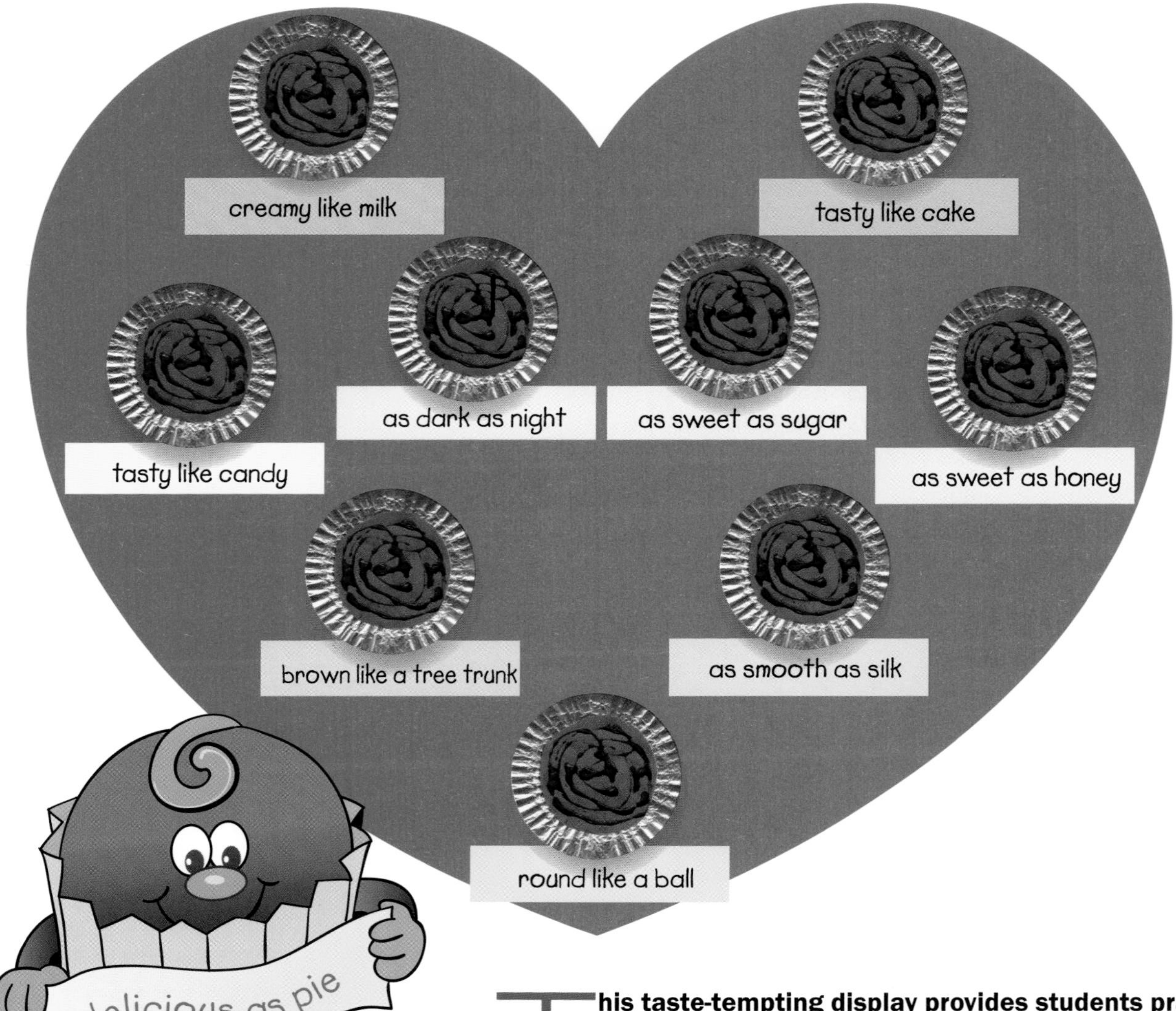

This taste-tempting display provides students practice with writing similes. In advance, use brown powdered tempera paint to tint a bottle of white glue brown.

Have each child glue a three-inch brown construction paper circle to a flattened cupcake liner. Then have her drizzle the brown glue over the circle to resemble a piece of chocolate candy. Set the resulting chocolates aside to dry. Next, ask each student to write on a seven-inch paper strip a simile about chocolate. Mount a large heart cut from bulletin board paper on the wall so that it resembles a candy box. Then attach each child's chocolate and simile strip to the heart and add the title shown.

adapted from an idea by Cindy Barber
Fredonia, WI

DISPLAYS

Reinforce math facts with this interactive display. Color and cut out several tagboard copies of the pattern on page 34. Carefully cut on the dotted line to make a slit. Then program each pattern with a different math fact. For each math fact, label a 4½-inch orange construction paper circle with the answer. Add details so that each circle resembles a basketball. Mount the basketball hoops on a board with the title shown. Place the basketballs and an answer key near the display. When a child visits the display, he places each ball in the corresponding hoop. After verifying all of his answers, he removes the balls for the next student.

adapted from an idea by Wendy Lunk, Bernice Young School, Burlington Township, NJ

Students share information about their favorite books with this dynamic display! Invite each child to use art supplies to transform a paper plate into a lion's face. Then have each student write on a speech-bubble cutout a short description of a favorite book. Showcase each lion with its speech bubble and the title shown.

Mederise Burke, Courthouse Road Elementary, Spotsylvania, VA

CLASSROOM

Caught Being Good!

To encourage positive behaviors, post a character and a paper fishing rod near a paper pond. Copy a fish (pattern on page 35) on colored paper for each child. Have each child cut out a fish and write his name on it. Post each fish in the pond. When a child is seen following a class rule or helping a classmate, move the child's fish to the fishing line. At the end of the day, return the fish to the pond.

April Fowler, Hunterdale Elementary, Franklin, VA

DISPLAYS

Have each child trim a sheet of green paper into a lily pad and then write her name on it. Mount the lily pads on a display as shown. A student reads a book that she would recommend to her classmates and completes a copy of the toad pattern on page 36. If desired, have her outline or lightly color the cutout. Then post the toad atop her lily pad.

Sarah Durspek, Skyview Elementary, Pinellas Park, FL

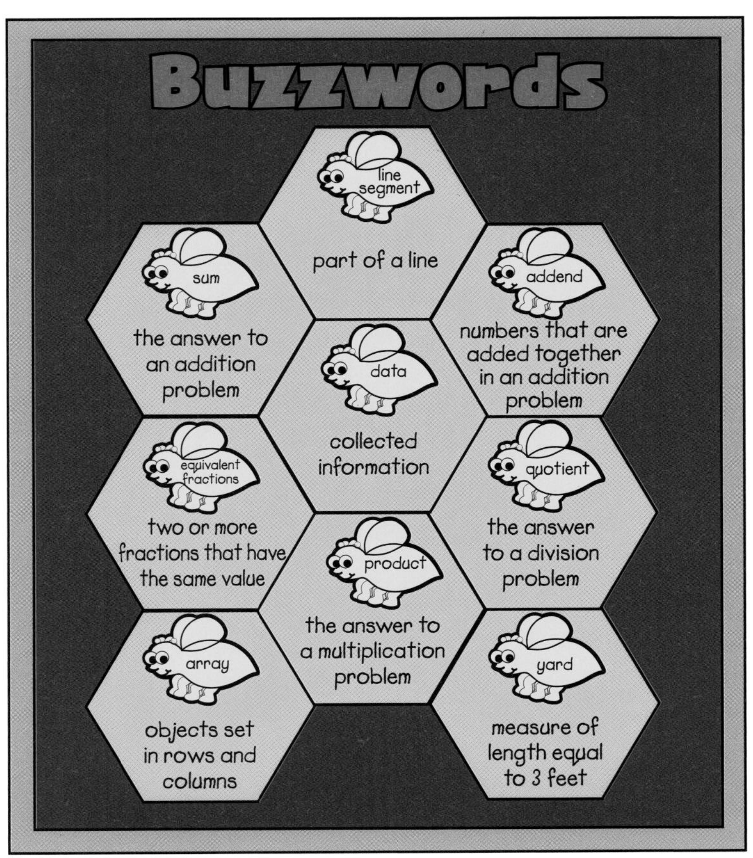

Review important vocabulary words with this interactive display. Enlarge and copy a supply of the honeycomb pattern on page 36. Also make an equal number of copies of the bee pattern on page 36. Cut out the patterns; then write a definition on each honeycomb. Mount the honeycombs side by side on a board. Next, write each matching word on a bee cutout and post the bees randomly around the display. A child visiting the display reads each definition and places the matching bee atop its definition on the honeycomb.

Reflect on one great year while preparing for the next with this easy-to-make display. Have each student create a list of her ten favorite memories from the school year. Then have her draw a small illustration next to each. Post the lists on a display and, if desired, include photos of the events as well. Keep the display posted throughout the summer to welcome new students in the fall.

Jessica Amend, McKenzie Elementary, Wilmette, IL

Reviewing verbs is the focus of this interactive display! Post two paper baseball mitts and label them as shown. Next, make a supply of the baseball patterns on page 35 and cut out the copies. Write a verb on each ball, being sure to include examples of both helping verbs and action verbs. Attach a small piece of the hook side of a Velcro fastener to the back of each ball; then attach pieces of the loop side of Velcro fasteners to each baseball mitt. Invite each child to visit this display and place each baseball on its corresponding mitt.

Antoinette Griffin, John G. Shedd Elementary
Chicago, IL

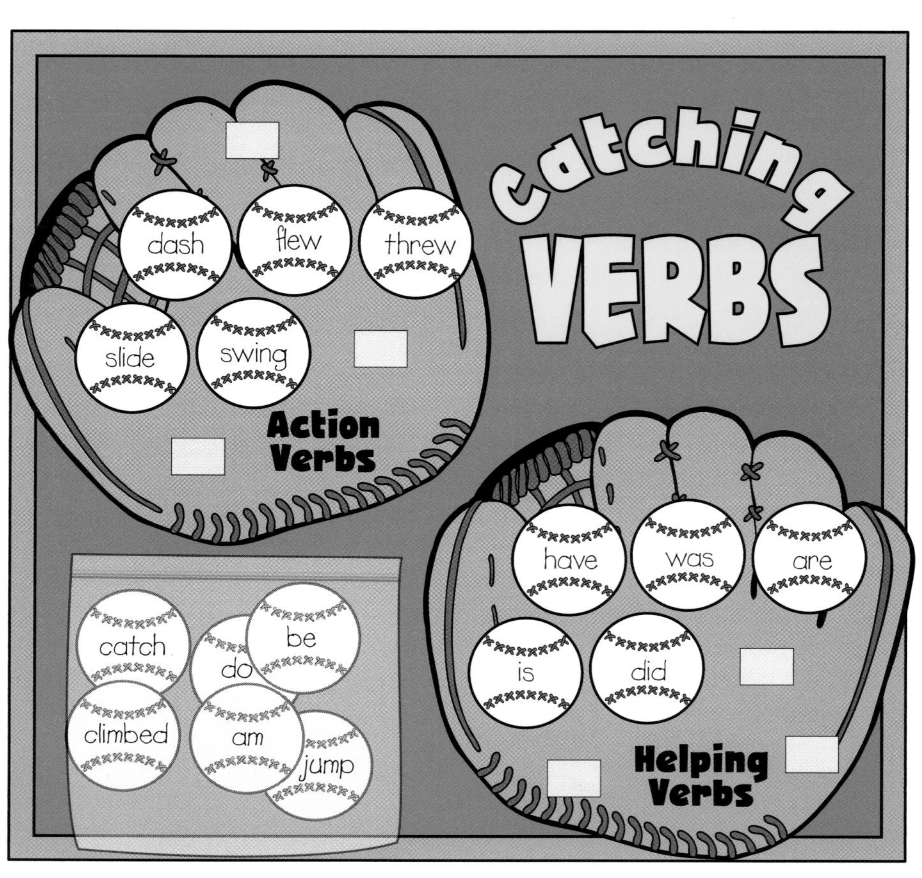

Cell Phone Pattern

Use with "Calling for an 'Ex-cell-ent' Year!" on page 21.

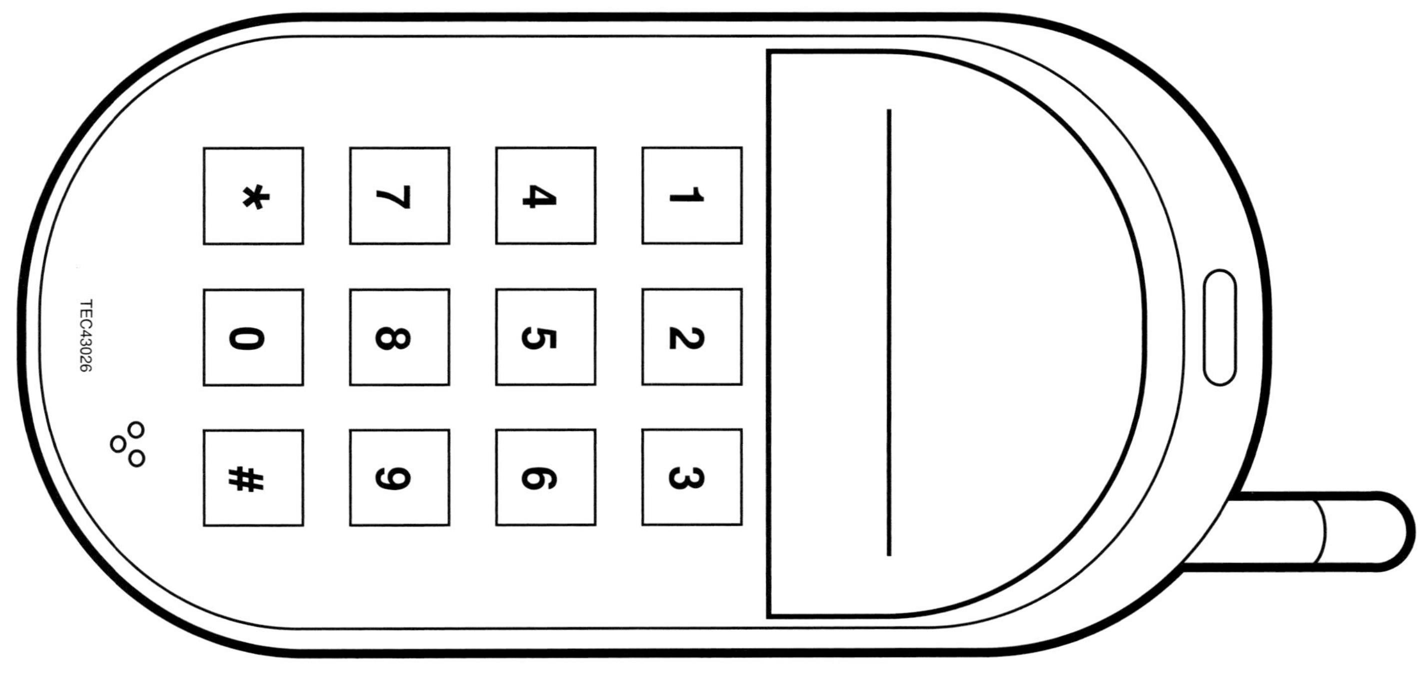

Apple Patterns

Use with "Apple Picking" on page 21.

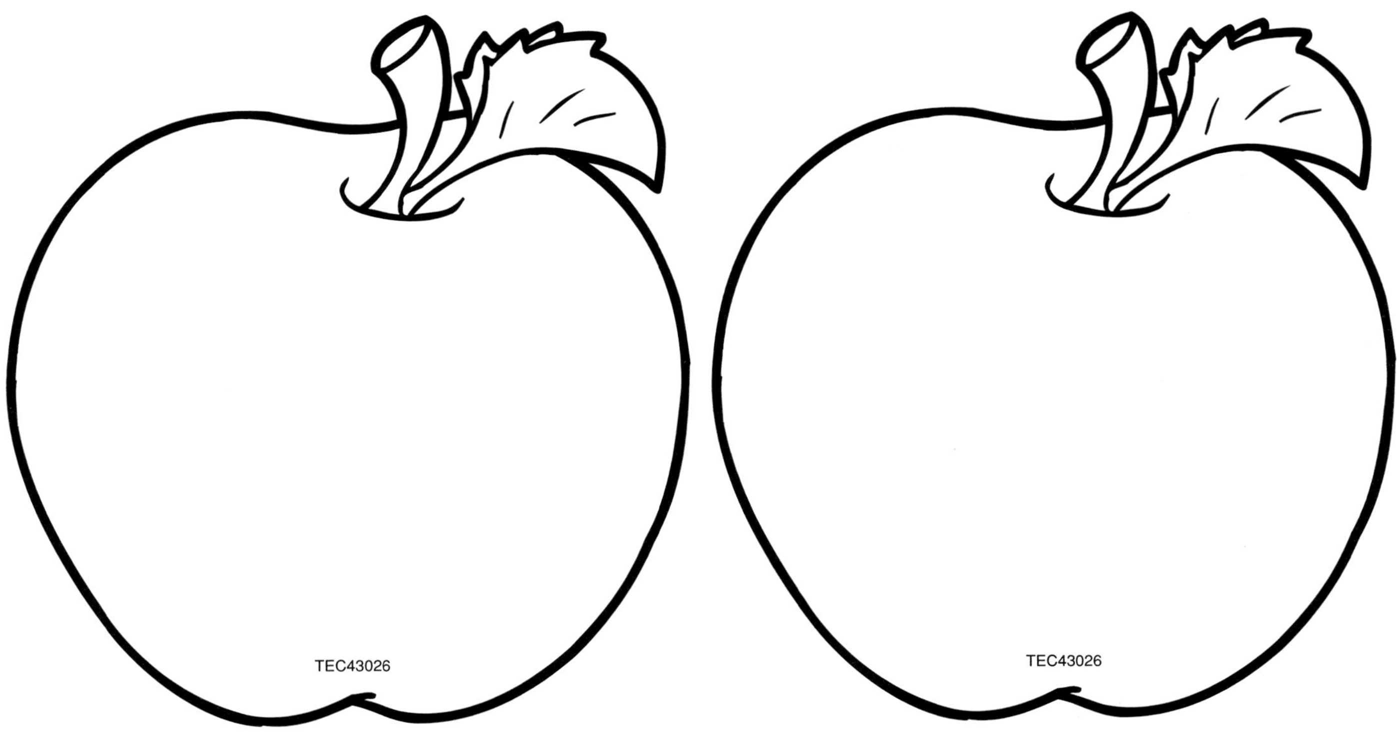

Bat Pattern

Use with "We've Gone Batty for Good Work!" on page 23 and "We're Batty!" on page 9.

TEC43027

Flashlight Pattern

Use with "Beam With Self-Esteem" on page 23.

TEC43027

Ornament Patterns

Use with "Trim the Tree" on page 24.

Noisemaker Pattern

Use with "Let's Hear It for the New Year!" on page 25.

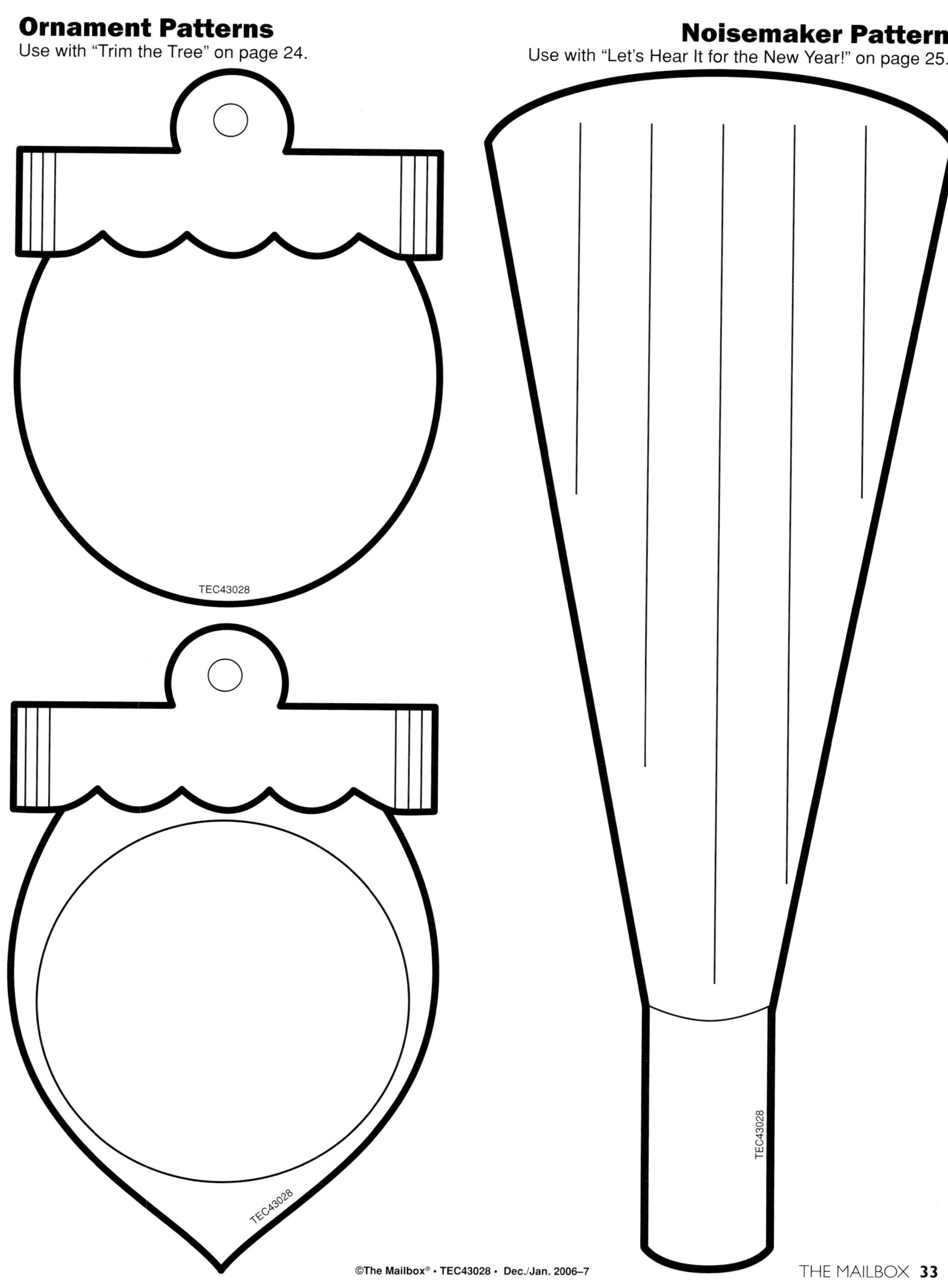

Basketball Hoop Pattern

Use with "Math Champs" on page 27.

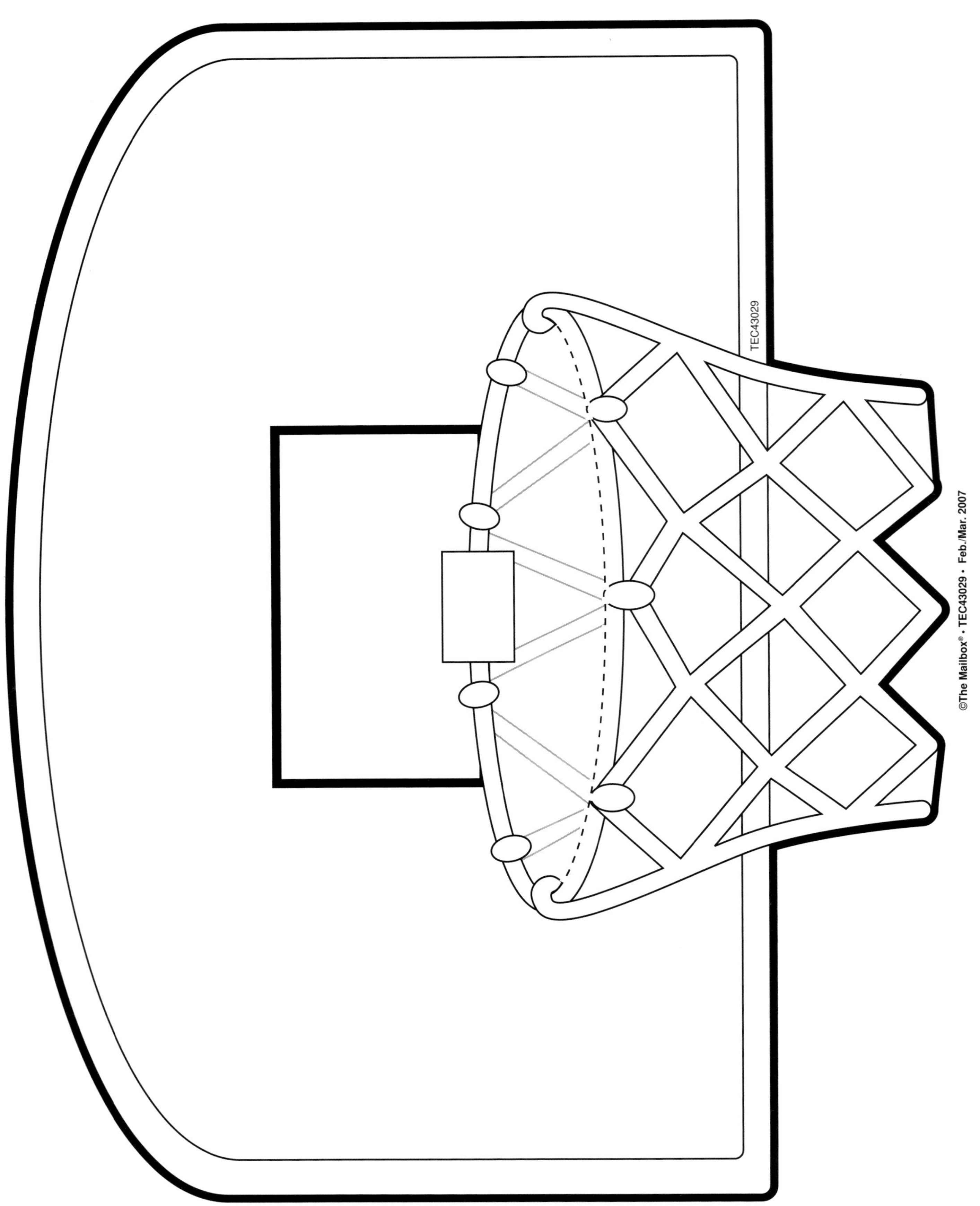

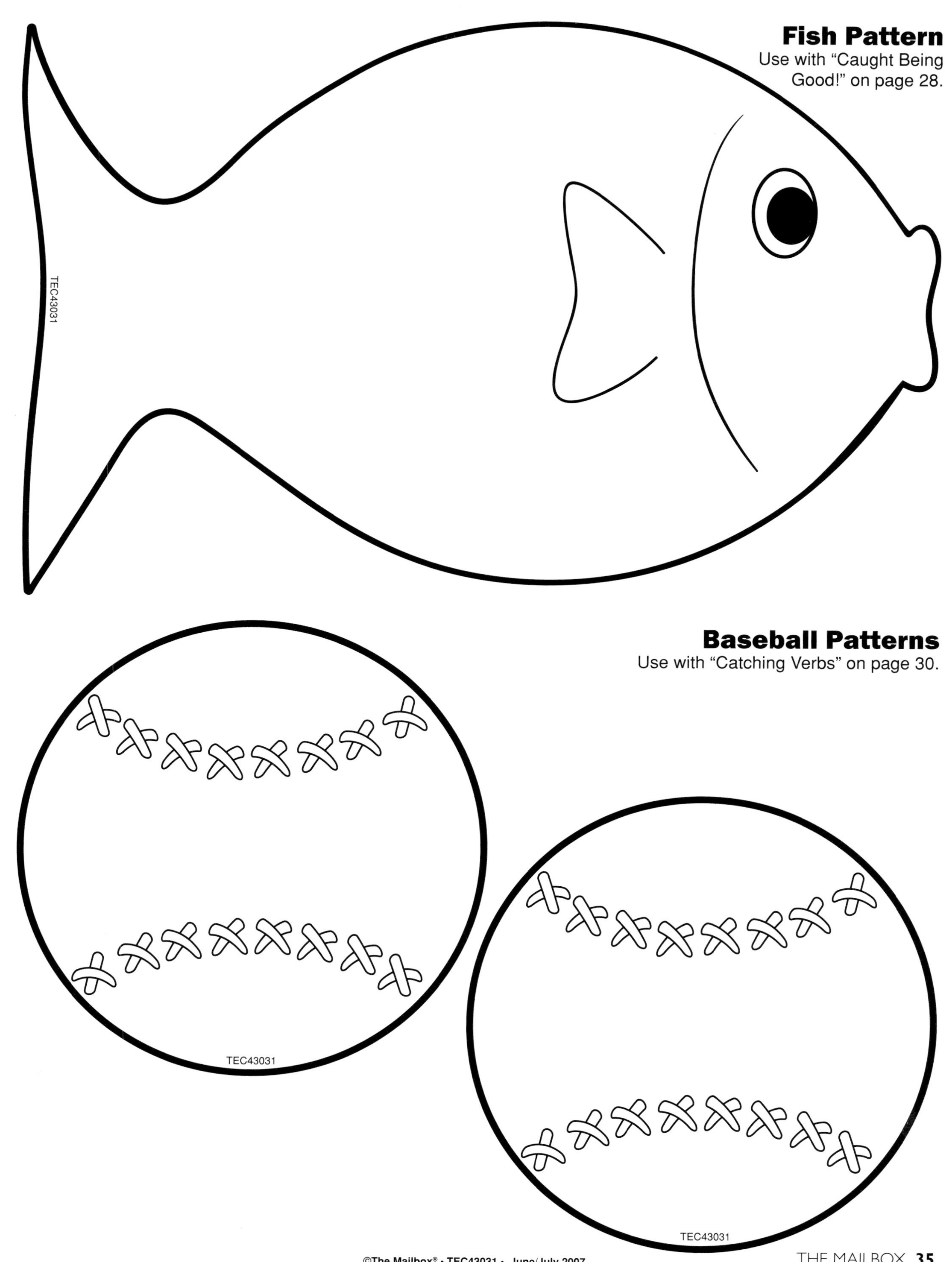
Fish Pattern
Use with "Caught Being Good!" on page 28.
TEC43031
Baseball Patterns
Use with "Catching Verbs" on page 30.
TEC43031
TEC43031

Toad Pattern

Use with "'Toad-ally' Cool Books" on page 29.

Honeycomb and Bee Patterns

Use with "Buzzwords" on page 29.

Learning Centers

Learning Centers

Peekaboo Numbers

Visualizing numbers in standard and expanded form is as easy as 1, 2, 3! In advance, cut a supply of sentence strips in half, making enough for each child to have two. Place the sentence strips and a die at a center. A child rolls the die and writes the number as the hundreds digit at the far left end of a sentence strip as shown. He repeats the process, writing the second number as the tens digit in the middle and the last number as the ones digit at the far right. Next, he fills in the value for each digit and adds plus signs where needed. He folds the first and last digits back and then creases the folded ends of the strip toward the tens digit. He reads the number with the strip closed and then opens the strip to reveal the number in expanded form. He repeats the process to show a new number with expanded and standard form.

Amanda Darmo, New Town Elementary
Owings Mills, MD

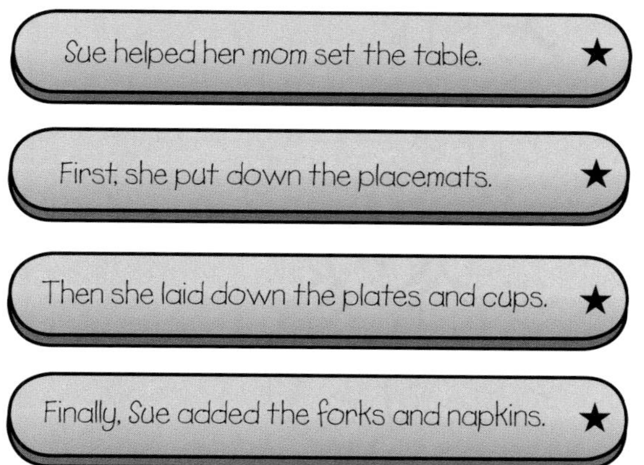

Story Sticks

Jumbo-size craft sticks are all you need to provide sequencing practice! To make one set, code each of four craft sticks with a small shape so that matching sticks can be returned to the same bag. Then use a fine-tip permanent marker to write one sentence of a sequential story on each stick; place the sticks in a resealable plastic bag. A student chooses a bag and reads the sentences. She arranges them in order from beginning to end and copies the story on her paper. Finally, she returns the sticks to the original bag.

Virginia Conrad, Bunker R-3 Elementary, Bunker, MO

Word Family Fun

Help students organize word families with this sorting activity. Place two six-section scrapbook pages in a photo album. Also write two word family endings on index cards. Place one card on each page as shown. Then write and illustrate a word that belongs to each word family on an index card. Make five cards per word family. Put the cards in a bag and place it with the photo album at a center. A child reads each card and slides it into the matching album page. When all of the words have been sorted, he copies the word families onto his paper.

Julie Larson, Jefferson Elementary, New Ulm, MN

Pattern Folders

To prepare this repeating pattern center, draw a two-column, ten-row grid on a file folder, numbering each row. Use stickers to create a pattern in the left column of each row. In the right column, provide a choice of three stickers to extend the pattern and label each one "A," "B," or "C." Turn the folder over and record an answer key; then laminate the folder for durability. A student looks at the first pattern, finds the sticker that completes the pattern, and writes its letter on her paper. She repeats the process with the remaining rows. Then she turns the folder over to check her work.

Virginia Conrad

Main-Idea Mobiles

Help students get the hang of main idea and supporting details! In advance, copy a nonfiction paragraph that correlates with a unit of study. Underline the paragraph's main idea and then place it at a center with 6" x 18" construction paper strips, crayons, a hole puncher, and yarn. A child reads the paragraph, looking for the supporting details. Next, he folds a strip into fourths, labeling the bottom of the first section with the main idea and the remaining sections with supporting details as shown. He illustrates each section; then he punches two holes at the top. Finally, he feeds a length of yarn through the holes and ties a knot.

Kelli Jones, East Clayton Elementary, Clayton, NC

In the Field

These seasonal scarecrows are just the thing to help students identify odd and even numbers. Make a copy of page 50 and mount it on construction paper. Laminate it and then cut out the cards. Color-code the backs of matching even cards with one color and odd cards with another; then place them at a center along with an overhead pen. A student chooses a crow card and determines whether the amount shown is odd or even. If needed, she uses the overhead pen to circle the pairs in the set. Then she finds the matching scarecrow card. When all matches have been made, she turns the cards over to check her work.

Sentences in a Stamp

Combine rubber stamping and imaginations to make sentence practice fun! Place a supply of seasonal rubber stamps, ink pads, and writing paper at a center. A child chooses a stamp, presses it on an ink pad, and stamps it on a sheet of writing paper. Then he writes a descriptive sentence about the object stamped. As an alternative, include stamps with seasonal phrases at the center. A child chooses a phrase stamp to go with his seasonal choice. He includes the phrase as dialogue in his descriptive sentence. He repeats the process until he has three sentences.

adapted from an idea by Julie Lewis, J. O. Davis Elementary, Irving, TX

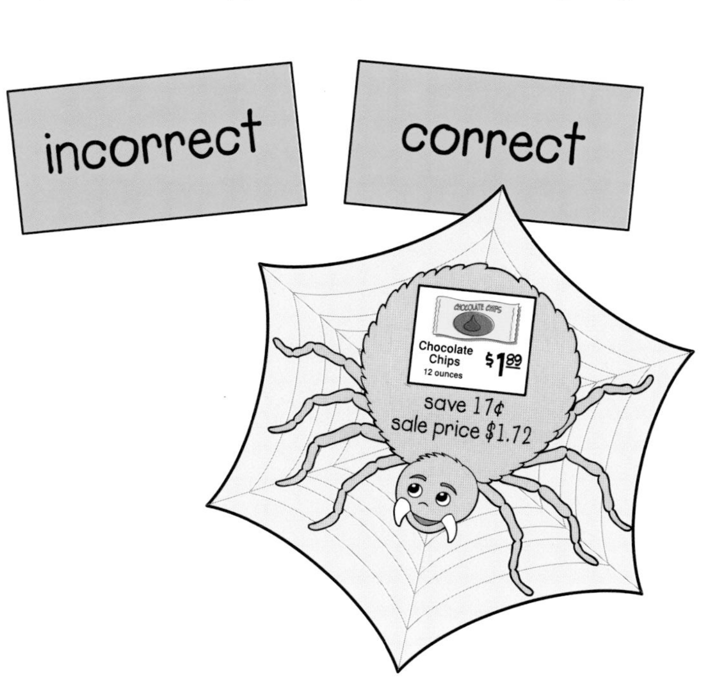

Spinning Up Bargains

Students weave together money and calculator skills with this activity! Make a supply of the spider pattern on page 51 and cut them out. Also cut out product advertisements from newspaper circulars and glue one at the top of each spider. Below each ad, write a savings amount and a sale price, making sure to program some with incorrect prices. Program the back of each cutout for self-checking. Then label each of two index cards "Correct" and "Incorrect." Place the cutouts, index cards, and a calculator at a center. A child chooses a spider and uses the calculator to find the sale price after the savings. She compares her answer to the one on the spider and places it on the matching pile. Then she turns the spiders over to check her work.

Virginia Conrad, Bunker R-3 Elementary, Bunker, MO

Learning Centers

Give 'em a Break

Identifying correct syllabication is in the bag with this simple center! Label two gift bags as shown. Also, copy the center cards on page 52 onto tagboard and cut them out. Place the cards and bags with paper and pencils at a center. A child reads the word on each card, decides whether the syllabication is correct, and then places it in the matching bag. After the cards are sorted, he removes the cards from the incorrect bag and rewrites each word with the correct syllabication.

Pin Down the Time

Practice telling time with this game for two! Copy 12 bowling pins and 18 clocks from the patterns on page 53 and cut them out. Program a time on each pin and then draw hands on a clock card to match each time. Label the remaining clocks with different times. To make a gameboard, glue six pins on each side of a file folder. Label the folder as shown and laminate it. Place the folder at a center with the clock cards and two dry-erase markers. Each child selects a side of the gameboard and writes her name on the corresponding line. Then she chooses a clock and determines whether the matching time is in her lane. If it is, she draws a line through the time on the pin and keeps the clock card. If not, she places the card at the bottom of the pile. Players take turns choosing a card until one player has crossed out all of her pins. Then the students wipe the gameboard clean for the next duo.

Jacqueline L. Jerke, Wynot Elementary, Wynot, NE

Stick With It

This easy-to-prepare partner activity provides extra practice with homophones. Copy the homophone sentence cards on page 53. Also program each side of a jumbo craft stick with a sentence number and one of the matching homophones from the pair listed. Place the sticks and the sentences at a center. A student reads a number and his partner locates the matching stick. Then the child reads the corresponding sentence and his partner displays the side of the stick with the matching homophone. After five sentences have been read, the students switch roles and continue with the activity.

Jennifer Winkelman, Tebbetts, MO

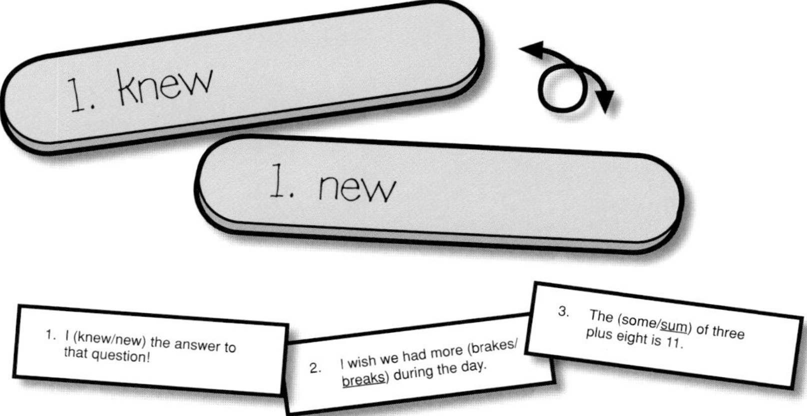

Three Times the Fun

Get on a roll with multiplication facts! Place five dice in a paper cup and store the cup at a center with a supply of paper and pencils. A child folds a sheet of paper in half three times and then unfolds the paper to reveal eight sections. She rolls the dice and sets aside any with matching amounts. Then she returns the remaining dice to the cup, rolls again, and keeps any dice matching those from the first roll. She repeats the process a third time; then she uses the number of dice and the repeated number on each to write a multiplication problem in one section of her paper. If necessary, she uses the dots on the dice to help her solve it. She repeats the steps to create seven more problems.

Jennifer Thoutt, Edmondson Elementary, Loveland, CO

Learning Centers

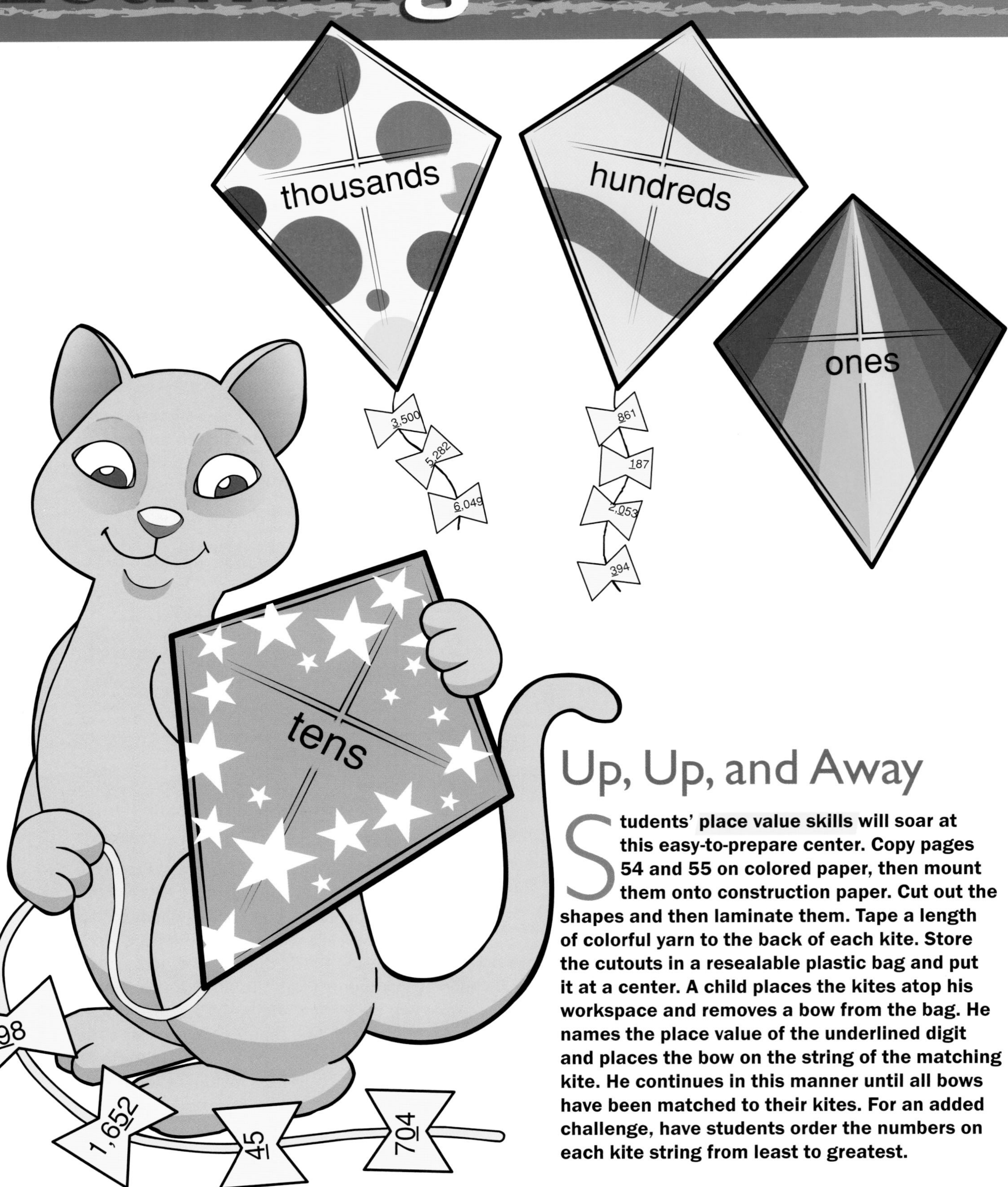

Up, Up, and Away

Students' place value skills will soar at this easy-to-prepare center. Copy pages 54 and 55 on colored paper, then mount them onto construction paper. Cut out the shapes and then laminate them. Tape a length of colorful yarn to the back of each kite. Store the cutouts in a resealable plastic bag and put it at a center. A child places the kites atop his workspace and removes a bow from the bag. He names the place value of the underlined digit and places the bow on the string of the matching kite. He continues in this manner until all bows have been matched to their kites. For an added challenge, have students order the numbers on each kite string from least to greatest.

adapted from an idea by Brooke Beverly
Dudley Elementary, Dudley, MA

Tap Into Contractions

This ready-to-go center gets students in tune with contractions. Make a copy of page 56; then mount the center mat and strip onto colored cardstock. Laminate the mat and strip. Cut out the patterns and cut the slits on the mat. Use a permanent marker to program each line of the strip with a contraction or two words that could make a contraction. Thread the strip through the slits and then place it a center with paper and pencils. A child visits the center and pulls the strip to reveal each set of words or contraction. Then she writes the matching contraction or words on her paper. To change the contractions, simply use hair spray or nail polish remover to wipe away the programming and then write the new words.

Name That President

Honor Presidents' Day and provide research practice at the same time! Use student-friendly references to locate interesting facts about U.S. presidents. Next, copy the center cards on page 57 and program each one with a question about a president. Record the matching answers on the key. Cut out the cards and put them in a resealable plastic bag. Place the bag and your reference materials at a center. A child chooses a card and reads the question. He uses the reference books to locate the answer and writes it on his paper next to the matching number. Then he chooses another question and repeats the process. If desired, have him use the answer key to check his work when finished.

Amanda Andrews, St. Joseph School, Marion, IA

Hot Dog!

Treat your students to word-building fun! Make a supply of the hot dog and bun patterns on page 57. Program the top of each bun with a root word and the bottom of each bun with an inflectional ending. Program the hot dog with the resulting word and cut out the shapes. To make the cutouts self-checking, place like-colored dots on the back sides of the matching pieces. Put each set of shapes on a paper plate and place them with a supply of paper and pencils at a center. A child chooses a bun and reads the words. Then she locates the matching hot dog and places it on the bun. She continues in this manner until she has made all of the matches. Finally, she turns the pieces over to check her work.

adapted from an idea by April Fowler, Hunterdale Elementary
Franklin, VA

Learning Centers

Get Going!

Encourage super spelling with this ready-to-go gameboard. Copy the gameboard on page 58, mount it onto construction paper, and laminate it. Write a commonly misspelled word or a spelling word on each of a supply of index cards. Place a die and two small toy cars with the cards and mat. A student pair places the cards facedown and each student chooses a car. Next, Player 1 selects a card and reads the word to Player 2. Player 2 spells the word aloud, and if correct, rolls the die and moves the appropriate number of spaces. If incorrect, he does not move. After each play, the card is returned to the bottom of the stack. Player 2 then selects a card for Player 1 to spell. Play continues in this manner until one child reaches the finish line.

adapted from an idea by Piper R. Porter
Mountain Way Elementary
Granite Falls, WA

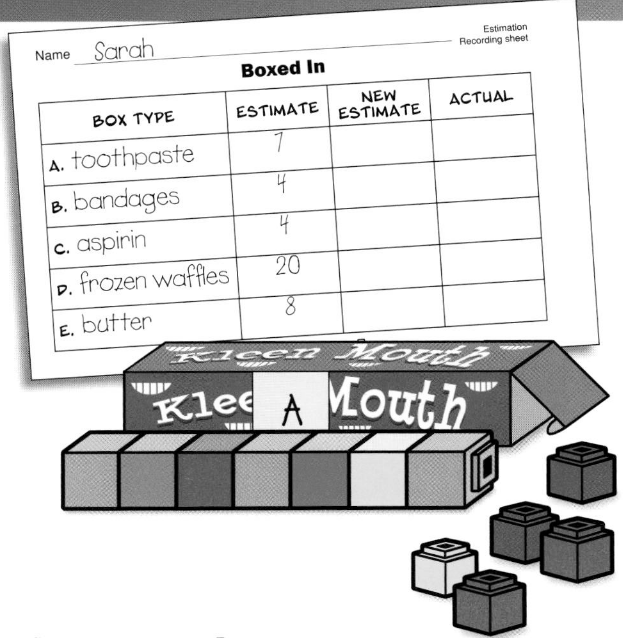
Name Sarah

Estimation Recording sheet

Boxed In

BOX TYPE	ESTIMATE	NEW ESTIMATE	ACTUAL
A. toothpaste	7		
B. bandages	4		
C. aspirin	4		
D. frozen waffles	20		
E. butter	8		

Boxed In

Discarded household boxes and some linking cubes make this estimation activity a snap! In advance, collect five empty boxes of different sizes and write a letter on each one. If desired, also cut off one set of flaps from each box. Next, place a class supply of the recording sheet on page 59 at a center with the boxes and a supply of Unifix cubes. A child records the box type next to each matching letter and records an estimate of how many cubes will fit inside for each. Then she stacks cubes inside the first box until she has filled half of it. Then she re-estimates the number of cubes needed and writes the new number. She continues adding cubes until she has filled the box and records the total used. She repeats the process with the remaining boxes.

Colleen Dabney, Williamsburg-JCC Schools, Williamsburg, VA

Light Reading

At their seats or at a center, students will flip for this table of contents practice. To prepare, cut out the table of contents page from a variety of student-friendly magazines. On the front of a large, decorative notepad sheet, write the magazine name and five questions that can be answered from the table of contents page. Then glue the table of contents page to the back of the notepad sheet. A student chooses a notepad sheet and numbers his paper from one to five. He reads each question and uses the table of contents to find the answer.

Virginia L. Conrad, Bunker R-III School District, Bunker, MO

Amazing Animals

1. On what page does the article on sharks start?
2. How long is the article "Meet a Zookeeper"?
3. In which article might you find pictures of young animals?
4. In which article might you find more information about emus and flamingos?
5. Which article is three pages long?

Amazing Animals
What's Inside?

2 Animal of the Month
4 Jokes and Riddles
5 Games and Mazes
7 Finding Fish
10 Animal Babies
12 Sharks
16 Meet a Zookeeper
18 How Pollution Hurts Animals
22 Big Birds

Name Sierra

Fact families

Spot Check

3 × 4 = 12
4 × 3 = 12
12 ÷ 3 = 4
12 ÷ 4 = 3

Spot Check

Review multiplication and division fact families with this easy-to-prepare center. Put a set of dominos in a paper bag; then make a class supply of the recording sheet on page 60. Place the bag and the recording sheets at a center. A child pulls a domino from the bag and writes on her paper the number of dots on each end. She multiplies the numbers together and records the product. If desired, have her check her work with a multiplication table. Next, she rotates the domino 180° and repeats the process. Then she uses the numbers from her multiplication sentences to create two related division problems. Finally, she draws the domino on her paper. Then she repeats the process with another domino.

Starin Lewis, Phoenix, AZ

Learning Centers

What's the Scoop?

Matching main ideas with supporting details will be a treat with this easy-to-make center. To prepare, copy the cone patterns on page 61 on brown paper and the ice cream scoop patterns on another color; then cut out the shapes. Make the shapes self-checking by adding like-colored sticky dots to the backs of corresponding pieces. Then put the pieces in a resealable bag and place the bag at a center with a supply of writing paper. A child removes the scoops from the bag and places them on his workspace. Next, he reads a scoop and locates the cone with the corresponding details, placing it below the scoop. After all matches have been made, he turns the cards over to check his work. Finally, have the student choose one matching set and use its information to write a complete paragraph.

Janet Brown, North Hills Traditional Academy, Winston-Salem, NC

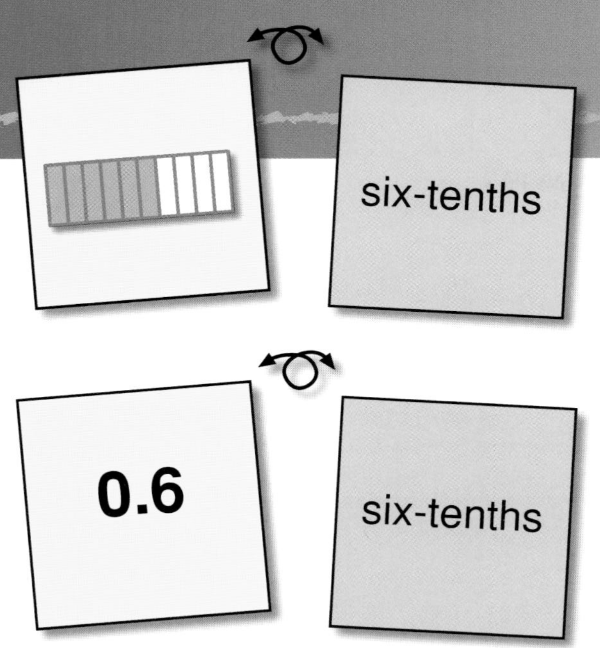

Meaningful Matches

Reinforce the relationship between fractions and decimals while providing vocabulary practice at the same time! Copy the cards on pages 62 and 63, then cut them out. Glue the matching cards front to back and laminate them for durability. Put the cards in a resealable plastic bag and place the bag at a center. A child removes the cards, placing them yellow side up. She matches each fraction bar to its decimal equivalent and places the cards together. When all matches have been made, she turns the cards over to check her work.

They're There!

Give students homophone practice while they create a resource they can use. To prepare the center, cut a supply of white paper in half. Next, write each word from a homophone pair on a separate index card, making one pair for each student. Place the paper and cards at a center with glue and crayons. A child chooses a homophone pair and glues each index card to a piece of paper. For each word, he writes across the bottom of the paper a sentence using the word and illustrates the sentence at the top. When each child has completed a pair, hang the sets alphabetically for an instant word wall reference!

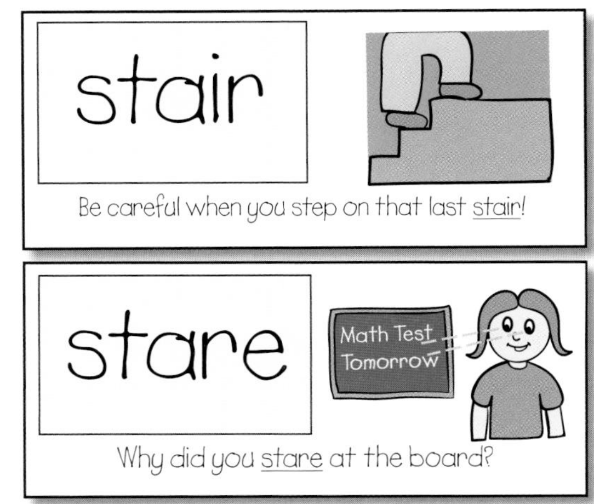

Allison Russell, Gleason Elementary, Houston, TX

Big on Bugs

Improve students' estimating and measuring skills with this hands-on center. Make a copy of the insect cards on page 64 and punch a hole in the top left corner of each card. Slide a metal ring through each hole and close the ring. Place the cards at a center with a meterstick and a supply of drawing paper. A child chooses a card and writes the insect's name on her paper. She measures out and draws a line equal to the insect's stated length, labeling the line with the length. Next, she estimates which objects in the classroom equal that length and then tests her estimates by measuring the objects. She records the name of each object and circles those that are about the same length as the line on her paper. If desired, have the student repeat the process with a different insect length on the back of her paper.

Center Cards

Use with "In the Field" on page 41.

Spider Pattern

Use with "Spinning Up Bargains" on page 41.

Center Cards

Use with "Give 'em a Break" on page 42.

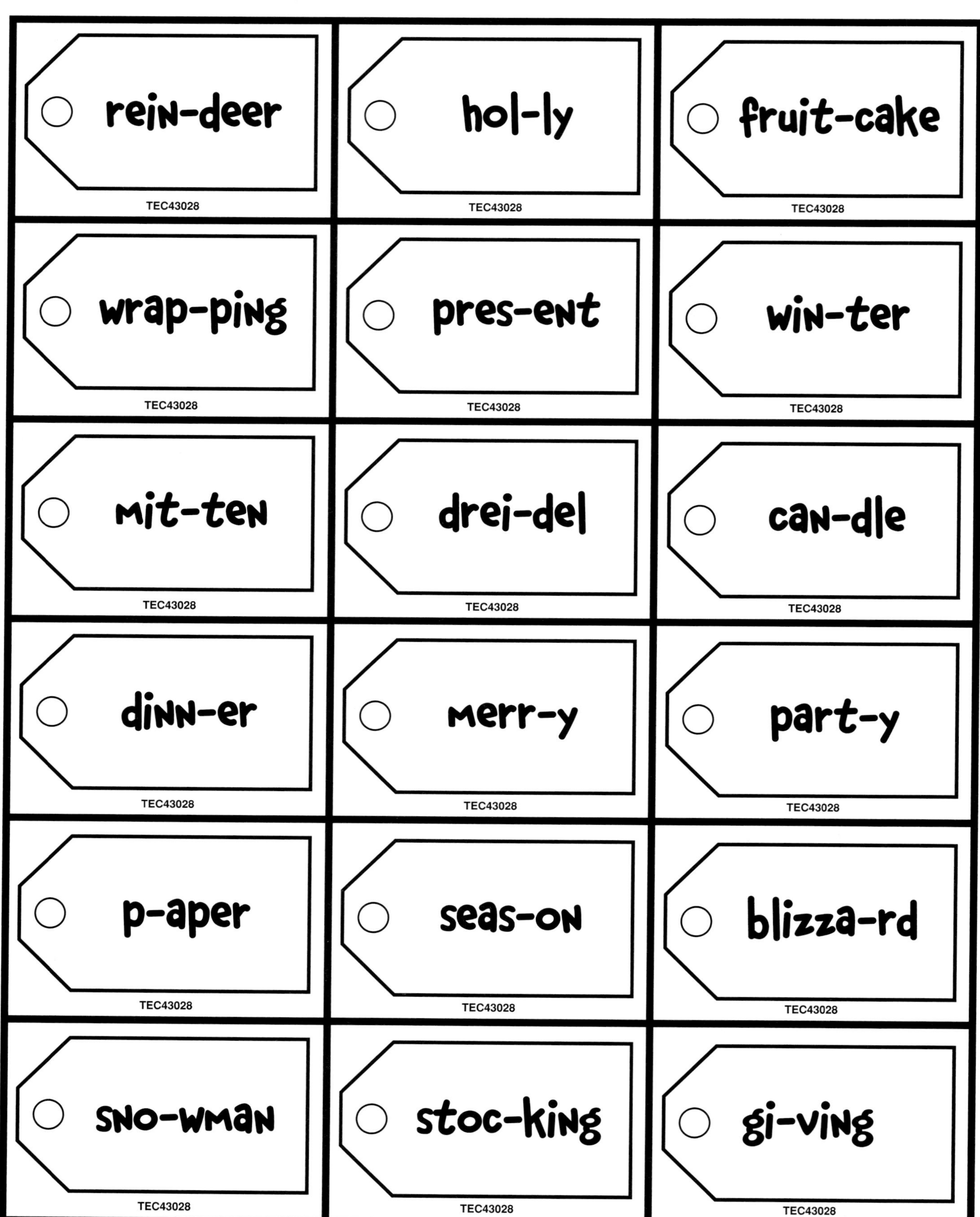

Bowling Pin Patterns and Clock Card

Use with "Pin Down the Time" on page 43.

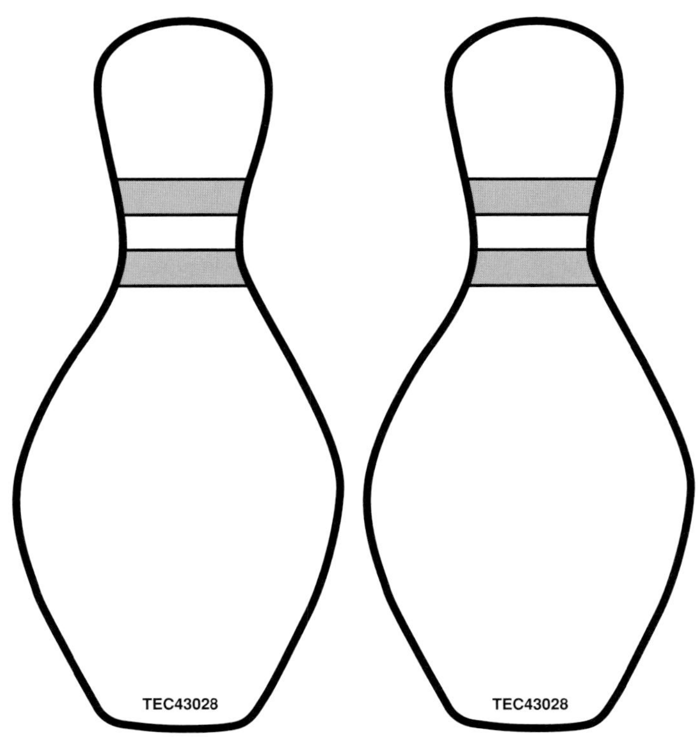

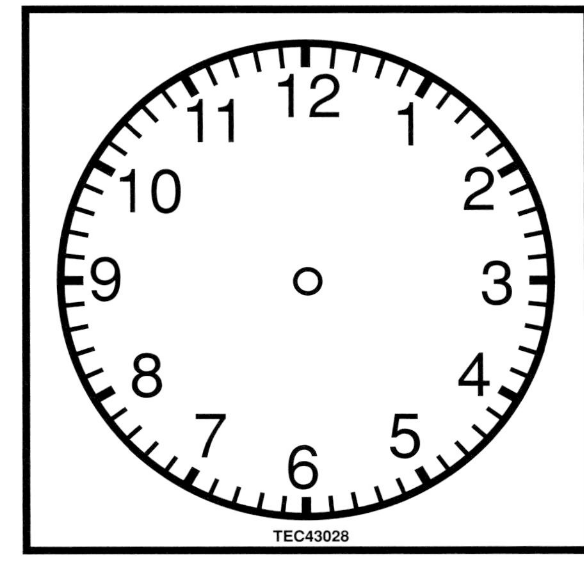

Homophone Sentence Cards

Use with "Stick With It" on page 43.

1. I (knew/new) the answer to that question! TEC43028	6. Saturday was a (grate/great) day! TEC43028
2. I wish we had more (brakes/breaks) during the day. TEC43028	7. I saw a large ship in the (sea/see). TEC43028
3. The (some/sum) of three plus eight is 11. TEC43028	8. I have a new puppy (to/too)! TEC43028
4. Did you (hear/here) me? TEC43028	9. We (ate/eight) pizza for lunch. TEC43028
5. The wind (blew/blue) very hard during the storm. TEC43028	10. It took me three (hours/ours) to do my homework. TEC43028

Kite Patterns

Use with "Up, Up, and Away" on page 44.

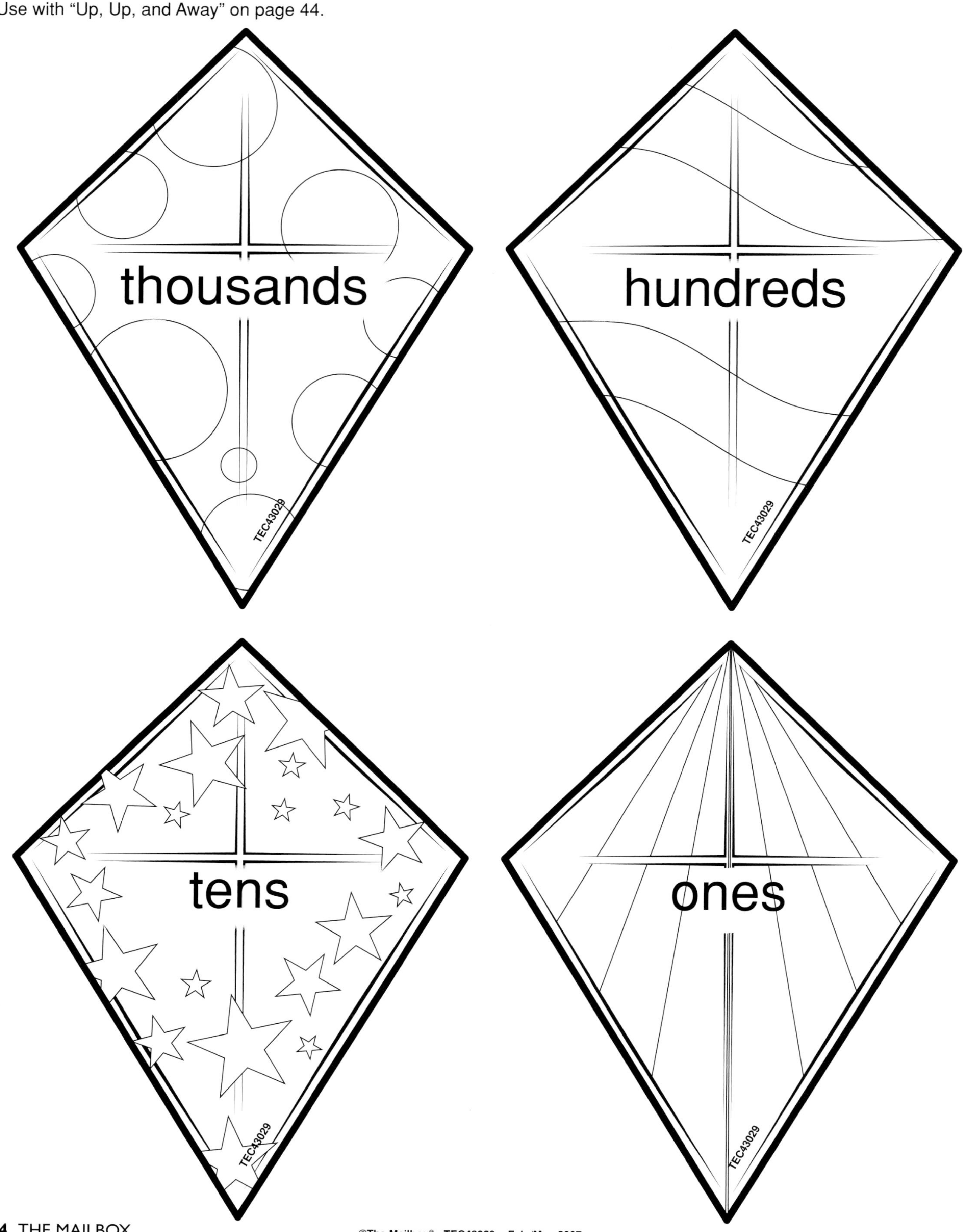

Kite Bows

Use with "Up, Up, and Away" on page 44.

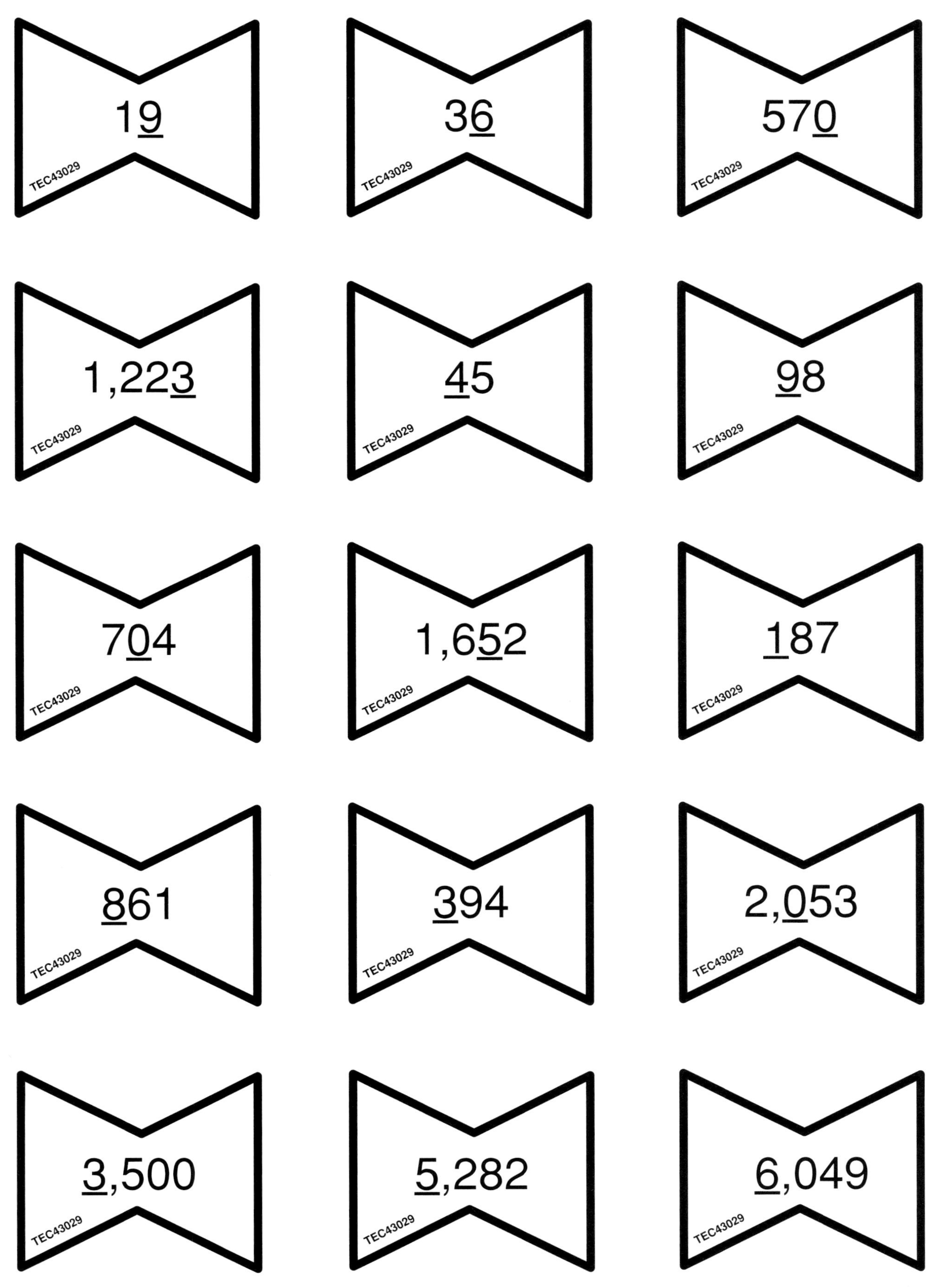

Center Mat and Strip

Use with "Tap Into Contractions" on page 45.

Tap Into Contractions

TEC43029

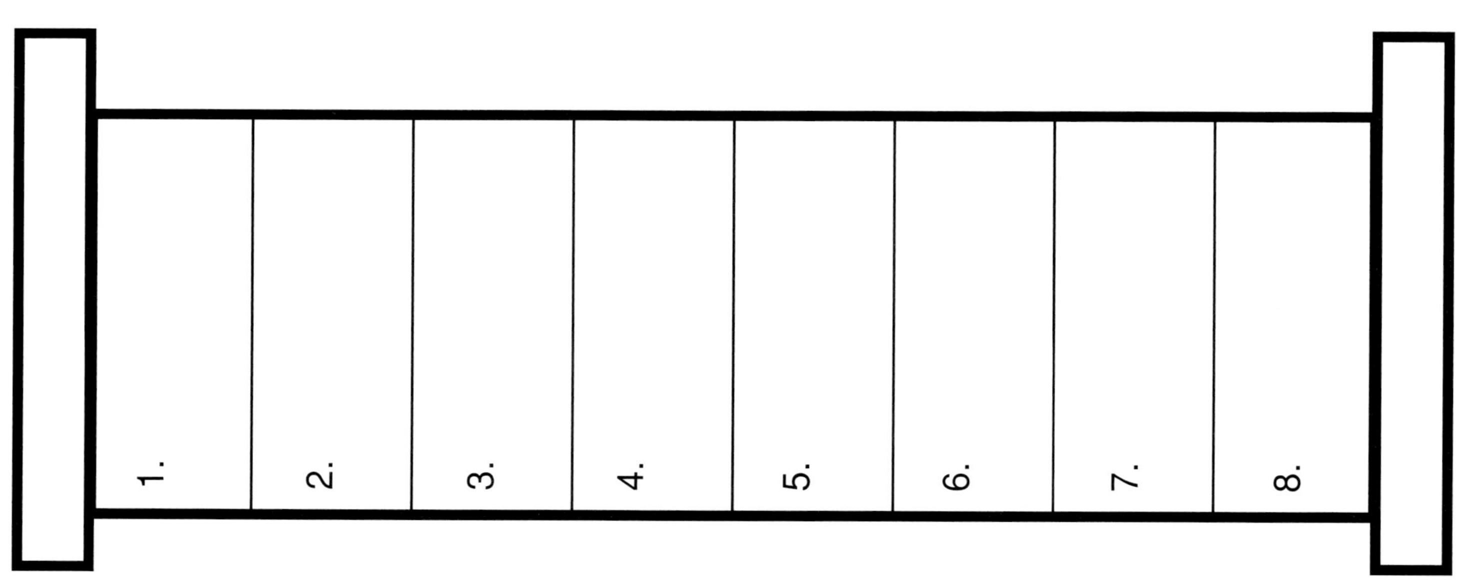

Center Cards

Use with "Name That President" on page 45.

		Answer Key
TEC43029	TEC43029	
TEC43029	TEC43029	
TEC43029	TEC43029	TEC43029

Hot Dog and Bun Patterns

Use with "Hot Dog!" on page 45.

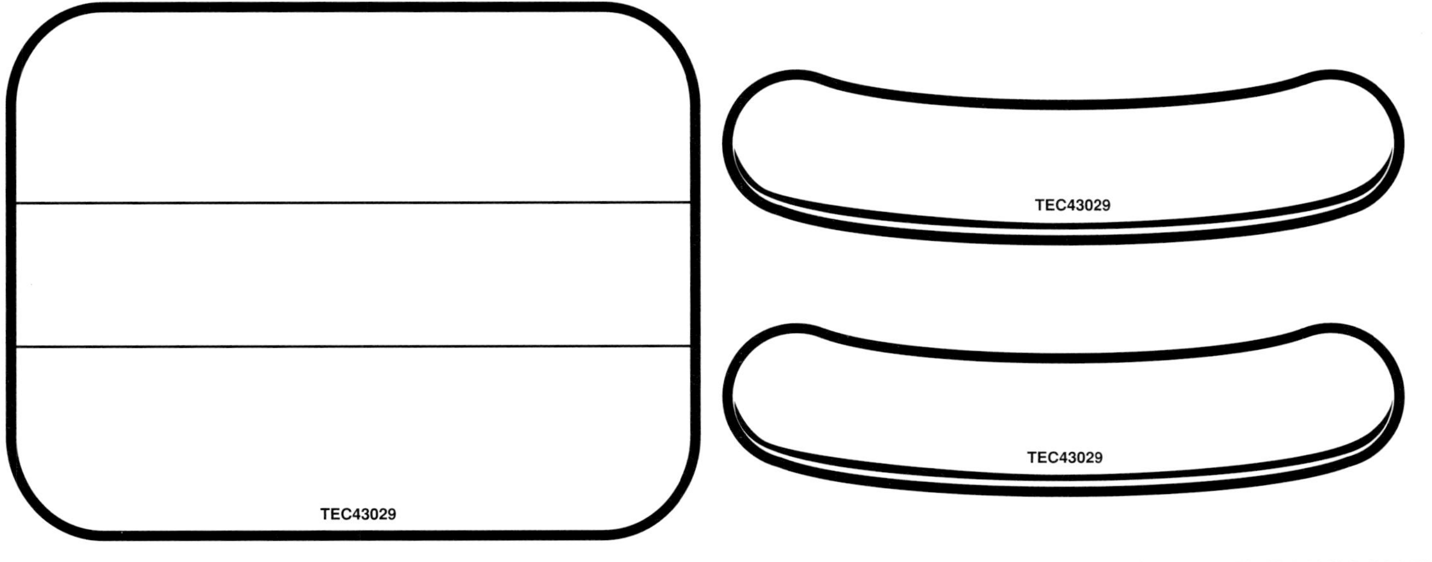

GET GOING!

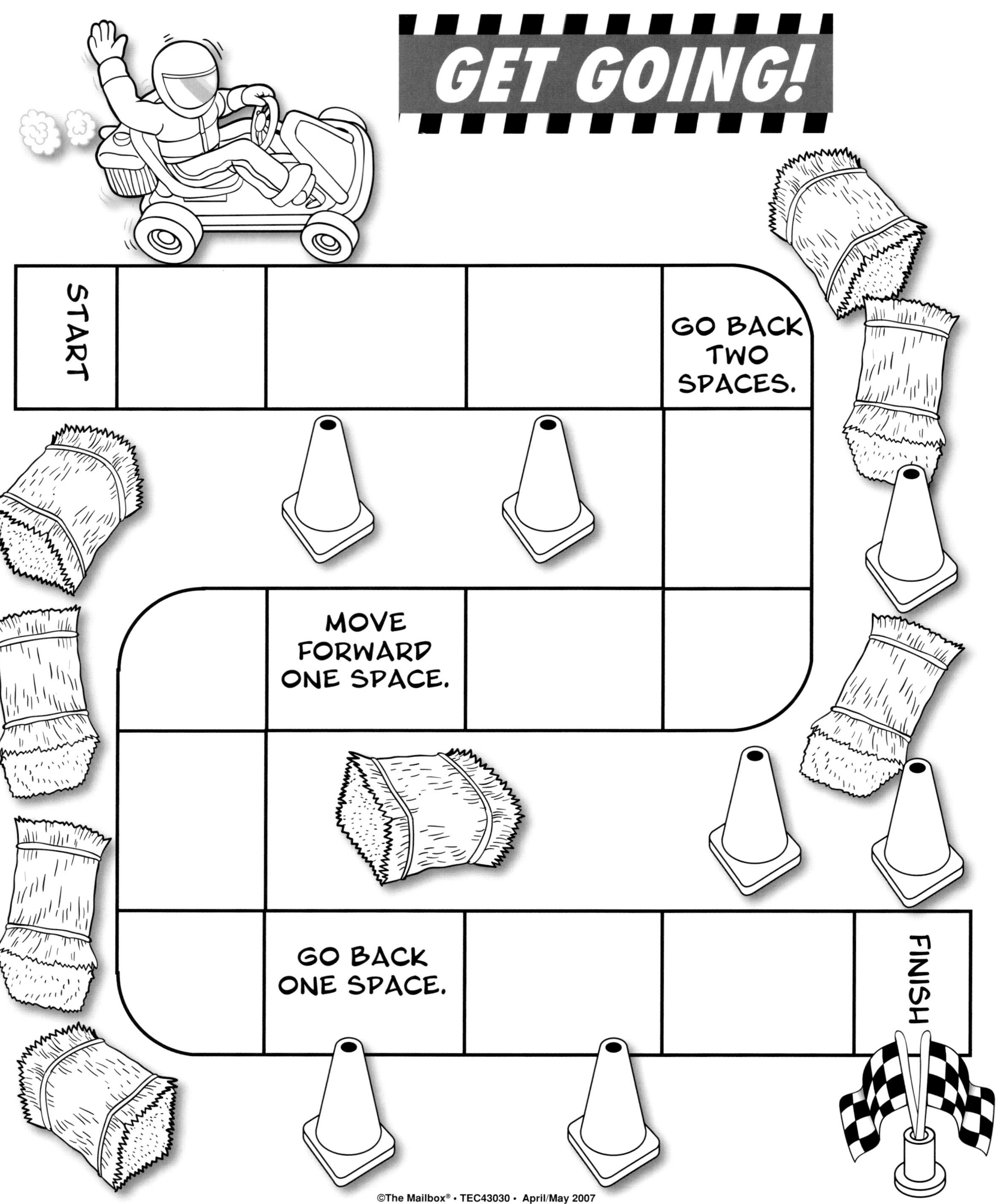

Note to the teacher: Use with "Get Going!" on page 46.

Name ______________________________

Estimation
Recording sheet

Boxed In

BOX TYPE	ESTIMATE	NEW ESTIMATE	ACTUAL
A.			
B.			
C.			
D.			
E.			

Name ______________________________

Estimation
Recording sheet

Boxed In

BOX TYPE	ESTIMATE	NEW ESTIMATE	ACTUAL
A.			
B.			
C.			
D.			
E.			

©The Mailbox® • TEC43030 • April/May 2007

Note to the teacher: Use with "Boxed In" on page 47.

Name ______________________________

___ x ___ = ___
___ x ___ = ___
___ ÷ ___ = ___
___ ÷ ___ = ___

___ x ___ = ___
___ x ___ = ___
___ ÷ ___ = ___
___ ÷ ___ = ___

___ x ___ = ___
___ x ___ = ___
___ ÷ ___ = ___
___ ÷ ___ = ___

___ x ___ = ___
___ x ___ = ___
___ ÷ ___ = ___
___ ÷ ___ = ___

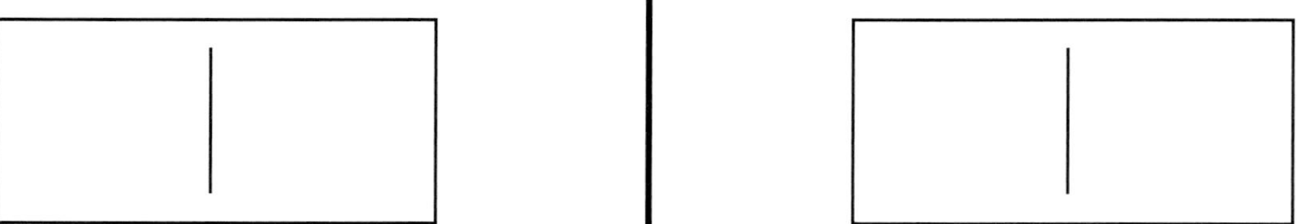

___ x ___ = ___
___ x ___ = ___
___ ÷ ___ = ___
___ ÷ ___ = ___

___ x ___ = ___
___ x ___ = ___
___ ÷ ___ = ___
___ ÷ ___ = ___

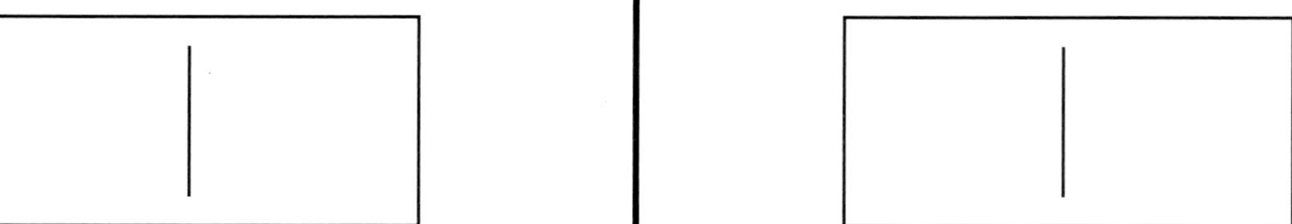

 Note to the teacher: Use with "Spot Check" on page 47.

Ice Cream Cone and Scoop Patterns

Use with "What's the Scoop?" on page 48.

The beach

TEC43031

The movie theater

TEC43031

Ice cream

TEC43031

Summer camp

TEC43031

Smell of sunblock
Crashing waves
Hot sand

TEC43031

TEC43031

Laughing and singing
Cabins in the woods
Fresh air

Sweet flavors
Cold treat
Sticky

TEC43031

TEC43031

Salty popcorn
Dark
Big screen

Fraction Bar and Decimal Cards

Use with "Meaningful Matches" on page 49.

	0.1		0.2
	0.3		0.4
	0.5	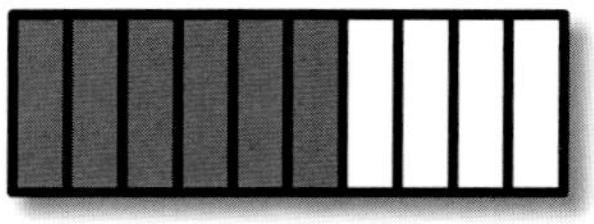	0.6
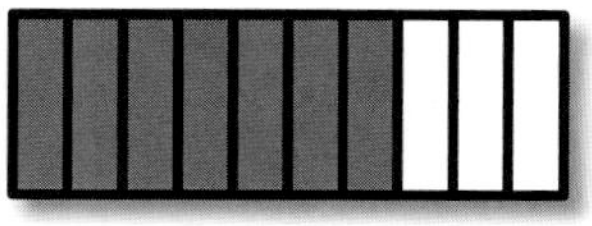	0.7	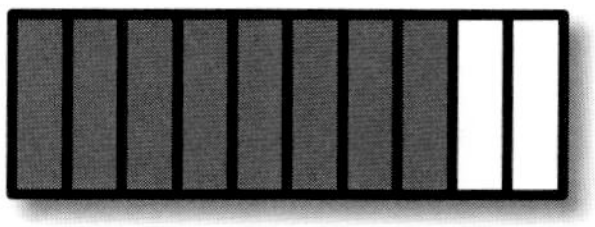	0.8
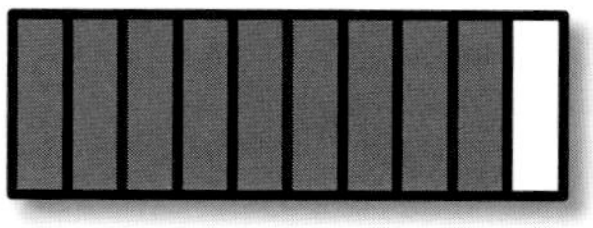	0.9		1.0

two-tenths	two-tenths	one-tenth	one-tenth
TEC43031	TEC43031	TEC43031	TEC43031
four-tenths	four-tenths	three-tenths	three-tenths
TEC43031	TEC43031	TEC43031	TEC43031
six-tenths	six-tenths	five-tenths	five-tenths
TEC43031	TEC43031	TEC43031	TEC43031
eight-tenths	eight-tenths	seven-tenths	seven-tenths
TEC43031	TEC43031	TEC43031	TEC43031
ten-tenths	ten-tenths	nine-tenths	nine-tenths
TEC43031	TEC43031	TEC43031	TEC43031

Insect Cards

Use with "Big on Bugs" on page 49.

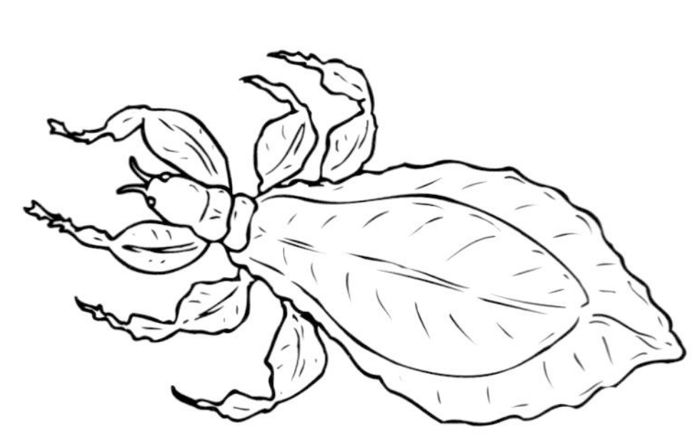

One kind of **leaf insect** can be about 8 cm long.

TEC43031

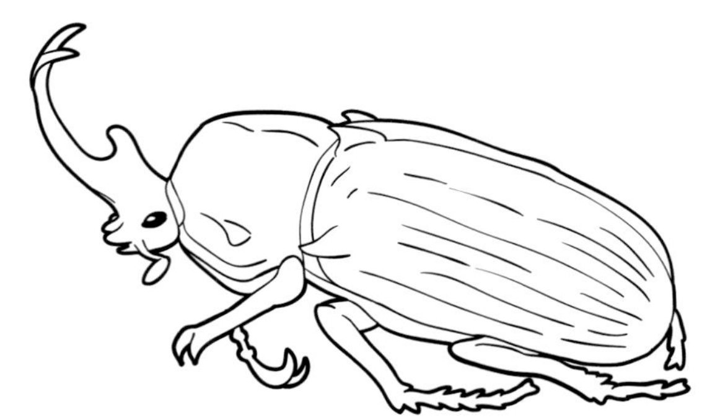

An **elephant beetle** can be up to 12 cm long.

TEC43031

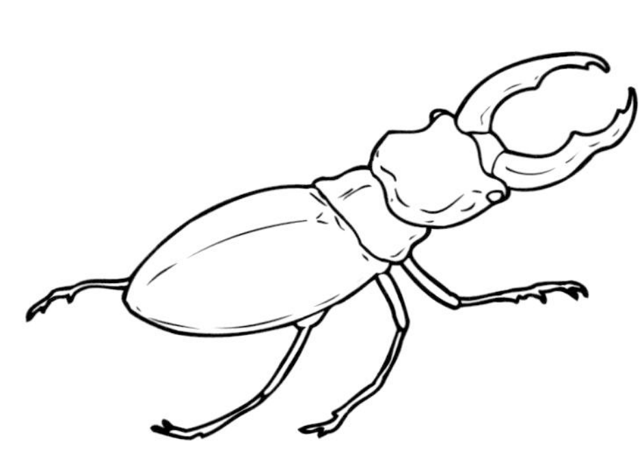

A **giant long-horned beetle** can grow to 21 cm long.

TEC43031

An **atlas moth** can have a wingspan of 24 cm.

TEC43031

A **white witch moth** can have a wingspan of 30 cm.

TEC43031

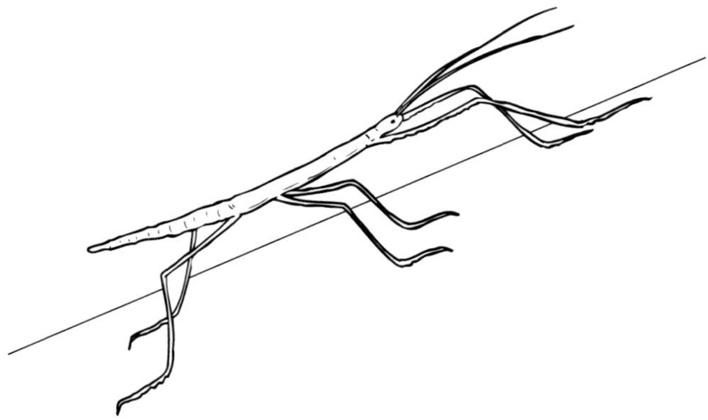

A **walking stick** can be up to 35 cm long.

TEC43031

Management Tips & Timesavers

Homework Credit Card

Motivate students to complete their homework on time! Make a class supply of the cards on page 74 and cut them out. Label each card with a child's name and an expiration date. Each time a student completes his homework on time, punch a hole in the card. When he has earned 20 punches, reward his responsibility by turning the card into a homework pass.

Kim Tenney, St. Luke's Lutheran School, Oviedo, FL

Work Zone Folders

Control the flow of paper traffic with this organizational idea! Gather three folders: one red, one yellow, and one green. Label each folder as shown. Place student work that needs to be reviewed immediately in the red folder. Then place work in progress, such as writing activities or projects, in the yellow folder. Finally, place in the green folder graded work that is ready to return to students.

adapted from an idea by Lori Knight, Adamston Elementary, Clarksburg, WV

Highlighter Alternative

Here's a way to easily highlight important words on big books, chart paper, or posters! Purchase at a discount store self-adhesive vinyl book covers and cut them to the size that you need. Then simply attach the cover to the word or phrase that you want to highlight. These covers are easy to remove and can be used again and again!

Kimberly Holt, Elfida P. Chavez Elementary, El Paso, TX

Filed Away

Organize word wall cards so they are easy to find year after year! At an office supply store, purchase a 5" x 8" file box and prenumbered file box dividers. Tape a list of the words posted each week to the divider that corresponds with that week of school. Then place each set of word cards behind its weekly divider. This easy system keeps a year's worth of words at your fingertips.

Heather Schumacher, Coronado Village Elementary, Universal City, TX

Grading Tip

Ensure that you always have the right supplies for grading papers at home! Purchase an inexpensive pencil case. Place inside markers, colored pens, stickers, and any other materials you use for grading. Then store the pencil case in your school bag. Now when you're checking papers at home, everything you need is readily available and not floating around at the bottom of your bag!

Jenny Massey, Sacred Heart School, Shelby, OH

Easy Identification

Use colored electrical tape to easily mark group materials! Purchase several rolls of different-colored electrical tape. After seating students by group, assign each group a color. Affix a piece of matching tape to the group's table, chairs, and any supplies that members share, such as markers, scissors, and storage containers. Now there's no doubt where materials belong!

Allison Wanaselja, Independence Charter School, Philadelphia, PA

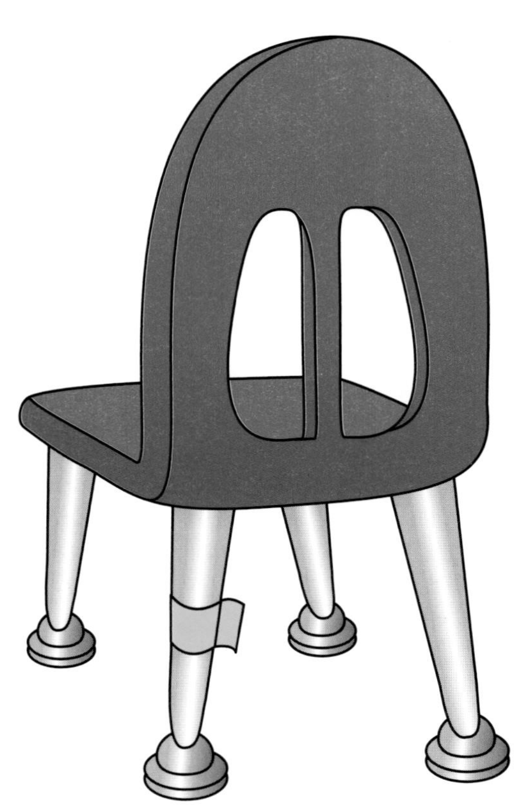

Which Books?

It's easy to remember the picture books to use during a unit of study with this organizational tip. Photocopy the cover of each picture book you plan to use during a unit of study. Then file the copies of the book covers in the corresponding unit's folder. When you're ready to teach the unit, you'll know just which picture books you'll need!

Barbi Kirk, Coral Springs, FL

Puzzling Behavior

Here's a noncompetitive way to encourage students to follow classroom rules. Puzzle-cut a large photograph or a magazine picture into a desired number of pieces and place the pieces in an accessible location. Each time your students exhibit exceptional behavior, present the class with one piece of the puzzle. Have a student volunteer begin assembling the puzzle in a designated classroom location. After all of the pieces have been collected and the puzzle is complete, reward the class with a privilege or a special treat.

Amy Rohr, Holy Family Elementary, Hays, KS

Management Tips & Timesavers

Easy Center Storage

Free up some extra space and organize your centers at the same time! Write each center name on a strip of masking tape. Place each strip on a drawer of a multidrawer rolling cart. Store all the center materials inside the drawer, including a class supply of any reproducibles needed. During center time, a child carefully removes a drawer and takes it to his assigned workspace. Then, when center time is over, the materials are returned to the drawer, and the drawer goes back in the cart. The drawers are easy to update when needed, and everything stays neat and organized!

Erin Santos, Foxborough Regional Charter School, Foxboro, MA

Mystery Student

Draw attention to classroom rules and expectations with this simple strategy. Write each child's name on one end of a craft stick and store the sticks name down in a cup labeled "Mystery Student." Choose a desired behavior and write it on the board. Then select a stick, but do not reveal the name to the class. Throughout the lesson, periodically monitor the named student for the desired behavior. If he achieves the goal behavior, reveal his identity and reward him with a special classroom incentive (sitting at the teacher's desk, writing with a special pen, etc). If the named student does not demonstrate the behavior, do not name the student; simply tell the class that there was not a winner this time. Choose another mystery student and repeat the process as desired.

Kara Mitchell, J. P. LeNoir Elementary, Donna, TX

Stick-On Supplies

This simple reminder helps students prepare materials for each lesson. Take pictures of commonly used classroom materials, mount each one on a piece of tagboard, and laminate for durability. Cut out each picture and add a piece of magnetic tape to the back of each one. Store the pictures in a bin near the board. Then, at the beginning of each lesson, post the pictures of the materials students will need. A quick glance is all it takes for students to be prepared for learning!

Erin Santos

Management Tips & Timesavers

Teacher Carryall

Avoid classroom interruptions by keeping frequently needed classroom supplies at your fingertips. Obtain a nail apron (sold at home improvement stores) or another type of short apron with pockets. Place items such as stickers, extra pencils, and tissues in the apron pockets, and decorate the apron if desired. Wear the apron each day, and when an item is needed, simply remove it from a pocket and hand it to the appropriate student. Restock the apron with additional supplies as needed.

Jane Walsh, Sweetwater Elementary, Lithia Springs, GA

Handy Highlights

For an easy way to keep track of your original copy of a skill sheet, try this bright idea! Draw an "X" over the skill sheet with a highlighter. Then copy the skill sheet as you normally would. The highlighter won't show up on the copies, and your copy won't be given away when the papers are passed out.

Laurel DeCastro, Wessagusset Primary, Weymouth, MA

Poster Storage

This idea is perfect for organizing your two-sided posters, such as those found in *The Mailbox* magazines. Slip each folded poster into a separate plastic page protector. Then attach a label to each page protector. On each label write a description of both sides of the corresponding poster. Not only will the posters be easy to locate, but you'll know at a glance the concepts each side of the poster reviews.

Rebecca Hagerty, Moore Elementary, Pittsburgh, PA

Pick a Partner

Give students the freedom to choose their own partners while ensuring they're not always paired with the same classmate. Before beginning a partner activity, announce a characteristic or preference, such as eye color or favorite food. If desired, have students jot down their responses on a piece of scrap paper. Then have each child find a classmate whose response corresponds with his own. Not only will students work with a variety of classmates, they'll enjoy finding out some things they have in common as well.

Vickie Loch, Moreland Elementary, West St. Paul, MN

Picture-Perfect Postcards

Use the photos you take of students throughout the year to share good news with parents! When a student meets a goal, does stellar work, or simply makes your day, choose a picture that includes the student. Then flip the photo, write a brief note on the left side, address the right side, add a stamp, and drop it in the mail!

Rebecca Boehler, Devaney Elementary, Terre Haute, IN

Group KWLs

To get more students involved in sharing what they know, what they want to know, and what they learn, create and laminate a KWL chart for each small group of students. Then, before beginning a new unit of study, give each group a laminated chart and a wipe-off marker. Introduce the topic and guide the students in each group to record on their chart what they know and what they want to know. After the unit, have the students in each group review their chart and write about what they learned. Then wipe the charts clean, and they're ready for your next unit of study.

Rebecca Boehler

Boxed for Use and Storage

Organize teaching materials for the coming year with this simple tip. Place resources in an empty copy-paper box on its side so that the spines face out and slide the lid under the box as shown. Set the box on a shelf near your desk for easy access. Then, when it's time to pack up your room, simply slide the lid out from under the box and put it on top. Materials are ready for storage. And, when it's time to set your room up in the fall, simply take off the lid and slide it under the box, and your materials are ready to use!

Rita Skavinsky, Minersville Elementary, Minersville, PA

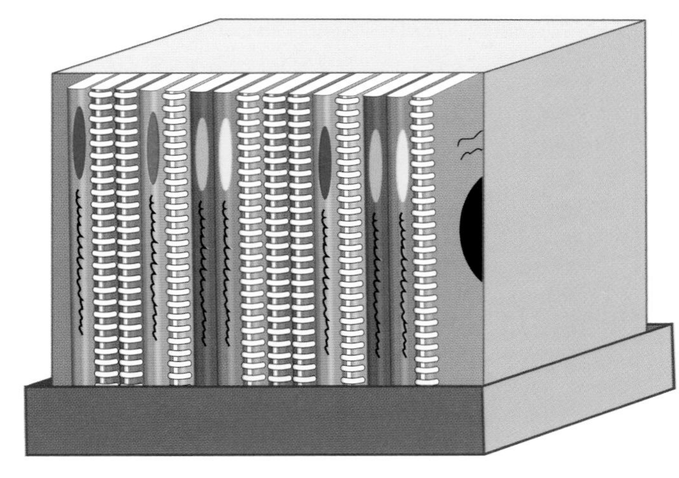

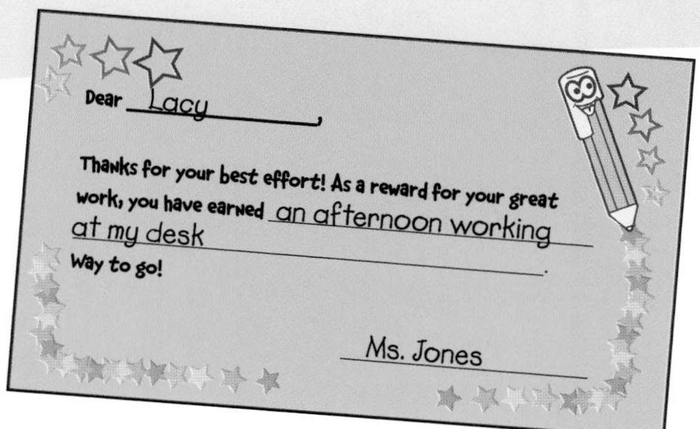

Best-Effort Notes

Encourage students to turn in quality work with this simple incentive. Copy a supply of the note on page 74 and cut each one out. Staple a note to a student assignment that is neat, correct, and complete. Then write a reward on the note, such as sitting at the teacher's desk, ten minutes of free time, or extra computer privileges. What an easy way to motivate students to turn in their best work!

Janelle Jones, Meadowcreek Elementary, Fort Worth, TX

Puzzle Predicament

Keep track of your puzzle pieces with this quick fix. Label each puzzle box with a different number (program all four sides of the box, if desired). The next time each puzzle is assembled, confirm that the correct pieces have been used. Then ask a student to dismantle the puzzle and write on each piece's back the number shown on the box. Whenever a puzzle is added to your collection, repeat the process. Now when a stray puzzle piece is found, returning it to the correct box is a snap!

Tania Czerkas, James B. McPherson Elementary, Chicago, IL

Student Groups

When it's time to organize students into groups, think of the days of the week. Divide students into five groups and assign each group a weekday (Monday through Friday). Use the group names to quickly organize students into cooperative learning groups. On their assigned day, allow group members special privileges, such as lining up first or serving as helpers.

Ashley Lovette, Warsaw Elementary, Warsaw, NC

Tiny Trash Cans

To reduce unnecessary trips to the trash can, try this tip! Give each student group an empty tissue box with the top cut off. Have the group members decorate and label their box and then place it in the middle of the table. Whenever a child needs to discard trash, he places it in the box. At the end of each day, have one group member empty the trash can.

Kathleen Brownlee, St. Matthew School, Wilmington, DE

Credit Card Patterns

Use with "Homework Credit Card" on page 66.

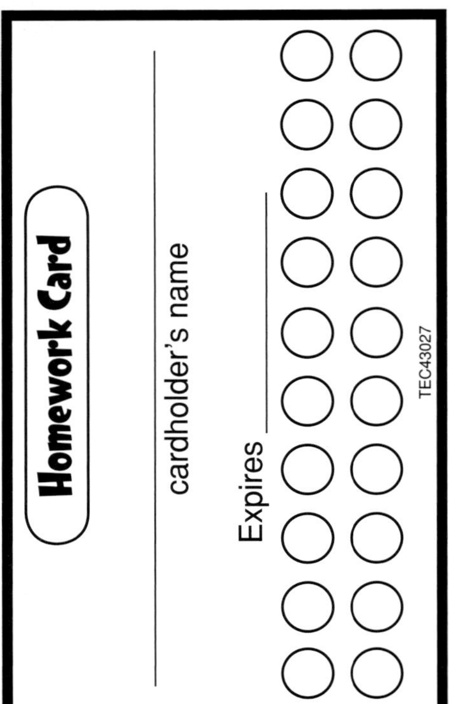

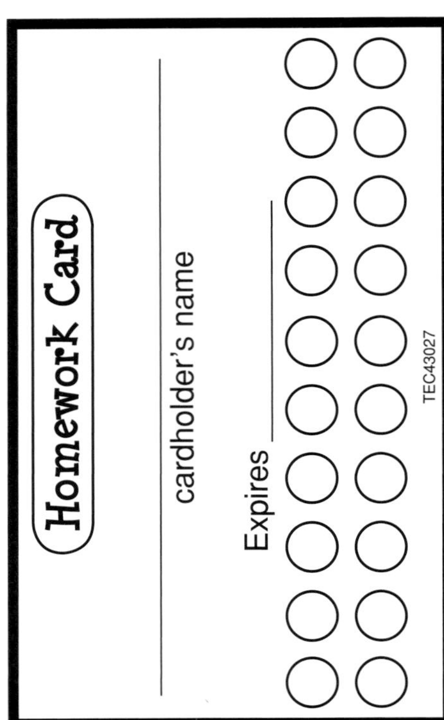

Best-Effort Note

Use with "Best-Effort Notes" on page 73.

Dear ______________________________,

Thanks for your best effort! As a reward for your great work, you have earned ______________________________

____.

Way to go!

____

TEC43027

Math Mailbag

It's greater than 15.

It's an even number.

It's a two-digit number.

There is an 8 in the ones place.

August

Sunday	Monday	Tuesday	Wednesday	Thursday	Friday	Saturday
		1	2	3	4	5
6	7	8	9	10	11	12
13	14	15	16	17		19
20	21	22	23	24	25	26
27	28	29	30	31		

Calendar Clues

Mathematical terms

Turn your class calendar into a gameboard! To play this whole-class game, give one blindfolded player a self-sticking note large enough to cover a date on the calendar. Have the child turn around several times and then place the note over a date. If the note lands between two spaces, adjust it to cover one of them. With the student still blindfolded, have his classmates give him clues about the date. Encourage students to use place-value and other mathematical terms like the ones shown. After several clues have been given, invite the child to guess the number. Then have him remove the blindfold to check his guess. Remove the note from the calendar; then pass it and the blindfold to a new student and repeat the process.

Vicki Dabrowka, Palm Harbor, FL

Revved Up!

Rounding to the nearest ten

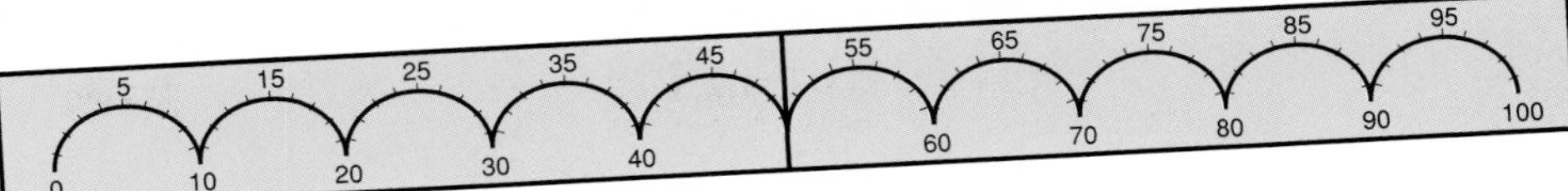

In advance, make a class supply of the strips and the reproducible on page 87. Give each child a set of strips. Have her cut them out; then tape them together to form one long strip. To use the strip for rounding, the student moves her finger along the scalloped line, pretending it's a car driving up hills and down into valleys to arrive at a specific number, such as 43. Once at that spot, explain that her car has run out of gas. If she's headed up a hill, as she would be on 43, her car would drift backward to 40. If she's at the top or headed down a hill, as she would be on 45, her car would roll into the valley below and stop at 50. After practicing rounding several times as a class, distribute copies of the half-page reproducible and have students use their strips to complete it.

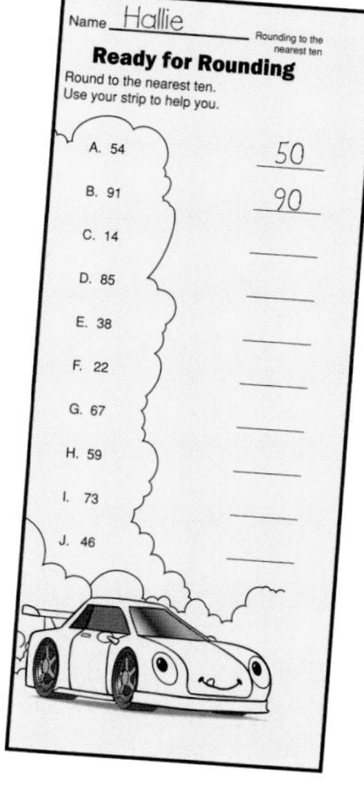
Name Hallie — Rounding to the nearest ten

Ready for Rounding

Round to the nearest ten.
Use your strip to help you.

A. 54 50
B. 91 90
C. 14
D. 85
E. 38
F. 22
G. 67
H. 59
I. 73
J. 46

Shelly Tamburro, Putnam Elementary School of Science, Fort Collins, CO

Which Is It?

AM and PM

eating breakfast
doing homework
eating dinner
making the bed
waiting for the bus to school
going to bed
helping Mom with dinner
packing your lunch

Help students distinguish between times of the day with this whole-class activity. Give each child two index card halves. Have him label one card "AM" and the other "PM." Then read aloud an activity from the list shown. Each child holds up the matching card to indicate the correct time of day.

Laura Wagner, Raleigh, NC

Who's Invited?

Problem solving

Joey invited three classmates to his birthday party. Each of those classmates invited two guests. If everyone who was invited came to the party, how many people were there?

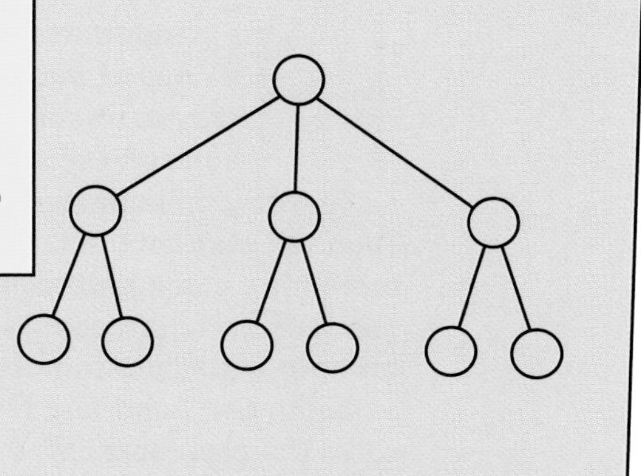

Use this party-themed puzzler to provide practice with the draw-a-picture strategy! Write the problem shown on the board. Then have each student draw a picture similar to the one shown to solve the problem. After discussing the answer *(10 students)*, vary the problem by changing the number of guests to three, five, and seven. Have students use the draw-a-picture strategy to find the solution to each problem *(13, 19, and 25)*.

Denine T. Carter, Greensboro, NC

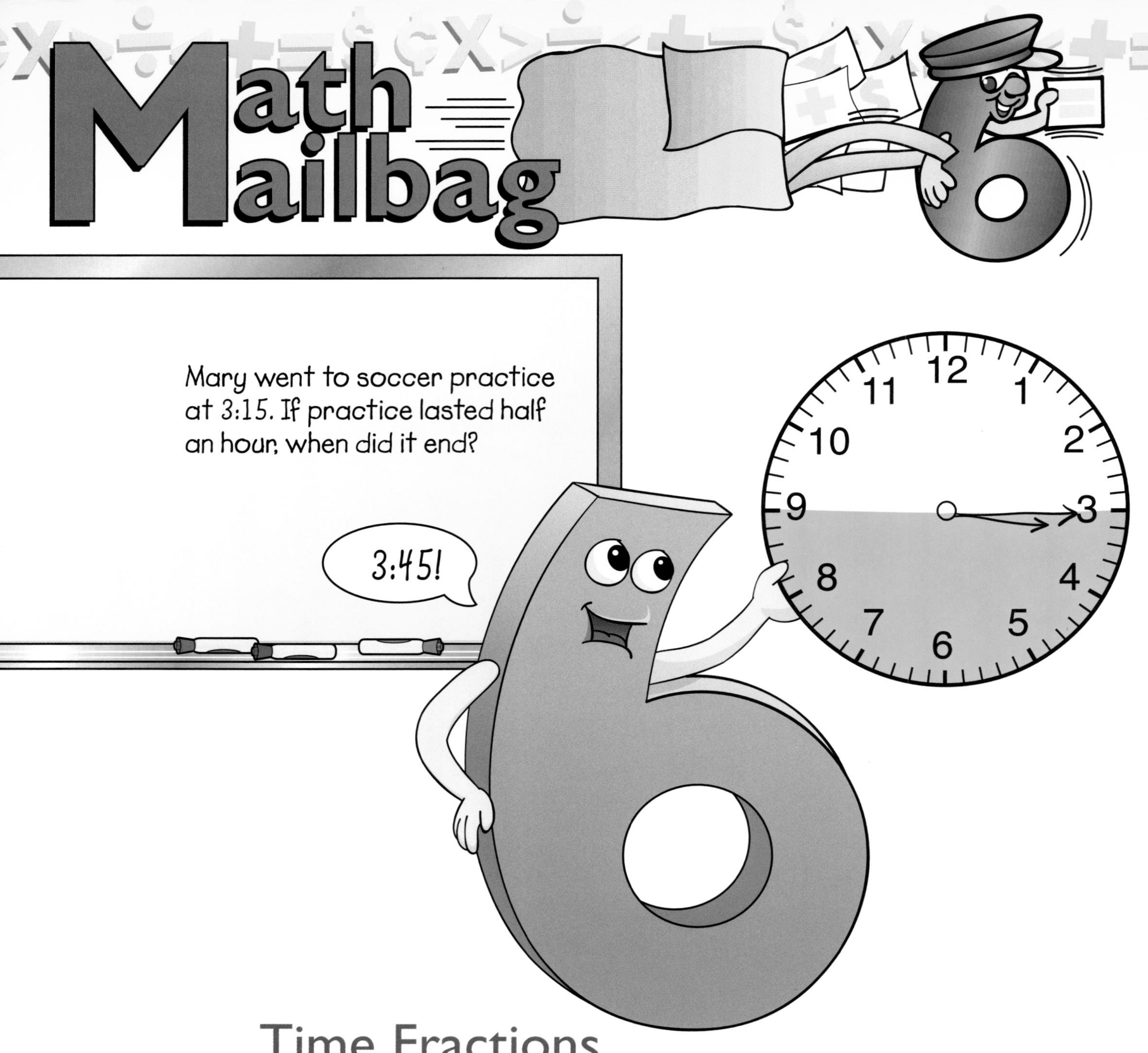

Time Fractions

Vocabulary, telling time

Help students understand the concept of half and quarter hours! Give each child a copy of the clock patterns on page 88. Begin by having the student use a crayon to color half of one clock pattern. Together count the minutes in the colored section and guide students to see that half an hour equals 30 minutes.

To introduce quarter of an hour, ask students how many quarters are in one dollar. Then tell students that there are four quarter hours in one hour. Have each child fold the remaining clock pattern in half twice, resulting in four sections. She colors one of the four sections and then counts the minutes in the clock's colored section to reveal that a quarter hour equals 15 minutes. Complete the activity by giving the class several blank clock patterns and posting a few problems like the one shown. Have students use the clocks to solve the problems.

Julie Lewis, J. O. Davis Elementary, Irving, TX

Where's the Pumpkin?

Problem solving, using mathematical terms

All that's needed for this activity is a hundred board and a wipe-off marker! In advance, write on the board a set of clues like the ones shown. Explain that a pumpkin is missing from the patch and the clues listed will help students find it. Then have each child read the clues, marking out numbers on her hundred board as she rules them out. When she discovers which number the pumpkin is hiding behind, she circles it. Afterward, discuss the results as a class. Then have students clean their boards and repeat the process with a new set of clues.

Cynthia Holcomb, Mertzon, TX

Hundred Number Board

1	2	3	4	5	6	7	8	9	10
11	12	13	14	15	16	17	18	19	20
21	22	23	24	25	26	27	28	29	30
31	32	33	34	35	36	37	38	39	40
41	42	43	44	45	46	47	48	49	50
51	52	53	54	55	56	57	58	59	60
61	62	63	64	65	66	67	68	69	70
71	72	73	74	75	76	77	78	79	80
81	82	83	84	85	86	87	88	89	90
91	92	93	94	95	96	97	98	99	100

The number has a five in the tens place.

The number is greater than 53.

The number is less than 57.

The number has a four in the ones place.

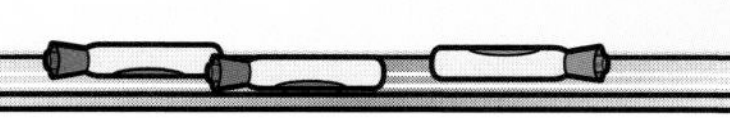

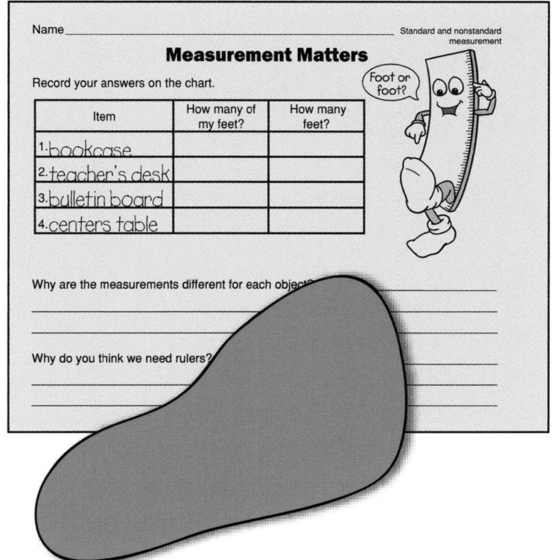

Name__________ Standard and nonstandard measurement

Measurement Matters

Record your answers on the chart.

Item	How many of my feet?	How many feet?
1. bookcase		
2. teacher's desk		
3. bulletin board		
4. centers table		

Why are the measurements different for each object?

Why do you think we need rulers?

Measurement Matters

Using standard and nonstandard units

Obtain a copy of *How Big Is a Foot?* by Rolf Myller. Also program the table on page 88 with four classroom items and then copy a class supply of the reproducible. Begin by having each student trace and cut out his stocking foot. Next, he uses his footprint to measure each item and records his answers on the chart. Invite students to share their answers, and ask them why some aren't the same. Then read the book aloud to students and pose the question again. After students have shared their thoughts, have each child measure the objects again with a ruler. Compare the results and discuss why these measurements are the same.

Joan Costello, William J. McGinn Elementary, Scotch Plains, NJ
Jane Hoogerwerf, St. Mary's Academy, Englewood, CO

Break Ten

Basic facts, fact families

Give each child a set of ten Unifix cubes. Have the student connect the cubes and break the stack in two. The child counts the cubes in each stack and uses the numbers to create an addition problem whose sum is ten. He writes the problem on his paper and then writes the remaining addition and subtraction problems in the fact family as shown. The child reconnects the cubes to form one stack. He repeats the process, breaking the cubes in a different place. Provide further basic facts practice by increasing the number of cubes.

Tiffany Hicks, Garfield Elementary, Parsons, KS

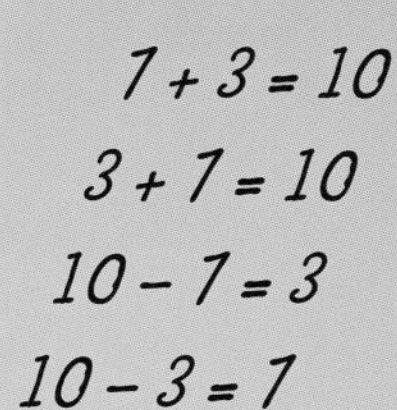

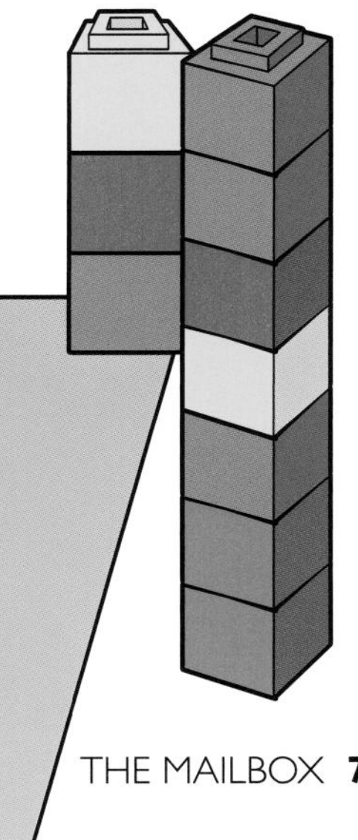

Math Mailbag

Mmm, Mmm Multiples

Multiplication facts

To prepare this partner game, first copy the game cards from page 89, mount them on construction paper, laminate them, and cut them out. Program each card in the left column with a multiple of a preselected factor, such as 4. Make an identical set of cards by programming the cards in the right column with the same multiples. Also write the chosen factor on a copy of page 90 and make a class supply. Place both sets of game cards, the recording sheets, a paper clip, and a pencil at a center.

To play, each child spreads a set of cards in front of him. Player 1 uses a paper clip and pencil to spin the spinner and then writes that number on the first line for problem A. He writes the number from the top of his page on the second line and solves the resulting multiplication problem. Next, he finds the card with that answer and turns it facedown. Then Player 2 takes a turn in the same manner. Players continue until one child has turned over all of his game cards. If a player spins a number that he has already spun, he loses a turn.

Valerie Wood Smith, Morgantown, PA

CD Check
Symmetry

Try using CDs instead of mirrors to test shapes for symmetry! In advance, collect a supply of CDs (such as the ones in junk mail). To check a shape for symmetry, a child simply places a CD along its suspected line of symmetry. If the reflection is identical to the shape on the other side of the CD, then the line of symmetry is correct.

Sherri Bradshaw, Fairfield Elementary, Fort Wayne, IN

Times That Tell About Me
Telling time

First, give each child a tagboard square with a clockface drawn or stamped on it. The child uses crayons to add hair, a neck, and shoulders that resemble her own. Then she cuts out two tagboard clock hands and uses a brad to attach them to her clock. Each day, post a question on the board like the ones shown. The student arranges the hands on her clock to show her answer. Invite each student to share her answer with the class by holding up her clock while saying the time correctly.

Courtney Heigele, Nottingham Elementary, Eudora, KS

What time do you brush your teeth at night?
When do you start getting hungry for lunch?
What's the earliest time that you've woken up?

Measurement Chant
Capacity

Write the chant shown on a sheet of chart paper and post it in your classroom. Have students refer to the chant for a quick reminder of liquid measurements.

Andrea Frost, Pensacola Christian Academy, Pensacola, FL

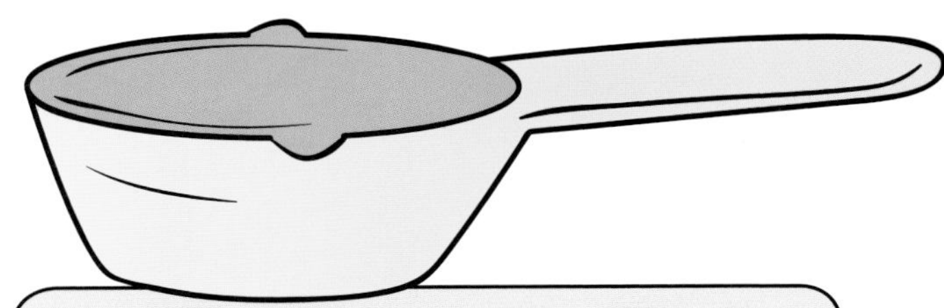

Measuring liquids is really fun!
Here's how it should be done.
Start with a cup; it's the first in line.
Two cups make a pint. Isn't that fine?
Two pints equal a quart. I'm happy to report!
To make a gallon, four quarts is all it takes.
Now I can measure liquids without a mistake!

Math Mailbag

All Suited Up

Skills review

Provide practice on a variety of skills with this sports-themed center. Make a class supply of the jersey patterns (page 91) on tagboard and a copy of the task cards. Cut out the cards and place them in a resealable plastic bag. Next, provide students with reference materials, such as Internet printouts or sports magazines, and have each child choose an athlete. He records the athlete's name and number on a copy of the jersey pattern. Then he decorates the jersey to his liking and cuts it out. Place the completed jerseys with the task cards at a center. A child selects a task card from the bag and completes the activity on a sheet of notebook paper. He continues in this manner for as long as desired.

Stacie Stone Davis, Lima, NY

Make the Match

Learning multiplication tables

This simple center makes learning multiplication facts fun! Use a marker to divide a shoebox top into ten sections as shown. Then select the multiple you'd like students to practice and label each section with a different answer. Trim a set of index cards to fit over the labeled sections. Program the cards with the multiplication facts that correspond to the answers on the lid, and store the cards in a resealable plastic bag. Repeat for as many multiples as desired. Place the box top(s) and the cards at a center. To use the center, a child selects a box top and card set. He matches each multiplication fact to its answer by placing the card atop the matching section. If desired, have the student consult a multiplication table to check his work.

Audrey Alligood, Mallard Creek Elementary, Charlotte, NC

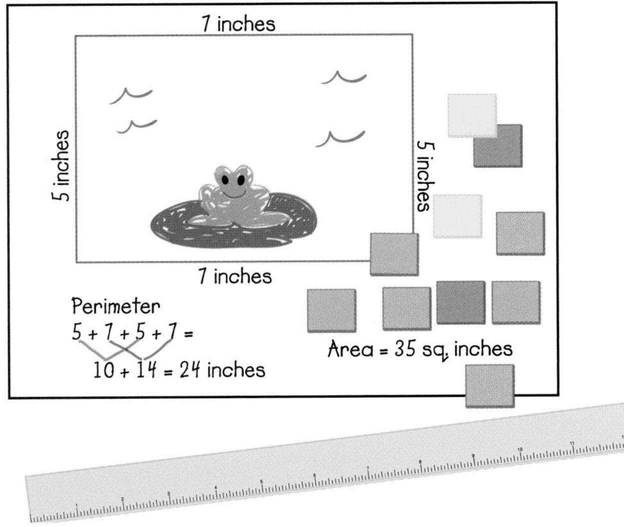

"Pond-ering" Measurements

Perimeter and area

Draw a 5" x 7" rectangle on the board and label each side with its measurement. Tell students that the rectangle represents a pond in Rectangle Town and have each student use a ruler to draw the same-size shape on a piece of paper. Next, model an addition sentence that shows the perimeter of the pond. Have students label their papers with that addition sentence. Then give each student a supply of one-inch tiles to represent lily pads. Tell students to cover the pond with lily pads to find its area. Review the students' solutions and then have each student draw a pond of his own on the back and find its perimeter and area.

Cynthia Holcomb, Mertzon, TX

On the Lookout

Reading and interpreting graphs

Display a graph on the board or overhead projector that is missing one component, such as a title, label, key, or set of numbers. Have each student write a sentence telling what is missing from the graph. Next, have her write three more sentences about the information the graph does provide. Then have students share their responses with a small group.

adapted from an idea by Kelly Hanover
Jane Vernon Elementary, Kenosha, WI

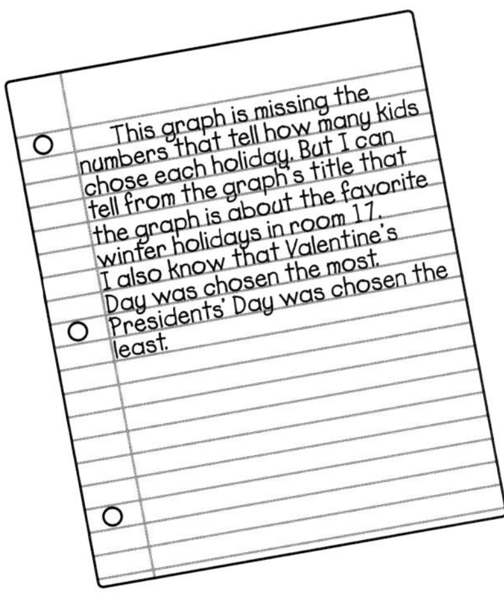

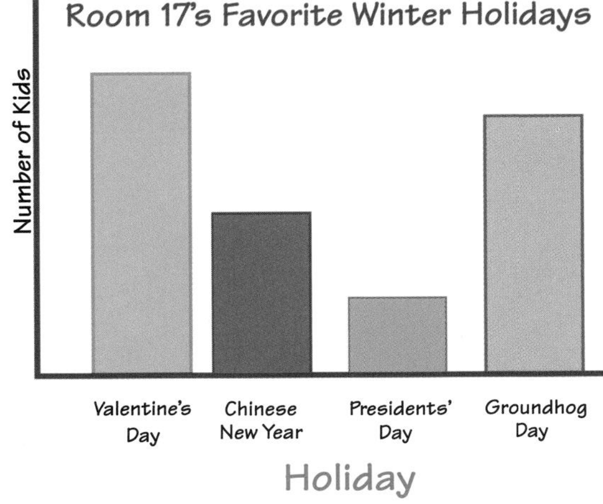

Math Mailbag

1. How many hours long is this movie?
2. How much time is there between movie showings?
3. What time will the last showing end?

NOW SHOWING

Now Showing

Solving problems with elapsed time

Get this partner activity started by listing on the board a variety of movie titles and the movies' lengths in minutes. Also list and explain directions for making a movie schedule, such as what time to start the first showing, the minimum amount of time to allow between showings, and the maximum number of showings per day. A student pair chooses a movie title and creates a schedule on a sentence strip. Then the duo creates a simple poster for the movie and attaches the schedule to the bottom. Display a different poster each day in an area titled "Now Showing." As a math warm-up, pose time-related questions for students to answer by referencing the poster's schedule.

adapted from an idea by Kim Minafo
Dillard Drive Elementary, Raleigh, NC

Angle Action
Identifying angles

To make a manipulative like the one shown, give each student three different-colored 1" x 12" paper strips, and a 1" x 9" strip of one of the colors used. Have each child trim one end of each paper strip to make a point. Next, he glues the two like-colored pieces to make a right angle. He places the remaining two strips behind the right angle and attaches them with a brad. He labels each strip as shown, then sets the manipulative at a desired angle. He uses the manipulative as a guide to draw a desired angle with a dark crayon; then he adds details to make a picture that includes the angle. He exchanges papers with a partner and uses his manipulative to determine if the angle in the drawing is greater than, less than, or equal to a right angle. He writes the angle description on a sticky note and attaches it to the picture. Finally, he shares his findings with a small group. If desired, follow up the activity by having each student complete a copy of page 97.

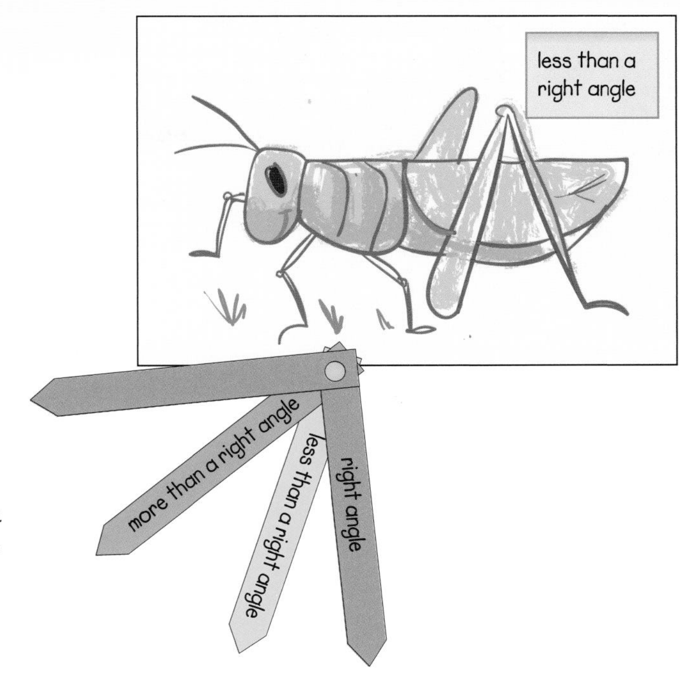

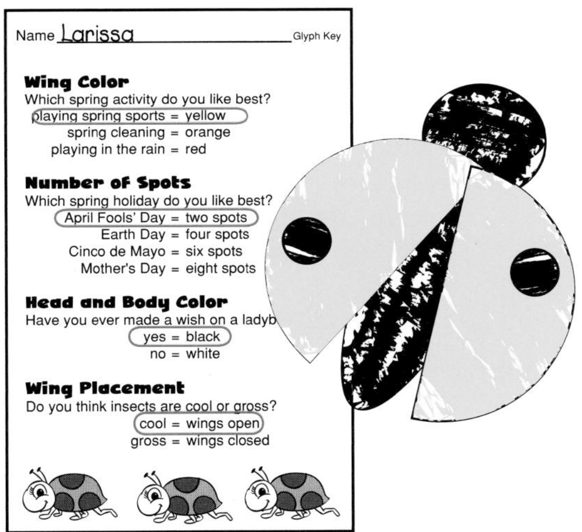
Name Larissa Glyph Key

Wing Color
Which spring activity do you like best?
playing spring sports = yellow
spring cleaning = orange
playing in the rain = red

Number of Spots
Which spring holiday do you like best?
April Fools' Day = two spots
Earth Day = four spots
Cinco de Mayo = six spots
Mother's Day = eight spots

Head and Body Color
Have you ever made a wish on a ladyb
yes = black
no = white

Wing Placement
Do you think insects are cool or gross?
cool = wings open
gross = wings closed

Looking at Ladybugs
Recording and interpreting data

To prepare these garden-creature glyphs, make a class supply of the ladybug patterns on page 92 and the glyph keys on page 93. Give each child a copy of a key and the pattern and have her read through the questions on the key. She circles her answer choices on the paper and then uses the matching directions to put together her glyph. Post the completed projects and pose questions to the class such as "How many students like spring cleaning?" or "Do more students think insects are cool or that insects are gross?" As an alternative, post your questions on the display and have each student record her answers on a sheet of notebook paper.

For Real?
Attributes of solid shapes

This activity for two helps students identify solid shapes by their faces. First, have each student pair trace on a piece of paper one face of a solid figure found in the classroom. Next, have the duo write below the drawing the name of either the solid shape used or an imposter. Then, on the opposite side of the paper, have the students create an answer key by drawing a picture of the solid shape. Also have them write a sentence or two naming the plane shape drawn on the front, the solid shape it is a part of, and the classroom object used. When all students are finished, have each student pair share its plane-shape drawing with the rest of the class. Have another student determine whether the solid shape named is correct, using his knowledge of solid shapes as part of his answer. Then have the student pair verify the answer.

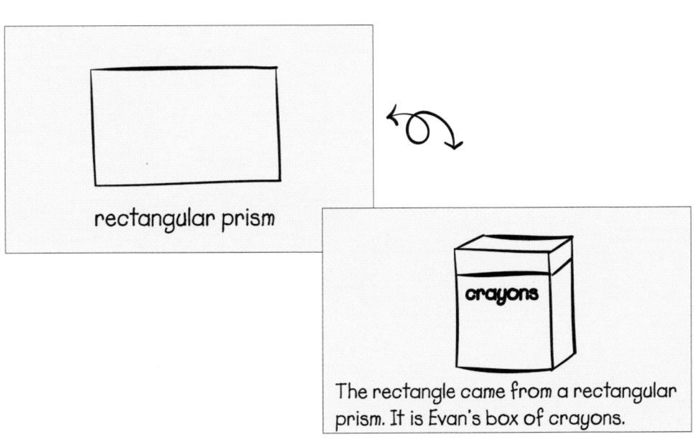

Math Mailbag

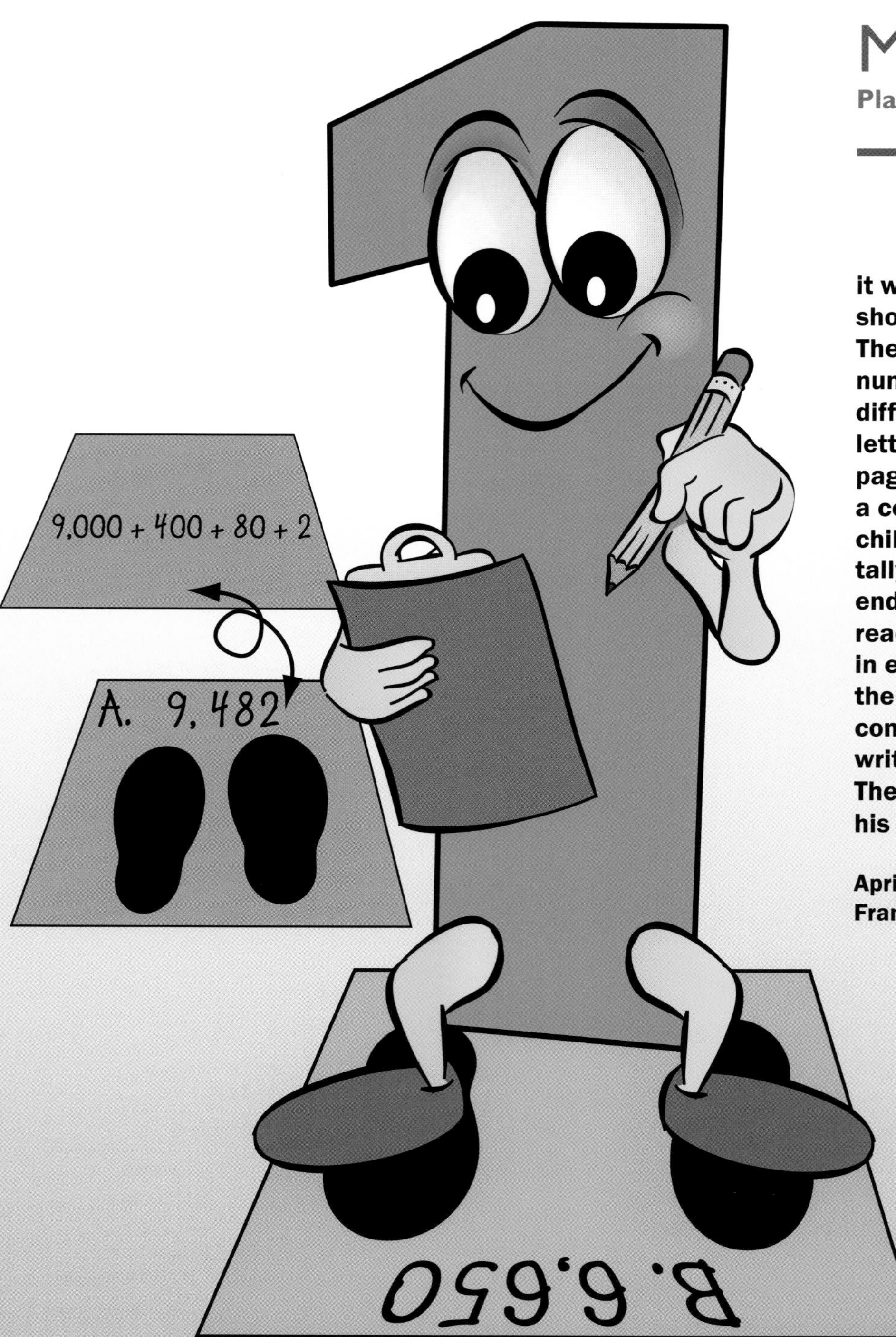

Moving On

Place value

To reinforce writing numbers in expanded form, write a number in standard form on a sheet of construction paper and label it with the letter *A.* Next, glue two shoe cutouts on the paper as shown. Then turn the paper over and write the number in expanded form. Make five different pages, each with a different letter and number; then laminate the pages for durability. Place the pages at a center with a clipboard and paper. A child puts the papers in order horizontally on the floor. Starting at the left end, he stands on the shoe cutouts and reads the number. He writes the number in expanded form on a piece of paper; then he moves to the next number. He continues in this manner until he has written each number in expanded form. Then he turns the papers over to check his work.

April Fowler, Hunterdale Elementary, Franklin, VA

Rounding Strips

Use with "Revved Up!" on page 77.

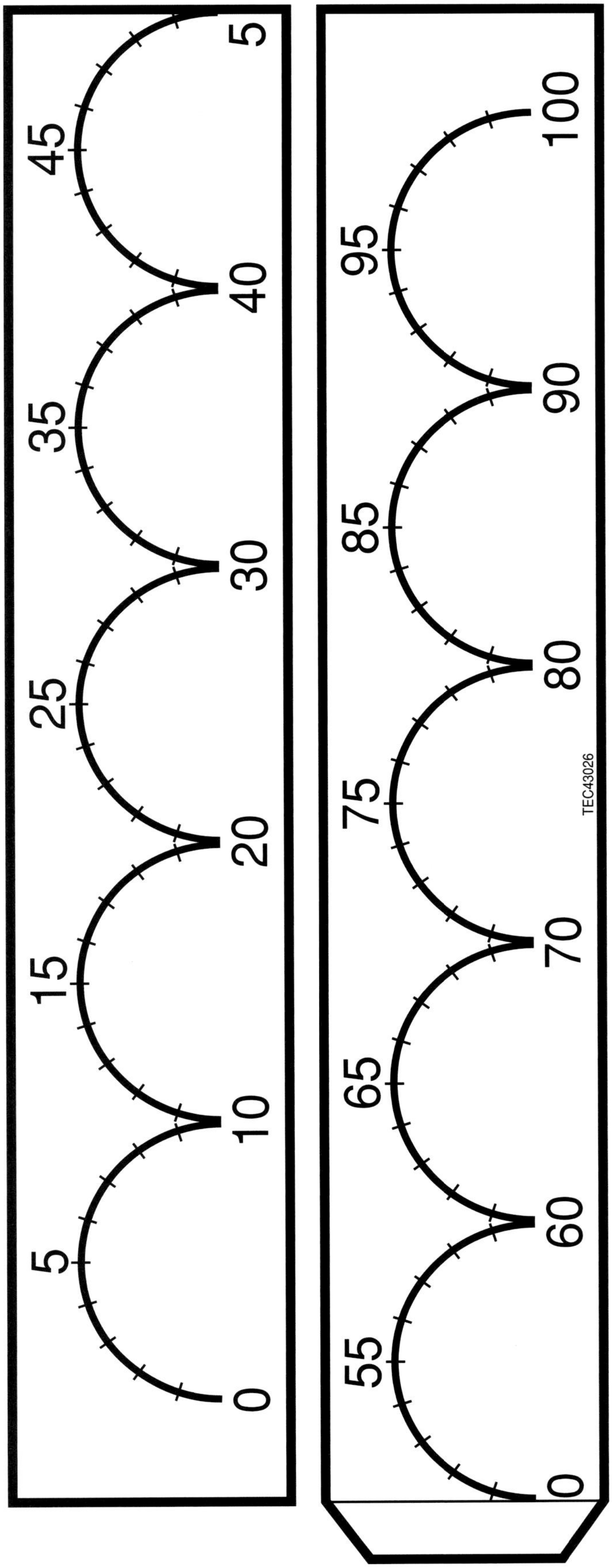

5 10 15 20 25 30 35 40 45 5

0 55 60 65 70 75 80 85 90 95 100

TEC43026

Name ______________________ Rounding to the nearest ten

Ready for Rounding

Round to the nearest ten.
Use your strip to help you.

A. 54 ________

B. 91 ________

C. 14 ________

D. 85 ________

E. 38 ________

F. 22 ________

G. 67 ________

H. 59 ________

I. 73 ________

J. 46 ________

Clock Patterns

Use with "Time Fractions" on page 78.

Name ____________________ Standard and nonstandard measurement

Measurement Matters

Record your answers on the chart.

Item	How many of my feet?	How many feet?
1.		
2.		
3.		
4.		

Why are the measurements different for each object? ____________________

____

____

Why do you think we need rulers? ____________________

____

____

 Note to the teacher: Use with "Measurement Matters" on page 79.

Game Cards

Use with "Mmm, Mmm Multiples" on page 80.

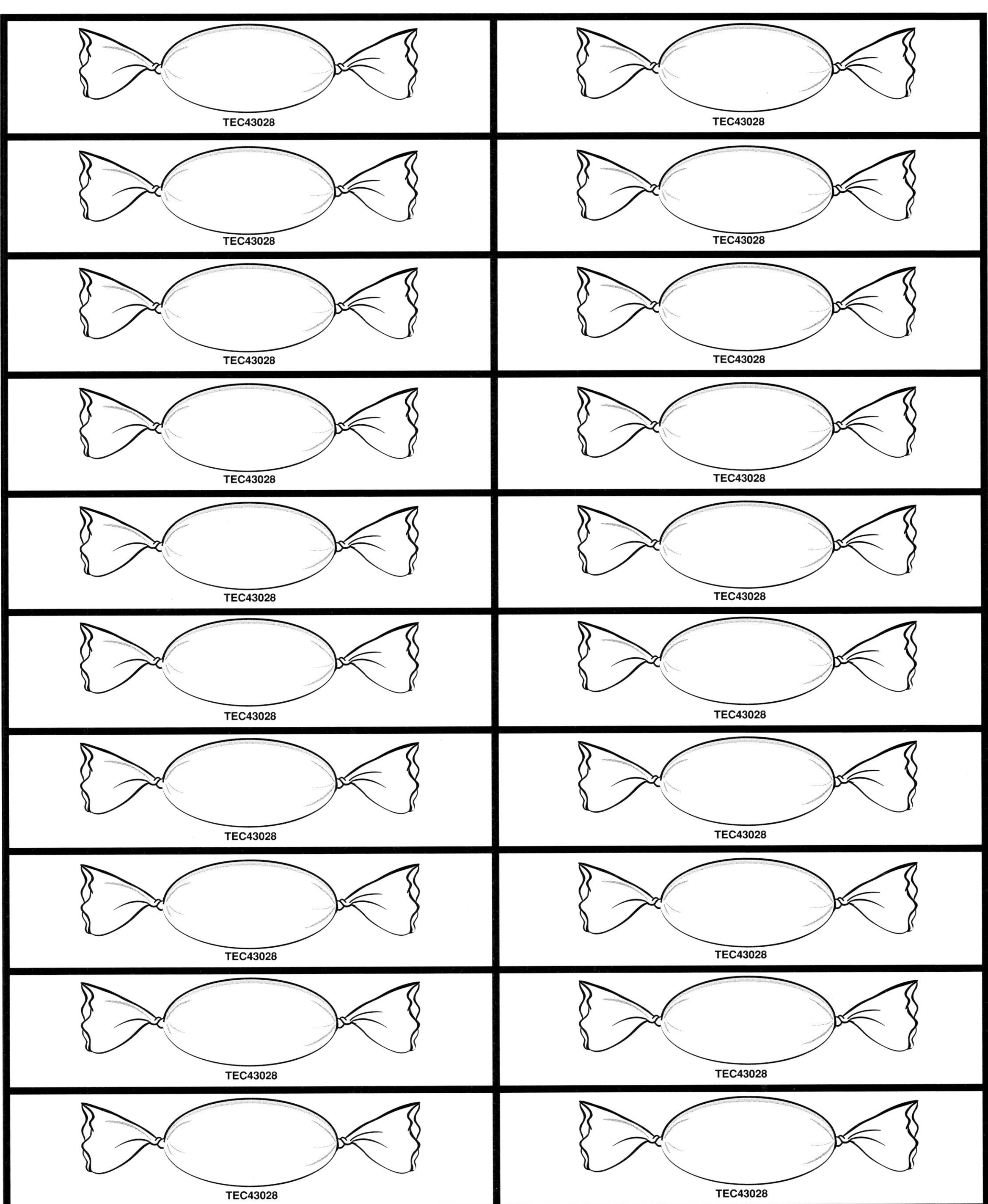

Name ____ Multiplication

Sweet Products

Spin the spinner.
Write the number in the first blank.
Multiply by ______.

A. ______ x ______ = ______

B. ______ x ______ = ______

C. ______ x ______ = ______

D. ______ x ______ = ______

E. ______ x ______ = ______

F. ______ x ______ = ______

G. ______ x ______ = ______

H. ______ x ______ = ______

I. ______ x ______ = ______

J. ______ x ______ = ______

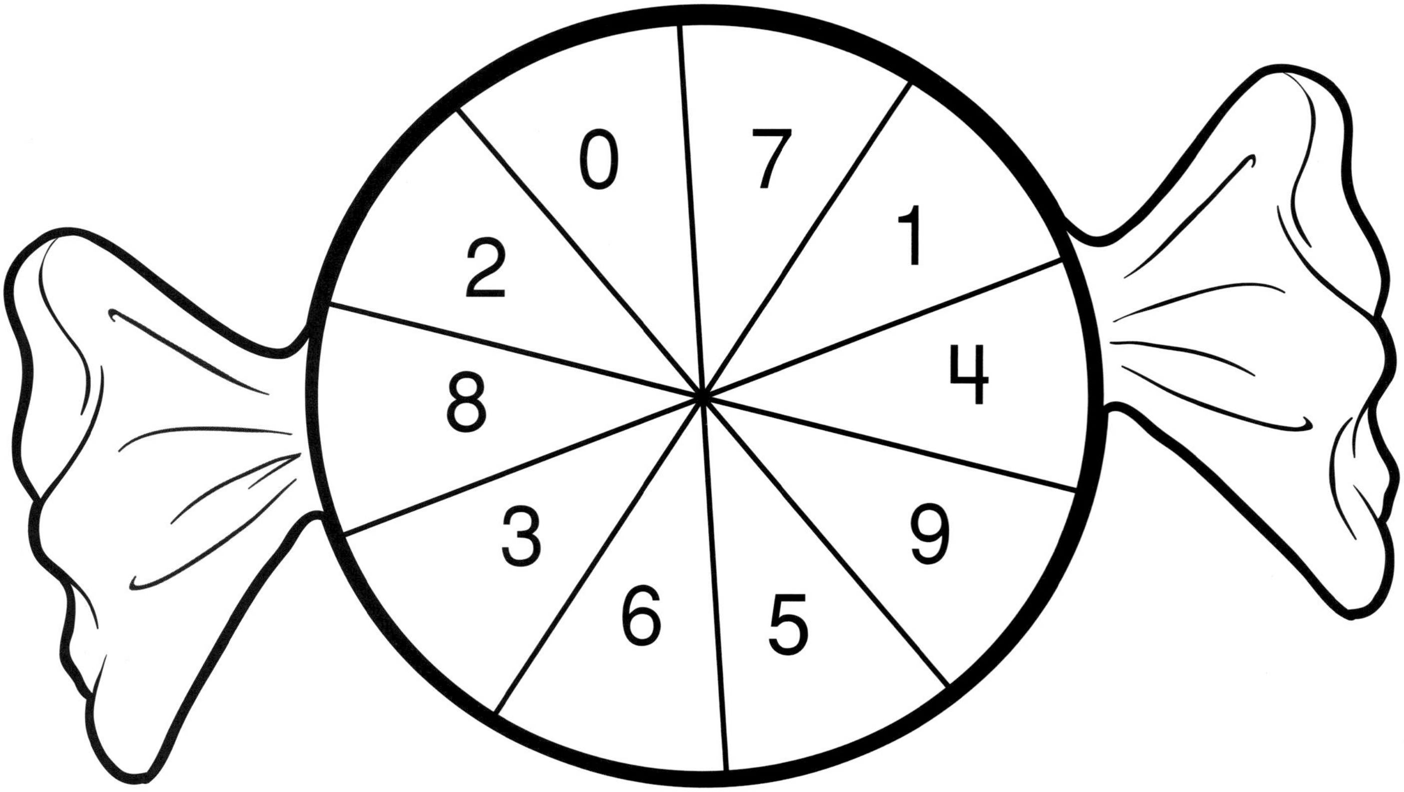

 Note to the teacher: Use with "Mmm, Mmm Multiples" on page 80.

Jersey Patterns and Task Cards

Use with "All Suited Up" on page 82.

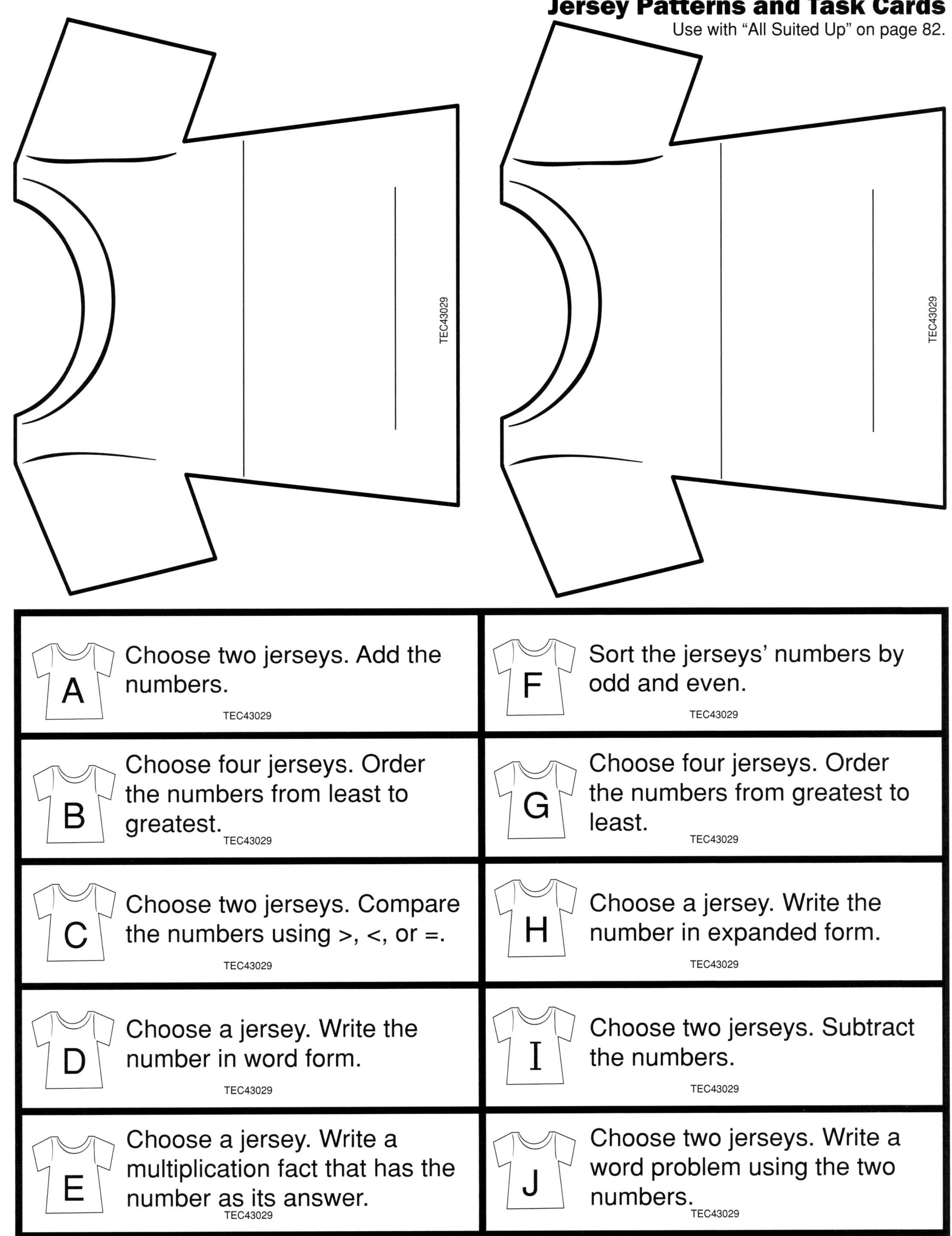

Ladybug Patterns

Use with "Looking at Ladybugs" on page 85.

spots

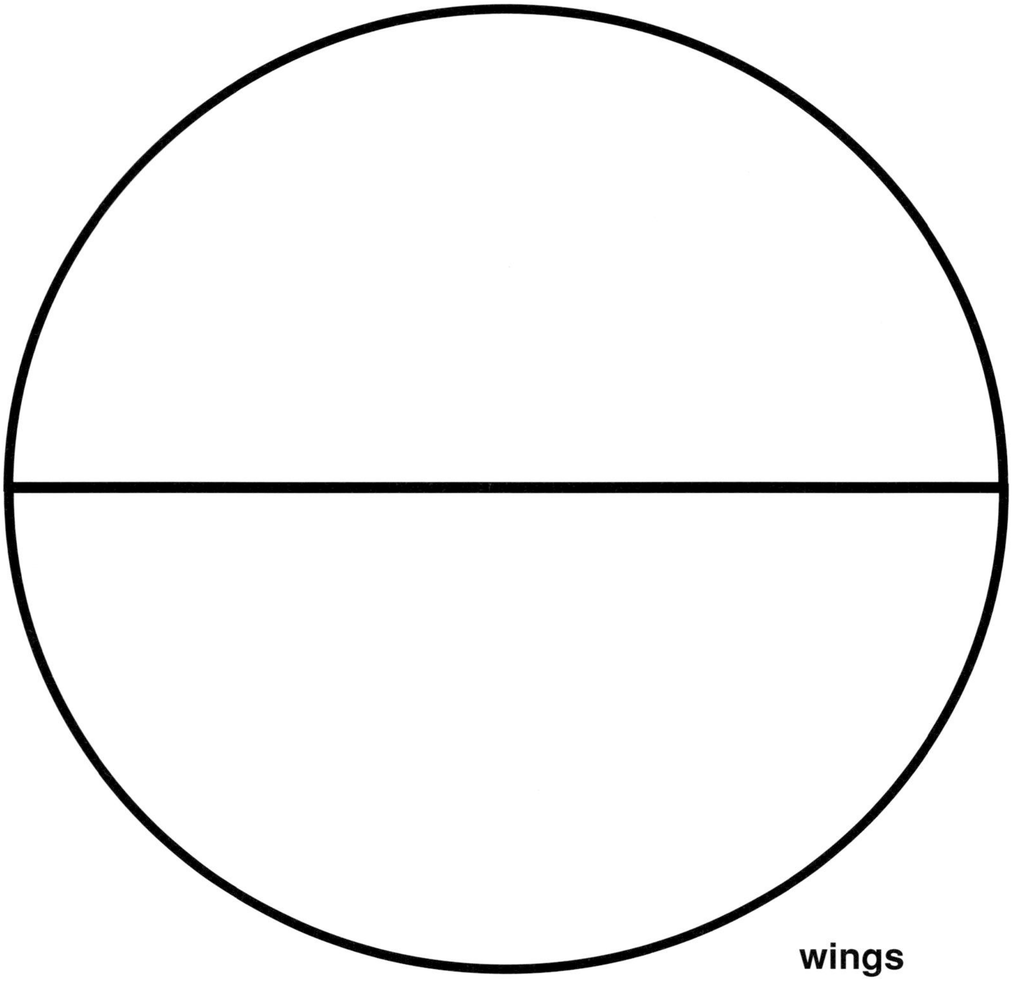

wings

head and body

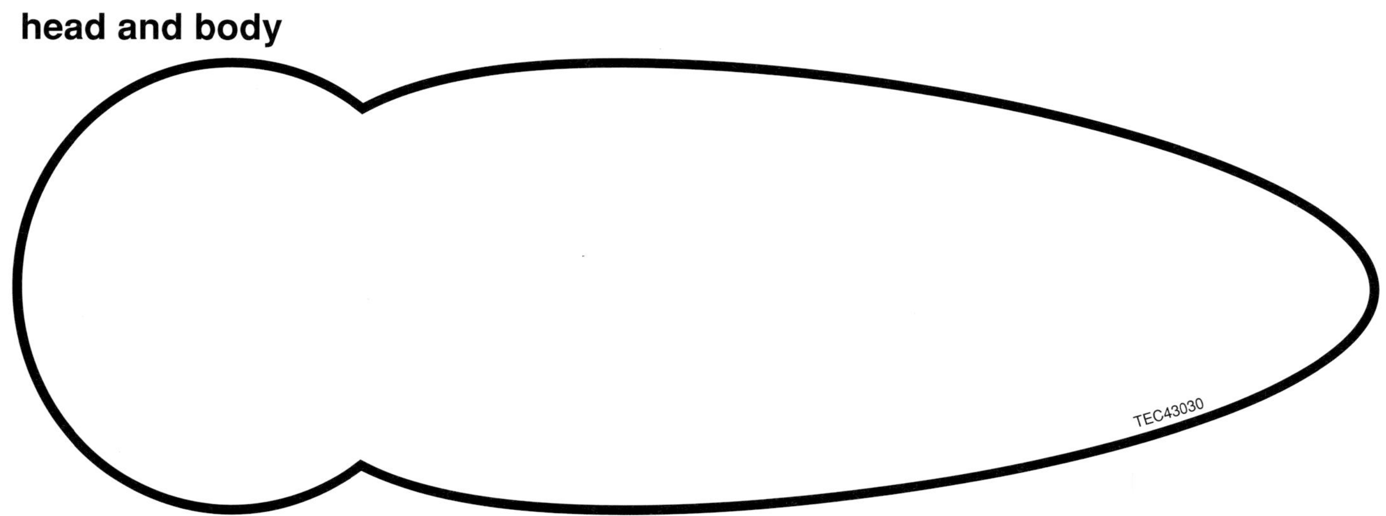

Name________________________ Glyph Key

Wing Color

Which spring activity do you like best?
playing spring sports = yellow
spring cleaning = orange
playing in the rain = red

Number of Spots

Which spring holiday do you like best?
April Fools' Day = two spots
Earth Day = four spots
Cinco de Mayo = six spots
Mother's Day = eight spots

Head and Body Color

Have you ever made a wish on a ladybug?
yes = black
no = white

Wing Placement

Do you think insects are cool or gross?
cool = wings open
gross = wings closed

Name________________________ Glyph Key

Wing Color

Which spring activity do you like best?
playing spring sports = yellow
spring cleaning = orange
playing in the rain = red

Number of Spots

Which spring holiday do you like best?
April Fools' Day = two spots
Earth Day = four spots
Cinco de Mayo = six spots
Mother's Day = eight spots

Head and Body Color

Have you ever made a wish on a ladybug?
yes = black
no = white

Wing Placement

Do you think insects are cool or gross?
cool = wings open
gross = wings closed

©The Mailbox® • TEC43030 • April/May 2007

Name ______________________________ Comparing numbers

Missing Mittens

Color the mitten in each pair that has the greater number.
Write < or > to make a true number sentence.

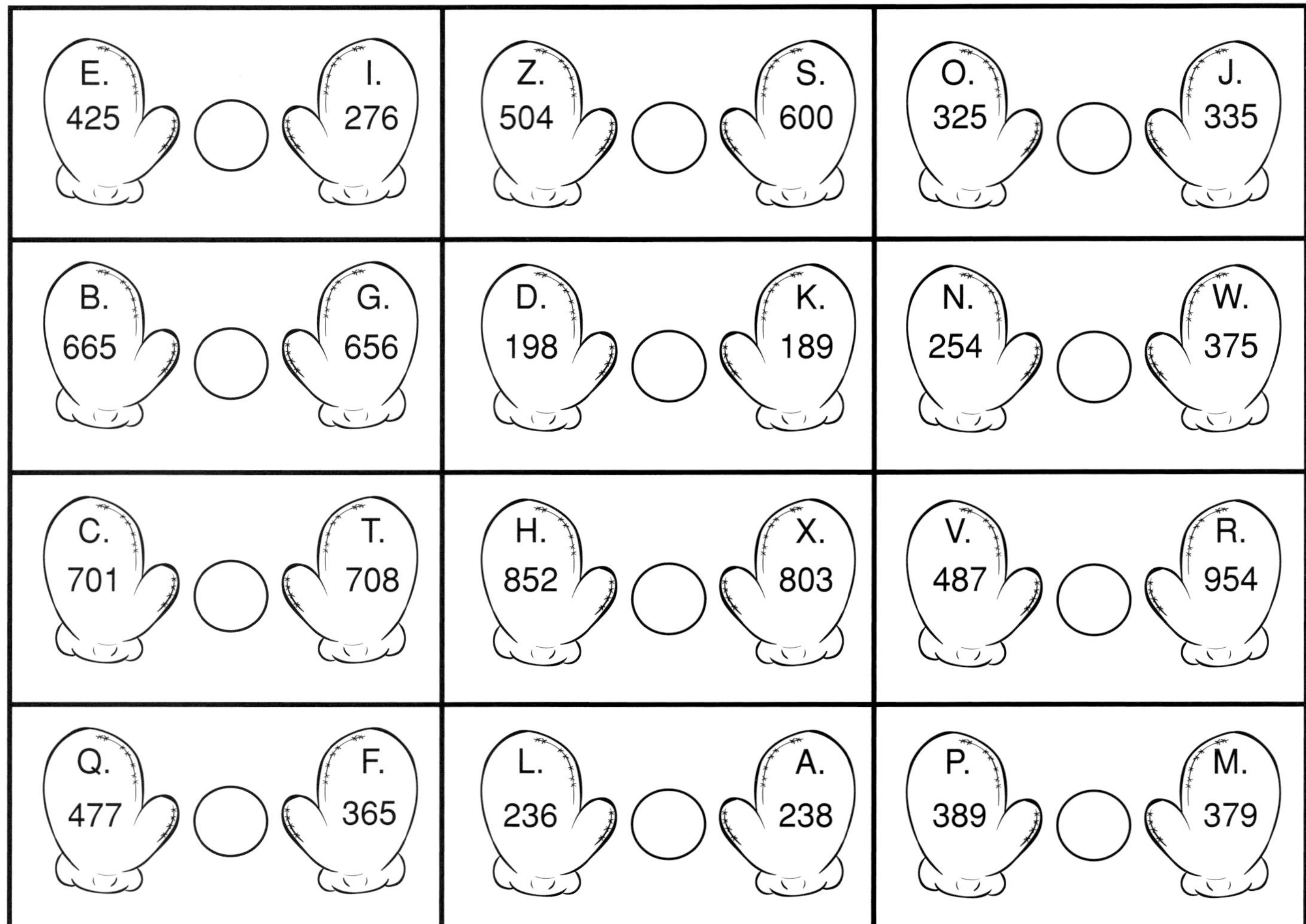

Why did the polar bear need his mittens?

To solve the riddle, match the letters for the colored mittens above to the numbered lines below.

Because his ___ ___ ___ ___
389 238 375 600

___ ___ ___ ___ "___ ___ ___ ___"!
375 425 954 425 665 425 238 954

Name ____ Metric Measurement

Heart Strings

Read the measurement on the heart.
Use a ruler to draw a matching line below the heart.
The first one has been done for you.

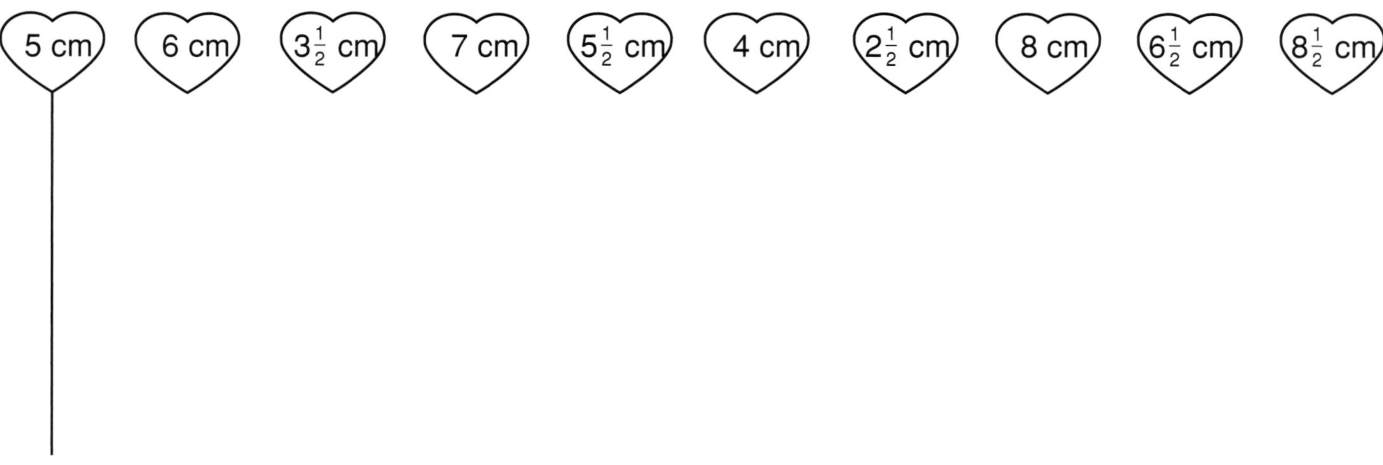

Measure the length of each arrow to the nearest half centimeter.

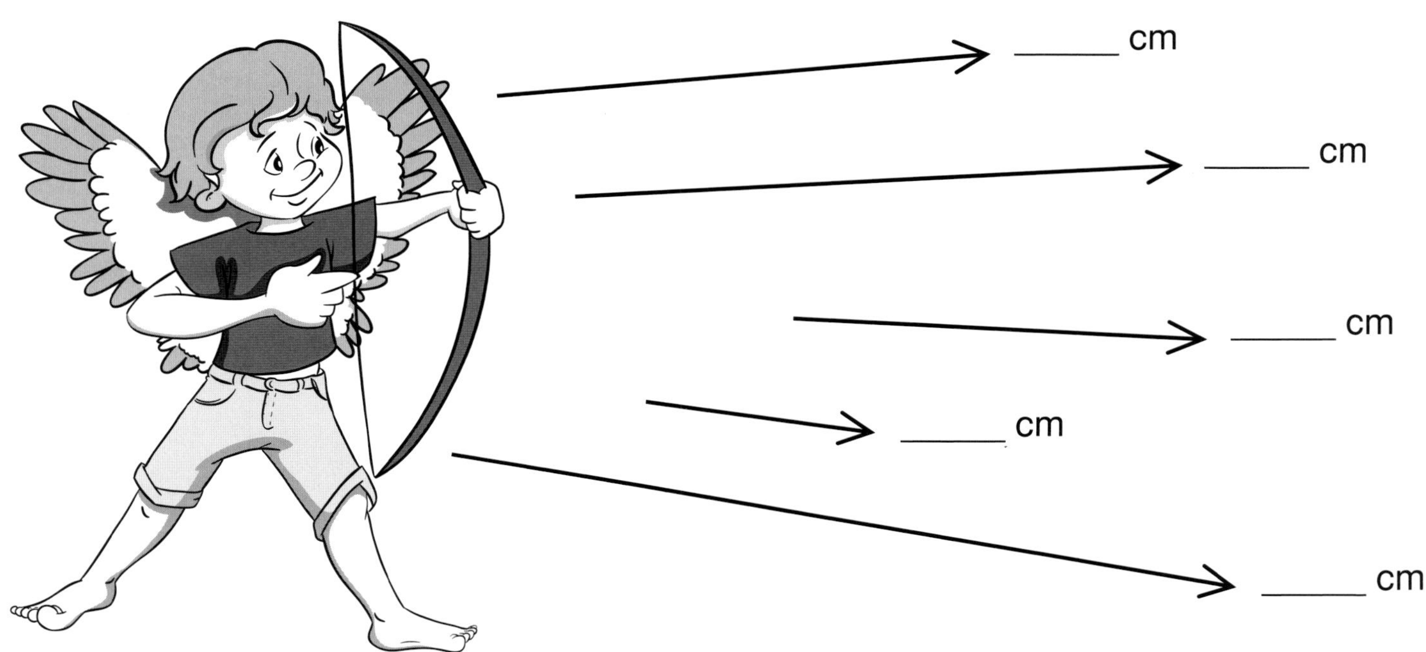

Name ____________________

Hide-and-Seek

How many pounds of gold did each leprechaun hide?
To find out, read the clues and complete the logic chart.
Put a ✓ in each box that is true and an **X** in each box that is not true.

Clues

- Luke hid the most gold.
- Louie hid the smallest amount of gold.
- Leon hid 90 more pounds than Louie.
- Lamar hid less than Luke but more than Liam.
- Liam hid 10 more pounds than Leon.

	10 lb.	100 lb.	110 lb.	111 lb.	1,000 lb.
Lamar					
Leon					
Liam					
Louie					
Luke					

Name ____________________

Beak Business

Write *equal to, less than,* or *greater than* on each matching line.

Name______________________________

The Heat Is On!

Write the temperature.

1. Burlington, VT

100
90
80
70
60

_____ °F

2. Washington, DC

100
90
80
70
60

_____ °F

3. Miami, FL

100
90
80
70
60

_____ °F

4. Fargo, ND

100
90
80
70
60

_____ °F

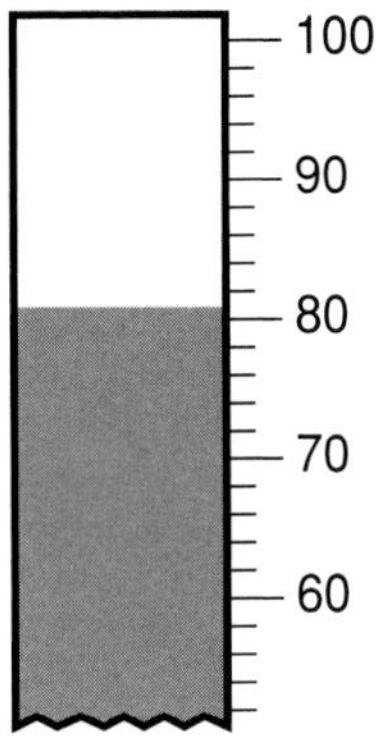

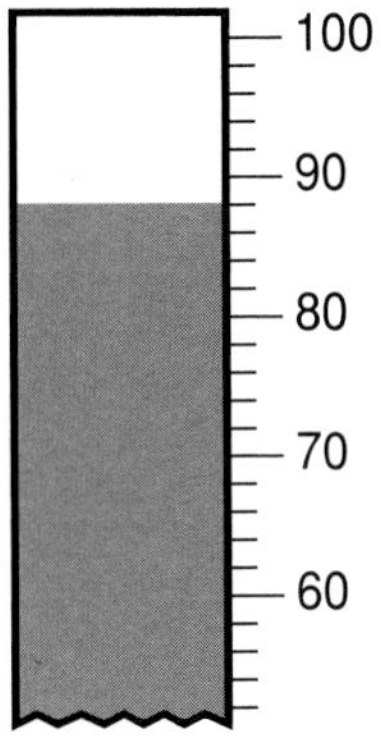

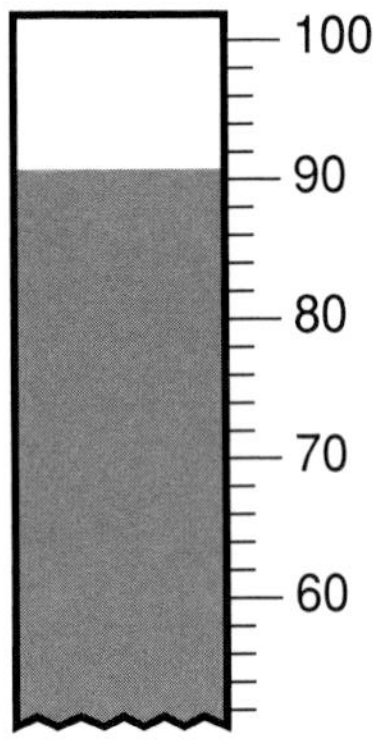

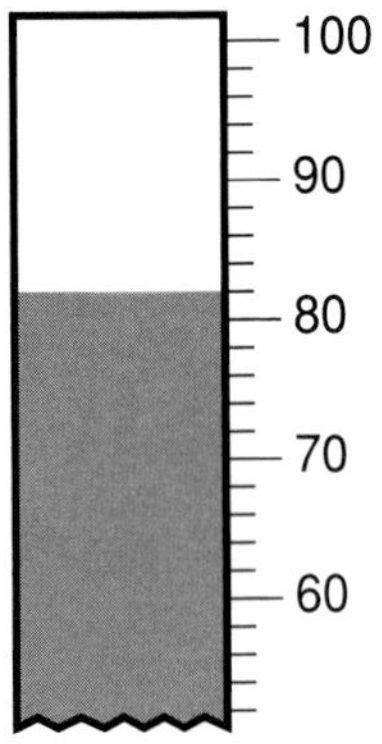

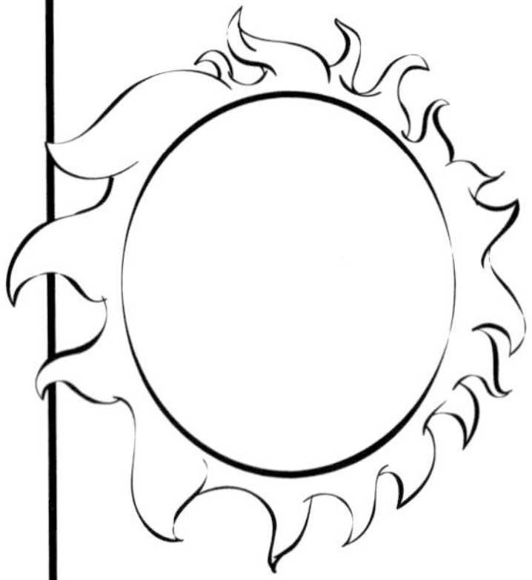

Show the temperature on the thermometer.

5. Kansas City, MO

100
90
80
70
60

89°F

6. Dallas, TX

100
90
80
70
60

96°F

7. San Francisco, CA

100
90
80
70
60

71°F

8. Hilo, HI

100
90
80
70
60

83°F

Average
High
Temperatures
in July

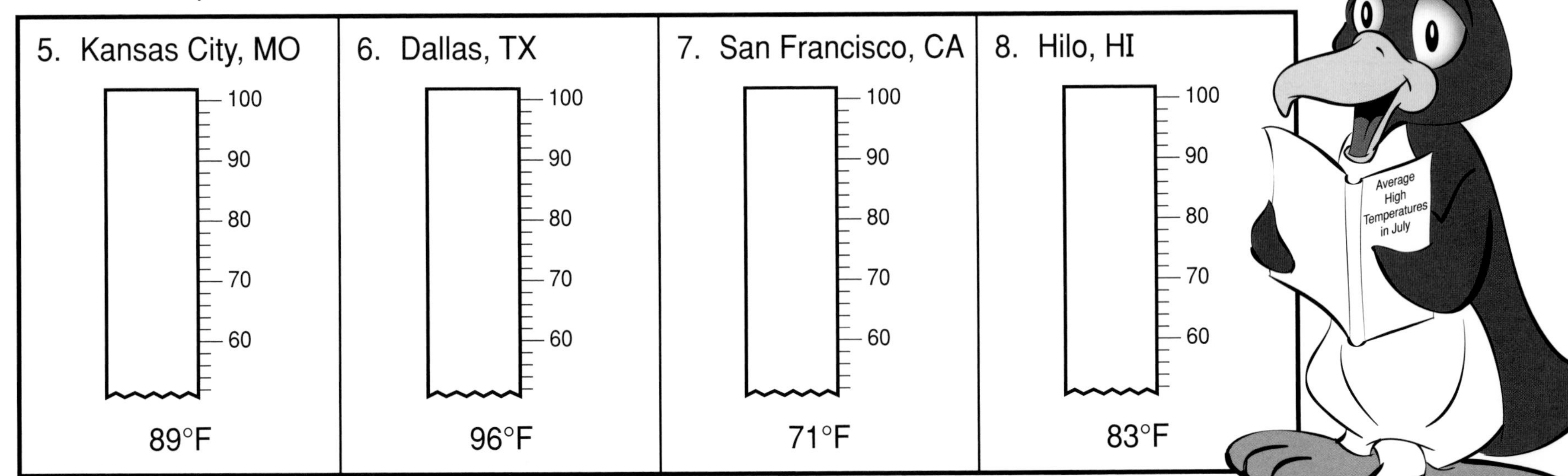

Our Readers Write

Our Readers Write

Personal Game Pieces

My students love using these simple markers to play their learning center games! First, I photograph each student. Next, I give each child his picture and have him cut out his head. Then he uses liquid glue to attach the photo to a one-inch pom-pom. He adds foam feet, and his game piece is ready for play!

Donna Zeffren, Torah Prep School, St. Louis, MO

Reading Chair

To add a special touch to my reading corner, I bought an inexpensive canvas camping chair. I used acrylic paints to decorate it with school-themed pictures and shapes. Each day, I choose one student to sit in the chair during silent reading time. Students love the privilege of sitting in it. What an easy motivator!

Amanda Blais, Holy Family Catholic School, Dayton, OH

Nametag Display

My school lacks hallway bulletin boards, so I create my own hanging displays for student work. On the first day of school I have each student create a colorful, personalized nametag. I glue the nametag to the top of a sheet of black construction paper and laminate it for durability. Next, I glue a small clothespin under the nametag. I hang each display outside of my classroom and simply clip on my students' good work.

Lisa Hammack, Curry Elementary, Jasper, AL

We Are Family

Make students feel welcome and part of your school family by displaying a school family tree. Write each child's and staff member's name on a different paper leaf. Post the leaves around a brown paper tree trunk. Then display the tree where everyone can see it. It's a great way to build community, and students love finding their names on the tree!

Beth Vos, St. Bonaventure School, Columbus, NE

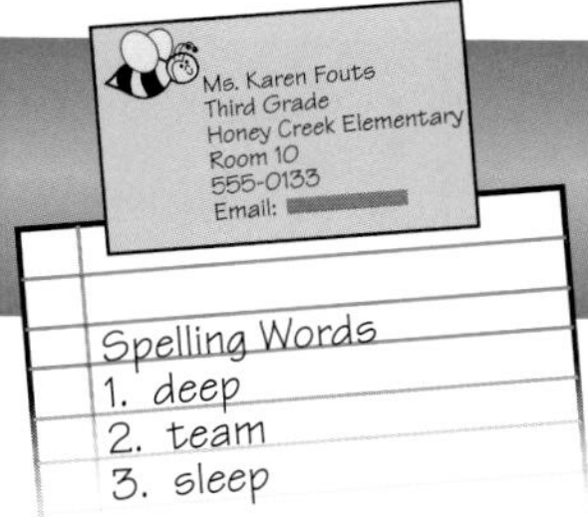

Making Contact

I build parent communication from day one by making my own magnetic business cards. I buy magnetic sheets at an office supply store. Then I use a word processing program to type my name and school contact information on them. I give the cards to parents at open house and ask them to use them to post weekly assignments or information on their refrigerators. It's a reminder that I'm always easy to reach.

Karen Fouts, Honey Creek Elementary, Conyers, GA

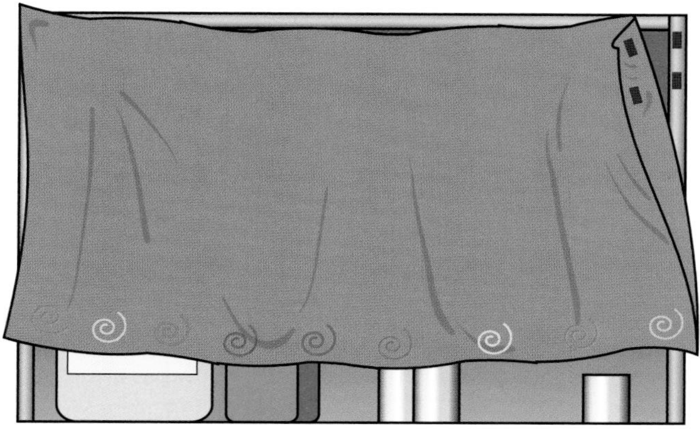

Creative Cover-Up

Want to hide all of your clutter? Make curtains without sewing a stitch! First, I cut burlap to fit the shelves that I want to hide. Then I use acrylic paints and stamps to decorate the burlap. To hang the curtains, I simply attach Velcro fasteners to the burlap and the shelf edge. Voilà! My clutter is out of sight!

Andrea Lovejoy, Goodrich Elementary, Milwaukee, WI

A New Year's Note

A few weeks before school starts, I use this simple idea to welcome students. After I get my class list, I mail a letter to my incoming students telling them how excited I am about the upcoming school year. I also copy my third-grade picture onto the letter. Both students and parents appreciate the letter, and they get a kick out of seeing my picture. It's a great way to break the ice and help students feel at ease!

Welcome to Third Grade!

Dear Friend,

Hi! I am so glad you are in my class. Third grade is awesome! You will explore rocks and minerals, read exciting books, write funny poetry, and learn to multiply.

I look forward to meeting you on August 15. Come prepared to work hard, learn a lot and have fun!

See you soon!

Your teacher,

Ms. Thackston

Tammy Thackston, Rossville Elementary, Rossville, IN

Classroom History

Each year, my students keep a journal timeline to track class events. I label the days of the school year in sets of five on colored sentence strips. I punch a hole under each number; then I post the strips around the perimeter of my room. Each afternoon I have students write about the day's events in their journals. After they record and share their journal entries, one student is chosen to transfer his entry onto a 4" x 6" index card. I punch a hole in the card's top and use an open paper clip to hook the entry to the timeline. It's a great visual reminder of all the learning that takes place throughout the year.

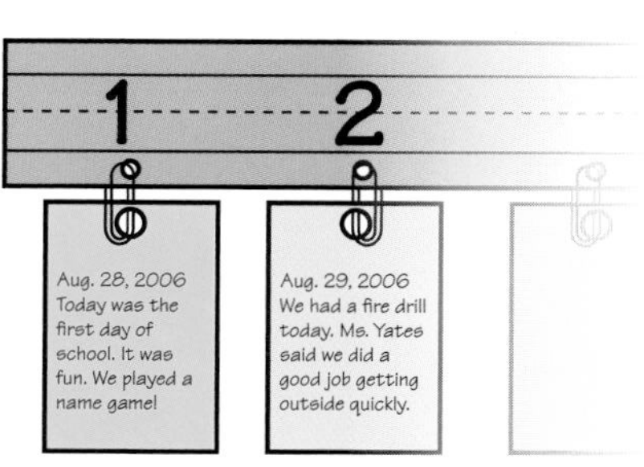

Trisha Yates, Erie Day School, Erie, PA

Everyone's Invited

To celebrate student birthdays, I designate the last Friday of each month as Birthday Time. The class sings "Happy Birthday" to the students who celebrate their birthdays during that month. I also give each honoree a birthday certificate. Then the birthday bunch leads the class in a preplanned activity of their choice, such as a class game or an art activity. Students who have summer birthdays may choose the first month of the school year, the last month, or their half-birthday month to celebrate. We all look forward to Birthday Time, and it replaces celebrations involving sugary sweets.

Jessica Amend, McKenzie Elementary, Wilmette, IL

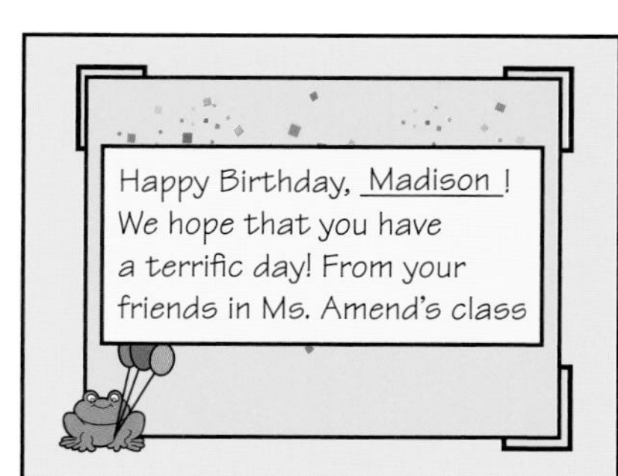

Our Readers Write

Pipe Cleaner Letters

My students love to get their hands on these cursive letters! After I teach the correct way to write a letter, I give each child a pipe cleaner. I show the class how to bend it to resemble the cursive letter they've learned. It's a great tactile reinforcer of the letter, and my students enjoy making them!

Chaya Silverstein, Bais Rivka, Brooklyn, NY

Halloween Treat

Instead of giving candy at Halloween, I give my students a comfort coupon. The coupon gives each child a chance to sit in our classroom library for an afternoon. They can sit in one of the comfortable chairs or work at the table there. What a treat!

Kelli Higgins, P. L. Bolin Elementary, East Peoria, IL

Quick and Easy Transparency

When I'm in a pinch for a clean transparency, I just grab a clear, gallon-size plastic bag. Then I write on it with a dry-erase marker or an overhead pen. It's readable and easy to clean!

Amy Ryan
Grace Lutheran School
St. Petersburg, FL

Nov. 13
Imagine that you are a leaf that's changing colors. Describe how you feel and what you hope to look like when you are done changing.

Clutter Control

I make use of every inch of my classroom with this space-saving idea! I bought several large shower baskets with suction cups. I hang the baskets on an available smooth surface, such as a spare window, whiteboard, or file cabinet. Students place completed work in the baskets. Neat and easy!

Amy Peluso
Minisink Valley Intermediate School
Slate Hill, NY

Name Garrett Date Oct. 3
Cleaning Crew
Write the missing numbers.

Communication Cassettes

I use cassette tapes to record get-well wishes for a sick student or thank-yous to parent volunteers. I keep a supply of tapes on hand and when the need arises, I have my students record their individual messages on a tape. Then I attach a personalized label before sending it on its way. What an extra special way to share your feelings!

Bonnie Gaynor, Franklin Elementary, Franklin, NJ

Budding Display

To help students spell seasonal words, I created a word tree. I use bulletin board paper to make the trunk and leaves. Then I post the tree in an area of the room that is easy to see. Each month, I write on seasonal cutouts words students may want to use in their writing and hang them on the tree. Students have easy access to words they want to spell!

Ashley Lovette, Warsaw Elementary, Warsaw, NC

Budget Boards

I've found a fast and inexpensive way to make a dry-erase board for each child. Simply place a sheet of copy paper inside a clear sheet protector. Students use a dry-erase marker to write their responses and then wipe them clean with a tissue or baby wipe.

Eva Perez, Franz Peter Shubert Elementary, Chicago, IL

The Bright Side

I use our Friday journals to help end the week on a positive note. Each Friday afternoon, I have my students reflect and write about the good things that happened at school that week. We share our journals, and we're all reminded of the joys of the past five days. It's a great way to start the weekend!

Ann Marie Stephens, G. C. Round Elementary, Manassas, VA

Nov. 17
Many good things happened at school this week, but the best happened yesterday. When we practiced our Thanksgiving program, we got a compliment from our principal. She said we sounded very grown-up. She also liked that we all knew our parts. That was a good feeling!

Teacher Time

To take away the stress of the day, the teachers at my school get together to work on craft projects. One teacher serves as the instructor, making a craft ahead of time. Then she teaches the rest of us how to make it. We all bring food to munch on while we craft. We leave these get-togethers feeling relaxed, and we each have a completed project to take with us.

Vicki O'Neal, Lincoln Elementary, Baxter Springs, KS

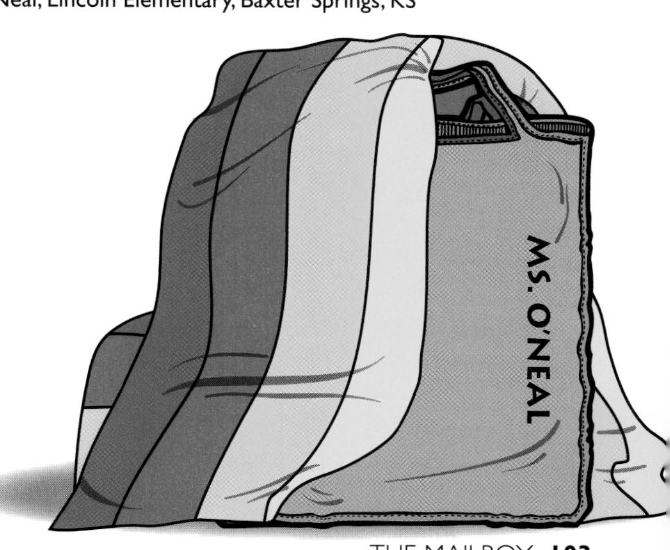

Our Readers Write

Ring of Review Questions

These review cards make great five-minute fillers! After completing a science or social studies lesson, I write a related question on one side of an index card and the answer on the other. I punch a hole in each card's top and store related cards on a ring. Whenever we have a few extra minutes, I grab a set of questions and pose them to students. I also keep the questions at a center. Student pairs visit and take turns asking questions of each other, using the answers on the backs to check their responses.

Sheila Criqui-Kelley
Lebo Elementary
Lebo, KS

Easy Directions

I use this idea for students who find multistep directions challenging. I laminate several index cards and then use a wipe-off marker to write each step on a different card. I punch a hole in the top of each card and store them on a ring. As a child completes one step, she flips the card to reveal the next one. After she completes the activity, I wipe the cards clean and program them for the next activity.

Jennifer Mross, Franklin Elementary, Franklin, NJ

Staying Put

To keep desks from sliding on the carpet in my classroom, I use this simple fix! I bought plastic ties from a home improvement store (the kind often used for bundling wires). After placing students' desks in groups, I wrap the ties around the legs of the desks, tying them together. Now the desks won't separate until I cut the ties.

Patty McKenna
Riverdale Elementary
Orlando, FL

The Gift of Time

I give my students a special holiday gift by distributing cards like the one shown. Each child selects a time for him and a friend of his choice to eat lunch with me. On that day, the three of us eat together and complete a simple holiday craft. My students really enjoy this unique gift!

Kelli Higgins
P. L. Bolin Elementary
East Peoria, IL

Durable Bookmarks

My students love these easy-to-make bookmarks. I laminate leftover strips of bulletin board border and trim them into appropriate-size pieces. Then I give one to each student to use with her personal reading book or her textbook. My students are always ready to open to the appropriate page!

Laura Walden, Carver Elementary
Greenville, TX

Melodic Review

I use this catchy tune to reinforce the difference between antonyms and synonyms in my classroom.

(sung to the tune of "London Bridge")

Antonyms are opposites:
Fast and slow, yes and no.
Antonyms are opposites:
Big and little.

Synonyms are similar:
Fast and quick, broad and thick.
Synonyms are similar:
Small and little.

Lisa Storm, Gilmour Elementary, Kingfisher, OK

Safe Web Surfing

To help my students find an appropriate Web site quickly, I use this time saving idea. In advance, I print each of several Web site addresses on separate paper strips. I laminate the strips and place them near my computers. When a student wants to visit a Web site, he takes the appropriate strip and places it in front of him as he types the address. Having the strip nearby helps to ensure that students will type the correct address and allows youngsters to practice their typing skills without distraction.

Jeanine Bulber, Belleville Schools, Belleville, IL

Super Silent Reading

To get my students excited about silent-reading time, I designed a schedule of activities that correspond with each day of the week. My students really look forward to silent-reading time now!

Suggested Activities

Munching Monday: Bring a snack to eat while reading.
Teddy Tuesday: Read with a favorite stuffed toy.
Wet-Your-Whistle Wednesday: Bring a drink to enjoy while reading.
Thematic Thursday: Read a book about a designated theme.
Friendly Friday: Sit next to a friend and read.

Suzette Pfanstiel, Forest Park Elementary, O'Fallon, MO

Beautiful Border

I have my students make seasonal borders for my classroom displays. I copy a four-inch seasonal drawing to make a large supply. Then I invite my students to color one (or more) picture(s) in their spare time. When I have a desired number of colored drawings, I staple the pictures around the outline of a seasonal bulletin board or display. What an easy, colorful border!

Mary Ann Gildroy, Roundup, MT

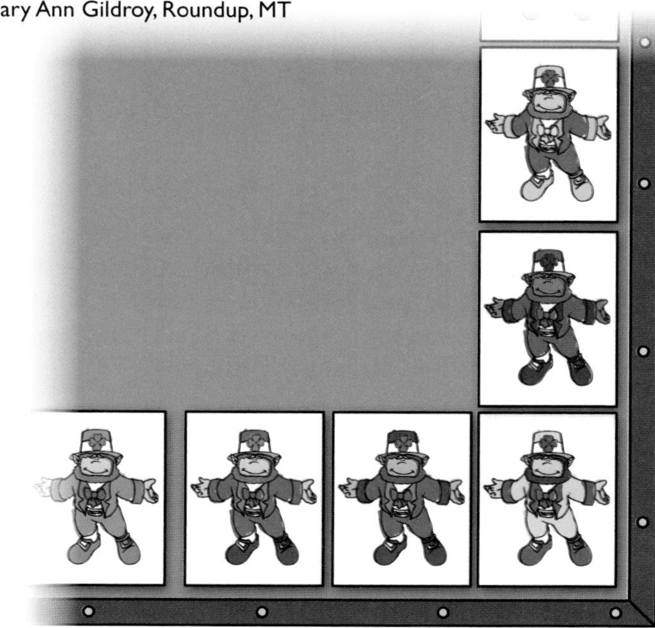

Our Readers Write

Handy Pointers

I like to use plastic drink stirrers as reading pointers. My students are excited to choose their favorite pointer, and the pointers make it easier for them to keep their place as they read. Plus, the pointers are small and easy to store.

Michelle Kessler
Wendell GT Magnet Elementary
Wendell, NC

Phone a Friend

To help students answer discussion questions, I let them "phone a friend." A student makes his hand into phone, pretends to dial a number, and asks another student to help him answer the question. After the other student gives the answer, I have the original student restate it. What a great way to build cooperation and student confidence!

Jolyn Haye, Peach Hill Academy, Moorpark, CA

Fun Geometry Review

To practice geometric terms, I give each of my students pretzel sticks, frosting, and a sheet of waxed paper. I call out a term, such as "right angle" or "parallel lines." Each student uses the frosting to adhere the pretzel sticks to the waxed paper to create an example of the geometric term. Then I make the shape on the overhead so students can check their work. Building the shapes using Wikki Stix yarn strands or dry spaghetti works well too!

Kate Alva, Jefferson Elementary, Carlsbad, CA

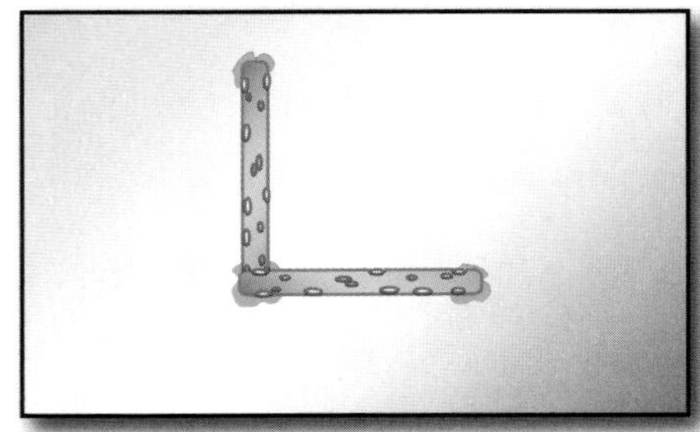

Easy Storage

When I need some extra storage space, I reuse plastic shopping bags. I simply hook the two handles on the indents of a plastic hanger. Then I store my items inside and hang them in my closet until I need them. The bags are easily replaced if torn. How simple!

Susan Marsh, White Township Consolidated
Belvidere, NJ

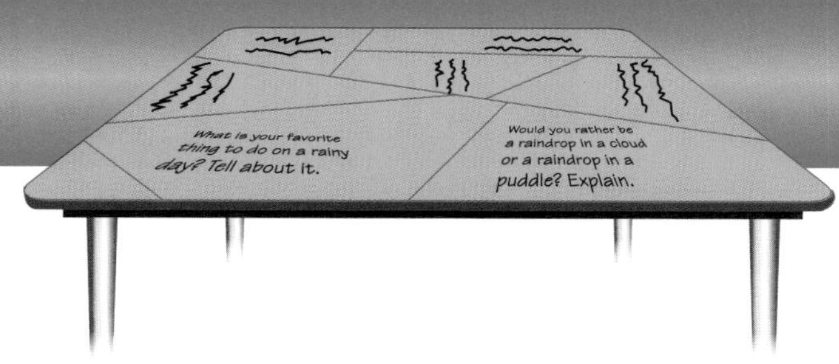

Topics Table

To motivate my students to write, I set up a topics table. I cover one of my large tables with brightly colored butcher paper. Then I write different journal topics on the paper. I also write down topics that students have shared with me. During journal-writing or free time, a student can visit the table and find just the right idea.

Karen Spano, Mount Sinai Elementary, Mount Sinai, NY

Cool Facts

I've found a fun way to get my students interested in research skills. Cut out a simple open book shape from a large piece of construction paper and laminate it. Post it near your reference materials. Periodically update the display with a seasonal or curriculum-based fact and picture. Then encourage students to find out more!

Lydia Hess, Providence School, Chambersburg, PA

Cleaning Time

I use Mr. Clean Magic Eraser cleaning pads to take permanent marker off my laminated posters. It saves me money since I can reuse my materials each year.

Rhonda Inzana, King George Elementary, King George, VA

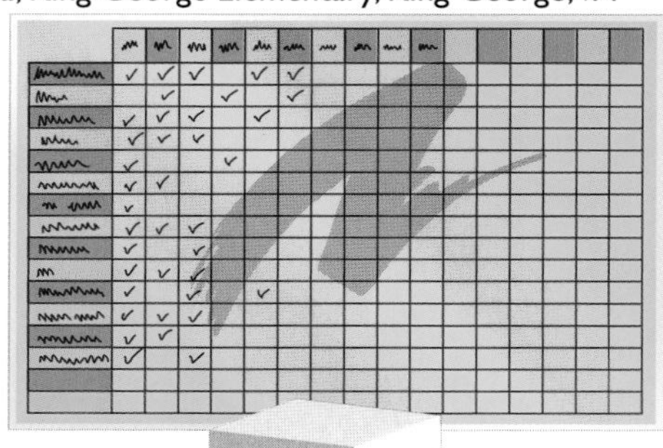

Word Wheel

Using a spinning card file, I create a word list for students to use when writing. First, I write a frequently used word on a card. If appropriate, I also glue a picture to demonstrate the word's meaning. I organize the cards by theme or topic; then I file them alphabetically in the card file. I keep the card file at my writing center for students to access when needed. As the year progresses, students help me add more words.

Deanna Higgins, George Washington School No. 1, Elizabeth, NJ

Treasure Keepers

When student artwork needs to go home but won't fit inside a backpack, I reuse plastic newspaper sleeves to keep them safe. I simply roll up the item, place it in a sleeve, and tie it to the student's backpack. Parents, friends, and family members pitch in by sending in empty bags, so I always have these plastic carryalls handy.

Mary Beth Bailey, Kirk Road School, Rochester, NY

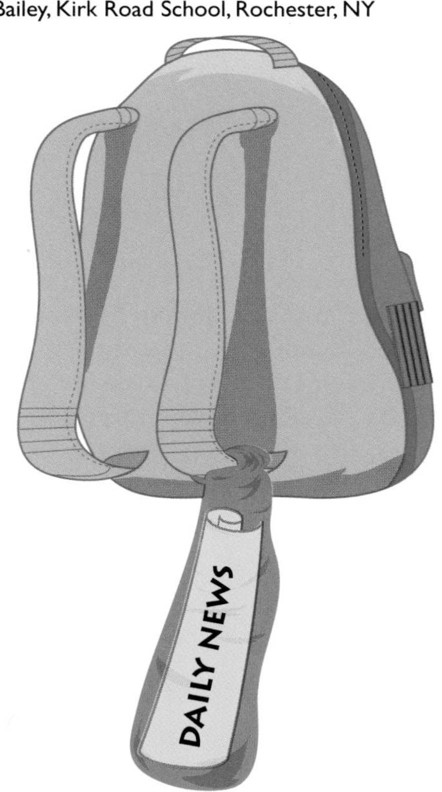

Autographed Beach Ball

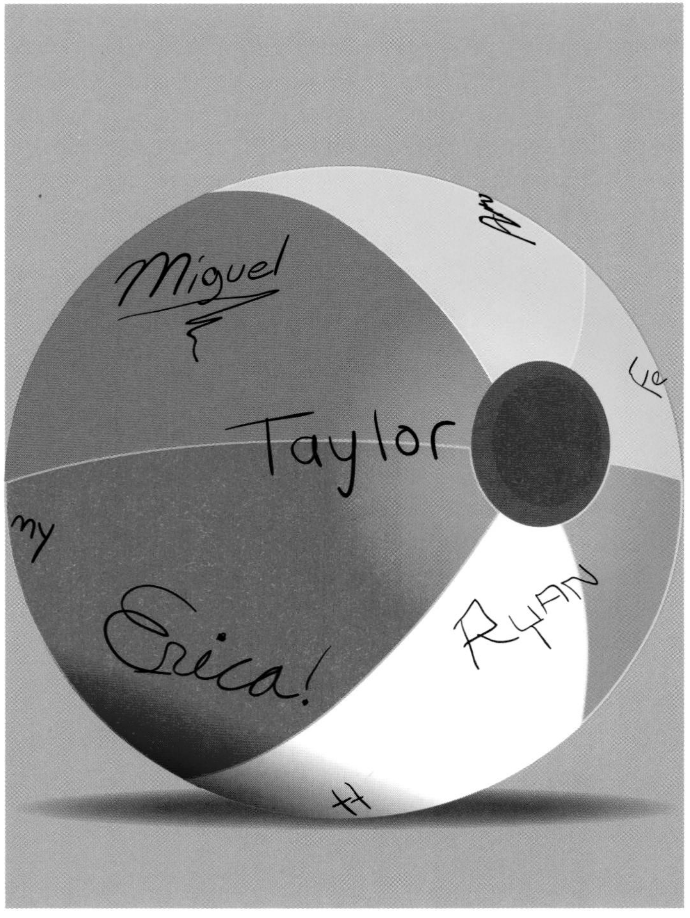

To celebrate the end of the school year and the beginning of summer, I give each child a six-inch beach ball. Then each student uses a permanent marker to sign his classmates' beach balls. My students have a great time getting the signatures, and when they're done, they take home a fun memento of their second-grade year.

Stephanie Hogle, Bronson Elementary, Bronson, FL

Retirement Gift

When a beloved colleague retired, I made her a gift to help us keep in touch. I wrote the name of a different local meeting place on each of 12 index cards and kept a copy of the locations for myself. I placed each card in a sealed envelope with the month written on the outside. I also wrote a letter explaining the gift. Then I placed the envelopes and the letter in a small, decorative box. On the first day of each month, she will open the corresponding envelope to find out where we will meet to catch up.

Dianne Pratt, Borah Elementary, Coeur D'alene, ID

Picture Magnet

To personalize my good-work display, I take a picture of each child. After the pictures are developed, I cut around each child's image and attach a self-adhesive magnet to the back. I use each child's picture magnet to post his work on a magnetic white board or chalkboard. When other students or classroom visitors look at the board, they can easily identify the student that completed the great work.

Rebecca Boehler, Devaney Elementary, Terre Haute, IN

Write On!

Write On!

All About Me

Using adjectives

These simple booklets help students get acquainted with their classmates! First, each child makes a flip booklet by stacking two half sheets of blank paper and then sliding the top sheet upward about an inch. He folds and staples the booklet as shown. On the top flap, the student writes his name and draws a self-portrait. On the bottom of each remaining flap, he writes an adjective that describes himself and a sentence that explains his choice. Then he illustrates the sentence at the top of the page. After each child's booklet is complete, invite him to share it with the class. Finally, post the booklets on a display titled "Adjectives That Tell About Me."

Rita Skavinsky, Minersville Elementary Center, Minersville, PA

Job Applications

Persuasive writing

Boost writing skills with this simple activity! On Friday, list on the board the classroom jobs that are available for the next week. Instruct each child to select a job she'd like to have. Then have her apply for the job by writing a short persuasive paragraph that includes the job title and the reasons why she would do the job well. Collect the finished paragraphs and read them. On Monday, assign a job to each child based on her response. Repeat the process every few weeks to fine-tune students' persuasive-writing skills.

I'd like to be the door holder next week. I would be really good at this job because I'm strong. It would be easy for me to hold the door. Plus, I'm nice to everyone. I also like to help people. That's why I think I would be a good door holder.

Jana

Moira Conway, Bennett Elementary, Chicago, IL

What It Is or What It Could Be

Descriptive writing

What It Is	What It Could Be

Have students brainstorm their way to better writing! In advance, write on a transparency a short story. Use the same word to describe the subject throughout the story. Also post a T chart and label it as shown. Begin by placing the story on the overhead and reading it aloud to students. As a class, identify the subject and then count the number of times the same word was used to describe it. Next, ask students, "We know what it is, but what could it be?" Write their responses on the chart. For instance, if the subject is a cat, suggestions might include furry feline, playful pet, green-eyed friend, or cuddly playmate. Then revise your story on the overhead, including students' suggestions where possible. Afterward, have each child repeat the process with a recently written story.

Mary Bryan, Poinciana Elementary, Naples, FL

Timely Prompts

Journal writing

Invite each student to respond to a prompt below. Then have students share their responses with the class.

- What is your favorite way to eat apples? Why?
- Imagine that you are a famous chef. Create a new apple dish to share with your friends. Give the dish a name and explain how to make it.
- People often use the idiom "apple of my eye" to describe something (or someone) that is very special to them. What's the apple of your eye? Write a short poem telling why this thing is so special.

Write On!

A Cat Tale

Beginning, middle, and end

This story activity is the cat's meow! To begin, review the three main parts of a story: beginning, middle, and end. Then have each child write a short story about a cat on a sheet of notebook paper. After proofreading his work, the child writes the final draft on a copy of the cat pattern on page 122, writing the beginning on the cat's head, the middle on its midsection, and the end on its tail. If desired, he outlines or lightly colors his creation; then he cuts it out. Post the completed stories atop a display board or along a window ledge, allowing each tail to dangle down.

Janette E. Anderson, Fremont, CA

		Abigail
Nouns	Verbs	Adjectives
bats	flying	fast
house	opens	dark
tree	blows	tall
pumpkins	rolling	orange
scarecrow	scaring	skinny

Picture It!
Prewriting

Set the scene for writing! Have each child use a white crayon to draw a detailed seasonal scene on a piece of black construction paper. Then, on another sheet of paper, have her list five nouns, five verbs, and five adjectives based on the picture. She uses her word list to create a poem. Post the completed poems with their pictures on a display titled "Seasonal Scenes."

Katie Robinson, Limestone Walters School, Peoria, IL

Helping Hands
Editing

Hand over editing responsibilities to your students! Pair students; then give each student a piece of construction paper and have him trace and cut out a hand shape. After reading his partner's writing, he writes a positive comment across each finger. Then he writes a suggestion for improvement across the thumb. He clips the hand to the paper before returning it to his partner for revision.

Terry Healy, Marlatt Elementary, Manhattan, KS

Timely Prompts
Journal writing

Invite students to respond to a prompt below. Then have students share their responses with the class.

- Imagine that you are a leaf that's changing colors. Describe how you feel and what you hope to look like when you are done changing.
- A pourquoi tale explains how and why things in nature are the way they are. Write your own pourquoi tale, explaining why leaves change colors in the fall.
- Pretend that you are a leaf at the bottom of a pile. Soon you will be bagged and put on the curb. Plan your escape.

Write On!

Reindeer Chatter

Writing dialogue

In advance, make a class supply of the reindeer pattern on page 123 onto brown construction paper. Begin by brainstorming with students what one reindeer might say to another, such as asking and answering a question or telling a joke and its punch line. List their ideas on the board. Next, have each student work with a partner to write a short dialogue between two reindeer. Then have each child make a reindeer by cutting out the pattern and adding decorative details such as wiggle eyes, a pom-pom nose, and a gift wrap hat. The child writes his part of the reindeer dialogue on a sheet of paper and cuts around it to make a speech bubble. Post reindeer pairs and speech bubbles side by side so others can read their conversations.

Janette E. Anderson, Fremont, CA

On the Lookout
Proofreading

Draw attention to students' writing with this easy-to-make poster. On a large sheet of construction paper, write "WANTED" in dark letters and name a specific writing skill underneath. Include examples or necessary information to give students a clear picture of what you are looking for in their writing. Then write a reward at the bottom of the poster for students who correctly include the skill in their work. Display the poster as a reminder when students are working on a writing project. Vary the posters as skills improve and new skills are introduced.

Terry Healy, Marlatt Elementary, Manhattan, KS

All Wrapped Up
Expository writing

Package students' past experiences into this eye-catching project! Start by having each student write about the best gift he received or tell how giving makes him feel. Then have him sandwich his completed draft between two sheets of construction paper. Next, he uses construction paper scraps, ribbons, and bows to make the front side of the paper resemble a wrapped gift. Then post the projects on a display titled "Wrapped Up in Writing."

Jennifer Cook,
Dr. N. H. Jones
Elementary,
Ocala, FL

Timely Prompts
Journal writing

Invite students to respond to a prompt below. Then have them share their responses with the class.

- Looking out the window one morning, you see animal tracks in the snow. You decide to follow the tracks. Where do they take you? What do you find?
- Would you rather have a warm and sunny winter vacation or a cold and snowy one? Tell why.
- What is your favorite winter activity? Write a letter to a friend describing the activity.

Krista Hatten, Forks Elementary, Easton, PA

Write On!

To Tell You the "Tooth"

Understanding point of view

Use National Children's Dental Health Month in February as an opportunity to discuss point of view. Have students think about good tooth care from the point of view of the tooth. For example, have them think about how it must feel to be brushed or flossed or how it would feel to be neglected. Then pair students and have them design a poster from a tooth's point of view that encourages children to brush their teeth. Hang the posters in the hallway throughout the month or ask other teachers in your school to each take one to display in their classrooms.

Kelly Hanover, Jane Vernon Elementary, Kenosha, WI

More Precious Than Gold!
Writing a paragraph

Share a leprechaun-related story from your school library and then discuss with students the value of gold. Next, challenge students to think of things that are even more valuable to them than gold. Encourage students to think about family, friends, and pets. Once each student has decided on one or two things, give him a copy of the pot-of-gold pattern on page 124. On the copy, he writes a paragraph telling about what he believes is even more precious than gold. Display the writings with a friendly leprechaun character under the title "More Precious Than Gold!"

Jennifer Cooper, Seoul Foreign School, Seoul, South Korea

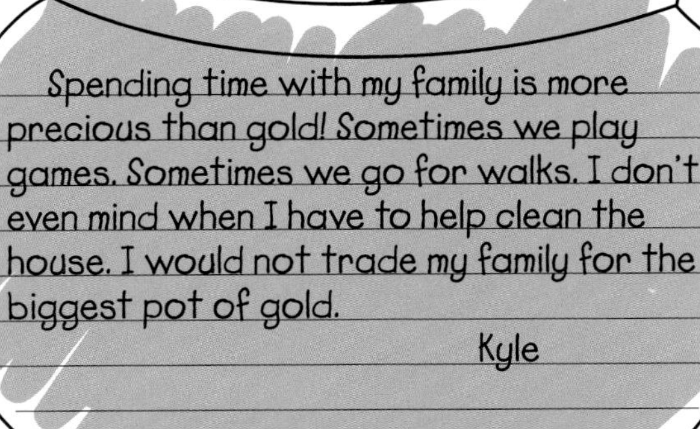

Biography Trading Cards
Writing an expository paragraph

Are your students into the trading-card craze? Then this idea is for you! For National Women's History Month, have your class create a set of women-in-history cards. Assign each child a woman to research. The child takes notes on a few statistics—such as date of birth, place of birth, and full name—then writes a brief paragraph that includes those statistics and other factual information about the woman's importance in history. She revises her writing and writes the final paragraph on an index card. Finally, she turns the card over, writes the woman's name, and illustrates her. Each day, invite students to exchange cards with another child. Continue trading until each child has had a chance to read every card. Then collect the cards and return them to their original owners.

Piper R. Porter, Mountain Way Elementary, Granite Falls, WA

Timely Prompts
Journal writing

Have each child respond to a chosen prompt below. Then allow students to share their responses with the class.

- Imagine that when the famous groundhog is pulled out of his hole on Groundhog Day, he begins to talk. Write about the conversation that takes place between him and the person who pulled him out.
- Would you rather have six more weeks of winter or not? Explain.
- Write about how a shadow is similar to your best friend.

Write On!

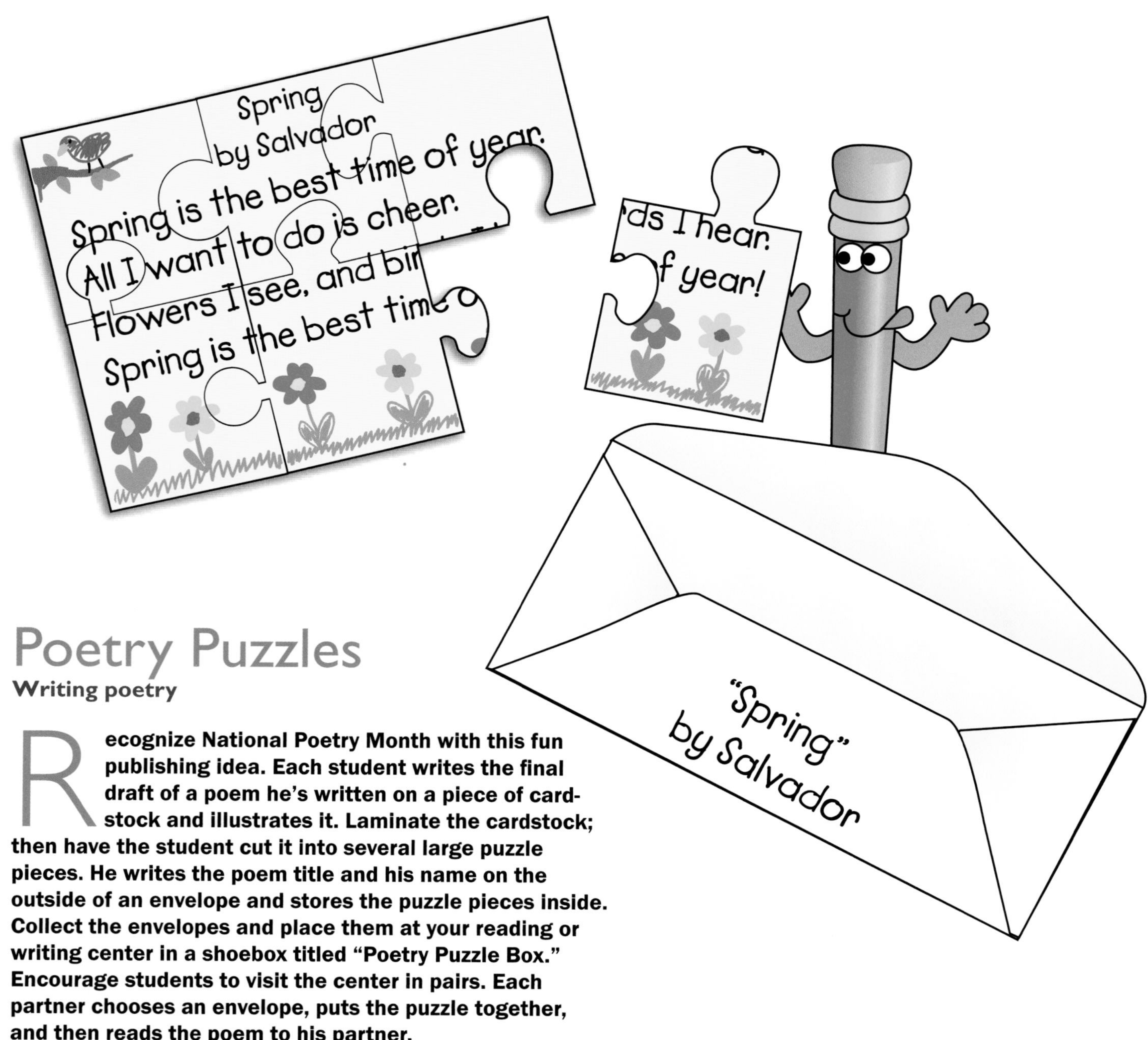

Poetry Puzzles

Writing poetry

Recognize National Poetry Month with this fun publishing idea. Each student writes the final draft of a poem he's written on a piece of cardstock and illustrates it. Laminate the cardstock; then have the student cut it into several large puzzle pieces. He writes the poem title and his name on the outside of an envelope and stores the puzzle pieces inside. Collect the envelopes and place them at your reading or writing center in a shoebox titled "Poetry Puzzle Box." Encourage students to visit the center in pairs. Each partner chooses an envelope, puts the puzzle together, and then reads the poem to his partner.

Crissie Stephens, Hunt Meadows Elementary, Easley, SC

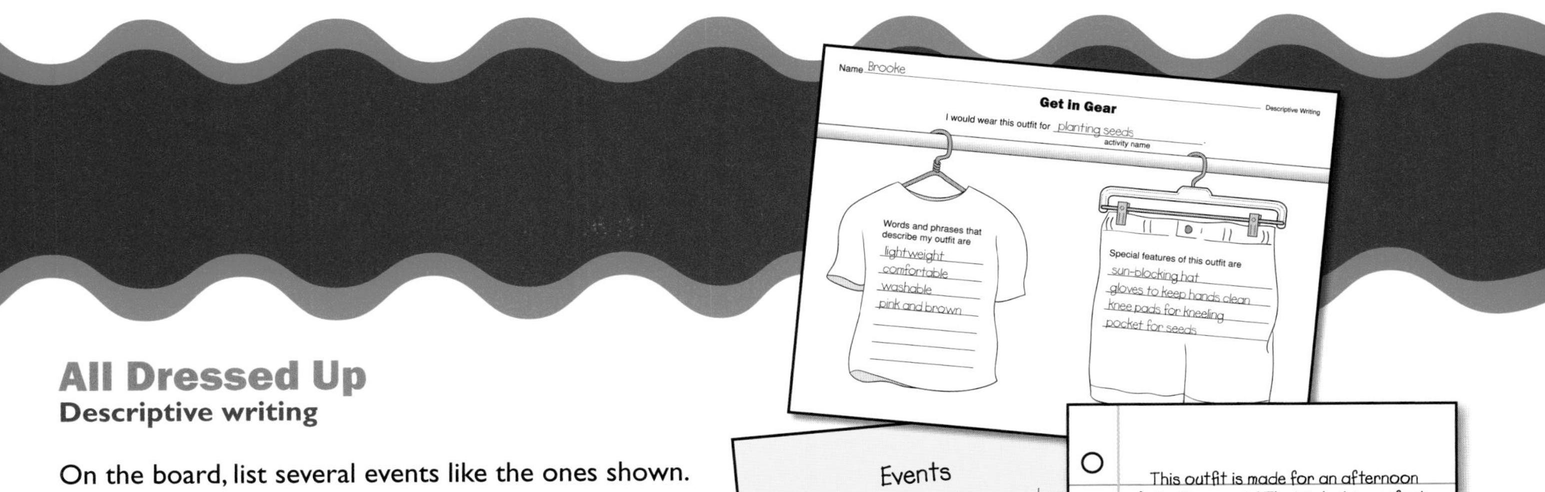
Name Brooke

Get in Gear

Descriptive Writing

I would wear this outfit for planting seeds
activity name

Words and phrases that describe my outfit are
lightweight
comfortable
washable
pink and brown

Special features of this outfit are
sun-blocking hat
gloves to keep hands clean
knee pads for kneeling
pocket for seeds

All Dressed Up
Descriptive writing

On the board, list several events like the ones shown. Have each child choose an event and draw a picture of the perfect outfit to wear while taking part in that event. Next, provide each child with a copy of page 125 and have her use her illustration to complete the organizer. Then she uses the ideas on the organizer to write a descriptive paragraph about her outfit. Post the completed paragraphs with the illustrations on a display titled "All Dressed Up and Somewhere to Go!"

Julia Alarie, Grand Isle School, Grand Isle, VT

Events
Planting seeds in the garden
Recycling
Taking a walk in the rain
Going to the park
Doing homework

This outfit is made for an afternoon of planting seeds! The big hat is perfect for blocking the sun. The brown gloves will keep my hands clean. The knee pads will keep my knees from hurting when I kneel to dig in the soil. My short-sleeved pink shirt is lightweight so I won't get too hot. Plus, it has a pocket. That's a handy place to keep my seeds. The brown pants won't show dirt stains. But if I get too dirty, the whole outfit is easy to wash.

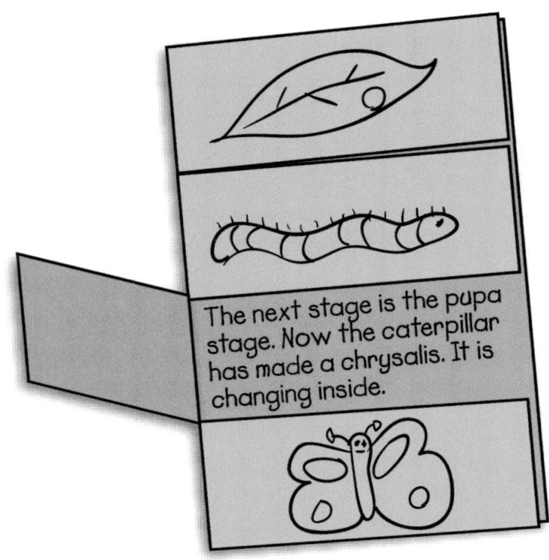

Flip Book
Prewriting, sequencing

To make this simple organizer, give each child a sheet of paper. Have him fold the paper in half horizontally to resemble a book and then fold it in half vertically twice. He unfolds the paper to return it to the book shape and cuts along the fold lines of the top layer, creating flaps as shown. Next, he thinks of the events of his story or the categories of a nonfiction topic. He draws a simple picture representing each one on a top flap, keeping his illustrations in sequential order. Then he lifts up each flap and writes matching text. When he is ready to write his draft, his ideas will be ordered and ready to go!

Bonnie Gaynor, Franklin Elementary, Franklin, NJ

Timely Prompts
Journal writing

Invite students to respond to a prompt below. Then have them share their responses with the class.

- The last Friday in April is Arbor Day. People are encouraged to plant and care for trees on this day. Write a letter to a friend telling him or her why this is an important day.
- A list poem is a list of ideas about a topic. Write a list poem that names the best uses for trees.
- How are trees and flowers alike? How are they different?

Write On!

Mystery Characters

Writing a description

Lead students to brainstorm a list of familiar fairy tale characters. Then guide each child to secretly choose one character and write a paragraph that describes but does not name the character. Next, the child cuts out the description pattern from a copy of page 126 and rewrites his paragraph on the left side of it. Then he draws a picture of the character in the middle section. Finally, the student folds the right section of the pattern over the drawing and paper-clips the flap closed. Post students' work on a board titled "Guess Who!"

If desired, tack an envelope beneath each student's work and place paper strips and pencils nearby. Then, as students read their classmates' work, they write their guesses on paper strips and drop them into the envelopes. After a set amount of time, have each student read aloud his work and reveal the mystery character.

Stacie Stone Davis, Lima, NY

Video Prompts
Responding to a prompt

Instead of writing a prompt on the board, try showing a short movie clip. Choose an excerpt from a movie version of a class read-aloud, an excerpt from a nonfiction film that supports a unit of study, or an excerpt that will inspire creative storytelling. After showing the clip, have each student write about it. A student might write about what happened before or after the excerpt. He might describe the excerpt. Or, he might write a story based on the excerpt. As time allows, have students share their responses.

Lori Knight, Adamston Elementary, Clarksburg, WV

Dazzling Books
Publishing

For a publishing project sure to inspire your young authors, provide access to a supply of 5½" x 8½" pieces of unlined paper, yarn, an assortment of beads, construction paper, a hole puncher, and scissors. When a student is ready to publish her work, she writes and illustrates it on the unlined paper. Next, the child folds a sheet of construction paper in half, slides her pages inside, and punches four holes along the folded edge. To bind her book, the student ties a bead to a length of yarn. Then she threads the yarn through the first hole and adds several beads. She threads the yarn down through the second hole and up through the third hole and adds more beads. Finally, she threads the yarn through the last hole, ties on a bead, and trims the excess yarn.

Kelli Higgins, P. L. Bolin Elementary, East Peoria, IL

Timely Prompts
Journal writing

Have each student respond to a prompt below. Then have students share their responses with the class.

- What is your favorite ice cream flavor? Describe it and explain why it's your favorite.
- Imagine that you are creating a new ice cream flavor. What ingredients would you use? How would it taste? What would you call it?
- Think about different ice cream flavors. How many can you name? Make a list.

Kelli Jones, East Clayton Elementary, Clayton, NC

Cat Pattern

Use with “A Cat Tale” on page 112.

Reindeer Pattern

Use with “Reindeer Chatter” on page 114.

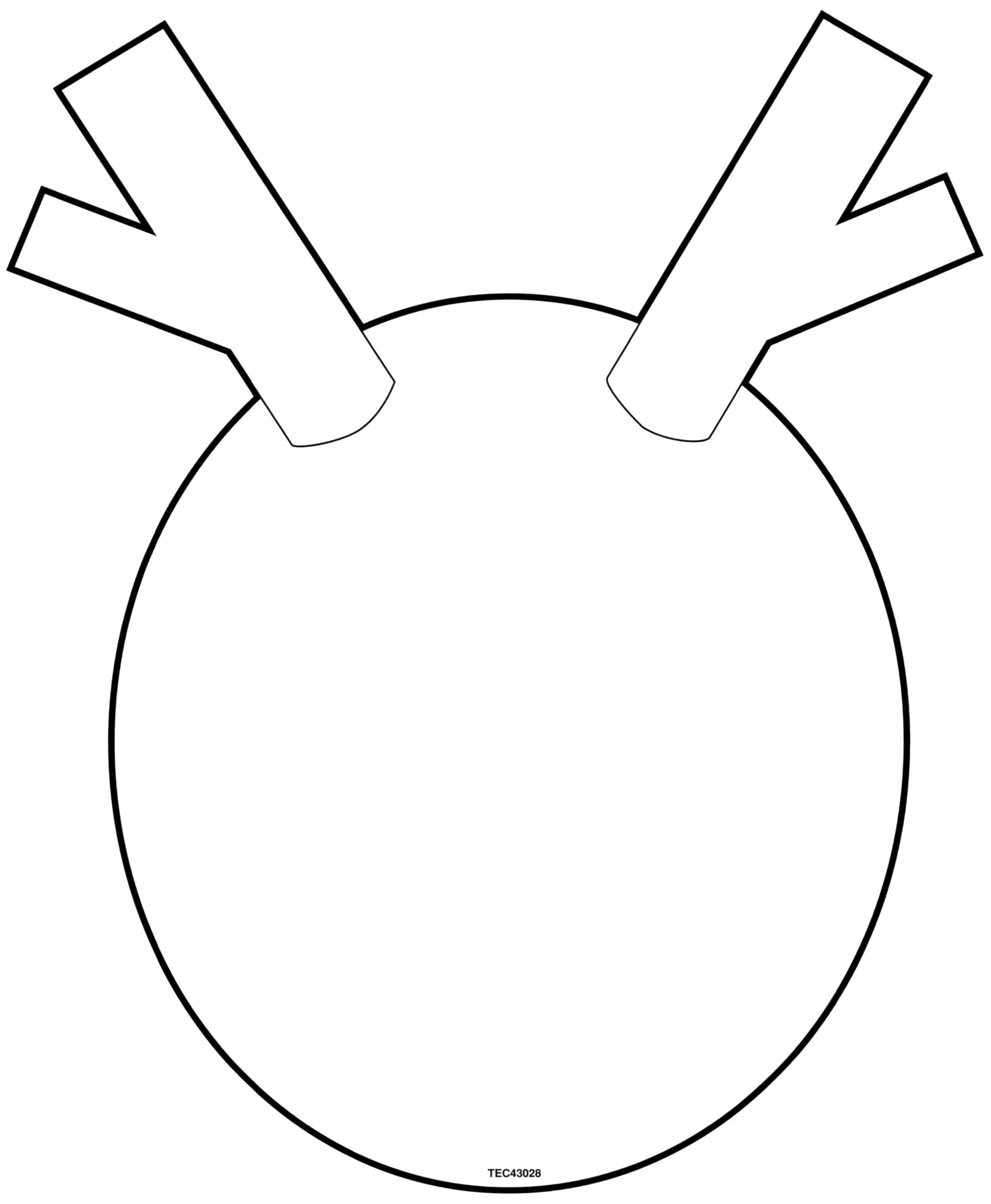

Pot-of-Gold Pattern

Use with "More Precious Than Gold!" on page 117.

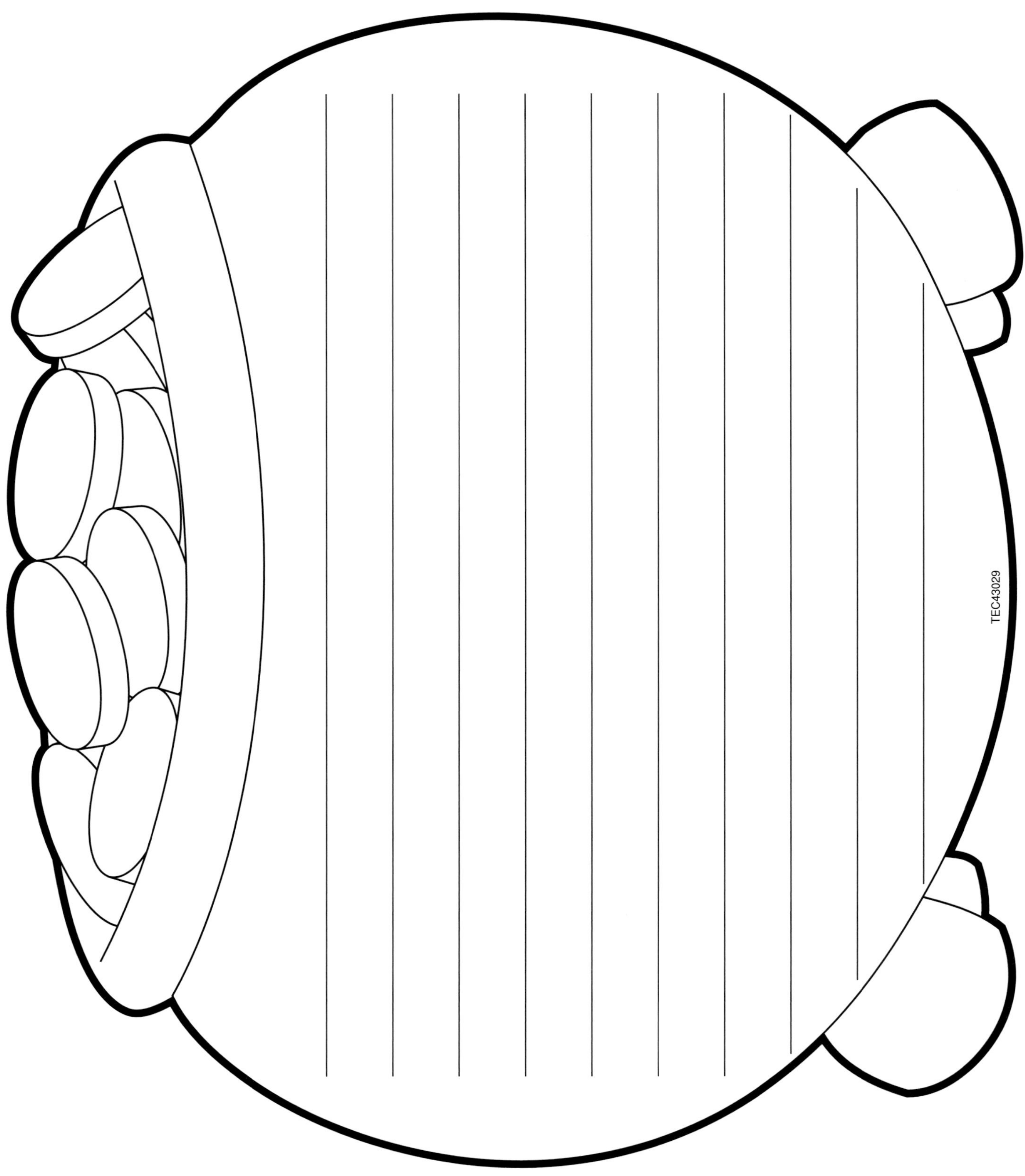

Name ______________________________

Get in Gear

I would wear this outfit for ______________________.
activity name

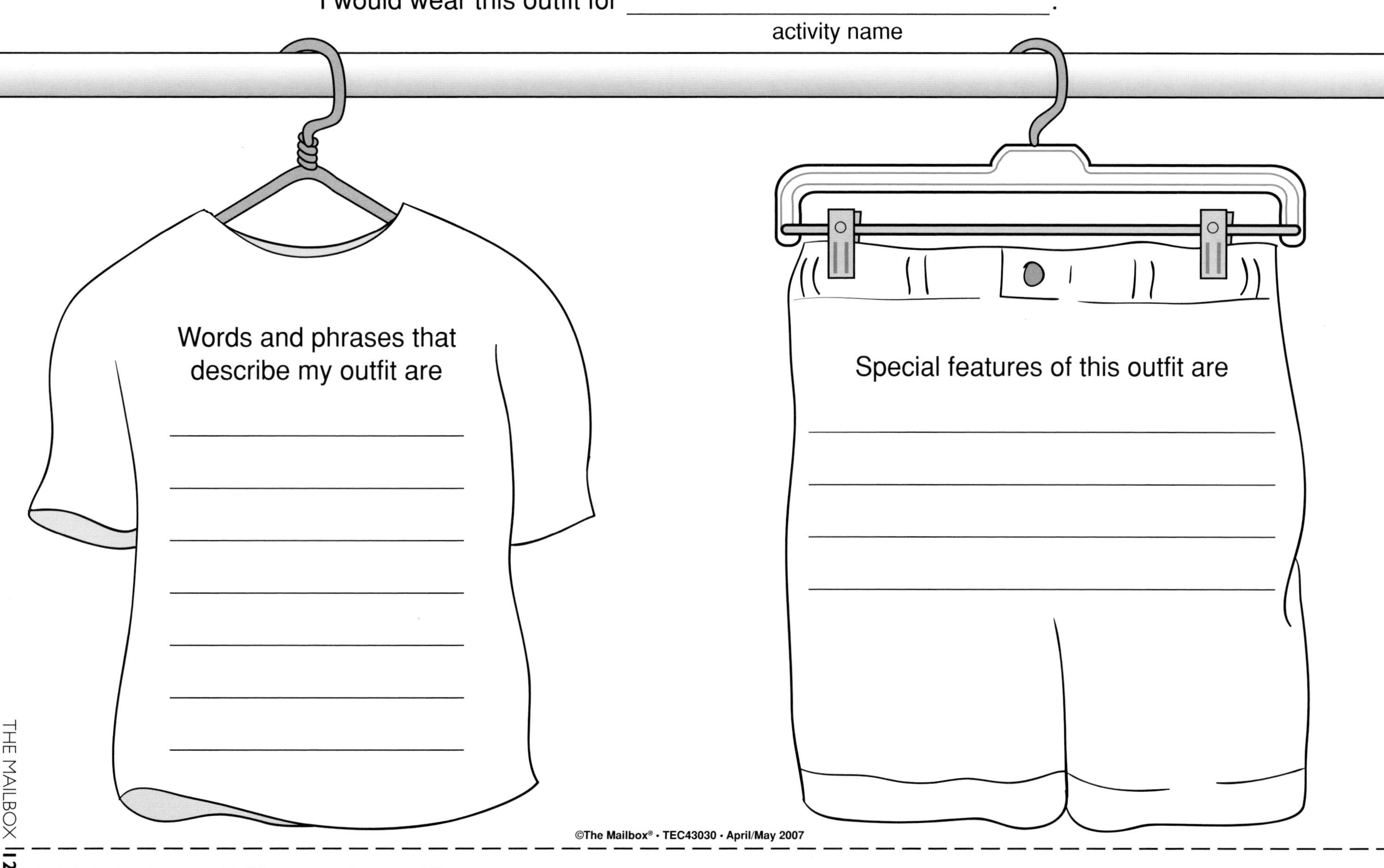

Note to the teacher: Use with “All Dressed Up” on page 119.

Description Pattern

Use with “Mystery Characters” on page 120.

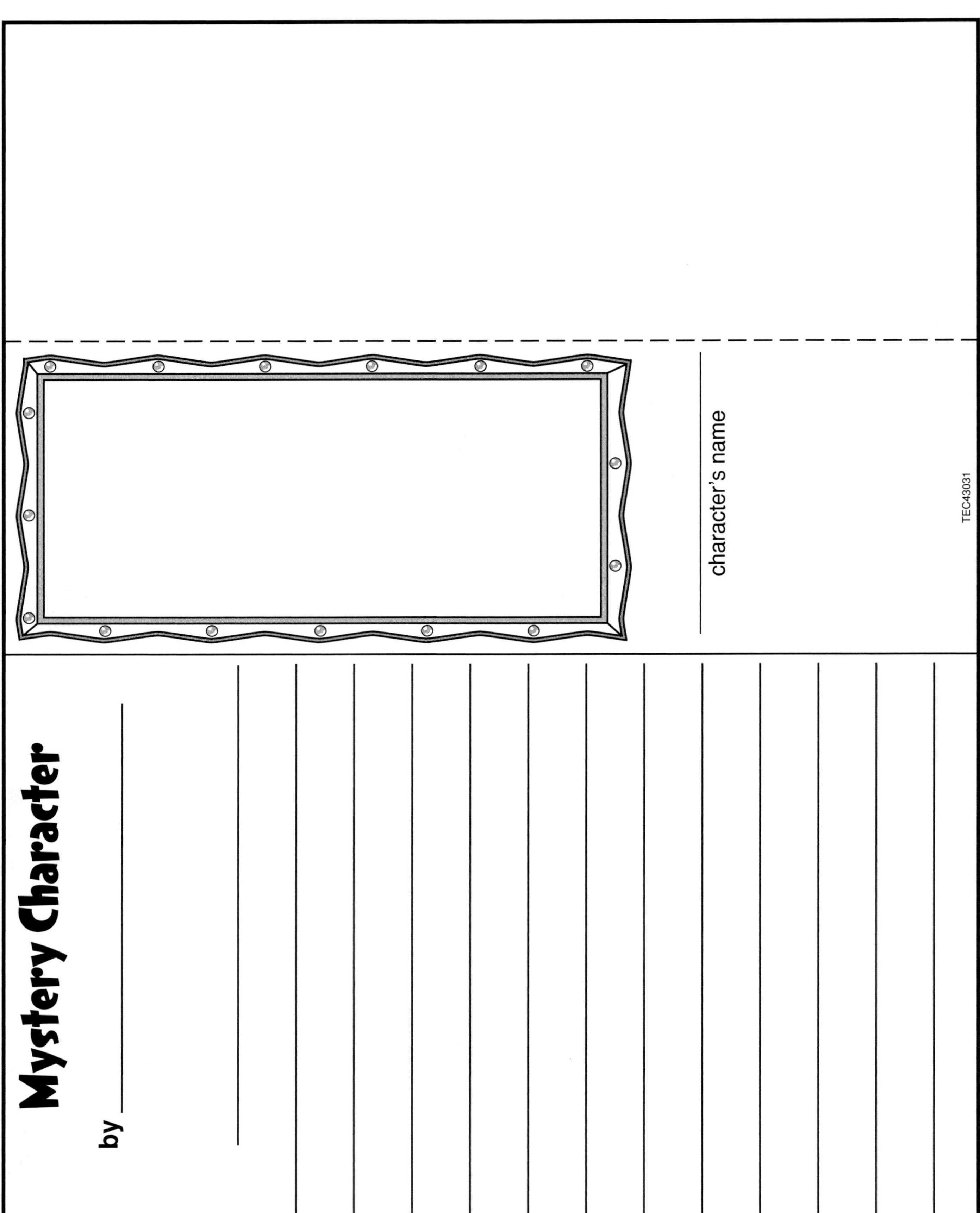

Language Arts Units

Building Up

High-Frequency Words

SORTING IT OUT
Categorizing words

To prepare this activity, make a copy of page 130 and mount it on construction paper. Laminate the page; then cut out the cards. To make two portable centers, place one card from each word pair in a plastic resealable bag. Also list the possible ways to sort the words, such as by beginning sound, ending sound, vowel sound, or number of syllables, and store the list in the bag. A child selects a bag of cards, chooses a sorting method from the list, and sorts the words. Then he writes the sorting method on his sheet of paper and records the words in each category. He repeats the process for as long as desired.

Reinforce reading skills with this collection of activities!

with ideas by Jennifer Kohnke, Nature Ridge Elementary, Bartlett, IL

MAKING THE MATCH
Word recognition

To prepare this independent or partner game, make a copy of page 130 and mount it on construction paper. Laminate the page; then cut out the cards. Store the cards in a resealable plastic bag and place them at a center. For independent practice, a student removes the cards from the bag and places them facedown. She turns two cards over at a time, reads the words aloud, and checks to see whether they match. If they do, she places the cards to the side and turns over two new ones. If the words are not a match, she turns the cards facedown and turns two different cards faceup. She continues in this manner until all cards are matched.

For a partner game, a pair uses the cards to play a memory-style game.

WORD BOX
Spelling and writing high-frequency words

Invite each child to create his own personal dictionary! Have each child bring in his own 3" x 5" index card file box and a supply of blank index cards. Create a master set of dividers, labeling each one with a different letter of the alphabet. Next, copy a set of dividers onto colored construction paper for each child. Have the student cut out the dividers and store them in his box. Each time you introduce a new set of high-frequency words, the child writes each word on one side of an index card. On the card's back, he illustrates the word and uses it in a sentence. Then he files the card in his box, behind the corresponding divider. He consults the box whenever he needs help with word meanings or spelling.

Word Cards

Use with "Sorting It Out" on page 128 and "Making the Match" on page 129.

about TEC43026	**about** TEC43026	**were** TEC43026	**were** TEC43026
again TEC43026	**again** TEC43026	**they're** TEC43026	**they're** TEC43026
because TEC43026	**because** TEC43026	**to** TEC43026	**to** TEC43026
people TEC43026	**people** TEC43026	**two** TEC43026	**two** TEC43026
there TEC43026	**there** TEC43026	**too** TEC43026	**too** TEC43026
their TEC43026	**their** TEC43026	**won't** TEC43026	**won't** TEC43026
was TEC43026	**was** TEC43026	**can't** TEC43026	**can't** TEC43026
said TEC43026	**said** TEC43026	**have** TEC43026	**have** TEC43026

Name ____________________

High-Frequency Words
Reading and spelling words

Working With Words

Write each word.

Use each word in a sentence.

1. ____________________
2. ____________________
3. ____________________
4. ____________________
5. ____________________

Use crayons to write each word.
Follow the code.

Color Code
vowels = blue
consonants = green

Note to the teacher: Use this page to provide practice with new sets of high-frequency words.

Check It Out

Story Elements

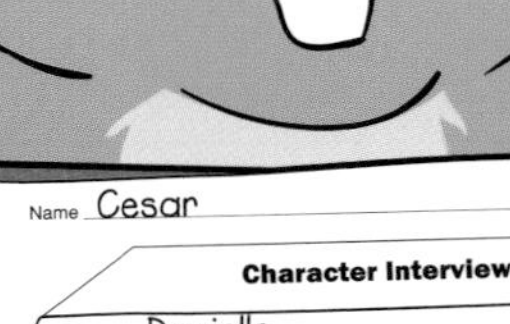

WHAT'S YOUR STORY?

Analyzing character traits

Have each student partner choose a different character from the same book. Next, give each child a copy of page 134. Have him review the questions and then add two of his own. Have one partner start the interview by asking a question from his paper. He listens as his partner responds as though she is the character she selected; then he records her answer. He continues in this manner until all of his questions have been answered. Then the students switch roles. When both interviews have been completed, have each student write a short summary of his interview and post the summaries with the interview questions on a display titled "What Are Their Stories?"

This collection of ideas will have students exploring all the parts of a good story.

with ideas by Dr. Jennifer Kohnke, St. Charles, IL

LISTEN UP
Associating setting with a story

List on the board stories all of your students have read or recent read-aloud books. Have each child choose a story and write a description of its setting. At the bottom of her paper, have each child also write the title of the book. Next, she tape-records her description and gives her paper to you. When each child has recorded her description, order the paper descriptions to match the tape-recordings. Then play each recording and have small groups of students work together to make a list of the story titles described. If desired, play four or five descriptions each day until all have been played. Use the written descriptions to verify the book titles and have student groups check their work. The group with the most correct titles is the winner.

IN THE CARDS
Naming an important event, plot

Discuss with students various occasions for which people send and receive greeting cards, such as for birthdays, holidays, good luck, congratulations, and condolences. If desired, show an example of each. Next, have each child name the main character and a major event from the story of his choice. Then he designs an appropriate greeting card for that character based on the main event. He decorates the outside of the card with a brief greeting and then writes a brief message to the main character inside the card. Store the completed cards in a basket for students to read in their free time.

ACTION!
Identifying problem and solution

Find out how well your students know your read-aloud stories. After hearing several stories, put students into small groups. Assign each small group a story and then divide each group into two smaller groups, one to represent the problem and the other to represent the solution. Provide time for each small group to practice acting out its story part and then have the groups present their skits. After each group has performed both acts, call on students to name the book presented.

Name ______________________________

Character Interview

Partner ______________________________

Book Title ______________________________

1. What is your name? ______________________________

2. Where do you spend your time? ______________________________

3. Name some things you like. ______________________________

4. Name some things you do not like. ______________________________

5. ______________________________

6. ______________________________

 Note to the teacher: Use with "What's Your Story?" on page 132.

Name ____________________

Story Elements
Making connections

Head-to-Head

Book Title ____________________

Main Character ____________	Me
Appearance	Appearance
Likes	Likes
Dislikes	Dislikes
Strengths	Strengths
Weaknesses	Weaknesses

Note to the teacher: Have the student draw the face of a main character in the left rectangle and draw her own face in the right rectangle. Then have the student complete the chart to make connections with the character.

In Its **Place**

Using Graphic Organizers With Nonfiction Text

STOP AND TALK ABOUT IT

Facts and details

To prepare this whole-class activity, create a large paper stoplight, as shown, and post it in an area accessible to students. Start the activity by giving each child several sticky notes and having him write his name on the back of each one. Next, each child reads an assigned selection. As he reads, he jots down interesting facts and details, recording each on a separate sticky note. When he finishes reading, he places his notes on the stoplight according to the labels. After all students have affixed their notes to the stoplight, invite each child to share his notes with the class. As a class, discuss the information on each note and its placement on the stoplight. Continue to use the organizer throughout the year as a way for students to respond to nonfiction text.

Helping students organize their thoughts is easy with these simple ideas!

with ideas by Jennifer L. Kohnke, Nature Ridge Elementary, Bartlett, IL

BRANCHING OUT

Main idea and supporting details

In advance, make a large brown construction paper branch for each group of three students. Also make a brown tree trunk and a supply of green construction paper leaves. Begin by assigning one paragraph from a multiparagraph science or social studies selection to each group. The group reads its assigned paragraph together. Then the group members identify the paragraph's main idea and supporting details. The students write the main idea on their branch and each supporting detail on a different leaf, and then attach the leaves to the branch. Label the trunk with the reading selection's title; then post it on a wall in your classroom. After each group shares the main idea and supporting details from its assigned paragraph, attach its branch to the tree.

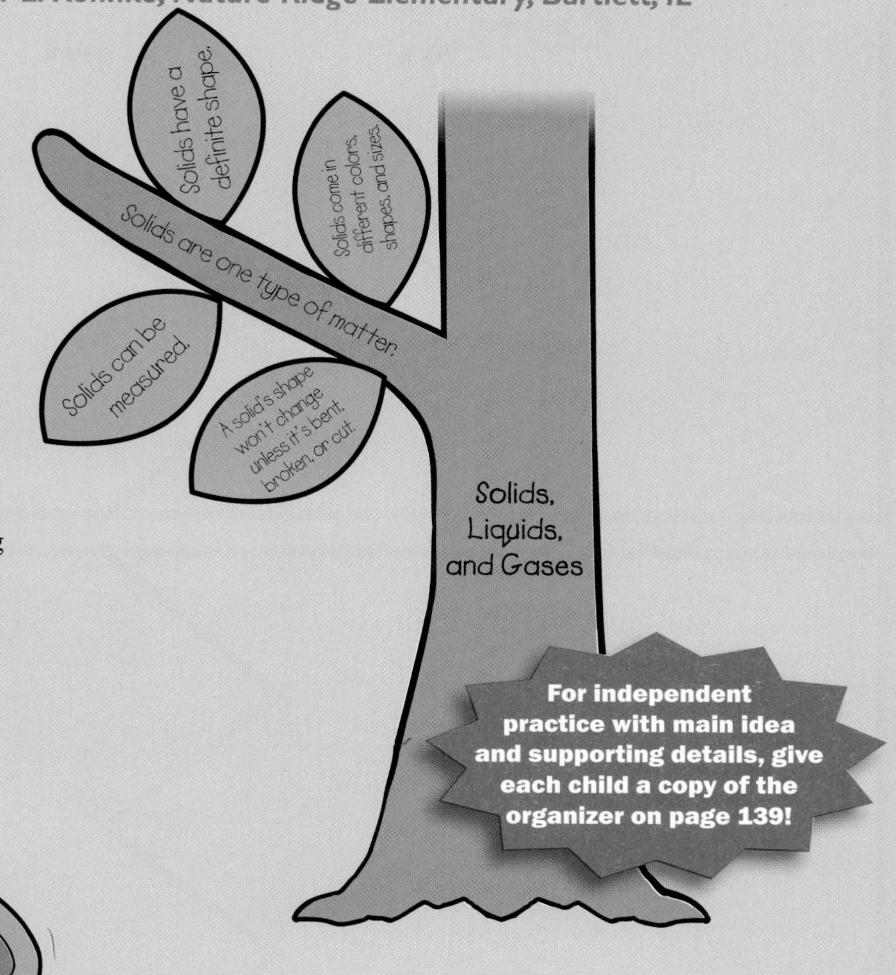

PIECING IT TOGETHER

Cause and effect

These puzzlers provide great practice with cause and effect! After students have finished reading a nonfiction passage, have each child list three events from the passage. Then have him identify the cause and effect of each one. Next, give him a copy of page 138. He programs the first puzzle piece with the first event's cause and the matching piece with the corresponding effect. He repeats the process for the remaining pieces. He cuts the pieces out and stores them in a resealable plastic bag. Pair students and have them exchange bags. Each child removes the pieces from the bag and matches each cause to its effect.

Puzzle Pieces

Use with "Piecing It Together" on page 137.

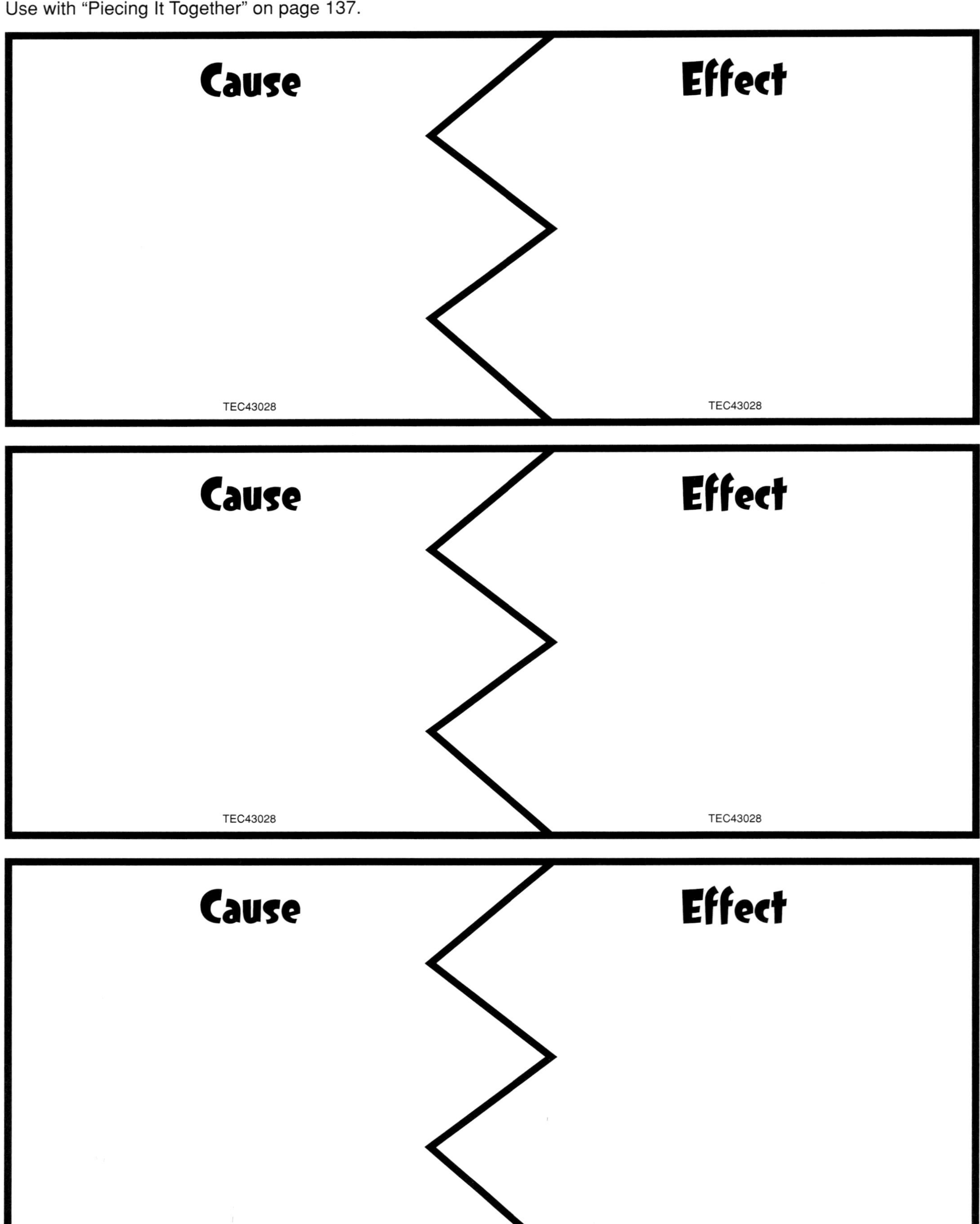

Name________________________________

Main Idea

Supporting Details

Detail 1:

Detail 2:

Detail 3:

Detail 4:

Note to the teacher: Use the organizer above with any nonfiction text.

Open the Door!

Making Inferences

WHAT'S INSIDE?

Using text clues to visualize setting

Have each child staple a copy of the door pattern from the top half of page 142 onto a half sheet of unlined paper as shown. Next, read aloud the selection at the bottom of page 142. As you read, guide each child to jot clues about the setting in the appropriate boxes on his door. Finally, have the student fold open the door and use the clues to draw the setting that he pictures.

adapted from ideas by Dr. Jennifer L. Kohnke, St. Charles, IL, and Melissa Pizirusso, PS 177K, Brooklyn, NY

Help students make inferences about what they read with these clever activities!

with ideas by Dr. Jennifer L. Kohnke, St. Charles, IL

WHAT DO YOU THINK?

Analyzing characters

What would a story character do if he or she were suddenly a member of your class? Guide students to think about just that with this quick activity. First, have each child choose a main character from a recent reading and then describe the character on a copy of the door hanger on page 143. Next, have each student complete the items on the hanger to describe how the character might act if he or she were to join your class. Then have the child flip the door hanger and draw a picture of the character as part of your class.

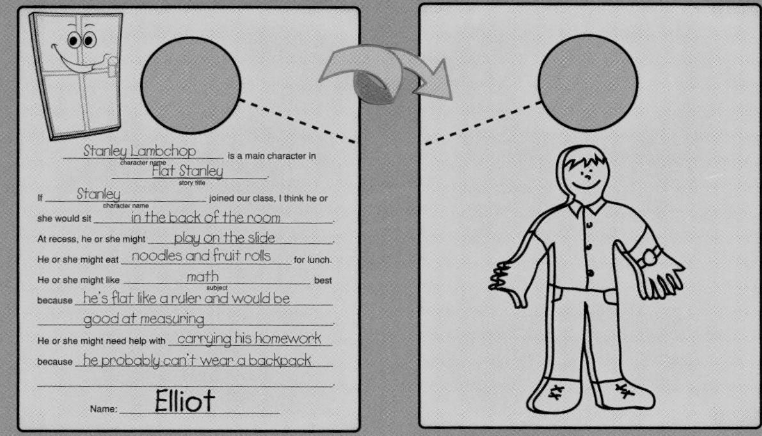

PROBLEM...SOLUTION

Making predictions

During your next read-aloud, guide each pair of students to listen for the story's problem. When each twosome identifies the problem, the partners curl their fists under their chins in poses similar to *The Thinker* statue. When all students have identified the problem, stop reading and have each duo fold a sheet of paper in thirds. Lead the partners to describe the story's problem in the top section and then use what they know about the characters to predict a solution and record it in the second section. Next, have students set their papers aside while you finish reading the story. Then have each duo reread its prediction and write about the problem's actual solution in the third section.

CLUED IN

Making and explaining inferences

For this simple center, copy for your files and make a class supply of the recording sheet on page 145. Copy page 144 and mount the mat and cards on construction paper; then laminate them and cut them apart. Place the cards, mat, and recording sheets at a center. A student reads each box on the mat and chooses the card that best answers its question. She places the card on the mat. Then she records and explains each choice on the recording sheet.

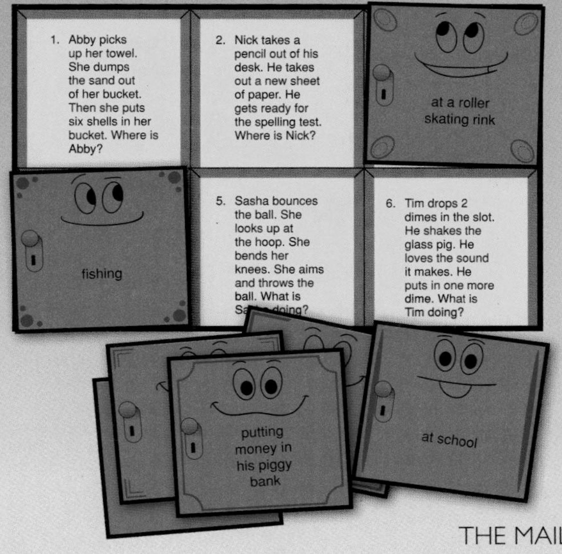

Door Pattern and Paragraph

Use with "What's Inside?" on page 140.

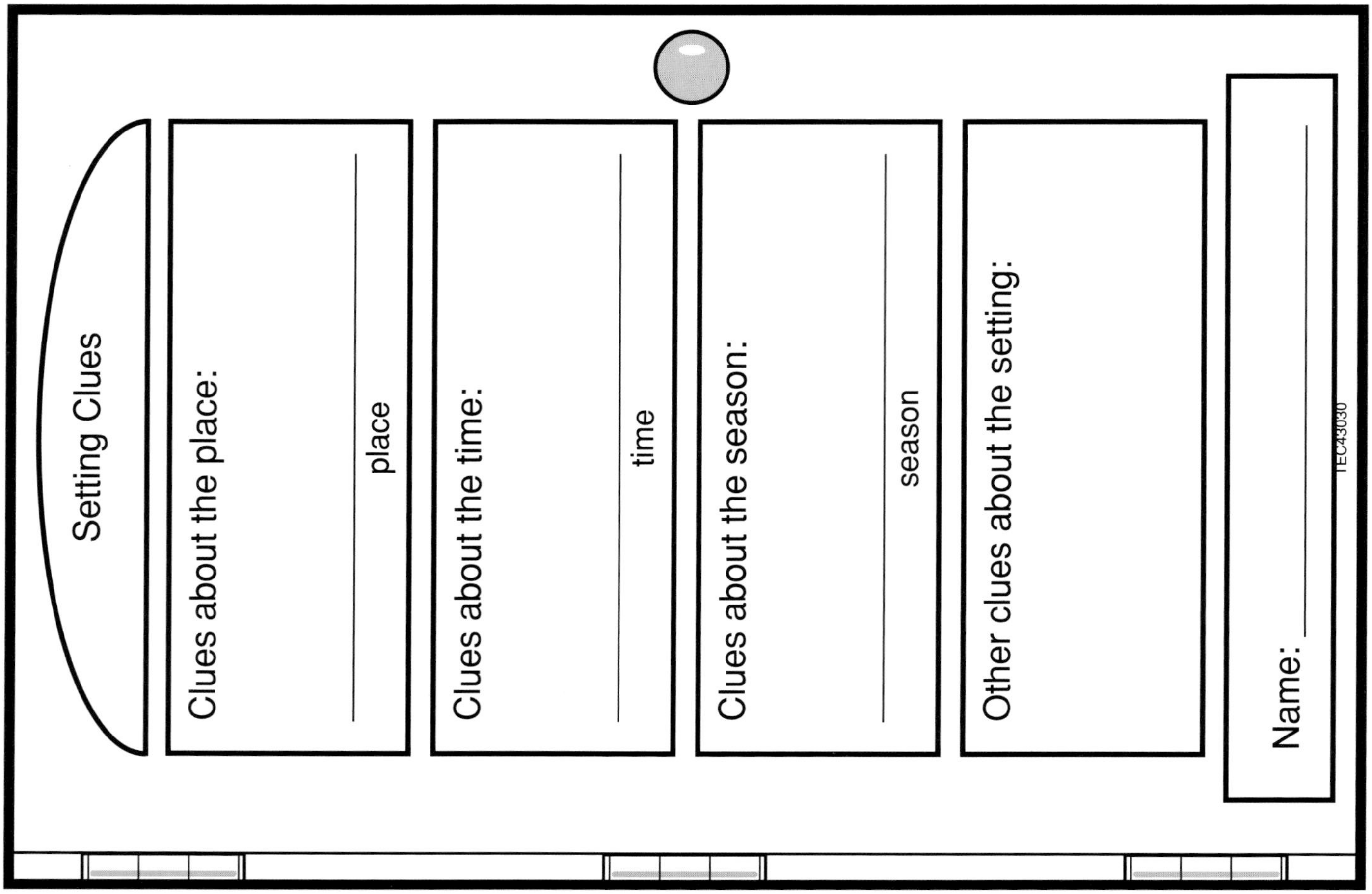

Setting Clues

Clues about the place: ____________ place

Clues about the time: ____________ time

Clues about the season: ____________ season

Other clues about the setting:

Name: ____________

TEC43030

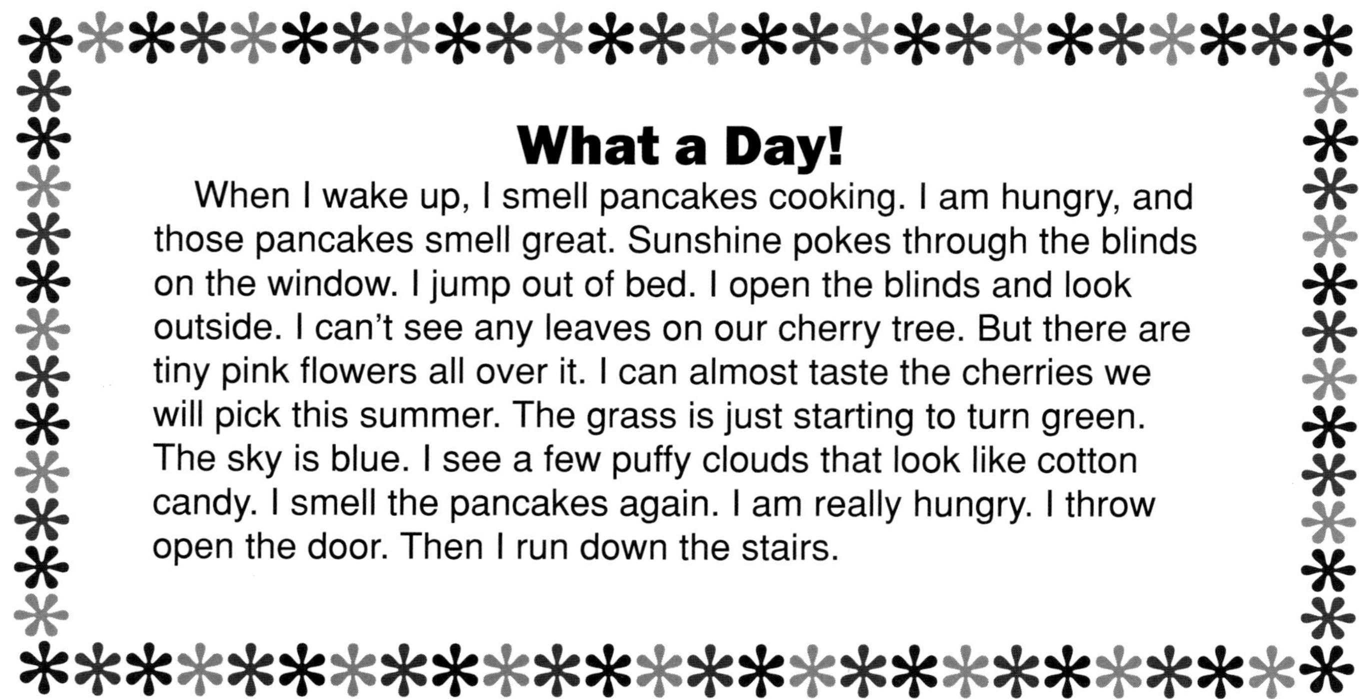

What a Day!

When I wake up, I smell pancakes cooking. I am hungry, and those pancakes smell great. Sunshine pokes through the blinds on the window. I jump out of bed. I open the blinds and look outside. I can't see any leaves on our cherry tree. But there are tiny pink flowers all over it. I can almost taste the cherries we will pick this summer. The grass is just starting to turn green. The sky is blue. I see a few puffy clouds that look like cotton candy. I smell the pancakes again. I am really hungry. I throw open the door. Then I run down the stairs.

Use with "What Do You Think?" on page 141.

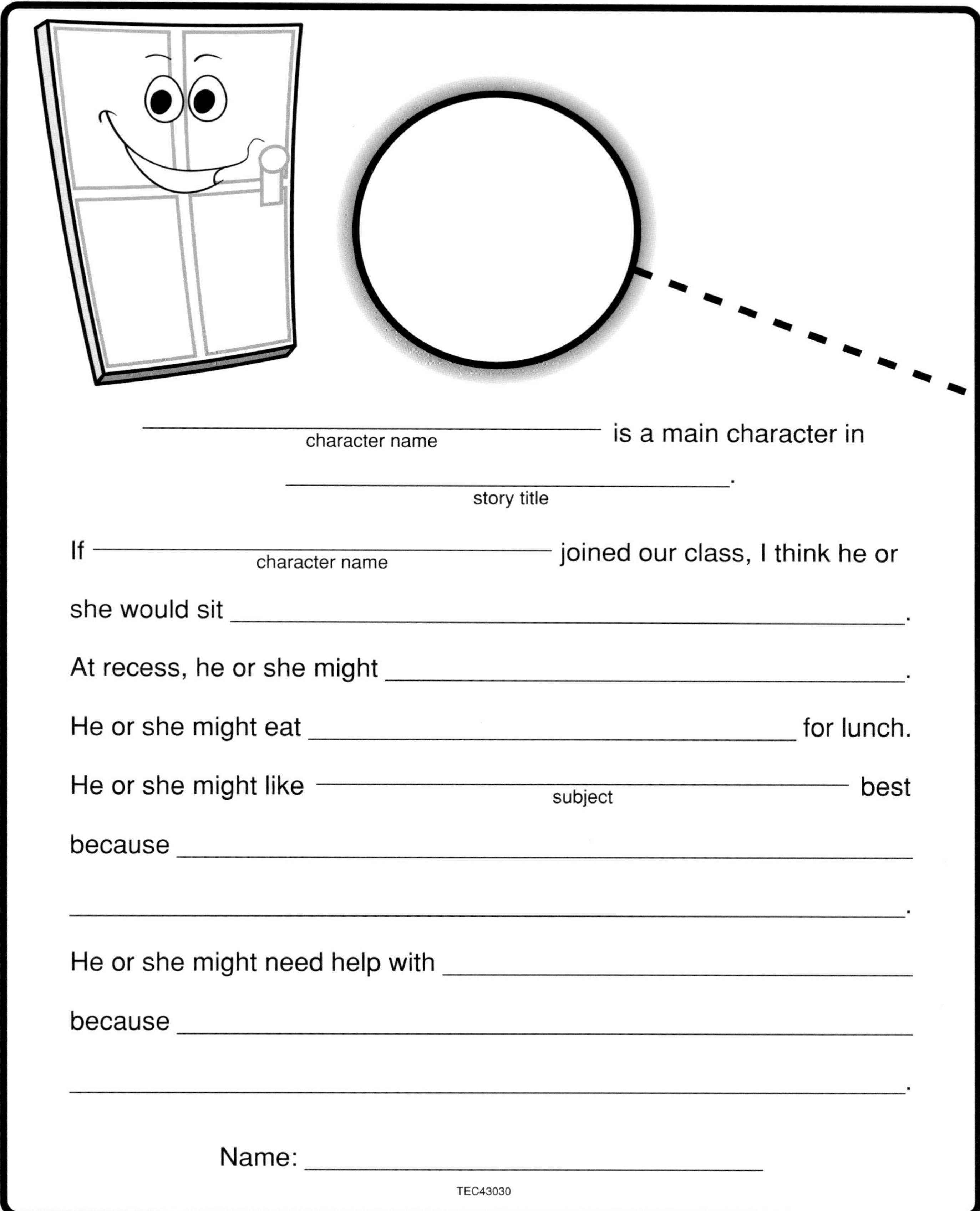

Sorting Mat and Cards

Use with "Clued In" on page 141.

1. Abby picks up her towel. She dumps the sand out of her bucket. Then she puts six shells in her bucket. Where is Abby?	2. Nick takes a pencil out of his desk. He takes out a new sheet of paper. He gets ready for the spelling test. Where is Nick?	3. Becky ties her laces in double knots. She rolls her feet back and forth. Then she glides onto the rink to join her friends. Where is Becky?
4. Alex digs the bait out of the jar. He puts it on the hook. Then he casts the line out into the water. What is Alex doing?	5. Sasha bounces the ball. She looks up at the hoop. She bends her knees. She aims and throws the ball. What is Sasha doing? TEC43030	6. Tim drops two dimes in the slot. He shakes the glass pig. He loves the sound it makes. He puts in one more dime. What is Tim doing?

Name ____________________

KNOCK, KNOCK!

Complete each item.

Note to the teacher: Use with "Clued In" on page 141.

All Together!

Making the Most of Reading Connections

Text-to-self connections, setting

Name James

Home, Sweet Home

Stink and the Incredible Super-Galactic Jawbreaker
story title

This is the story's setting.

The story starts out in a big candy store. The shelves are full of different kinds of candy. The floor is shiny. There is a couch that used to be a car's seat. There's even a TV.

This is how the places are alike.

Both places are stores. Both places sell candy. There is a lot of candy that a kid might want to buy at both places.

This is what the setting reminds me of.

The store in the story reminds me of the store where my mom always gets gas. Sometimes I get to go inside and choose a piece of candy. There is a whole row of candy. Most of the candy is in boxes on the shelves. So, it's easy to pick out a piece and go buy it. But sometimes it seems like there's too much candy to just pick one.

HERE AND THERE
Text-to-self connections

To help students identify with a story's setting, give each child a copy of page 148. Guide the student to review a recently read story and describe or draw its setting in the diagram's left section. Then have the child describe or draw in the diagram's right section a place the setting reminds him of. After that, lead the student to list in the overlapping section ways the two places are similar. Invite students to share their work in small groups.

Build students' comprehension skills with ideas for making connections that count!

with ideas by Dr. Jennifer L. Kohnke, St. Charles, IL

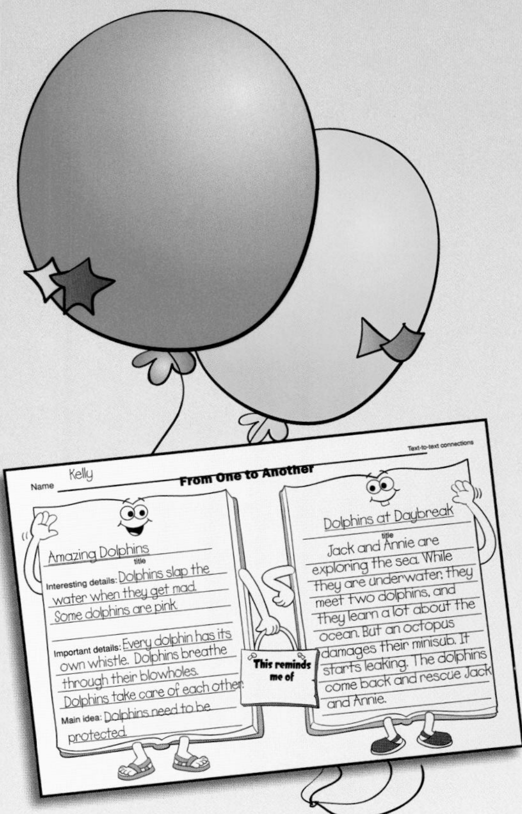

CHARACTERS AND FRIENDS

Text-to-self connections

During your next read-aloud, lead students to brainstorm traits that describe the story's characters. Next, guide each child to choose one character who reminds him of someone he knows. The student decorates the first figure on a copy of page 150 so that it resembles the character. Then the child decorates the second figure on the page so that it resembles the person he's thinking of. Finally, the student fills in the blanks as directed and lists in the big balloon shape qualities the character and the child's acquaintance share. Post the completed papers on a board titled "Connecting What We Read With What We Know."

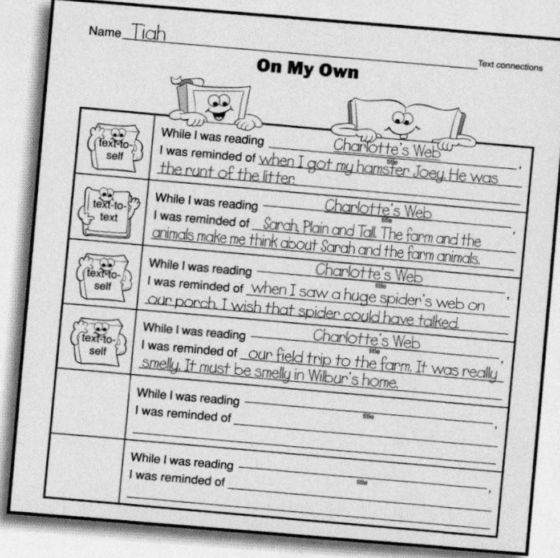

ON THE PAGE

Text-to-text connections

Stock a center with a class supply of copies of page 149 and several books on the same topic, in the same series, of the same genre, or by the same author. At the center, each student reads the books for a set amount of time. Then the child chooses one book. She writes about the book as guided on the left side of her reproducible. Next, the student chooses another book from her reading, thinks about the connections between the books, and records her ideas on the right side of the page. Follow up by having each student share her connections with a partner.

KEEP IT UP!

Text connections

To help students make and record connections when they read independently, have each child keep a copy of page 151 handy while she reads. Each time the student makes a connection, she writes it on the page. Then she cuts out the appropriate stamp from the bottom of the page and glues it beside her connection.

Name ________________________________

Home, Sweet Home

story title

This is
the story's setting.

This is
how the places
are alike.

This is
what the setting
reminds me of.

Note to the teacher: Use with "Here and There" on page 146.

Name____ Text-to-text connections

From One to Another

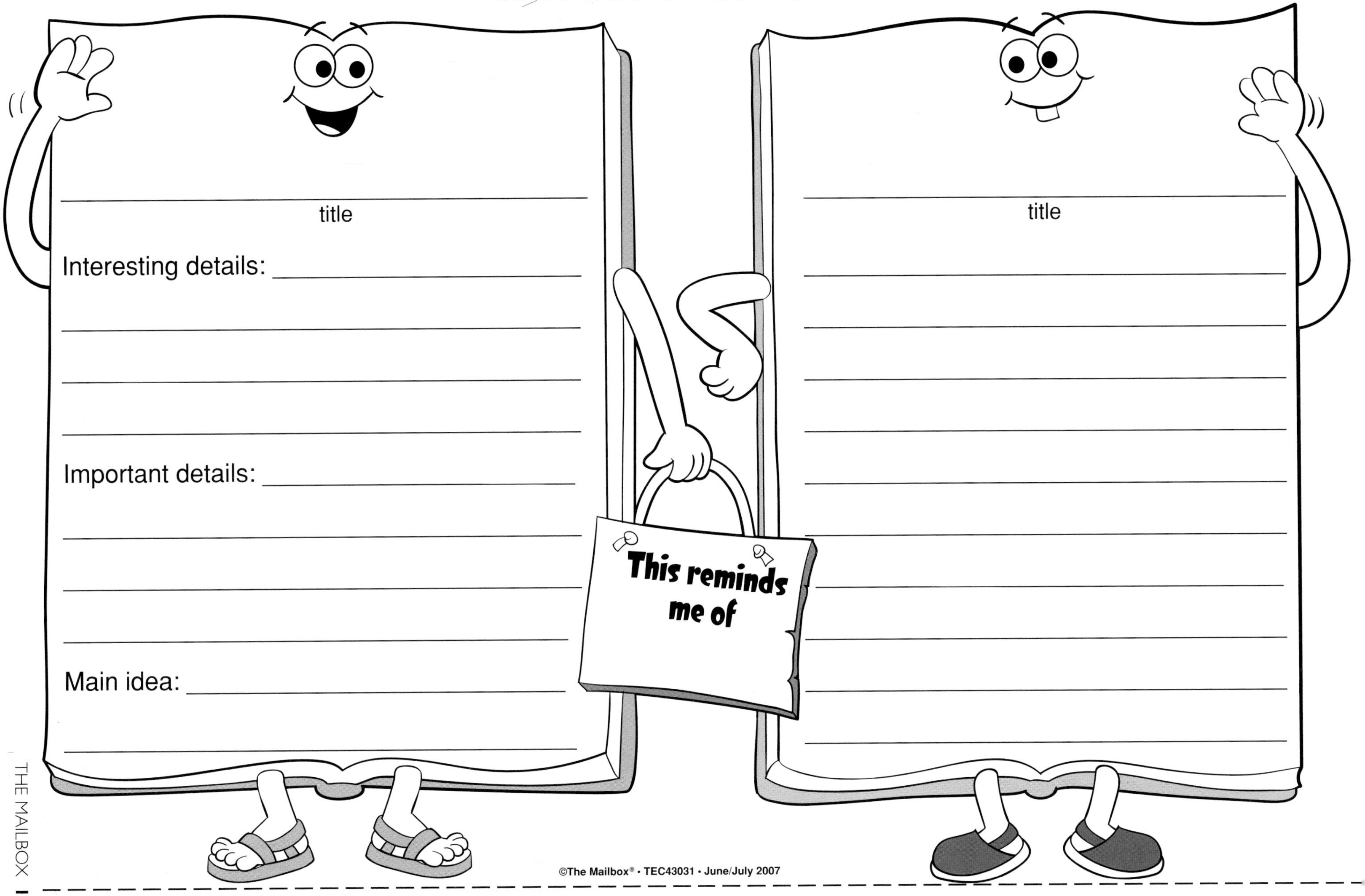

title
Interesting details:
Important details:
Main idea:
This reminds me of
title

©The Mailbox® • TEC43031 • June/July 2007

Note to the teacher: Use with "On the Page" on page 147.

Name ______________________ Text-to-self connections

Up, Up, and Away!

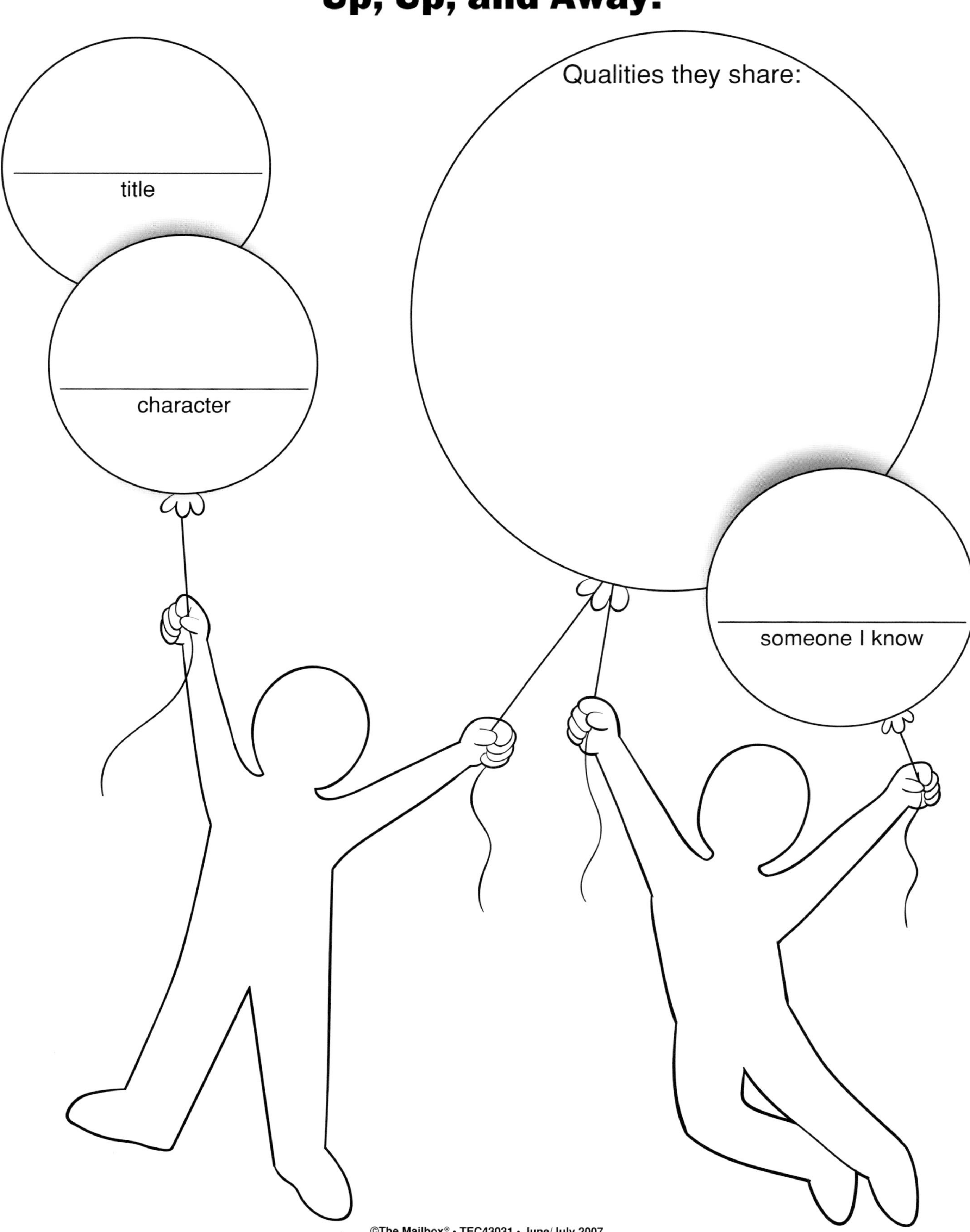

 Note to the teacher: Use with "Characters and Friends" on page 147.

Name ________________________________ Text connections

On My Own

	While I was reading ____________ (title), I was reminded of ____________ ____________
	While I was reading ____________ (title), I was reminded of ____________ ____________
	While I was reading ____________ (title), I was reminded of ____________ ____________
	While I was reading ____________ (title), I was reminded of ____________ ____________
	While I was reading ____________ (title), I was reminded of ____________ ____________
	While I was reading ____________ (title), I was reminded of ____________ ____________

Note to the teacher: Use with "Keep It Up!" on page 147.

Reel Them In

Hooking Students on Capitalization

CATCH OF THE DAY

Capitalization rules

To prepare this partner game, program two sets of index cards, one with capitalized words and the other with matching rules. Put each set of cards in a plastic bucket and place the buckets at a center. Player 1 chooses a card from each bucket. He shows the word card to his partner and then reads the rule aloud. If the rule card matches the word card, he keeps the pair and takes another turn. If the rule and word cards don't match, he returns them to the buckets. The player with more pairs wins.

Melinda Smith, Cypress Ridge Elementary, Clermont, FL

These "al-lure-ing" activities help students cast a line for correct capitalization skills.

with ideas by Mederise Burke, Courthouse Road Elementary, Spotsy, VA

GEARING UP
Capitalization rules

Give students the equipment they need for correct capitalization! Give each child a copy of the tackle box pattern on page 154 and have her cut it out. She glues the cutout to a sheet of folded construction paper and stands it on her desk. Then she uses the tackle box as a reference when working on capitalization or writing activities.

GONE FISHING
Capitalizing beginning of sentences, months, days, and people's names

Send students trolling for capital letters with this graphic organizer! In advance, make a class supply of the fish pattern on page 156 on colored paper. Give each student a copy of the organizer, several magazines or newspapers, scissors, and glue. He cuts out an example of each rule from a magazine or newspaper. Then he glues the cutout on the matching line. Post the completed organizers on a display titled "A Catch of Capital Letters!"

ANGLER ACTION
Capitalizing places, holidays, special events, and times in history

Fishing for correct capital letters is the focus of this center activity. Copy page 155; then mount the sorting mat and cards on construction paper. Cut out the mat and cards; then program each card's back for self-checking. Place the cards and the mat at a center. A child decides whether each card uses correct capitalization and places it on the corresponding space on the mat. Then she flips the cards over to check her work.

Tackle Box Pattern

Use with "Gearing Up" on page 153.

TEC43026

_______________'s Capital Letters Tackle Box

Beginning of Sentences We love to fish!	**Special Places** Bear Lake
People's Names Fred Fisherman	**Holidays** Labor Day
Months August	**Special Events** Falls Lake Fishing Contest
Days Sunday	**Times in History** Boston Tea Party

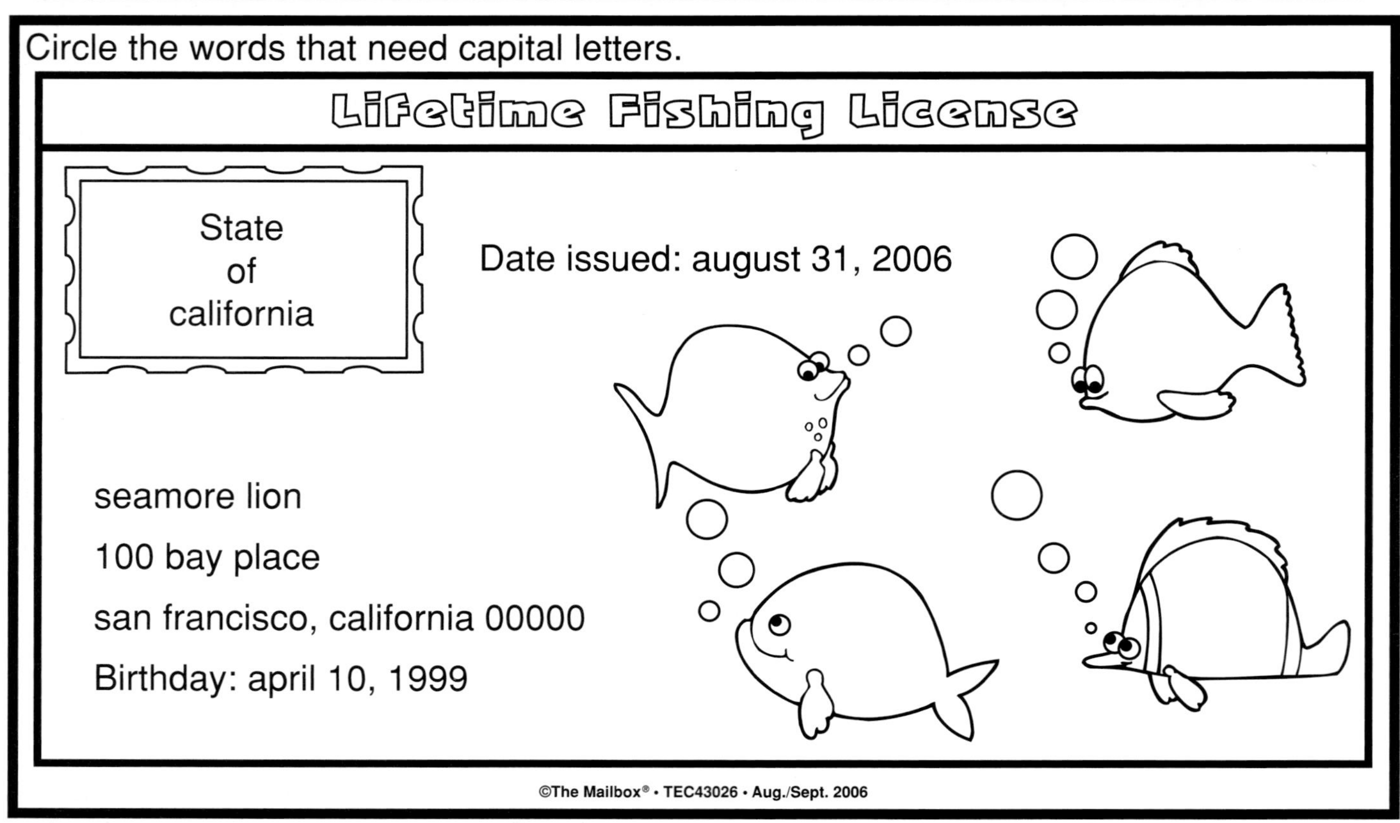
Circle the words that need capital letters.

Lifetime Fishing License

State of california

Date issued: august 31, 2006

seamore lion

100 bay place

san francisco, california 00000

Birthday: april 10, 1999

 Note to the teacher: Copy and laminate this card. Place the card and a wipe-off marker at a center for extra practice.

Sorting Mat and Cards

Use with "Angler Action" on page 153.

Fish Pattern

Use with "Gone Fishing" on page 153.

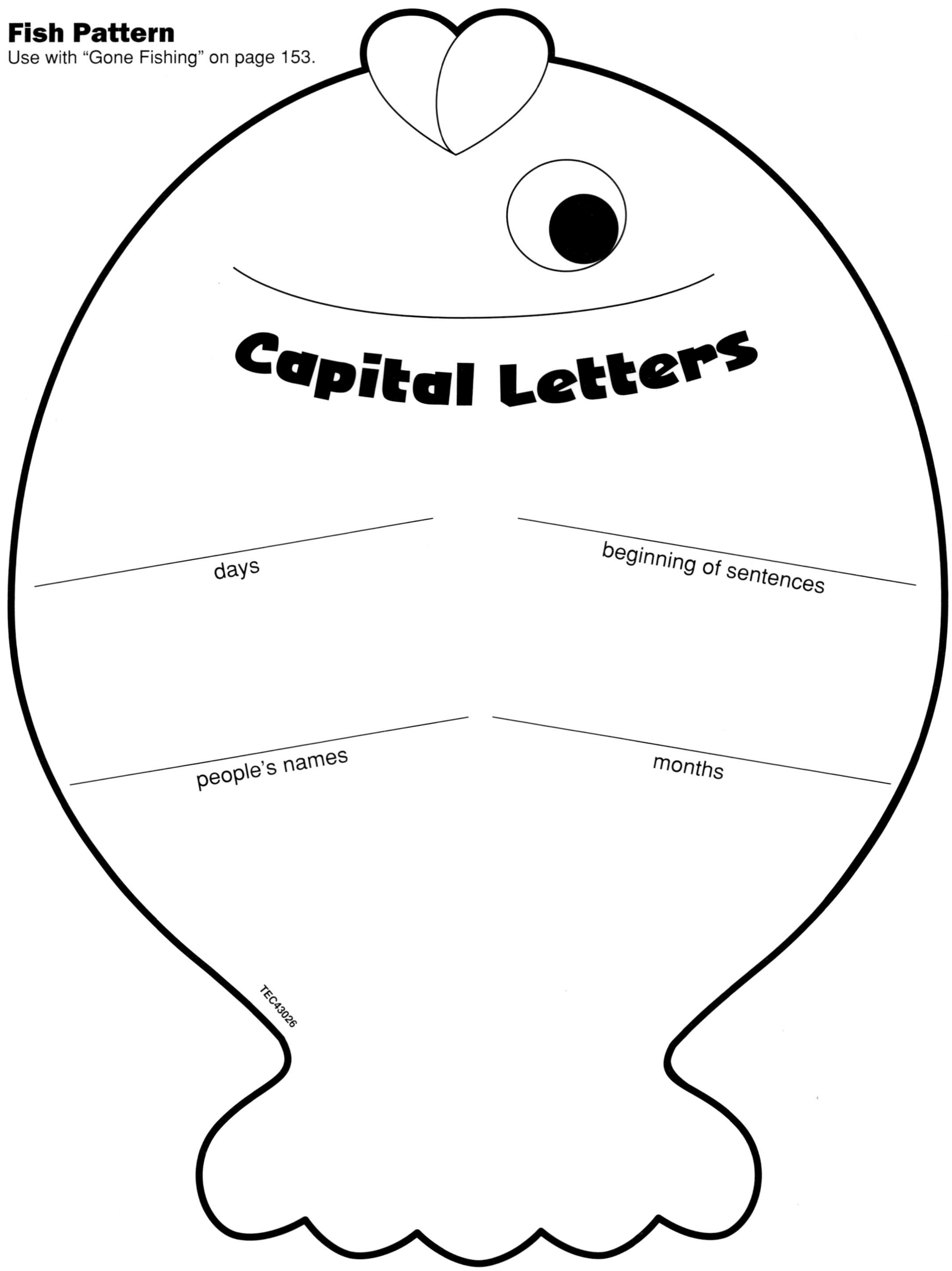

Name ____________________

Good Times

Circle each word that needs a capital letter.
Write it correctly on a matching line below.

My Summer on the Coast

by Seamore Lion

i had a great summer! It started in westport, Washington. I went fishing and surfing there. that was fun! Then I swam to seaside, oregon. while I was there, I fed the seagulls. I also went crabbing. Next, I moved south through the pacific Ocean. I stopped in oceanside, California. I picked up seashells there. I made new friends too. my busy summer went by too fast. I'll never forget it!

Beginning of Sentences	Special Places
____________________	____________________
____________________	____________________
____________________	____________________
____________________	____________________
____________________	____________________

On Your Feet

Noun Activities to Cheer About

SONG AND DANCE

Identifying nouns

Get students in tune with people, places, and things! Choose a kid-friendly song and make a class supply of its lyrics. Give a copy to each child and have him locate and circle each noun in the song. Next, have the class sing the song. Each time a noun is sung, students make a predetermined gesture, such as raising their hands or tapping their feet. After singing the song a few times, challenge each child to use the color code shown to trace the circles according to the type of noun named.

With these activities and games on your schedule, your students will be fans of nouns!

with ideas by Stacie Stone Davis, Lima, NY

PRONTO!

Common and proper nouns

This fast-paced activity will have students wanting more! To prepare, make a nine-space grid as shown. Program each space with an age-appropriate common noun. (If desired, make four different versions of the grid to ensure different student outcomes.) Organize students into small groups and give each child a grid. Then have students fill in as many spaces as possible with corresponding proper nouns. After a predetermined amount of time, signal students to stop writing. Have each child pass her grid to the classmate on her left. Continue in this manner until each child has written on all the grids. Finally, challenge each student to write a paragraph using as many of the proper nouns on her grid as possible.

holiday	cereal	month
Thanksgiving Halloween	Frosted Puffs	October May June
restaurant	**teacher**	**planet**
McBurger	Ms. Davis	Mars
author	**state**	**day**
Kevin Henkes	New York	Sunday

PEANUT PROMENADE

Plural nouns with *-s*, *-es*, and *-ies*

Students stroll through correct endings with this center activity! Copy page 161. Mount the cards and mat on construction paper; then laminate them and cut them out. Program each card's back for self-checking and then place them at a center with the mat and a wipe-off marker. A child chooses a card and decides which ending will make the underlined word plural. Then he writes the noun on a corresponding peanut. He continues in this manner until all spaces have been filled in. Then he flips the cards over to check his work.

NOTHING BUT NOUNS

Irregular plural nouns

To prepare this partner activity, label each of two index cards with a singular irregular noun and its plural, such as those shown. Make enough cards so that each student has one. Place the cards in a paper bag, and have each student select one. Provide time for each child to locate the classmate who has the matching noun. Once paired, give each duo two sheets of white paper. Each partner folds the paper about two inches from the bottom as shown. She writes a sentence atop the resulting flap, drawing a line to indicate where her assigned word should go. Then she unfolds the flap and writes the missing word. The student then illustrates her sentence above the fold. Bind the completed pages across the top. Title the resulting book "Nothing but Irregular Nouns," and place it in your classroom library.

Name ____________________

Falling for Peanuts

Read each word.
If the word is a noun, color the peanut yellow.
Write each noun on the matching bag.

shell
peanut
eat
baseball
pitcher
stadium
loud
dugout
pennant
umpire
coach
player
skybox
sit
outfield
hungry

People

____
____
____
____

Places

____
____
____
____

Things

____
____
____
____

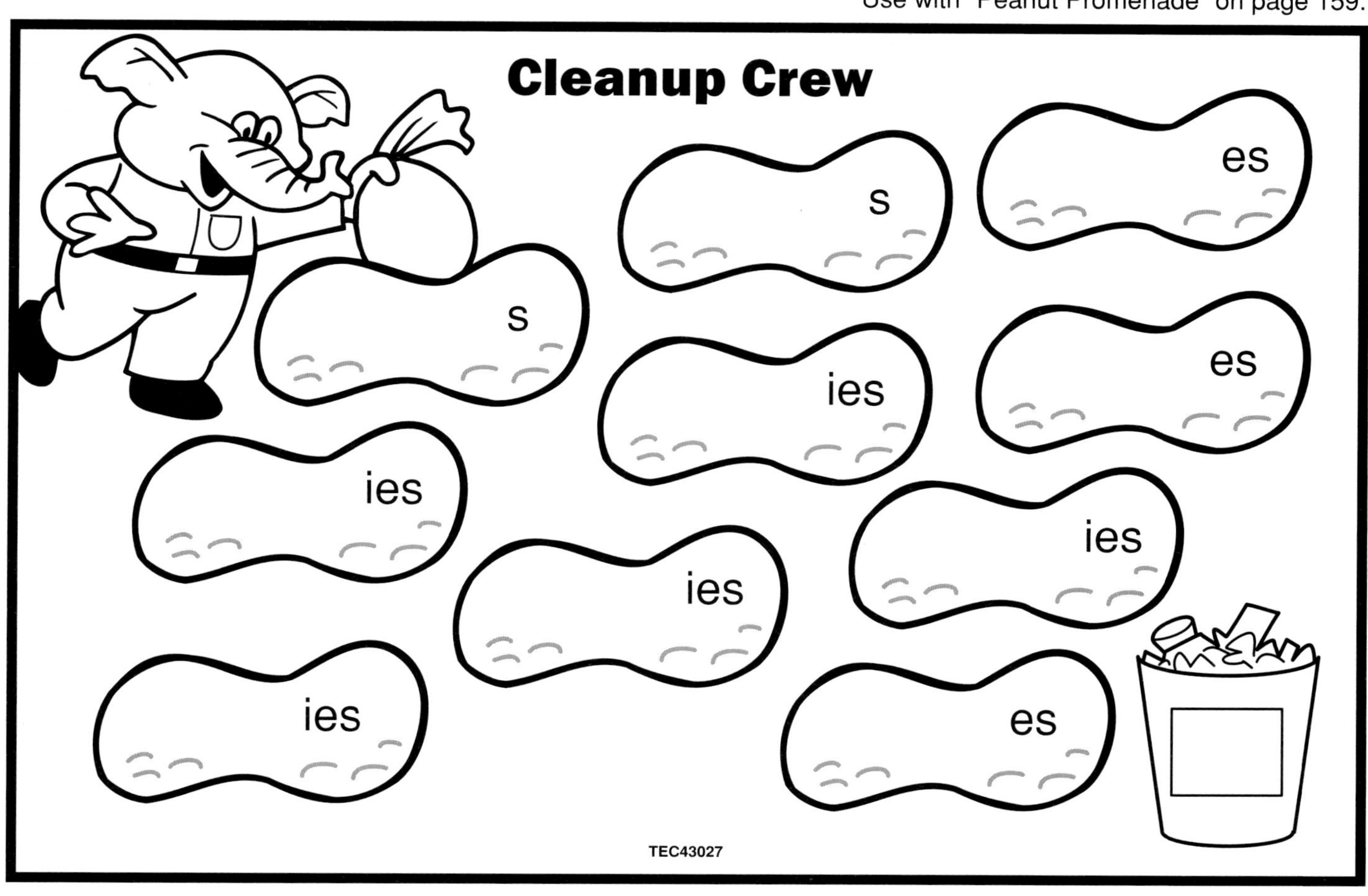

Ed has four jersey. TEC43027	Sometimes there are baby at the games. TEC43027
He loves to eat snack at the game. TEC43027	He visits different city to see his favorite team play. TEC43027
Ed has been to 30 ball game. TEC43027	Ed tells many story about baseball. TEC43027
He buys box of peanuts. TEC43027	Sometimes he has ice cream with lots of cherry on top. TEC43027
Many fans take bus to the game. TEC43027	Once in a while, a batter hits a ball into the bush. TEC43027

Name ____

Play Ball!

Read each sentence.
Look at the underlined noun.
Circle the letter to show whether the noun is singular or plural.

	Singular	Plural
1. Tonight's game starts at 7:00.	N	B
2. The two best teams are playing.	M	E
3. The fans are excited.	S	P
4. Some are eating hot dogs.	A	O
5. Others are reading their programs.	F	N
6. The batboy is getting ready.	E	K
7. The mascot is dancing around.	N	L
8. The players are warming up.	P	E
9. A coach is talking.	H	C
10. Some umpires are stretching.	I	O
11. Is everyone in his or her seat?	A	Y
12. Let's play ball!	L	D

How do elephants call each other?

To solve the riddle, match each circled letter above to a numbered line below.

___ ___   ___ ___   "___ ___ ___ ___ ___ ___ ___ ___"!
4 1   11 5   6 12 8 3 9 10 7 2

Some Assembly

Prefixes and Suffixes

Prefixes	Base Words
re-	treat
dis-	agree
un-	appear
mis-	approve
pre-	count
	lodge
	play
	able
	adjust
	judge
	tie
	happy
	named
	used
	arrange
	wrap
	charge
	organized
	inform
	view
	do
	lock
	assign

PREFIX MIX

Using prefixes

Label a class supply of blank cards, each with a common prefix or base word (such as those shown). Punch two holes in each card, thread a length of yarn through the holes, and tie the yarn to make a necklace. To begin, have each child put on a necklace. If his necklace has a base word on it, he finds a spot in the classroom to stand. If his necklace has a prefix on it, he finds a student with a base word and stands beside her. The two students put their necklaces together and read the resulting combination. If it is a word, one of the youngsters lists it on the board. If it is not, the child with the prefix on his necklace waits for your signal and then moves to a different child. After a desired amount of time, have students trade necklaces. Continue to have students make words in this manner until each youngster has had a turn to wear a prefix necklace.

Shasta Looper, Live Oak Elementary, Watson, LA

Challenge your students to build their vocabularies with this collection of activities.

CLASSROOM COMPARISONS

Using suffixes -er and -est

Gather similar classroom items that differ by a characteristic such as size in groups of three. Also have each student make a recording sheet similar to the one shown. Show a group of three items to the class and announce an adjective, such as *big.* Have students compare the items and add the suffixes *-er* and *-est* to the adjective to create comparative words such as *bigger* and *biggest.* Then have each child draw pictures of the items on his recording sheet and label each illustration with the appropriate word. Continue with different groups of objects and adjectives as desired.

Jean Erickson, Grace Christian Academy, West Allis, WI

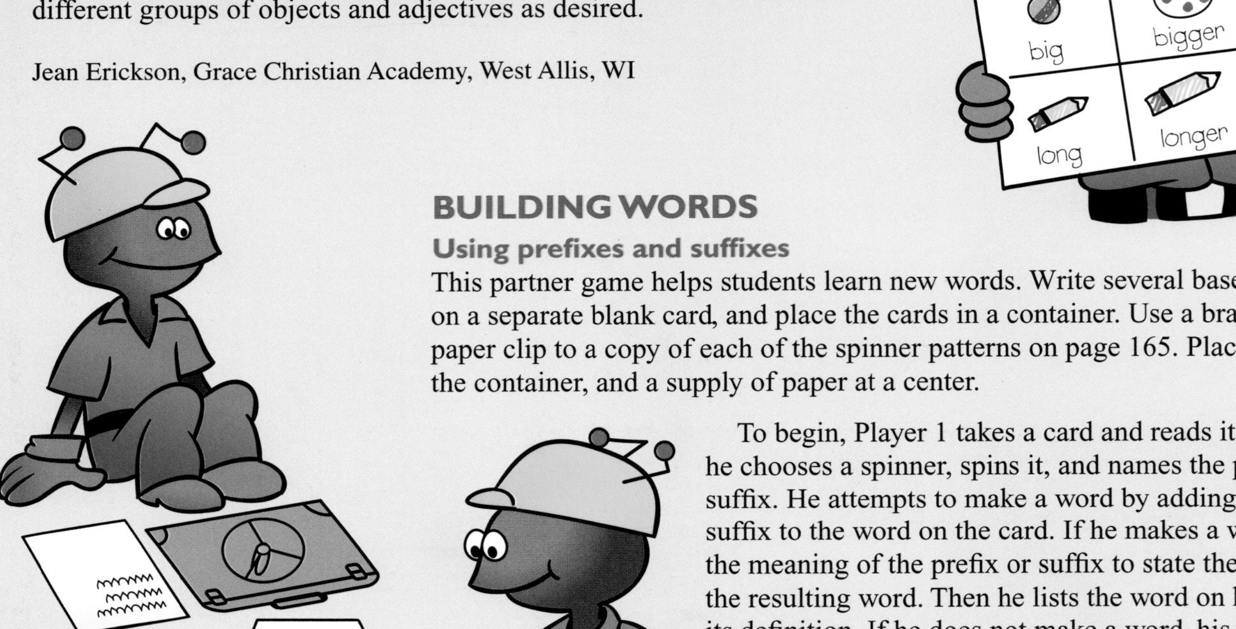

BUILDING WORDS

Using prefixes and suffixes

This partner game helps students learn new words. Write several base words, each on a separate blank card, and place the cards in a container. Use a brad to secure a paper clip to a copy of each of the spinner patterns on page 165. Place the spinners, the container, and a supply of paper at a center.

To begin, Player 1 takes a card and reads it aloud. Next, he chooses a spinner, spins it, and names the prefix or suffix. He attempts to make a word by adding the prefix or suffix to the word on the card. If he makes a word, he uses the meaning of the prefix or suffix to state the definition of the resulting word. Then he lists the word on his paper with its definition. If he does not make a word, his turn is over. Player 2 takes a turn in the same manner. Alternate play continues in this way as time allows.

QUICK THINKING

Using prefixes and suffixes

To prepare for this small-group activity, gather four different-colored sheets of construction paper. Write a different prefix or suffix at the top of each sheet. Designate four stations in the classroom and place one of the papers at each station along with a pencil. Divide students into four groups, and have each group assemble at a different station. At your signal, invite the groups to list on the paper words containing the corresponding prefix or suffix. After a short amount of time, have the groups stop and rotate to the next station. Continue in this manner until each group has visited each station.

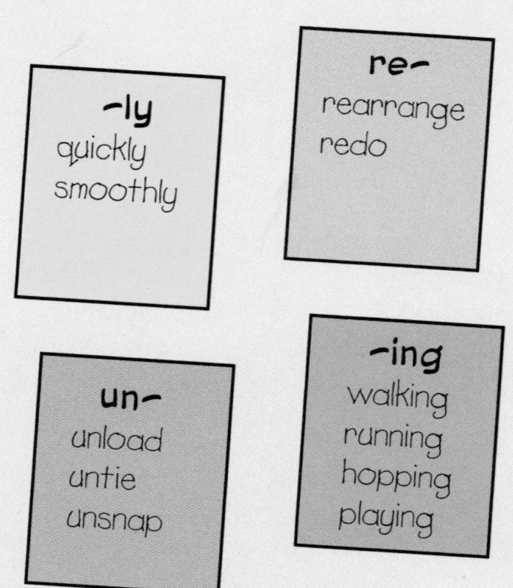

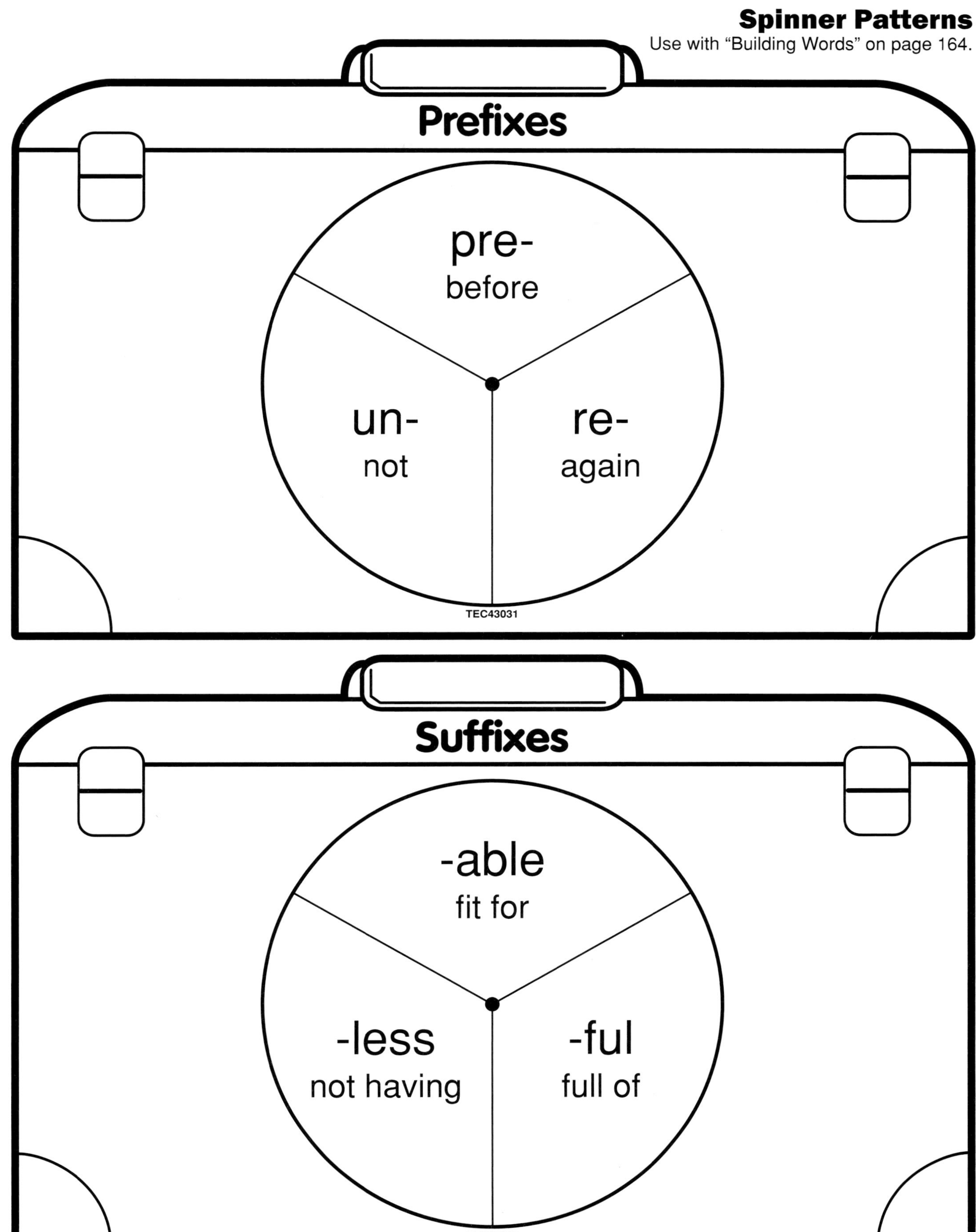
Prefixes
pre-
before
un-
not
re-
again
TEC43031
Suffixes
-able
fit for
-less
not having
-ful
full of
TEC43031

Name______________________________

Hard at Work

Write a prefix or suffix to make a new word.

Write Now!

Motivating Students to Write

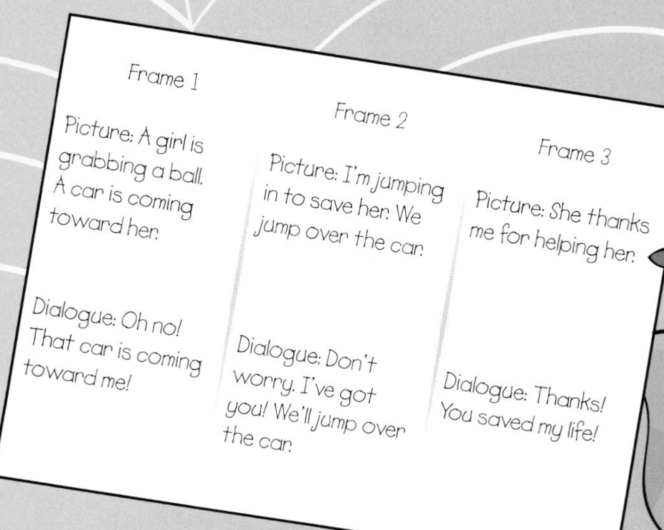

EVERYONE'S A HERO

Start the activity by reviewing comic strips with students, pointing out that the story is told with pictures and dialogue. Next, tell students they will **create a short comic strip** that features themselves as superheroes. To do this, each child creates an alliterative superhero name for himself such as "Jumping Juwan" or "Bobby the Brave." Then he plans his strip by completing an organizer like the one shown. To make the strip, he folds a sheet of white paper in half vertically and then folds it into thirds, creating six equal boxes. The student uses his notes to write the dialogue for the first frame in the top left box. Below it, he draws the corresponding picture. He repeats the process twice, writing each frame's text in the top box and drawing the matching picture in the box below it. Finally, give each child a sentence strip and have him label it with his superhero name and his real name and attach it to his comic strip. Post students' comics on a display titled "Super Student Writers."

Collette Pechous, North Pointe Elementary, Houston, TX

Put a new spin on writing that will excite even your most reluctant writers!

with ideas by Jennifer L. Kohnke, Nature Ridge Elementary, Bartlett, IL

LIFE AS A SPIDER

Engage students' imaginations with this activity! Before starting the activity, copy the prompts shown onto chart paper and post it in the room. Begin by having each child imagine that she received a special treat. When she ate it, she suddenly turned into a spider! Then have her choose a prompt and respond to it. After revising and editing her paper, she cuts it out and mounts it on a large black construction paper circle (spider's body). To complete the spider, she attaches a smaller black circle with eyes (head) and black construction paper legs. Invite each student to share her writing with the class. Then display the spiders around the room to showcase students' super writing skills.

- How is your life as a spider different from your life as a person? Explain three ways your life has changed.
- You've just received the TSA, or the Top Spider Award. Why was this award given to you?
- You're a new spider and you need some helpful hints. Write five questions you would ask an experienced spider in an interview.

SPACE EXPLORATION

Boost students' **descriptive-writing skills** with a visit to a newly-discovered planet! In advance, make a class supply of page 170. Start by telling students they are astronauts and their spaceship has just landed on a new planet that no one from Earth has ever explored. Have each child imagine what the planet looks like; then give him a copy of the reproducible and have him complete it. He uses his answers to write a descriptive paragraph about the planet on story paper. Then he draws a picture of the planet as it appeared when he landed on it. Attach the child's paper to his paragraph and then post the paragraphs on a display titled "Stellar Descriptions."

Imagine that you own a new restaurant. Write and design an ad that will make people want to eat there.

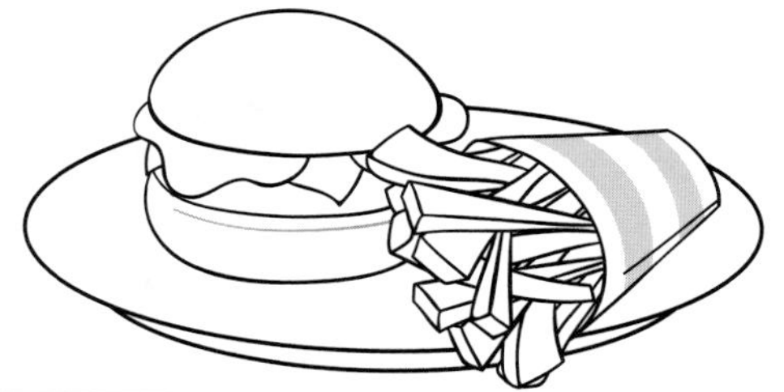

TEC43027

You are a film critic. This means you watch movies and explain whether you like them. Write about the last movie you saw. Use examples from the movie to support your feelings.

TEC43027

Where would you like to go for your next class field trip? Write a letter to your teacher. Try to talk her into taking your class to this place.

TEC43027

What healthy snack or meal do you like best? List the items needed to make it. Then write steps that explain how to make the meal.

TEC43027

Think about a business you could start with a friend that would help other kids. What kind of business is it? Why will it succeed?

TEC43027

Write a friendly letter that could be given to a new classmate when he or she joins your class. Make sure your letter includes these things:

- a welcome
- classroom rules and procedures
- advice on how to succeed in the classroom

TEC43027

Note to the teacher: Make a copy of this page. Glue the strips onto construction paper, laminate them, and cut them apart. Place the strips, writing paper, and pencils at a center.

Name ______________________________ Descriptive Writing
Planning sheet

First Visit Facts

What do you see as you step out of your spaceship? ______________________________

____

____

Are there plants, animals, and people? ____________

If there are, what do they look like? ______________________________

____

What color is the ground? ______________________________

What color is the sky? ______________________________

What sounds do you hear? ______________________________

____

What odors do you smell? ______________

____

____

How is this place like Earth? ____________

____

____

____

How is it different? ______________

____

____

____

 Note to the teacher: Use with "Space Exploration" on page 168.

"Snow" Wonder

Narrative-Writing Tips

COLOR-CODED STRIPS

Writing a paragraph

These simple strips help students write strong paragraphs with supporting details! For each child, gather two different-colored construction paper strips and three same-colored construction paper strips. Start by giving the student a topic such as "The Time I Was the Most Surprised" or "The Best Gift I Ever Received" and have him plan his story. Next, he chooses one event and thinks about the details he wants to include in his paper. On one colored strip he writes the paragraph's topic sentence. On each of the three same-colored strips he writes a different supporting detail that relates to the topic sentence. He programs the last strip with a concluding sentence. Then the child reads the strips to himself, rearranging the order of the supporting details if desired. Finally, he glues the strips in order onto a large sheet of construction paper. If desired, give students extra paper strips to help them organize and write the remaining paragraphs. After revising his sentences, he copies them onto his draft.

Susanne Poppe, McKinley School, Cicero, IL

Use these cool ideas to improve students' writing!

CATCHY SENTENCES
Writing a strong beginning

Help students write creative sentences that grab the reader's attention! Explain that a story can start in several different ways, including asking a question or using onomatopoeia, dialogue, or action words. Then share with students a personal narrative title such as "The Best Day of My Life." As a class, list examples of onomatopoeia, actions, or questions that could be used in the first sentence of the story. Then divide students into four groups. Assign each group one of the methods for starting a story and have it use examples from the class list to write three different beginning sentences. Finally, invite each group to share its sentences with the class.

Peggy Hurd, McKinley Elementary, Boise, ID

The Best Day of My Life

1. Boom, boom, boom! I woke up to the sound of someone knocking on my door.
2. Rip! I tore into the paper wrapped around a huge box.
3. Thud! A strangely shaped box landed at my feet.

TO-DO LISTS
Parts of a personal narrative

These student-created posters make perfect reminders! Begin the activity by discussing with students what makes a good personal narrative, such as an attention-grabbing beginning, strong details, and good action words. Next, pair students and give each twosome a 12" x 18" sheet of colored construction paper. The pair designs a poster that names two or three elements of a good narrative and includes an example of each. Allow each twosome to present its poster to the class; then display the posters around the room as handy references for students.

Name ______________________________ Personal Narrative
Revising

Making Changes

Write details in the blanks to make the narrative more interesting.

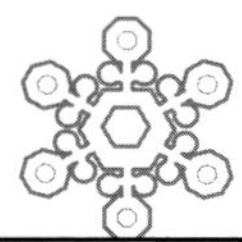

The Time I Lost My Scarf

Whoosh! The wind whipped all around me as I walked to hockey practice. I was freezing. Suddenly, I realized that my scarf was missing. It was my lucky scarf. I just had to find it!

First, I looked in my room. I couldn't find it.

Then I searched the living room. There was no scarf in there.

Finally, I looked in my sister's bedroom. There it was!

I was so scared when I thought I had lost my lucky scarf. I'm so glad I finally found it. I knew I would need it for my hockey game!

Where did you search in your room? ______________________________

____

How did you feel while you were searching the living room? ______________________________

____

Where did you find it in your sister's room? ______________________________

____

How did it get there? ______________________________

____

Bonus Box: On the back of this page, rewrite the narrative. Include the details to make it more interesting.

Save the Day
Activities for Writing Poetry

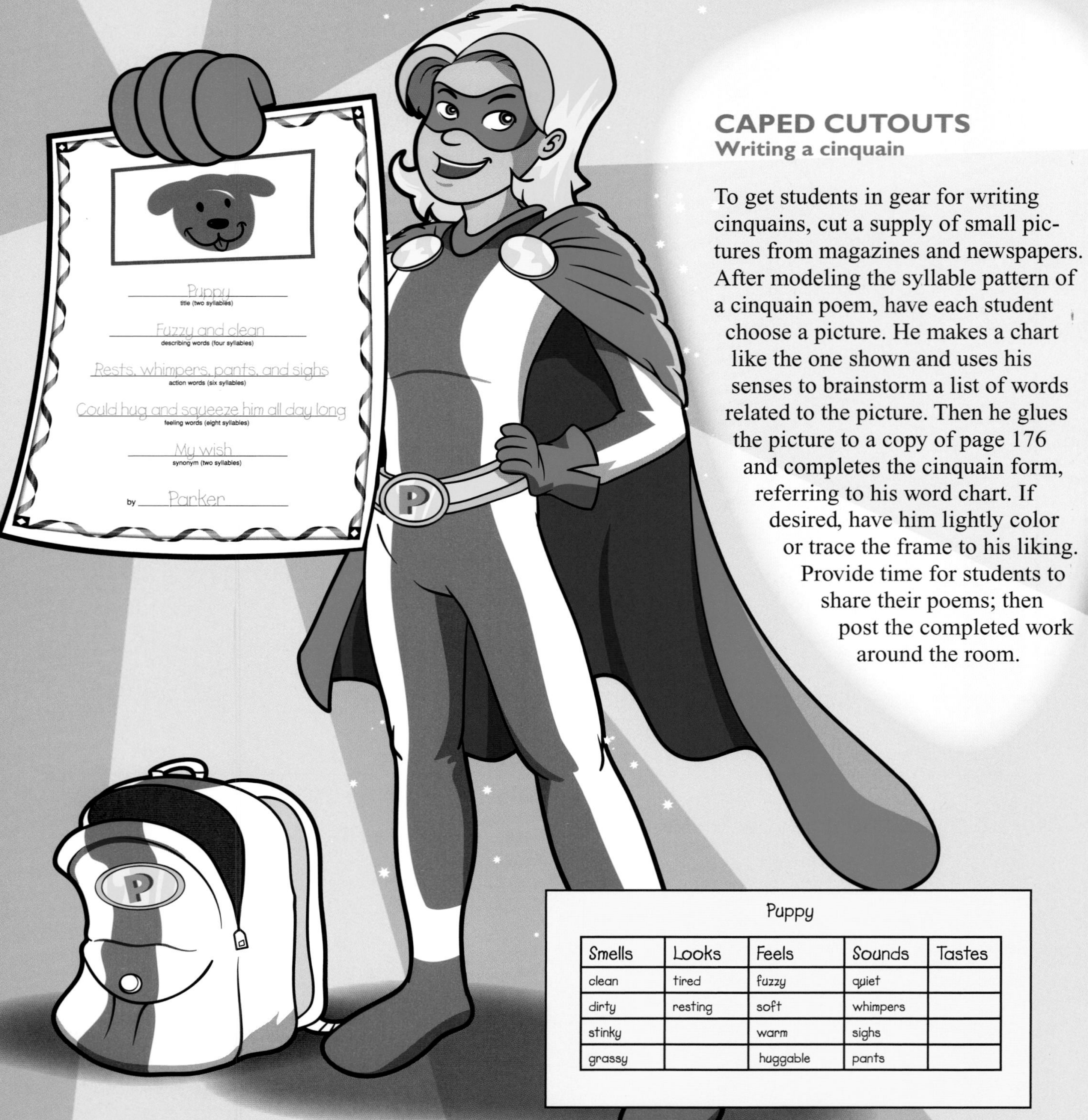
Puppy
title (two syllables)
Fuzzy and clean
describing words (four syllables)
Rests, whimpers, pants, and sighs
action words (six syllables)
Could hug and squeeze him all day long
feeling words (eight syllables)
My wish
synonym (two syllables)
by Parker

CAPED CUTOUTS
Writing a cinquain

To get students in gear for writing cinquains, cut a supply of small pictures from magazines and newspapers. After modeling the syllable pattern of a cinquain poem, have each student choose a picture. He makes a chart like the one shown and uses his senses to brainstorm a list of words related to the picture. Then he glues the picture to a copy of page 176 and completes the cinquain form, referring to his word chart. If desired, have him lightly color or trace the frame to his liking. Provide time for students to share their poems; then post the completed work around the room.

Puppy

Smells	Looks	Feels	Sounds	Tastes
clean	tired	fuzzy	quiet	
dirty	resting	soft	whimpers	
stinky		warm	sighs	
grassy		huggable	pants	

Rescue your students from poetry writer's block with these inspiring ideas.

with ideas by Jean Erickson, Grace Christian Academy, West Allis, WI

OUR HERO
Rhyming couplets

Remind students that a couplet poem is made up of pairs of lines that usually rhyme at the end. To start the activity, have each pair of students choose a common hero—such as an athlete, an entertainer, a historical figure, or a comic book superhero—to write about. Have students brainstorm a list of words that describe their chosen hero, focusing on the five Ws. Next, have the duo list rhyming words for each brainstormed word, referring to a rhyming dictionary if needed. Then have the pair use the words to write a couplet poem and illustrate it. Post the completed pages on a display called "Dynamic Duos at Work."

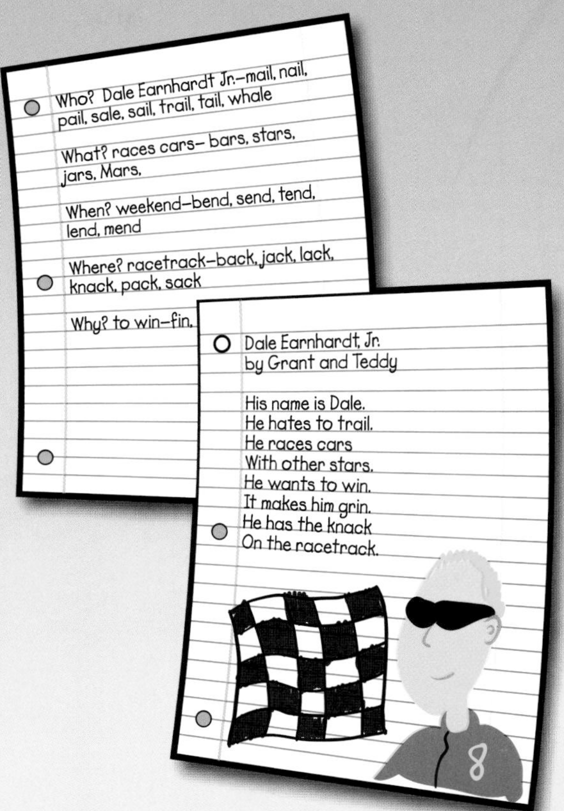

SUPER SIDEKICKS
Using alliteration

Explain that alliteration is a series of words that begin with the same sound. Next, have each student select a letter of the alphabet. She brainstorms a list of words that begin with that letter's sound and uses the words to write an alliteration poem on a sheet of construction paper. Then she draws the letter with a crayon and uses the letter as part of her illustration. Bind the completed poems in a book called "The ABCs of Alliteration."

title (two syllables)

describing words (four syllables)

action words (six syllables)

feeling words (eight syllables)

synonym (two syllables)

by

 Note to the teacher: Use with "Caped Cutouts" on page 174.

In the Swing!

Revising Ideas

Name LaQuinton

checklist

Hit It Out of the Park!

Use each item below to revise your story.

My beginning will grab my readers.

The details I use help tell the story.

My words will help my readers see the story.

My story makes sense.

My story has a clear ending.

UP TO BAT!

Using a checklist

To give revising hands-on appeal, make several copies of the checklist on the top half of page 179 and provide a supply of cotton balls. When a student is ready to revise a story, he takes a copy of the checklist and six cotton balls. Next, he reads the first item on the checklist, checks his writing for that element, and makes any necessary changes. Then he glues a cotton ball to the end of the bat and moves on to the next item. When the student is finished, he puts his checklist in his writing folder for a three-dimensional reminder of what it takes to hit a writing home run!

Turn students into seasoned pros with these revising activities!

Stacie Stone Davis, Lima, NY

PINCH HITTERS

Word choice

Lead students to brainstorm a list of words to use in the place of overused words, such as *good, fun,* and *big.* Post the list and provide a supply of small sticky note strips. Next, have each child review a story she is writing and place a sticky note strip over each overused word she finds. Then guide the child to choose a more specific or descriptive word for each one and write it on the strip.

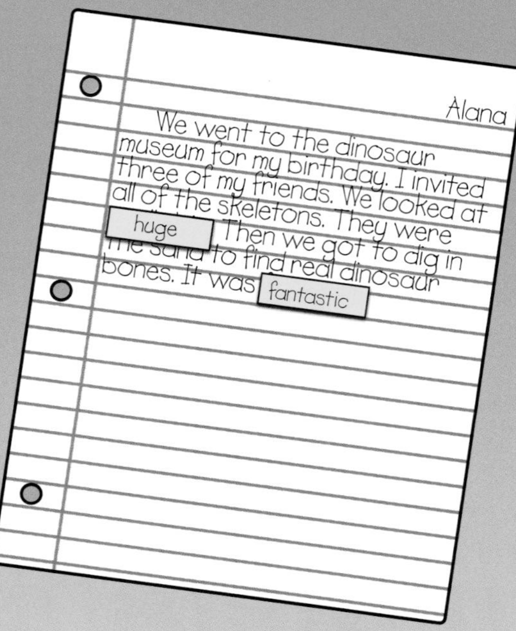

STEP UP TO THE PLATE!

Peer review

To begin, have each pair of students trade and read each other's stories. Next, guide each child to identify the story's strengths and write compliments about them on a copy of the bottom half of page 179 as directed. Then lead each child to write on the page as directed three questions about what he read or ideas to help improve his partner's story. Finally, have each child read his partner's comments and use them to guide his revisions.

Name ______________________________ Revising

Big League Review

Write in each ball one thing you like about the story.

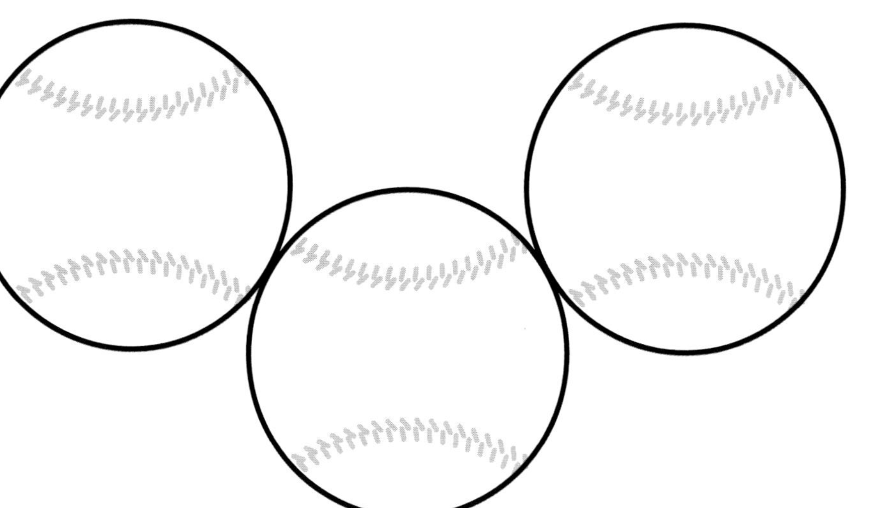

Write in each ball one question about the story.

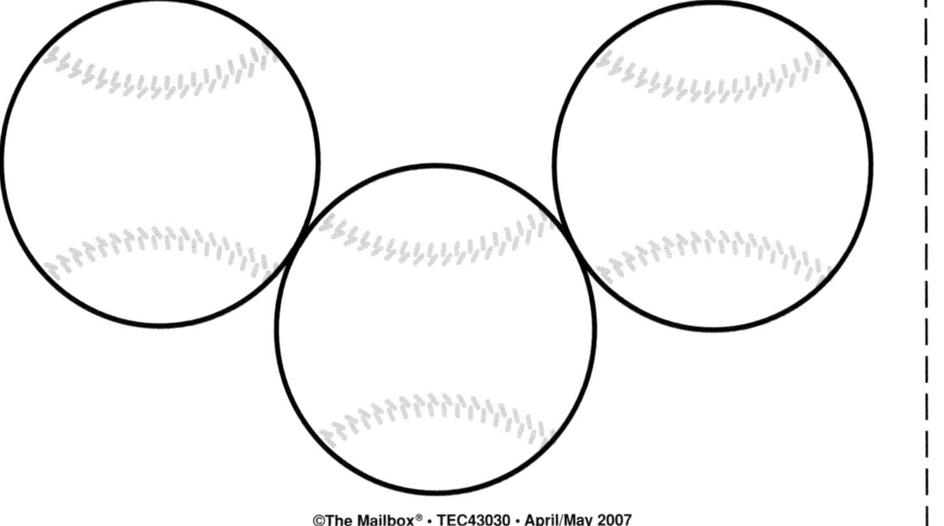

Note to the teacher: Use with "Step Up to the Plate!" on page 178.

Name ______________________________ Revising

Hit It Out of the Park!

Use each item below to revise your story.

My beginning will grab my readers.

The details I use help tell the story.

My words will help my readers see the story.

My story makes sense.

My story has a clear ending.

Note to the teacher: Use with "Up to Bat!" on page 177.

Name________________________________ Word choice

A Whole New Ball Game

Color the best word to take the place of the underlined word.
Follow the path to find out what happens.

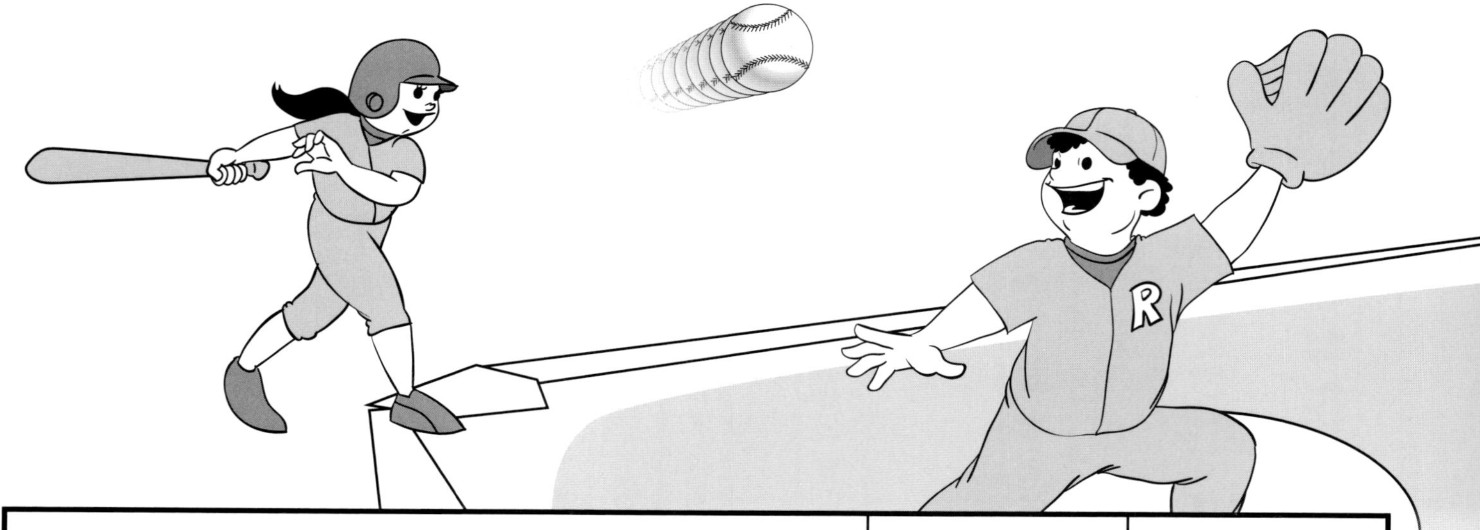

1. Abby <u>goes</u> up to home plate.	marches	moves
2. Ryan is a <u>good</u> pitcher.	fine	terrific
3. He thinks he can <u>get</u> Abby out.	put	strike
4. Abby <u>wants</u> to hit a home run.	hopes	gets
5. Ryan <u>says</u>, "I'm ready! Let's go!"	states	shouts
6. He takes a <u>big</u> step and throws the ball.	large	giant
7. Abby <u>moves</u> her bat.	waves	swings
8. Ryan hears a loud <u>sound</u>.	crack	hum
9. It is the bat as it <u>hits</u> the ball.	touches	whacks
10. Abby and Ryan watch the ball <u>go</u> into the air.	move	fly

Abby hits a foul ball.

Abby hits a home run.

Math Units

Place to Place

Monkeying Around With Place Value

Key
standard form = pink
written form = green
expanded form = purple
picture form = yellow

658
600 + 50 + 8
six hundred fifty-eight

NUMBER KITES

Number forms

In advance, cut a class supply of 9" x 9" white construction paper squares. Begin by giving each child a square and having him fold it in half twice, creating four equal sections. Also assign each child a different three-digit number. To complete the activity, the student places the unfolded square diagonally in front of him. In each section he uses a black crayon to write his number in a different form: standard, expanded, written, and picture. Then he lightly colors each section a different color and creates a key like the one shown. Finally, he attaches a length of yarn as a tail. Post students' completed number kites and keys on a bulletin board titled "Flying High With Place Value."

Get students into the swing of place value!

with ideas by Jean Erickson, Grace Christian School, West Allis, WI

CALL-AND-RESPONSE GAME

Understanding place value

This take-off of a popular game is an easy way to review number values! Write on the board several three-digit numbers. Next, tell students that they will be playing a game similar to Marco Polo. Explain that you will circle a digit in one of the numbers on the board and say, "Place." Students will respond by saying the place (ones, tens, or hundreds) that the number is in. Then you will say, "Value." Students will respond with the circled number's value. Repeat the process for as long as desired. Continue to play the game throughout the year as a simple way to review place value.

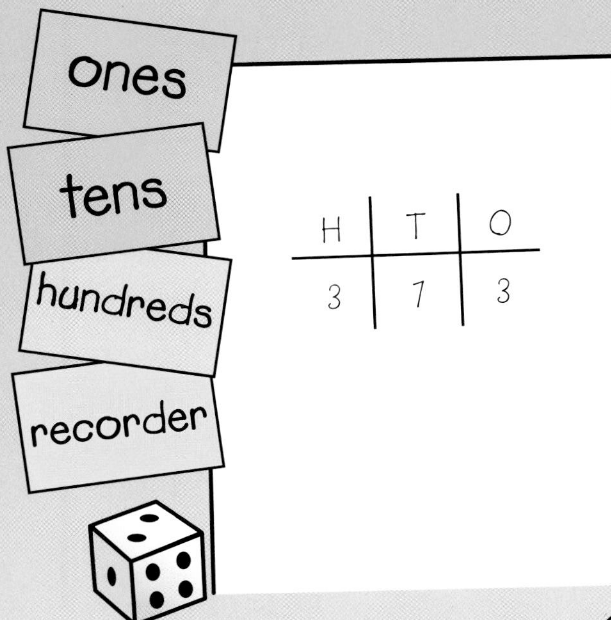

ROLLING ALONG

Understanding place value, writing numbers

Before the activity, create a set of index cards labeled as shown for each group of four students. Start by giving each group a die, a set of cards, and a sheet of paper. Have each child draw a card. The student who has the recorder card draws a three-column place-value chart like the one shown. Each student with a place-value card rolls the die, in turn, and holds it up for the recorder to list on his paper in the corresponding column. After each number is recorded, the recorder reads the three-digit number aloud. Then the students switch cards and repeat the process. Groups continue working in this manner until time is called. If desired, challenge students to make the largest and smallest numbers possible for each roll.

SIMPLE SAYING

Identifying place value

When introducing the order of ones, tens, and hundreds, teach students the chant shown. It makes place value easy to remember!

Karen Marklein
Saints Andrew-Thomas School
North Potosi, WI

Name ____

Place Value
Value of digits

Monkey Munchies

Write the value of the underlined digit.
Color the matching banana.

A. 23 ________ 87 ________ 94 ________ 102 ________

B. 567 ________ 235 ________ 741 ________ 96 ________

C. 243 ________ 899 ________ 620 ________ 158 ________

D. 964 ________ 753 ________ 148 ________ 359 ________

8 30 40
100 300 4
1 700
500 90
20 600
60 7 200 800

Activity 1

1. Draw three cards from the bag.
2. Use the cards to make the largest number you can. Write it on your paper.
3. Put the cards back in the bag.
4. Repeat the steps three more times.

TEC43026

Activity 2

1. Draw three cards from the bag.
2. Use the cards to make the smallest number you can. Write it on your paper.
3. Put the cards back in the bag.
4. Repeat the steps three more times.

TEC43026

Activity 3

1. Draw three cards from the bag.
2. Use the cards to make a number. Write it on your paper.
3. Write the number in word form.
4. Put the cards back in the bag.
5. Repeat the steps three more times.

TEC43026

Activity 4

1. Draw three cards from the bag.
2. Use the cards to make a number. Write it on your paper.
3. Write the number in expanded form.
4. Put the cards back in the bag.
5. Repeat the steps three more times.

TEC43026

0 TEC43026	1 TEC43026	2 TEC43026	3 TEC43026	4 TEC43026	5 TEC43026	6 TEC43026	7 TEC43026	8 TEC43026	9 TEC43026
0 TEC43026	1 TEC43026	2 TEC43026	3 TEC43026	4 TEC43026	5 TEC43026	6 TEC43026	7 TEC43026	8 TEC43026	9 TEC43026
0 TEC43026	1 TEC43026	2 TEC43026	3 TEC43026	4 TEC43026	5 TEC43026	6 TEC43026	7 TEC43026	8 TEC43026	9 TEC43026

Note to the teacher: Make a copy of this page and mount it on construction paper. Cut out the cards and store the number cards in a paper bag. Place the cards, the bag, paper, and pencils at a center. A child follows the directions on each card to complete the activity.

Puzzle Pieces

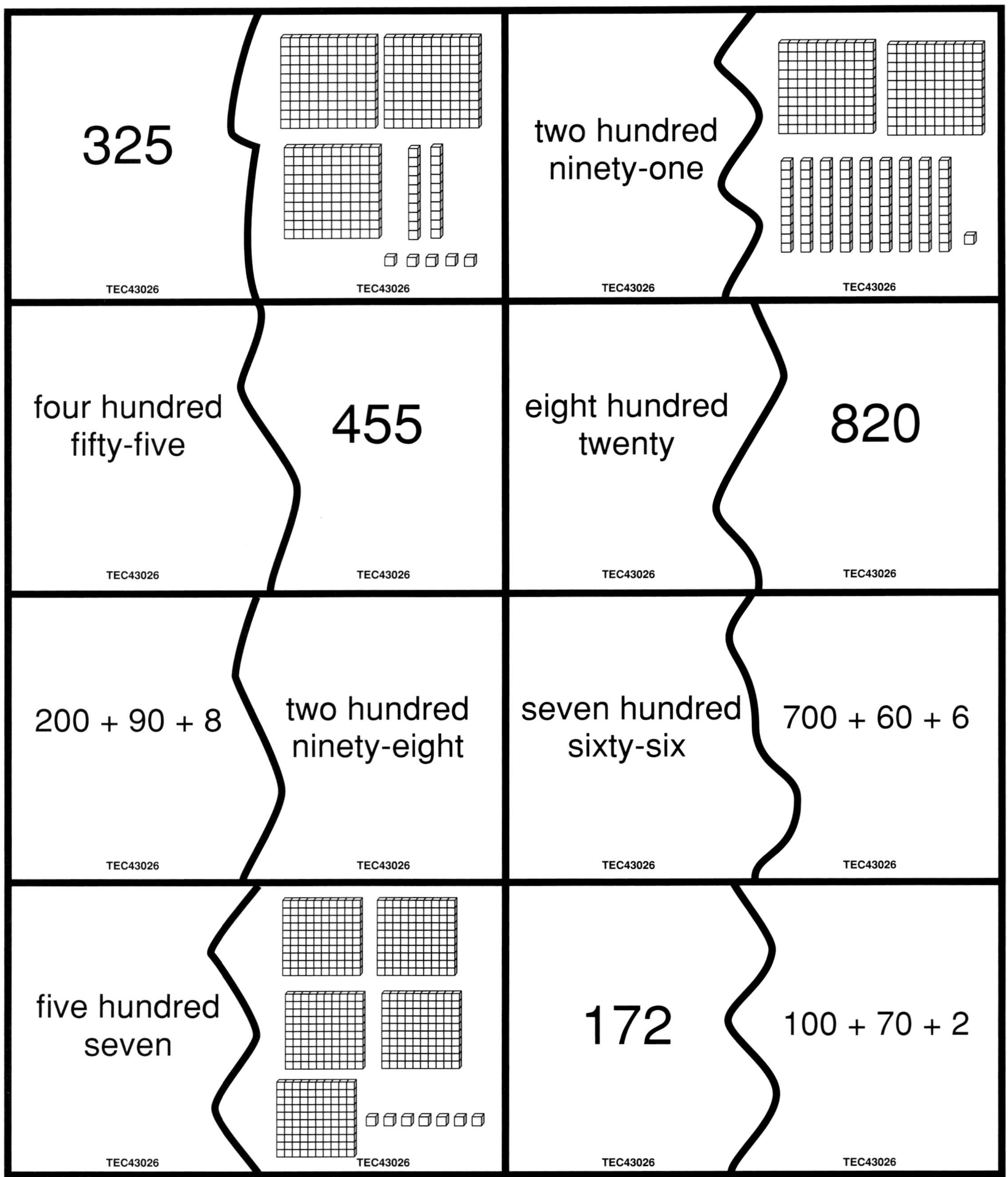

Note to the teacher: Make a copy of this page and mount it on construction paper. Cut out the puzzle pieces. Program each piece's back for self-checking and place the pieces at a center. A child finds matching number forms, places the pieces together, and then turns them over to check his work.

Name ____________________

In the Right Order

Color the matching number.

A. 1 hundred
3 thousands
2 tens
9 ones

3,129 1,329

B. 6 thousands
0 tens
4 ones
7 hundreds

6,704 6,074

C. 9 tens
2 hundreds
7 thousands
2 ones

9,272 7,292

D. 5 thousands
0 ones
0 hundreds
4 tens

5,040 5,004

E. 9 tens
3 thousands
7 hundreds
0 ones

3,790 9,370

F. 8 ones
9 hundreds
6 tens
4 thousands

4,896 4,968

G. 5 ones
5 thousands
4 tens
3 hundreds

5,543 5,345

H. 7 tens
0 ones
7 hundreds
7 thousands

7,707 7,770

I. 9 thousands
0 hundreds
0 ones
3 tens

9,030 9,003

J. 8 hundreds
8 tens
1 thousand
1 one

8,811 1,881

Just the Facts

Investigating Basic Facts

PRACTICE PARTNERS
Addition to 18

These simple cards are a great way for pairs to brush up on basic facts! To make one practice card, glue a sheet from a theme-shaped notepad (such as an apple-shaped notepad) on tagboard. Cut out the shape and write several different basic addition facts on its front. Also punch a hole beside each problem where the answer would be. On the back, write each fact's answer next to its corresponding hole. Then glue the shape to a tongue depressor, and place it at a center along with a golf tee.

To use the card, one child holds it with the answers turned toward him and the problems turned toward his partner. The partner selects a problem, places the golf tee in the corresponding hole, and says the answer aloud. The student holding the card checks the answer by looking at the number beside the tee. The pair repeats the process until each problem has been solved. Then the partners select a new card, change jobs, and continue practicing.

Virginia Conrad
Bunker R-3 Elementary
Bunker, MO

Use these arresting ideas to strengthen students' knowledge of basic facts!

GIVE ME THE SIGN

Completing number sentences

This whole-class activity provides practice with addition and subtraction! Give each child two index card halves. Have her label one card with an addition symbol and the other with a subtraction symbol. Next, write on the board a basic fact number sentence like the one shown, omitting the operation sign. Each child holds up the card with the matching sign. Repeat the process for as long as desired. Then follow up the activity by having each child complete the reproducible on page 190.

Julie Lewis, J. O. Davis Elementary, Irving, TX

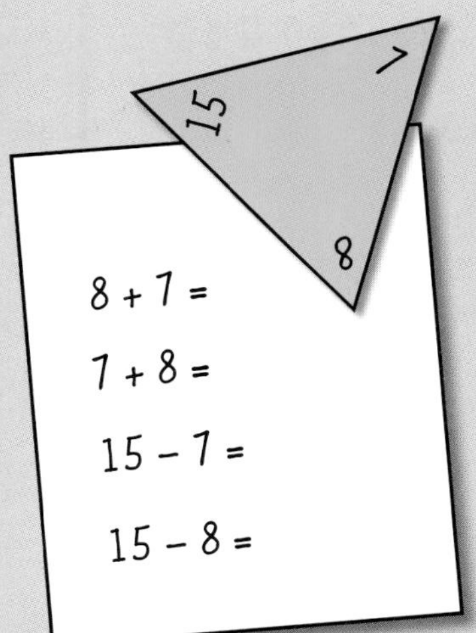

CHOOSE YOUR FACTS

Individualized practice

Easily adjust your basic facts practice to meet each student's needs! On Monday, each child chooses four facts to practice, makes a triangular flash card for each one, and stores the cards in a resealable plastic bag. Then he creates a quiz by writing the four corresponding addition and subtraction facts for each card on a sheet of paper, leaving the answers blank. (Collect students' papers for use later in the week.) He reviews the cards during the week by placing his thumb on one number, reading the problem aloud, saying the answer, and lifting his thumb to check it. At the end of the week, have him complete his premade quiz. If he's mastered all four facts, he repeats the process the following week with a new set of facts. If he needs extra practice, he continues working with those facts.

Sue McDonald, John W. Armstrong Elementary, Sachse, TX

STAMP A PROBLEM

Representing problems pictorially

This simple idea helps students see what they're adding and subtracting! Place at a center a basic fact master sheet, a set of stamping markers, paper, and pencils. To represent an addition problem, a child selects a number sentence from the master sheet and stamps the number of each addend. Then he counts the number of stamps to find the sum. To create a subtraction problem, he stamps the minuend and then uses his pencil to cross out the subtrahend to find the difference. After creating and solving the problem, he writes the corresponding number sentence below it. He repeats the process as long as desired.

Julie Lewis

Name ____

What's the Sign?

Write "+" or "–" to complete each number sentence.

A.	2 ☐ 3 = 5	8 ☐ 9 = 17	7 ☐ 4 = 3	6 ☐ 7 = 13
B.	6 ☐ 3 = 3	2 ☐ 5 = 7	4 ☐ 4 = 8	4 ☐ 7 = 11
C.	8 ☐ 6 = 2	6 ☐ 5 = 1	1 ☐ 8 = 9	8 ☐ 2 = 10
D.	16 ☐ 8 = 8	9 ☐ 5 = 4	9 ☐ 9 = 18	9 ☐ 7 = 16
E.	5 ☐ 2 = 3	9 ☐ 3 = 12	6 ☐ 1 = 5	15 ☐ 6 = 9

 Note to the teacher: Use with "Give Me the Sign" on page 189.

Name ____________________

Missing Numbers

Write each missing addend.
Cross off the matching answer.

A.	2 + □ 10	3 + □ 12	□ + 3 9	□ + 1 5	8 + □ 11	7 + □ 13
B.	9 + □ 15	□ + 6 12	□ + 7 7	3 + □ 5	□ + 1 10	
C.	2 + □ 6	5 + □ 13	6 + □ 7	□ + 9 17	4 + □ 8	
D.	3 + □ 3	□ + 7 8	□ + 9 13	8 + □ 16		

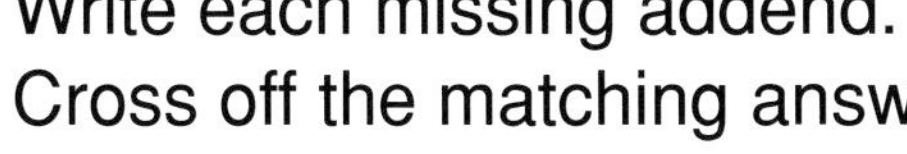
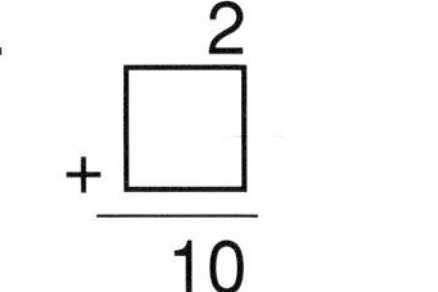
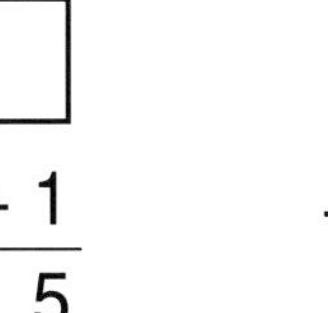
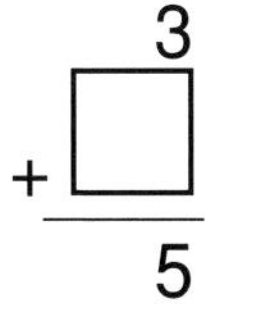
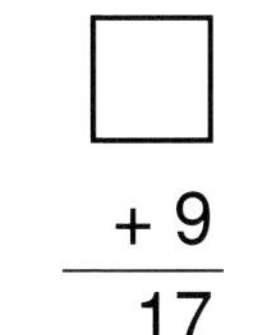

Name ____________________

Basic Facts
Subtraction facts through 18

Foot Patrol

Solve.
Help the police officer get to the station.
If the answer is 5 or greater, color the box blue.

	12 − 4	10 − 5	8 − 6	9 − 5
11 − 7	4 − 3	14 − 6	6 − 4	3 − 1
7 − 4	15 − 8	11 − 3	5 − 2	8 − 7
13 − 9	7 − 1	10 − 8	12 − 9	
8 − 4	12 − 5	18 − 9	9 − 2	

Climbing Up

Addition and Subtraction

SUM'S MISTAKES

Addition with regrouping

In advance, gather a stuffed animal or an action figure. Begin the activity by introducing the character to the class as Sum. After reviewing with students the meaning of the character's name, write on the board an addition problem with an incorrect sum like the one shown. Tell students that Sum added the numbers together, but his answer isn't correct. Then challenge each child to find Sum's mistake by copying the problem onto his paper and solving it correctly. After students have found the answer, discuss Sum's mistake and the correct answer as a class. Repeat the activity once a day to provide practice with addition and regrouping. Also keep Sum on display to remind students to check their work. If desired, introduce a second character named Difference and repeat the process with subtraction problems.

Help students reach new heights with these computation activities!

with ideas by Jean Erickson, Grace Christian School, West Allis, WI

GET THE DIFFERENCE

Subtraction

To prepare this partner game, draw on poster board a simple gameboard like the one shown below. Also copy the game markers below and color them if desired. Place the gameboard and the markers at a center. To start, give each child two index cards. Have him program the front of each card with a different subtraction problem and the card's back with the answer. Have him use a calculator to ensure that his answers are correct. Collect students' cards and place them faceup at the center along with paper and pencils. To play, each child places his marker on Start. Then he draws a card, writes the problem on his paper, and solves it. When he is finished, he turns his card over to check his answer. If his answer is correct, he keeps his card and moves forward one space. If his answer is incorrect, he returns the card to the bottom of the stack and keeps his marker in the same space. Students continue in this manner until one child collects ten cards and reaches the mountaintop.

More on the floor?
Go next door and borrow ten more.
More on the top?
There's no need to stop.

35 (top)	78 (top)
− 18 (floor)	− 12 (floor)

REGROUPING RULE

Subtraction

This simple rhyme is the perfect regrouping reminder! Before starting the activity, write the rhyme shown on a sheet of chart paper. Also write on the board two subtraction problems: one that involves regrouping and one that doesn't. Label each problem's minuend and subtrahend as shown. Begin by reviewing regrouping with students. Next, teach them the rhyme, pointing to the corresponding part of the problem as students recite it. Solve the problems as a class and then give each child a copy of the reproducible on page 196. Have the student look at each problem and write "R" beside it if it involves regrouping. Then have her complete the page.

Rebecca Joslin, Whispering Pines Elementary, Humble, TX and Carrie Billings, Brentwood Elementary, Victorville, CA

Game Markers

Use with "Get the Difference" on this page.

Name ______________________________

Addition of Larger Numbers
With and without regrouping

Reaching the Summit

Add.

Why did the goat go over the mountain?

To solve the riddle, write the letters above on the matching numbered lines below.

Because ___ ___ couldn't ___ ___ ___ ___ ___ ___ ___ ___ ___!

48 96 881 199 97 168 891 102 114 423 73

Name ____________________

Missing Gear

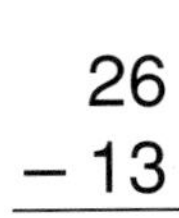
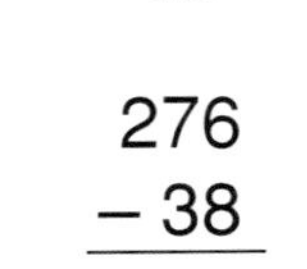
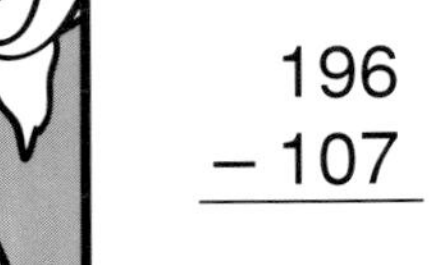

Subtract.
If the answer is 50 or greater, color the box.

26 − 13	48 − 29	276 − 38	196 − 107
36 − 19	55 − 24	302 − 111	78 − 26
296 − 135	556 − 448	823 − 351	87 − 32
943 − 796	290 − 188	77 − 29	346 − 137

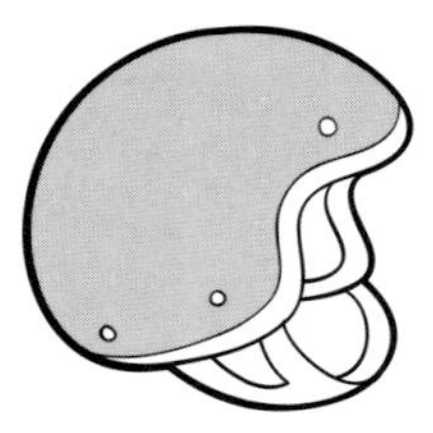
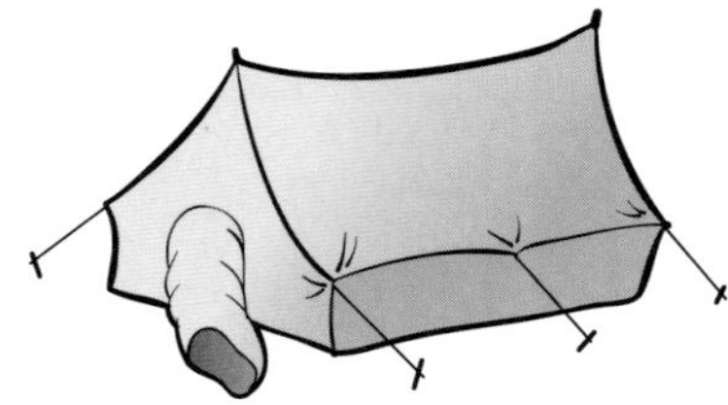

Find the column with the most colored boxes.
Circle the item below it. It's what Gary forgot to pack!

 Note to the teacher: Use with "Regrouping Rule" on page 194.

Get Hopping

Computation Games and Puzzles

This will be a double if you get it right. 44 + 35 equal what?

single double triple

Keegan Kendra 1st Home

ROUND THE BASES

Addition and subtraction

To prepare this whole-class game, program a supply of index cards with addition and subtraction problems of varying difficulties. Sort the cards into three stacks: singles (easiest), doubles (more difficult), and triples (most difficult). Next, give each pair of students two different-colored linking cubes and a large sheet of paper. Have one child draw a simple baseball diamond in the middle of the paper and write one player's name on each side to make a scoreboard as shown.

To play, choose any student to select a card from one of the piles. Name the stack the card came from and read the problem aloud. Have Player 1 from each pair solve the problem on a piece of paper. Then announce the correct answer and have Player 2 check Player 1's work. If Player 1 is correct, he moves his cube the appropriate number of bases (one for a single, two for a double, three for a triple). If incorrect, he does not move his cube. Choose another student to select a card, and repeat the process with Player 2. Players continue taking turns solving the problems. Each time a player passes over home plate, he adds a tally mark to his score. Play continues until time is called, and the player with more points is declared the winner.

Play up your students' addition and subtraction skills

with these interactive activities.

with ideas by Laura Johnson, South Decatur Elementary, Greensburg, IN

HOP, SKIP, AND JUMP

Estimating sums and differences

Use this partner game to improve students' estimation skills. Make a copy of the gameboard on page 199 and the cards on page 200. Mount the gameboard and cards on construction paper, cut them out and place the cards in a resealable plastic bag. If desired, place the answer key cards in the bag for self-checking. Then place the bag and the gameboard at a center. A student places the cards facedown in a stack. Player 1 chooses a card and tries to match the estimated answer on the card to one of the problems in her section. If she makes a match, she places the card on the matching problem. If she cannot make a match, she returns the card to the bottom of the stack. Player 2 takes a turn in a similar manner. Play continues until one player has covered all of her problems or until time is called.

'ROO RACES

Computation

To prepare for this variation of Leapfrog, have each student write an addition problem with its solution on one side of a sheet of paper and a subtraction problem and its solution on the other. Collect the papers and then take students outside or to a large indoor space. Mark off starting and finish lines and then divide the class into four teams. Have each team line up in a row behind the starting line and give the first person on each team a mini dry-erase board, a marker, and an eraser. Randomly choose a paper and read aloud a problem. The first player from each team writes and solves the problem on the dry-erase board. When all four players are finished or time is up, they show their answers. Each child with the correct answer hops forward one time and then sits down. If a child's answer is incorrect, he moves to the end of his line. The next players continue in this manner with a new problem. Each additional player who gets a correct answer stands beside the teammate seated farthest away and then hops forward. If all team players are seated but none have reached the finish line, the next turn goes to the seated player closest to the starting line. Play continues in this manner until one team reaches the finish line.

Hop, Skip, and Jump

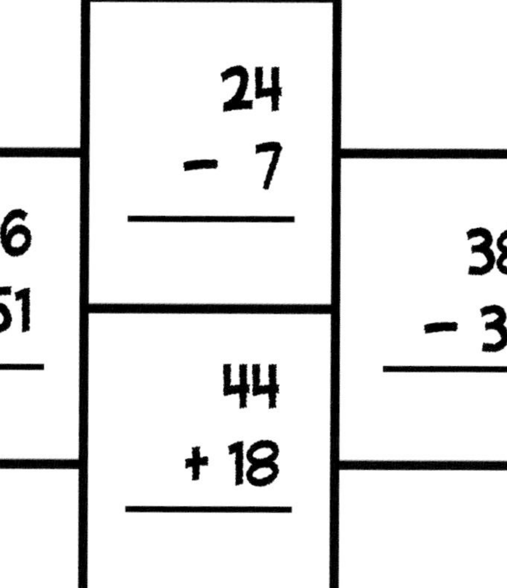

Start

38 + 12	25 + 35 / 60 − 56	22 + 17	47 − 32	81 + 4 / 99 − 68	66 − 23 / 52 + 45	33 − 18

Start

96 − 51	24 − 7 / 44 + 18	38 − 31	51 + 25	91 − 34 / 79 + 9	67 + 23 / 73 − 48	86 + 13

Game Cards and Answer Key Cards

Use with "Hop, Skip, and Jump" on page 198.

40 + 10 60	30 + 40 70	20 + 20 40	80 + 0 80	50 + 50 100
40 + 20 60	50 + 30 80	80 + 10 90	70 + 20 90	90 + 10 100
60 − 60 0	50 − 30 20	100 − 70 30	70 − 20 50	70 − 50 20
100 − 50 50	20 − 10 10	40 − 30 10	90 − 30 60	30 − 20 10

Top

- 30 + 40 = 70
- 80 + 0 = 80
- 70 − 20 = 50
- 40 + 10 = 50
- 20 + 20 = 40
- 50 − 30 = 20
- 30 − 20 = 10
- 60 − 60 = 0
- 100 − 70 = 30
- 50 + 50 = 100

TEC43029

Bottom

- 20 − 10 = 10
- 90 − 30 = 60
- 70 + 20 = 90
- 100 − 50 = 50
- 40 − 30 = 10
- 50 + 30 = 80
- 90 + 10 = 100
- 40 + 20 = 60
- 80 + 10 = 90
- 70 − 50 = 20

TEC43029

Name ______________________________

Jumping for Joy

Add or subtract.

R.	L.	I.	
41 + 37	69 − 15	22 + 65	
U.	D.	P.	A.
99 − 76	34 + 43	52 + 36	87 − 22
A.	E.	N.	R.
75 + 14	83 − 72	66 − 31	41 + 11
E.	Y.	A.	G.
12 + 4	60 + 36	96 − 22	78 − 37

When does a kangaroo jump the most?

To solve the riddle, write the letters from above on the numbered lines below.

___ ___ ___ ___ ___ ___ ___ ___ ___ ___ ___ ___ ___ ___ ___.
77 23 52 87 35 41 89 54 16 65 88 96 11 74 78

Name ____

Reporting Results

Write the missing numbers.

Kalani

```
   1 7
+  3 □
   ---
   □ 9
```

Kalil

```
   4 5
+  □ 1
   ---
   6 □
```

Kara

```
   8 0
+    9
   ---
   □ □
```

Karl

```
   2 4
+  6 □
   ---
   □ 8
```

Kayla

```
   3 1
+  □ 6
   ---
   9 □
```

Keaton

```
   □ 6
+    3
   ---
   9 □
```

Kelsey

```
   5 3
+  4 □
   ---
   □ 8
```

Kevin

```
   7 2
+  □ 3
   ---
   9 □
```

Keshawn

```
   1 8
+  6 1
   ---
   □ □
```

Kyle

```
   3 4
+  1 □
   ---
   □ 6
```

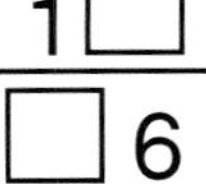
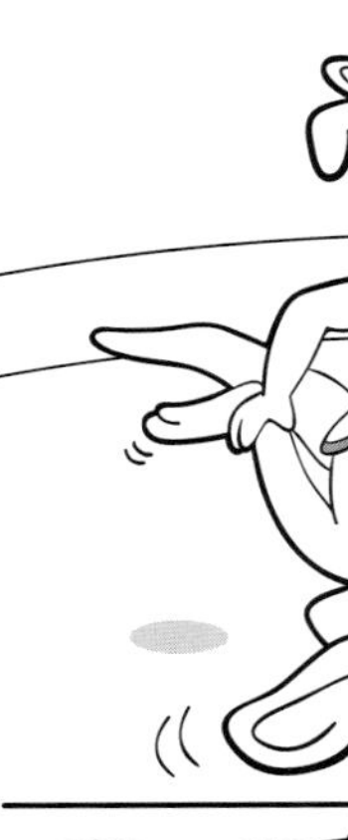

Look at the score sheets above.

Who had the longest jump?

____

Who had the shortest jump?

____

In Training

Strategies for Understanding Multiplication

SPIN, SORT, AND SOLVE

Modeling multiplication with equal groups

Students model multiplication with this hands-on partner game. Have each student pair cut out a copy of the spinner, multiplication table, and bone cards on page 205. Then give the twosome a paper clip and five small paper plates (dog bowls). To play the game, Player 1 uses a pencil and the paper clip to spin twice. The first spin shows the number of groups, or dog bowls, needed, and the second spin shows the number of bones to place on each bowl.

Player 1 uses the bowls and bones to model and solve a multiplication problem. After naming the product, he uses the multiplication table to check his answer. If he's correct, he colors the product on the table with a crayon. If he's incorrect, his turn is over. Player 2 repeats the process, coloring her product on the table a different color. If a player spins a pair of numbers that his partner has already spun and given a correct answer for, he does not color the table. The first player to color ten products is the winner.

Help students understand the basics of multiplication
with these interactive ideas.

TIMES TENTS
Relating skip-counting to multiplication

This activity for two puts skip-counting skills to work. Have each student pair cut out a copy of the skip-counting strips on page 206. If desired, program the blank strip with another skip-counting pattern prior to copying. Have each pair fold each strip along the center line to create a long tent. Player 1 chooses a tent and turns it so Player 2 only sees the number pattern. After Player 2 names the skip-counting pattern shown, Player 1 rotates the tent so that Player 2 sees the multiplication problems. Player 1 points at a problem, and Player 2 uses skip-counting or her knowledge of multiplication facts to name its product. Player 1 uses the number pattern on the opposite side to check his partner's answer. When Player 2 has answered each problem, she chooses a new tent, the partners switch roles, and the process is repeated.

adapted from an idea by Bonnie Gaynor, Franklin, NJ

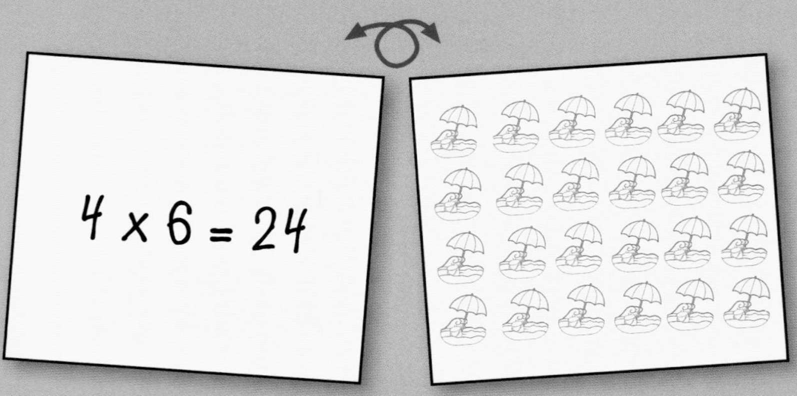

ALL LINED UP
Using arrays

In advance, make a class supply of paper rectangles of different sizes. Then explain to students that an array is an arrangement of objects in columns and rows. This arrangement can be used to show a multiplication fact. After modeling some arrays and their corresponding multiplication facts, have students make their own arrays. To do this, give each student a paper rectangle and access to an ink pad and stamps. The student stamps a shape across the rectangle, leaving a small space between each shape. Then he continues on the following rows, lining up each shape under the one above it until he has filled the paper. Next, he counts the number of stamps in one row and one column and then uses the numbers to write a multiplication fact on the back of the paper. Collect the completed arrays and place them at a center for students to use as flash cards.

Spinner, Multiplication Table, and Bone Cards

Use with "Spin, Sort, and Solve" on page 203.

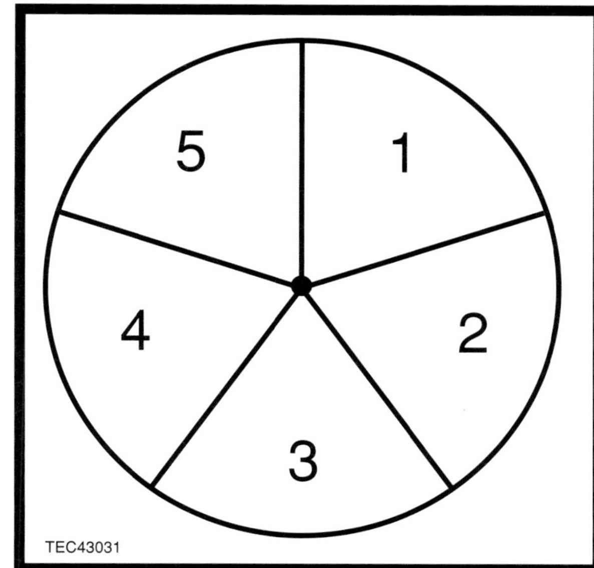

X	1	2	3	4	5
1	1	2	3	4	5
2	2	4	6	8	10
3	3	6	9	12	15
4	4	8	12	16	20
5	5	10	15	20	25

TEC43031

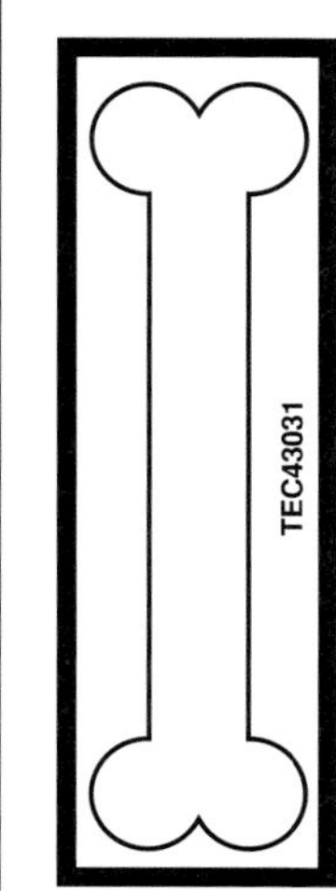

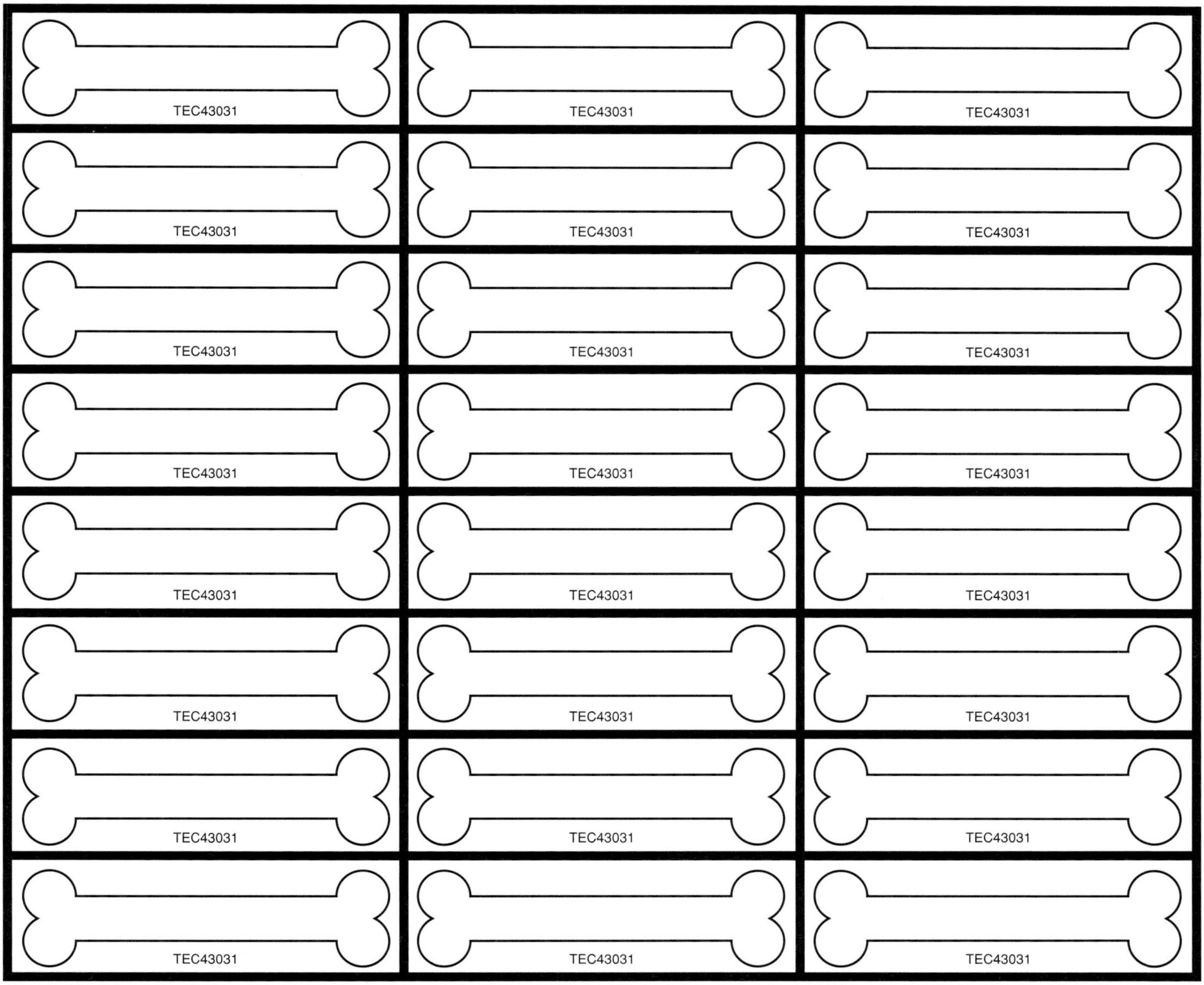

TEC43031	TEC43031	TEC43031
TEC43031	TEC43031	TEC43031
TEC43031	TEC43031	TEC43031
TEC43031	TEC43031	TEC43031
TEC43031	TEC43031	TEC43031
TEC43031	TEC43031	TEC43031
TEC43031	TEC43031	TEC43031
TEC43031	TEC43031	TEC43031

Skip-Counting Strips

Use with "Times Tents" on page 204.

2 x 0	2 x 1	2 x 2	2 x 3	2 x 4	2 x 5	2 x 6	2 x 7	2 x 8	2 x 9
0	2	4	6	8	10	12	14	16	18 TEC43031

3 x 0	3 x 1	3 x 2	3 x 3	3 x 4	3 x 5	3 x 6	3 x 7	3 x 8	3 x 9
0	3	6	9	12	15	18	21	24	27 TEC43031

5 x 0	5 x 1	5 x 2	5 x 3	5 x 4	5 x 5	5 x 6	5 x 7	5 x 8	5 x 9
0	5	10	15	20	25	30	35	40	45 TEC43031

10 x 0	10 x 1	10 x 2	10 x 3	10 x 4	10 x 5	10 x 6	10 x 7	10 x 8	10 x 9
0	10	20	30	40	50	60	70	80	90 TEC43031

x	x	x	x	x	x	x	x	x	x
									TEC43031

Name ____________________

Multiplication
Repeated addition

Well-Earned Rewards

Count the amount in each set.
Write a repeated addition sentence.
Then write a multiplication sentence.
The first one has been done for you.

A.

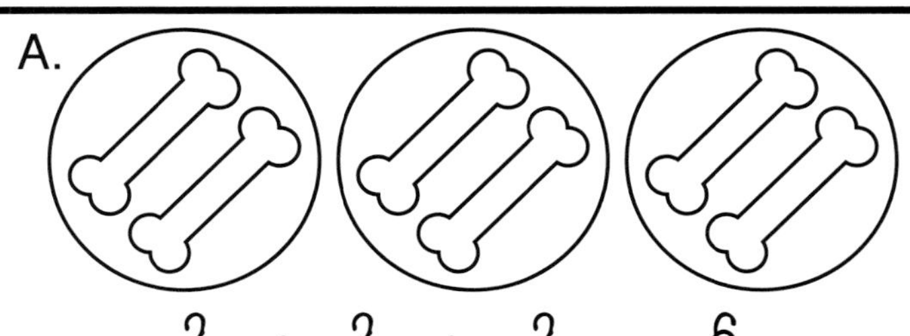

2 + 2 + 2 = 6

3 x 2 = 6
sets of

B.

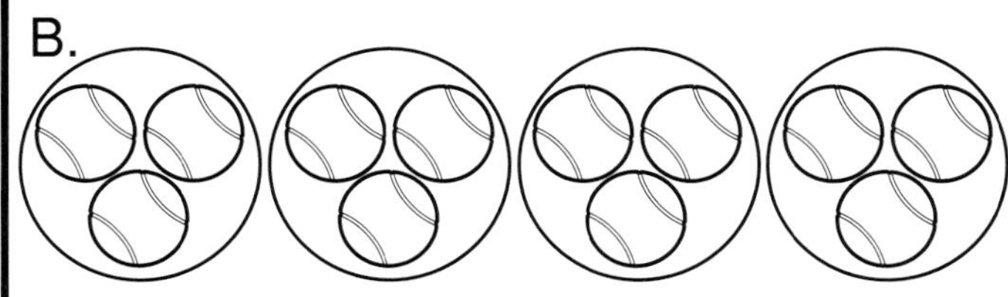

____ + ____ + ____ + ____ = ____

____ x ____ = ____
sets of

C.

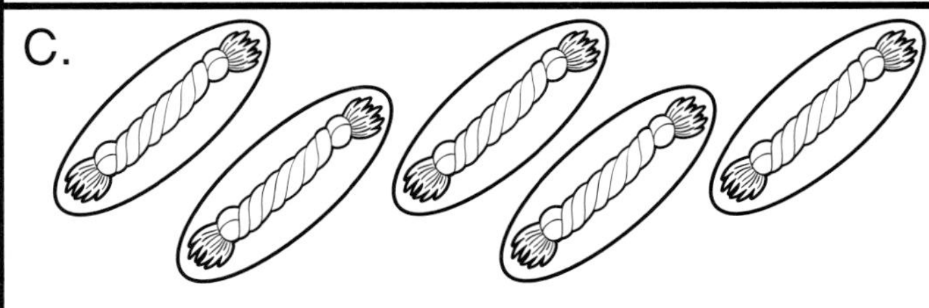

____ + ____ + ____ + ____ + ____ = ____

____ x ____ = ____
sets of

D.

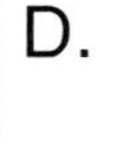

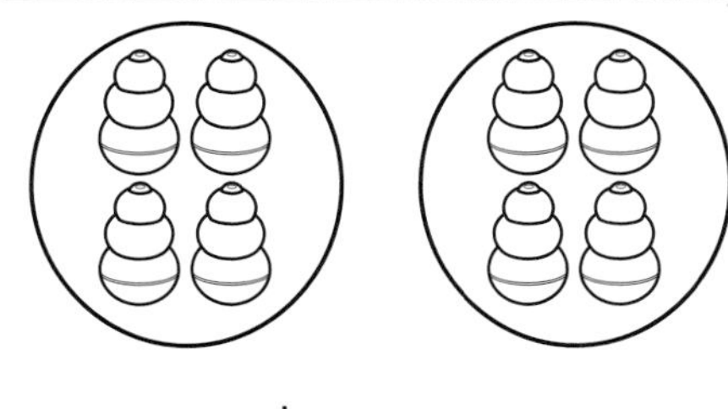

____ + ____ = ____

____ x ____ = ____
sets of

E.

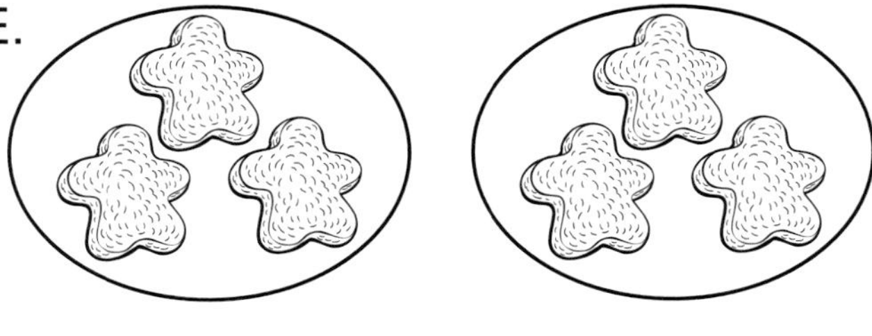

____ + ____ = ____

____ x ____ = ____
sets of

F.

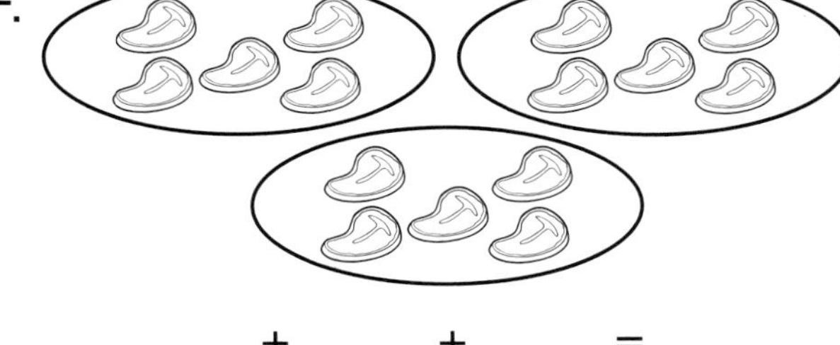

____ + ____ + ____ = ____

____ x ____ = ____
sets of

Sumatran Tigers	Bengal Tigers	Siberian Tigers	South China Tigers
12	10	13	11
8	11	9	11

Keeping Fit

Computation Review

HOW MANY WAYS?

Adding, subtracting, multiplying, and dividing

Set up a computation tournament with this mathematical variation of the Boggle game. In advance, write a number on each of a supply of index cards. Divide your class into small teams. Then choose a card and read the number aloud. Give the team members three minutes to each write down as many number combinations as they can name that equal that number. When time is up, have each child share his combinations with the rest of his team to determine how many unique combinations the team made. Award one point for each correct combination and record each team's total on a class scoreboard. Continue the game with more numbers. Play for as long as desired. The team with the most points at the end of the game wins.

Phylene Fizzuoglio
William Sidney Mount Elementary
Stony Brook, NY

Maintain a healthy understanding of computation skills with these fun review activities.

with ideas by Stacie Wright, Millington School, Millington, NJ

HIGH ROLLER
Multiplying, adding

To get this partner activity rolling, give each student pair two dice and a copy of the recording sheet on page 210. Player 1 rolls the dice and multiplies the values together. She records her product on the sheet, then rolls again. After recording the second product, she adds the products together. Then Player 2 rolls the dice and records his totals. The player with the higher sum circles the number and wins the round. The duo continues in this manner until all rounds have been played or time is called. The player who wins more rounds wins the game.

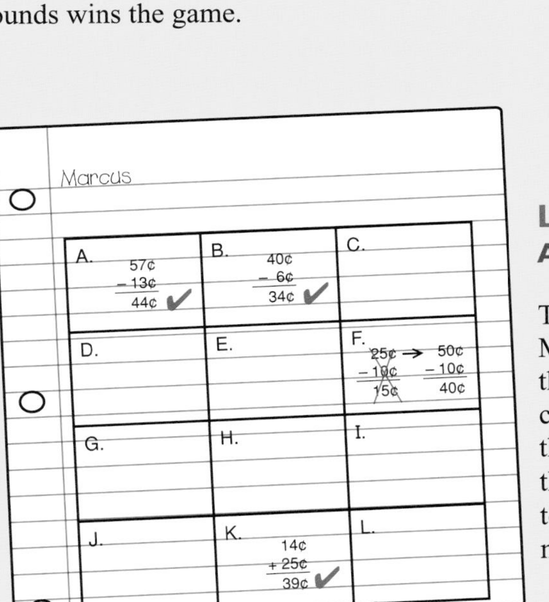

LOOSE CHANGE
Adding and subtracting money

To prepare this center activity, first copy the center cards on page 211. Mount the center cards on construction paper, laminate them, and cut them apart. Program each card's back for self-checking and store the cards in a resealable plastic bag. A child makes a recording sheet like the one shown. Next, he chooses a card, sets up the problem next to the matching letter, and then solves the problem. He flips over the card to check his work and then chooses another card. He continues in this manner until all problems have been solved.

MEMORABLE FACTS
Adding doubles and near doubles

To prepare this center for two, remove the face cards and aces from a deck of playing cards. Player 1 shuffles the deck and places each card face-down on the workspace. Player 2 turns over two cards, looking for a set of doubles (5 + 5) or near-doubles (5 + 6 or 4 + 5). If she makes a match, she states its sum and places the cards in her own stack. If desired, have Player 2 check Player 1's answers with a calculator or hundred chart. If a match is not made, the cards are turned over in their original locations. Player 2 takes a turn in a similar manner and play continues until all possible matches have been made. The player with more cards wins.

Five Times the Fun

Player 1: ____________________ Player 2 : ____________________

	T		I		M		E		S	
	Player 1	Player 2	Player 1	Player 2	Player 1	Player 2	Player 1	Player 2	Player 1	Player 2
Roll 1										
Roll 2										
Total										

Note to the teacher: Use with "High Roller" on page 209.

Center Cards

Use with "Loose Change" on page 209.

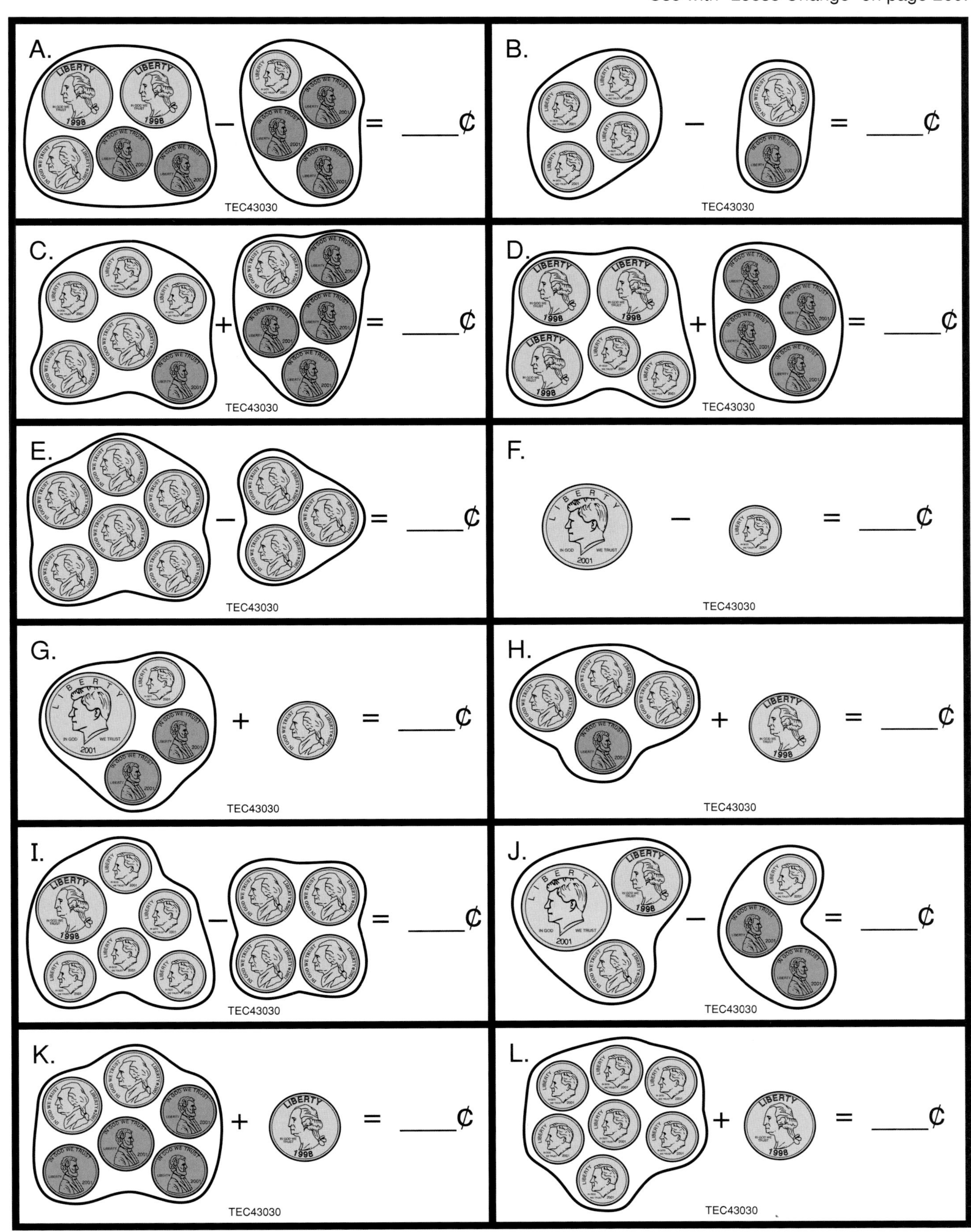

Name______________________________ Computation Review
Division

Working Hard

Divide.
Cross out the correct answer.

A. 9 ÷ 3 = _____ B. 30 ÷ 5 = _____ C. 28 ÷ 4 = _____ D. 15 ÷ 3 = _____

E. 42 ÷ 6 = _____ F. 18 ÷ 2 = _____ G. 40 ÷ 5 = _____ H. 6 ÷ 6 = _____

I. 14 ÷ 7 = _____ J. 16 ÷ 4 = _____ K. 3 ÷ 1 = _____ L. 16 ÷ 2 = _____

M. 54 ÷ 6 = _____ N. 36 ÷ 4 = _____ O. 64 ÷ 8 = _____ P. 63 ÷ 7 = _____

Q. 12 ÷ 6 = _____ R. 32 ÷ 8 = _____

S. 45 ÷ 9 = _____

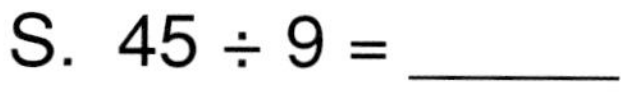

T. 24 ÷ 4 = _____

Cool Rules

Properties of Addition and Multiplication

ACTING IT OUT

Associative property

Program a class supply of index cards as follows: one-third with a digit and an addition sign (2 +), one-third with a digit (3), and one-third with an addition sign and a digit (+ 5). Separate the cards into three different stacks. Invite three students to choose a card, ensuring that a card is selected from each stack. Have the students stand side by side as shown. Student 1 raises his right arm to create the left parenthesis and holds his card with his left hand. Student 2 raises her left arm, forming the right parenthesis, and holds her card with her right hand. Student 3 holds up his card. The remaining students solve the problem. The students switch roles, with Student 1 holding up his card, and Students 2 and 3 forming the parentheses. Have the class solve the new problem; then point out that the answers were the same even though the grouping of the addends changed. Continue the process until each child has had a chance to act out the associative property. Extend the activity by programming other cards with a multiplication sign instead of an addition sign.

Reinforce the properties of addition and multiplication with this collection of ideas.

with ideas by Jean Erickson, Grace Christian School, West Allis, WI, and Laura Wagner, Raleigh, NC

HANDS-DOWN FUN
Commutative property

To prepare this partner activity, copy page 215. Then mount it on construction paper. Laminate the page; then cut out the cards. Sort the cards by operation; then place each set in a resealable plastic bag and store the bags at a center. To play, a pair selects a bag, removes the cards, and places them facedown on the playing surface. Player 1 turns over three cards. If all three cards correspond, as shown, then a match has been made, and he keeps the cards. If the cards are not a match, he turns them facedown, and Player 2 takes a turn. Play continues in this manner until all the cards have been matched. The student with more cards wins.

DRESS FOR SUCCESS
Reviewing the properties of addition and multiplication

All students need to make these simple reminders is a copy of page 216. Before starting the activity, copy the key shown on the board. Begin by reviewing each of the properties listed with the class. Then have each child cut out the polar bear and the clothing patterns and use the key to label each piece with an example of a property and the property's name. She lightly colors the clothing and then glues it to the polar bear. After her bear is complete, she keeps it in her math book as a handy reminder of the different properties.

Hat = Property of Zero
Scarf = Identity Property
Gloves = Commutative Property
Boots = Associative Property

Game Cards

Use with “Hands-Down Fun” on page 214.

7 + 9 = TEC43028	3 + 7 = TEC43028	2 + 4 = TEC43028	8 + 5 = TEC43028
9 + 7 = TEC43028	7 + 3 = TEC43028	4 + 2 = TEC43028	5 + 8 = TEC43028
16 TEC43028	10 TEC43028	6 TEC43028	13 TEC43028
6 + 1 = TEC43028	3 + 8 = TEC43028	4 + 5 = TEC43028	8 + 7 = TEC43028
1 + 6 = TEC43028	8 + 3 = TEC43028	5 + 4 = TEC43028	7 + 8 = TEC43028
7 TEC43028	11 TEC43028	9 TEC43028	15 TEC43028
2 x 9 = TEC43028	3 x 4 = TEC43028	6 x 5 = TEC43028	4 x 7 = TEC43028
9 x 2 = TEC43028	4 x 3 = TEC43028	5 x 6 = TEC43028	7 x 4 = TEC43028
18 TEC43028	12 TEC43028	30 TEC43028	28 TEC43028
3 x 6 = TEC43028	5 x 8 = TEC43028	2 x 6 = TEC43028	4 x 5 = TEC43028
6 x 3 = TEC43028	8 x 5 = TEC43028	6 x 2 = TEC43028	5 x 4 = TEC43028
18 TEC43028	40 TEC43028	12 TEC43028	20 TEC43028

Polar Bear Patterns

Use with "Dress for Success" on page 214.

Name ____

On the Rise

Solve each problem.
Color by the code.

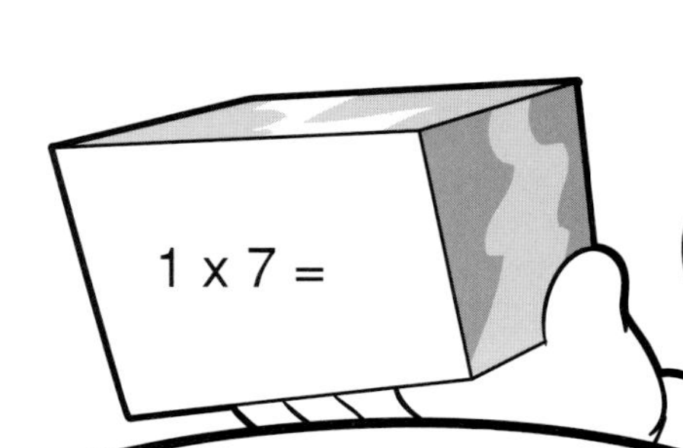

1 x 7 =

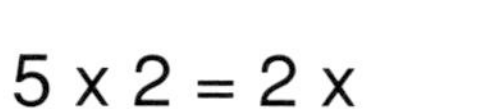

5 x 2 = 2 x ____

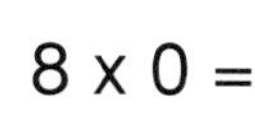

8 x 0 =

5 x (4 x 2) = (5 x ____) x 2

0 x 12 =

3 x 5 = ____ x 3

(3 x 3) x 6 = ____ x (3 x 6)

7 x 4 = 4 x ____

6 x 8 = ____ x 6

1 x 4 =

2 x 7 = 7 x ___

6 x 1 =

9 x 1 =

0 x 6 =

(5 x 6) x 8 = 5 x (____ x 8)

Color Code

Property of Zero = blue
Identity Property = red
Commutative Property = yellow
Associative Property = green

On the Farm

A Graphing-Skills Roundup

The question is "What kind of food did students eat the least?"

The answer is breakfast bars.

What We Ate for Breakfast

Foods	Students
Cereal	7
Toast	5
Pancakes	2
Breakfast Bars	1
Eggs	3
Fruit	2

WHAT'S THE QUESTION?

Interpreting data from a graph

In advance, create a bar graph like the one shown on a sheet of chart paper (or post a recently made class bar graph). Begin by reviewing with students the parts of a bar graph, including the title, number scale, and labels. Also discuss the information on the graph as a class. Then ask students to think of a question they could ask about the graph that has an answer of 7. Confirm that the question is "How many students had cereal for breakfast?" Then continue the activity by giving the class two or three additional answers and having students provide the corresponding questions. Extend the lesson by pairing students and having each child write a question and answer for his partner to solve. In turn, each student shares the answer with his partner. His partner uses the graph to figure out the matching question.

Ropin' graphing skills is a cinch with these activities!

with ideas by David Green, North Shore Country Day School Winnetka, IL

"CENTS-IBLE" GRAPHS

Collecting data, creating a bar graph

Before starting this partner activity, gather ten pennies for each student pair. Also create on the board a large class tally chart like the one shown. Begin by giving each twosome ten pennies and a magnifying lens. Also have the pair create a small version of the tally chart shown. The partners use the magnifying lens to find the year that each coin was minted and mark it on their tally chart. After they have recorded each coin's date, the partners add their data to the class chart. As a class, discuss how the data could be recorded on a bar graph and give the graph a title, a scale, and labels. Then give each pair a sheet of grid paper on which to create a bar graph showing the class results. When each duo has completed its graph, review the results together. Invite students to explain why there are more coins from some decades than others.

Felicia Arnold, Rolling Hills Primary, Vernon, NJ

When Our Pennies Were Minted	
1950s	I
1960s	II
1970s	
1980s	II
1990s	IIII
2000s	I

TRANSPORTATION TRENDS

Creating a graph, interpreting data

Prepare this whole-class activity by gathering several large, identical, transparent containers; a supply of sand; index cards; and a small scoop. Start by discussing with students how they arrive at school each morning. List each of their responses on a different index card, and place each card in front of a container. Next, invite each child, in turn, to place a scoop of sand in the container that corresponds with her transportation to school each day. Afterward, compare the results as a class, pointing out the most popular and least popular methods of transportation. Then ask students what could have made the results inaccurate, such as using different-size scoops or not filling the scoop completely. Finally, have each child write three statements describing the graph.

Name ____________________________________

Down on the Farm

Use the tally chart to complete the graph.

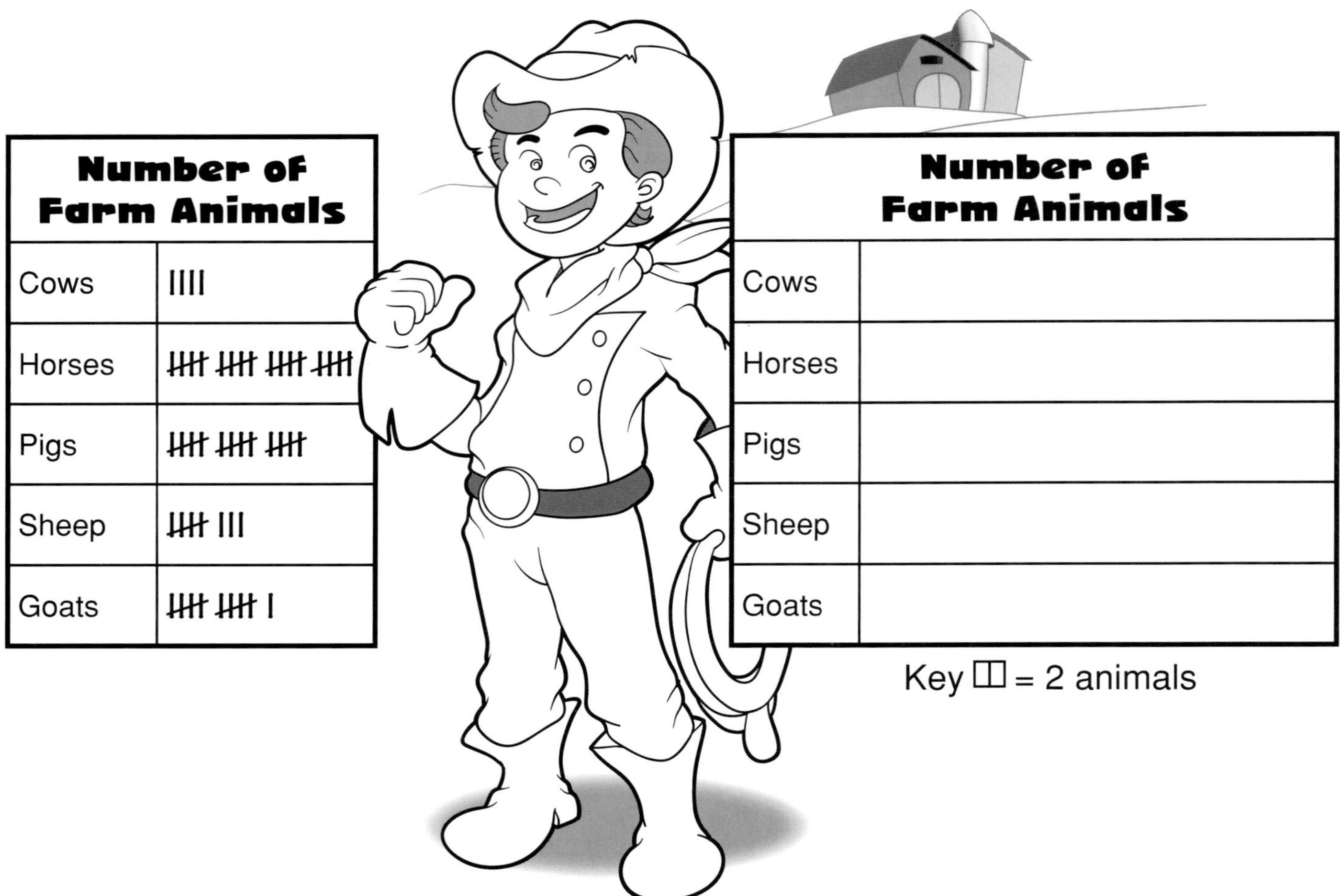

Number of Farm Animals	
Cows	IIII
Horses	𝍸 𝍸 𝍸 𝍸
Pigs	𝍸 𝍸 𝍸
Sheep	𝍸 III
Goats	𝍸 𝍸 I

Number of Farm Animals	
Cows	
Horses	
Pigs	
Sheep	
Goats	

Key ◫ = 2 animals

Use the graph to answer the questions.

1. How many pigs live on the farm? __________
2. How many sheep live on the farm? __________
3. Are there more sheep or goats? __________ How many more? ___________
4. How many more pigs than goats are there? __________
5. How many horses and cows are there in all? __________
6. How many animals are there in all? __________

Name____________________

Chow Time!

Use the graph to answer the questions.

1. How many pounds of food does a sheep eat each day? __________

2. How many pounds does a pig eat in two days? __________

3. Circle the animal listed below that eats the most food.

   a. sheep b. horse c. pig

4. How much more food does a cow eat than a pig? __________

5. Which animals eat less than five pounds each day? __________

   ____

6. How many pounds do a pig and a sheep eat in one day? __________

Cold Cash

A Store of Money-Related Centers

POCKET CHANGE

Making coin sets, writing values

In advance, write a different money amount on each of a supply of index cards. Place the index cards, coin reproducibles or stamps, and 4" x 12" construction paper strips at a center. A child folds a piece of paper into thirds as shown and writes his name across the top flap. Next, he cuts out a small paper circle and glues it to the bottom of the flap for a closure. Then he opens the paper and copies onto the top section the value from a card. If desired, have him write it using the cents sign as well as the dollar and decimal point notation. Then he glues on or stamps the coins that make that money amount. He repeats the process with two new values on the remaining sections.

Check out these on-the-money center activities!

with ideas by Stacie Wright, Millington School, Millington, NJ

BUYING POWER

Equivalent values

Place at a center grocery store circulars, paper lunch bags, coin reproducibles or stamps, scissors, and glue. A student cuts out an item from a circular (staying within a preset spending limit) and glues it to one side of the bag. Next, she cuts out, draws, or stamps coins to equal the cost of the item. Then she draws a line and shows another combination of coins that represents the same amount. She repeats the process on the opposite side of the bag with another grocery cutout.

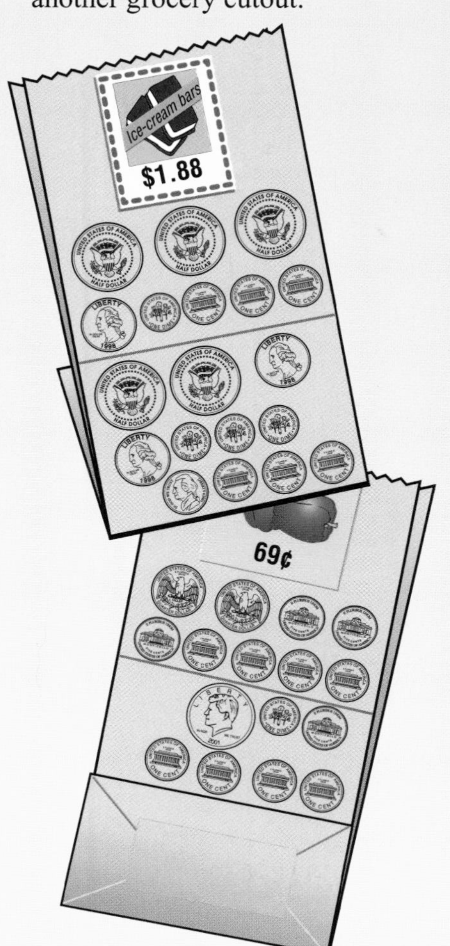

MAKING A BUNDLE

Counting coins with mixed values

This fun variation of War challenges student pairs to look out for big money! Use coin stamps or coin clip art to program an even number of index cards with different money amounts; then place the cards at a center. To begin, each player receives half of the deck with the cards facedown in a stack. At a predetermined signal, both players turn over their top cards. The player with the greater coin value takes both cards. If both cards show equal values, each player takes the top card off his pile and places it facedown on the card at play. At the signal, the cards are turned over. The player with the greater value takes all four cards. Play continues in this manner until one player has all the cards or until time is called and the player with more cards wins.

A FAST BUCK (OR TWO)

Determining value

To get rolling with coin values, make two copies of the die pattern on page 224 on card stock. Cut out the patterns, fold on the dotted lines, and glue the sides together at the tabs. Place the cubes at a center with scrap paper and pencils. Each student takes a turn rolling the dice and recording the amount rolled while tallying the total. Students continue in this manner until one student reaches $2.00 and is declared the winner.

Cube Pattern

Use with "A Fast Buck (or Two)" on page 223.

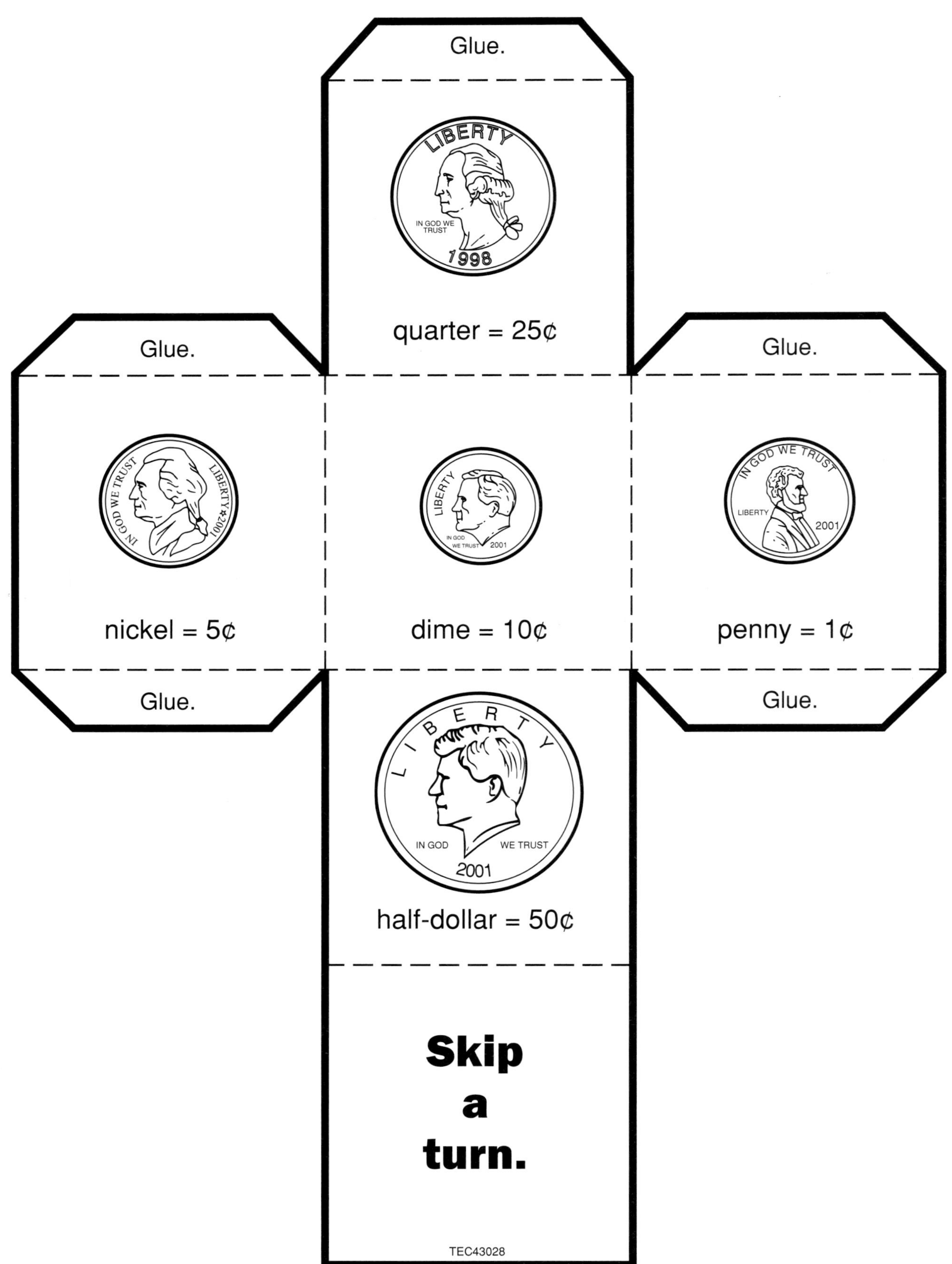

Name ________________________________ Counting coins

What a Deal!

Write the value of the coins on the line.

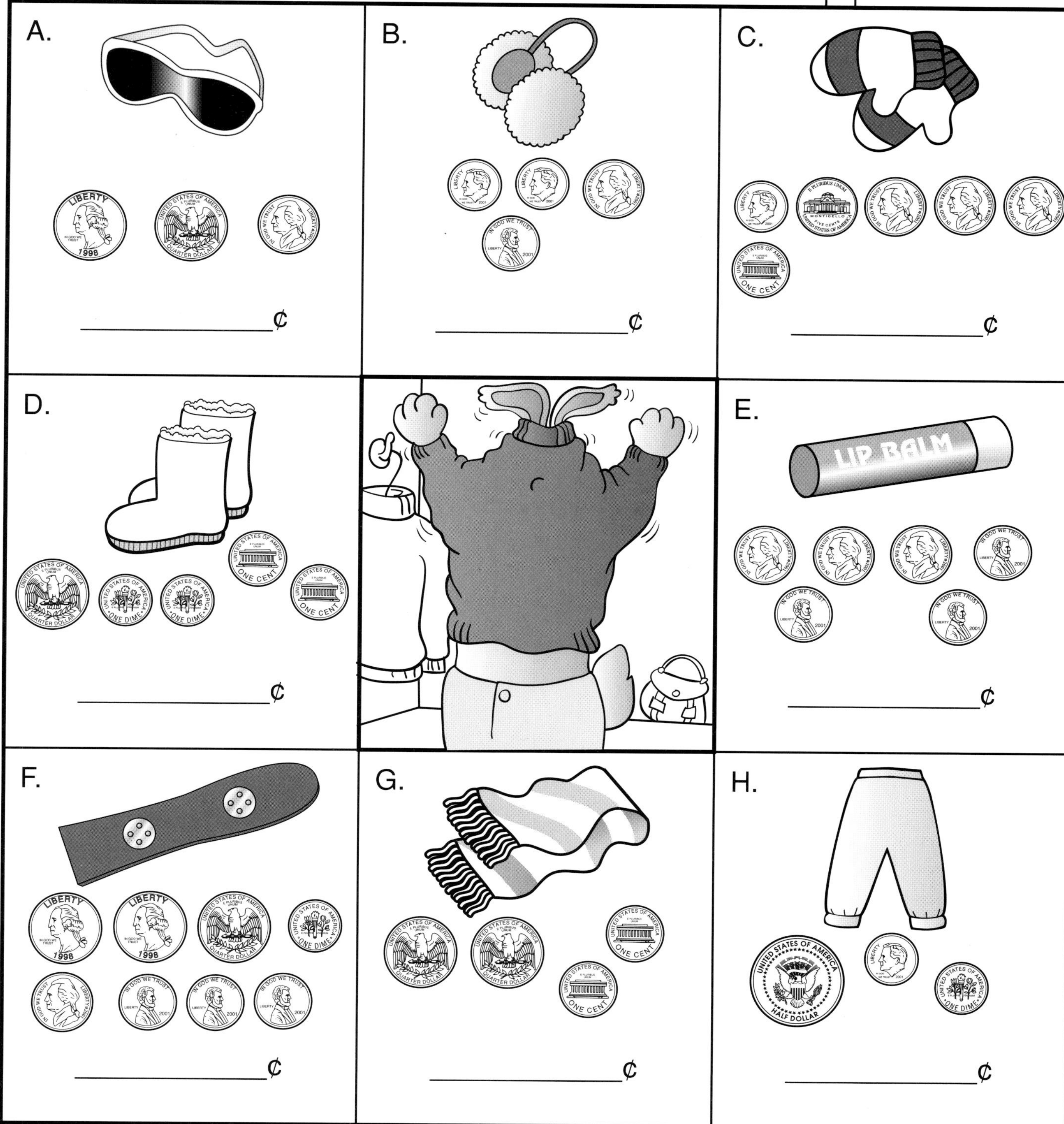

Bonus Box: Write the value of the coins under the price using a dollar sign and decimal point.

Smart Cookies

Fractions

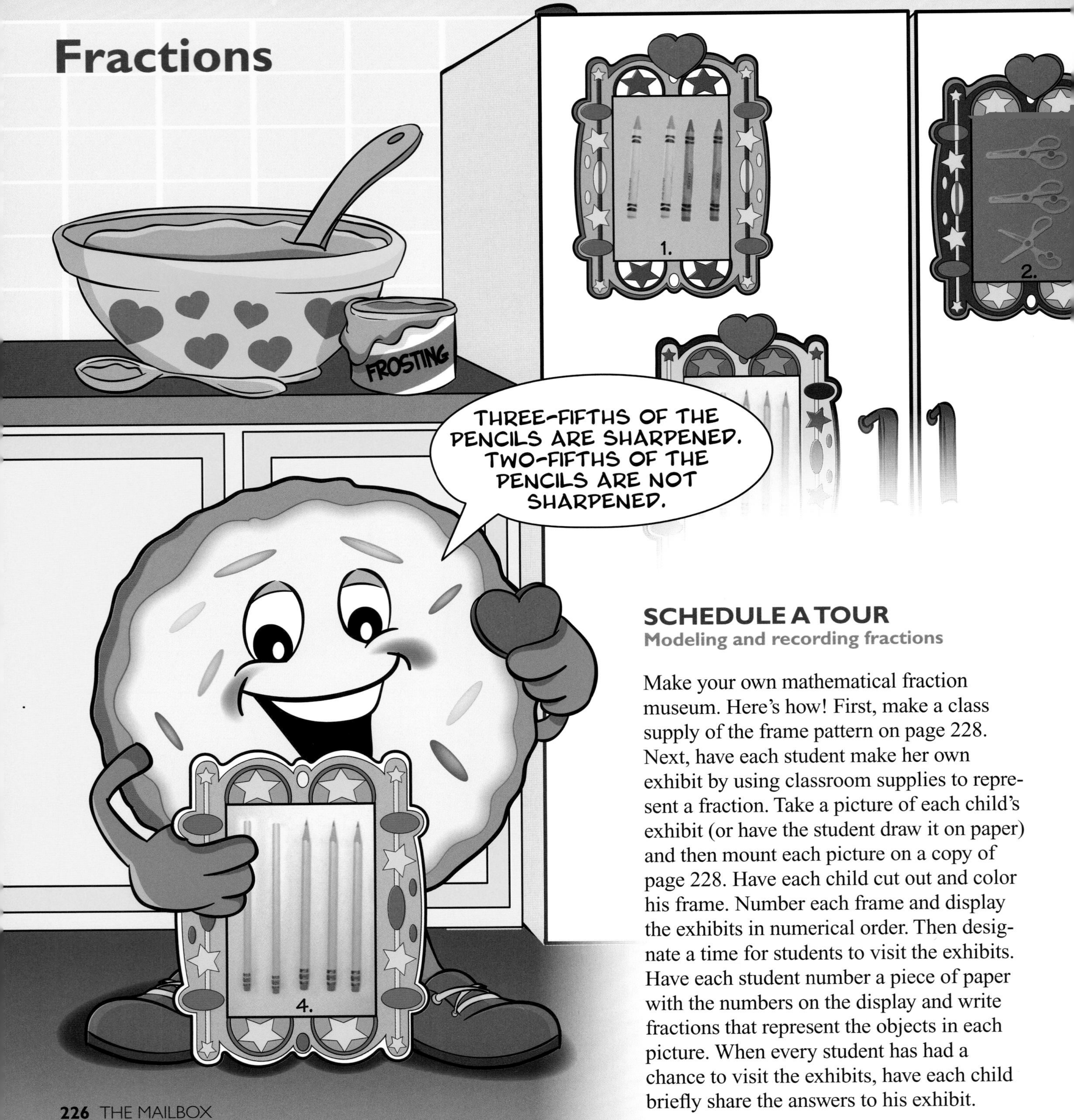

SCHEDULE A TOUR

Modeling and recording fractions

Make your own mathematical fraction museum. Here's how! First, make a class supply of the frame pattern on page 228. Next, have each student make her own exhibit by using classroom supplies to represent a fraction. Take a picture of each child's exhibit (or have the student draw it on paper) and then mount each picture on a copy of page 228. Have each child cut out and color his frame. Number each frame and display the exhibits in numerical order. Then designate a time for students to visit the exhibits. Have each student number a piece of paper with the numbers on the display and write fractions that represent the objects in each picture. When every student has had a chance to visit the exhibits, have each child briefly share the answers to his exhibit.

Sweeten up your fractions instruction with these interactive ideas.

With ideas by David Green, North Shore Country Day School, Winnetka, IL

WHO KNEW?

Identifying parts of a set

Practice fractions and share fun facts about your students at the same time. Select four students to sit in chairs placed at the front of the room. Pose a statement, such as "If you have a pet, please stand." After those students have stood, ask the class, "What fraction of the group has a pet?" Have a child share her answer and write the fraction on the board. Have the four students sit; then pose another statement. If desired, repeat the activity with a different number of students to model different fractions.

"One-half of these bears are sitting. One-half of these coats are blue. One-half of the sodas are diet. One-half of the juices are orange."

ON DISPLAY

Parts of a whole, parts of a set

Incorporate real-world fractions with these easy-to-make student posters. Assign each small group a common fraction. Provide students with newspapers, magazines, and a large sheet of construction paper. Have the students look for pictures that represent their assigned fractions. Group members cut out the pictures and glue them to the construction paper as shown. Then, when the poster is complete, have each group share its poster and explain some of the pictures. Post the completed posters on a display titled "Fractions Are Everywhere!"

SPY EYES

Identifying fractions

Looking for a quick, fun, and engaging fraction game? Then this is the one for you! To begin, secretly identify a fraction occurring in your room. For example, you might see that three of your four computers are on. Then announce to students, "I spy with my fraction eye, the fraction three-fourths." Students ask yes-or-no questions to figure out what you are referring to. If a child asks a question that equals the fraction you named but does not represent the objects you are looking for, accept the answer and start a new round. However, if a child correctly identifies the objects you are thinking of, that child takes over the role as spy and starts a new round.

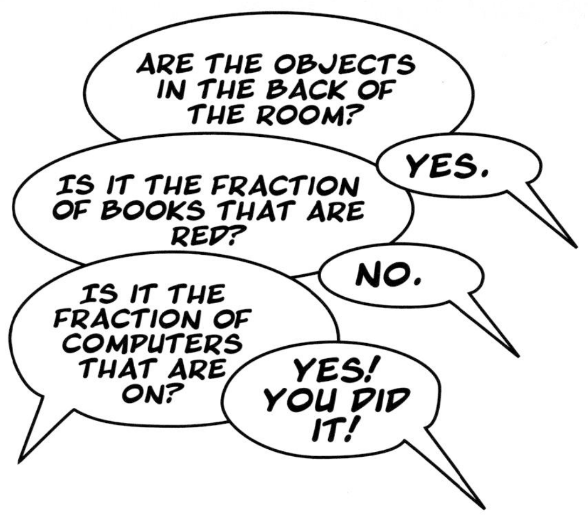

Frame Pattern

Use with "Schedule a Tour" on page 226.

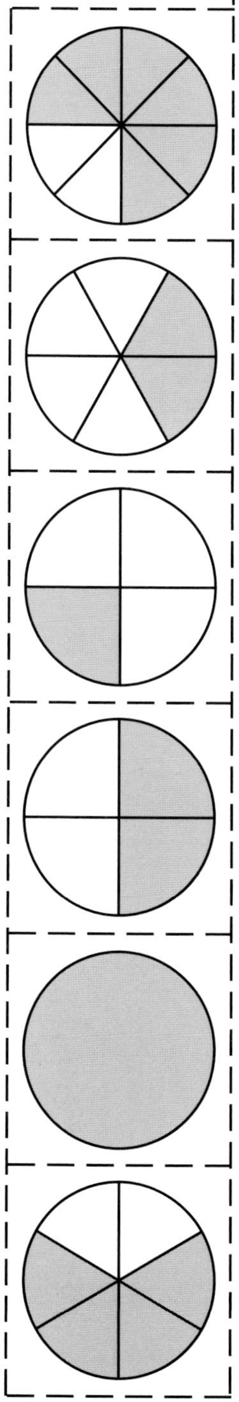

Name ______________________________

Same-Size Sweets

Cut apart the cards on the left.
Glue each card next to its equivalent fraction.
Write a fraction for the shaded amounts.

A. 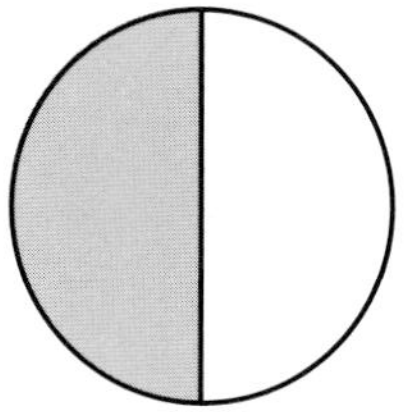 = ____ = ____

B. 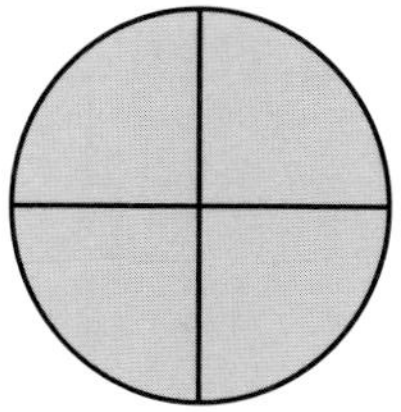 = ____ = ____

C. 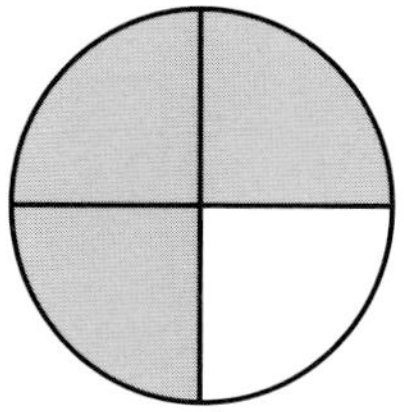 = ____ = ____

D. 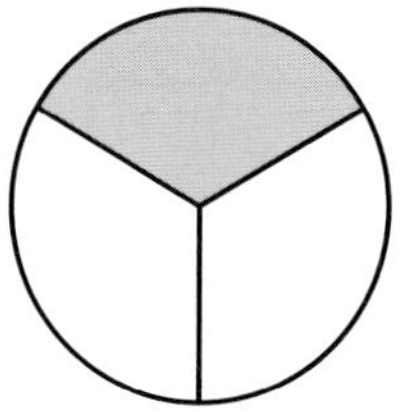 = ____ = ____

E. 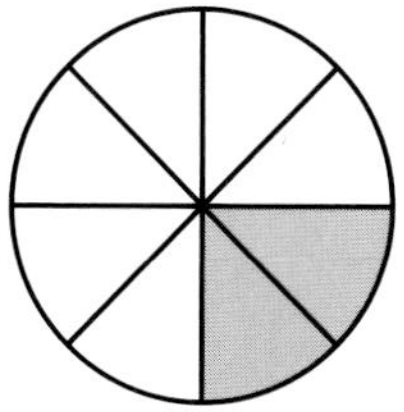 = ____ = ____

F. 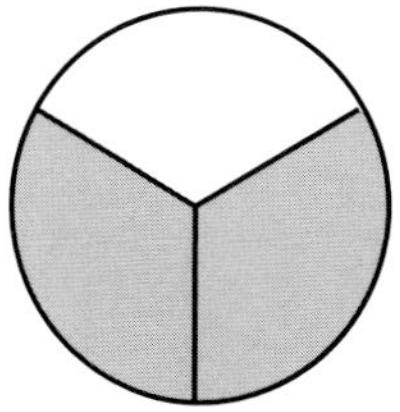 = ____ = ____

Name ______________________________

Baked to Perfection

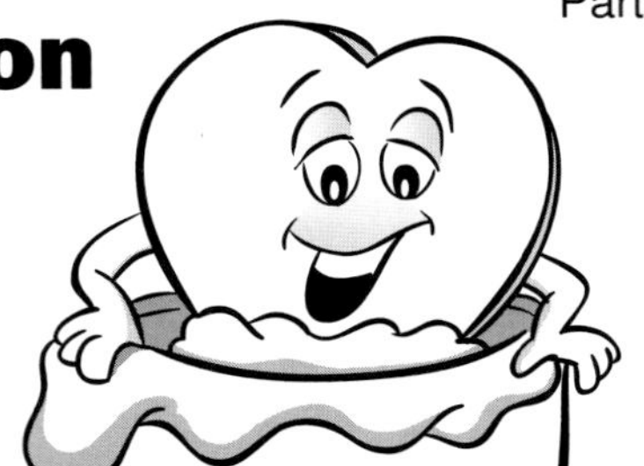

Write the fraction for each cookie tray.
The first one has been done for you.

A.

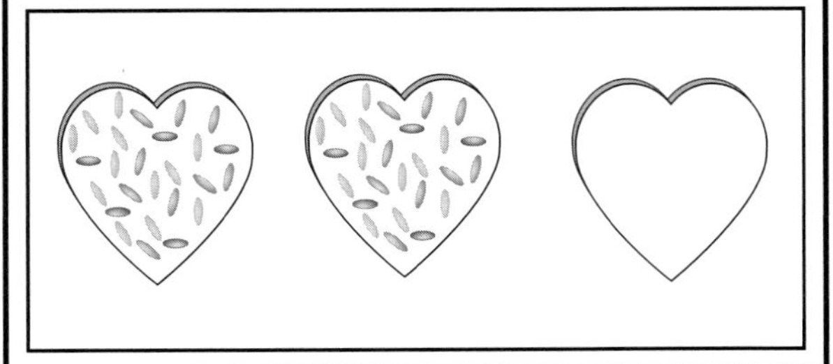

$\frac{2}{3}$ = sprinkles

$\frac{1}{3}$ = no sprinkles

B.

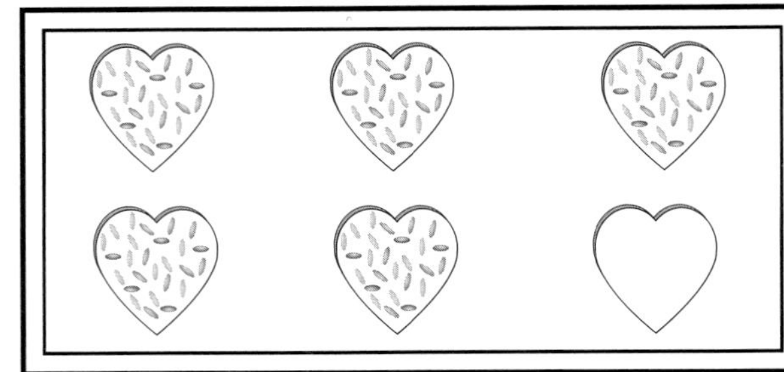

_______ = sprinkles

_______ = no sprinkles

C.

_______ = icing

_______ = no icing

D.

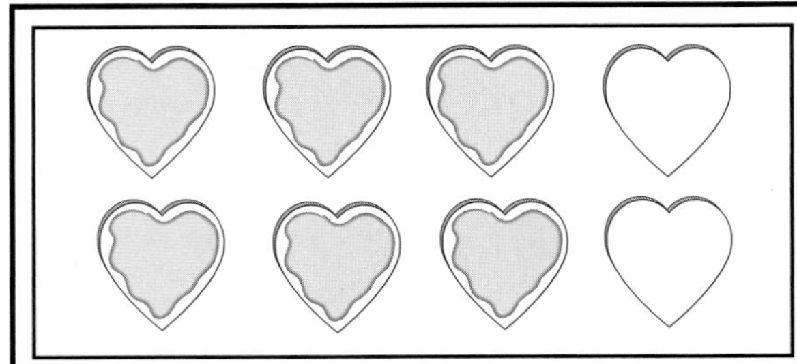

_______ = icing

_______ = no icing

E.

_______ = sprinkles

_______ = no sprinkles

F.

_______ = icing

_______ = no icing

Taking Shape

Plane Figures

MOVING ALONG

Identifying and demonstrating slides, turns, and flips

Give each child a sentence strip and a parallelogram pattern block. Have the student mark an X on one side of the parallelogram to indicate its front and then place the parallelogram atop the sentence strip. To start, have each student demonstrate a slide by dragging the parallelogram from one end of the strip to the other, a turn by placing his fingers on the shape and rotating his wrist clockwise, and a flip by picking up the shape and turning it over. Next, have the student return the parallelogram to the left side of the strip and trace the shape. He slides, turns, and flips the shape as desired across the sentence strip, tracing the shape each time. Then he trades strips with a partner. Each partner works independently to write the name of each movement across the bottom of the strip.

Laura Mihalenko, Holmdel, NJ

Help students gain a better understanding of plane shapes with these hands-on activities!

THREE IN A ROW

Identifying attributes of plane shapes

To prepare this variation of Go Fish, copy the cards on page 233 onto cardstock and cut them apart. To play, partners sit face-to-face and one partner deals five cards to both players. The remaining cards are placed facedown in a stack between them. Each child puts up a file folder barrier and lays out her cards, looking to see if she has all three cards for a shape (word, picture, and description). If she does, she places the cards to the side where her partner can see them. If no matches can be made, Player 1 asks her partner for all cards related to a certain shape. If Player 2 has any of those cards, she hands them over. If not she replies, "Take a shape," and Player 1 selects the top card from the draw pile. Play continues in this manner until one player is out of cards or there are no cards left in the stack. The player with more completed sets wins.

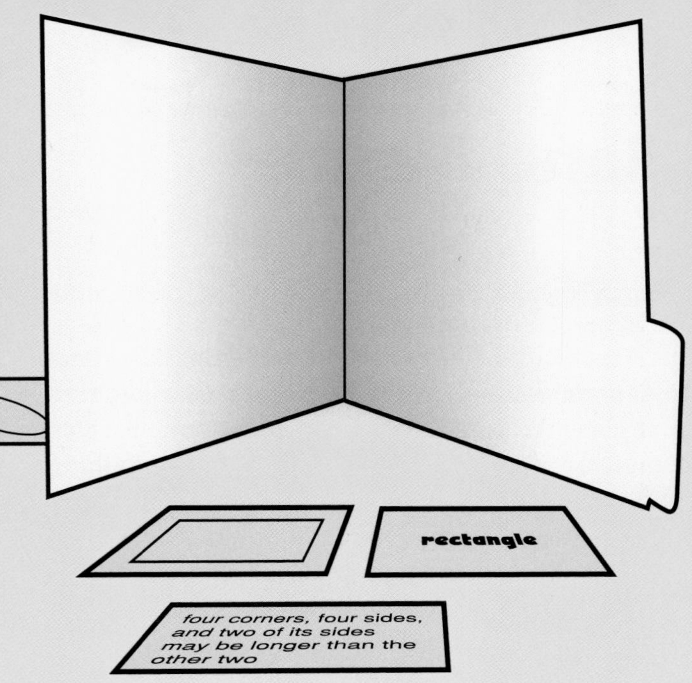

adapted from an idea by Tracy Lawson, Cassopolis, MI

SHAPE BUILDING

Using plane shapes to create another shape

Shapes Needed	Shape Made
A. Three ________	trapezoid
B. Six ________	hexagon
C. Two ________	rectangle
D. Two ________	hexagon
E. Two ______ and two ______	parallelogram

Shapes Needed	Shape Made
A. Three triangles	
B. Six triangles	
C. Two squares	
D. Two trapezoids	
E. Two triangles and two rhombuses	

In advance, copy one of the charts shown on an overhead transparency. Next, provide each student with the following pattern blocks: six triangles, two squares, two trapezoids, and two rhombuses. After reviewing the chart, have each student use his blocks to find the missing information and record his responses on a sheet of paper. Finally, review students' responses, inviting a different student to use his pattern blocks to demonstrate each answer on the overhead.

Laura Wagner, Hebrew Academy Day School
Austin, TX

Game Cards

Use with "Three in a Row" on page 232.

circle TEC43030	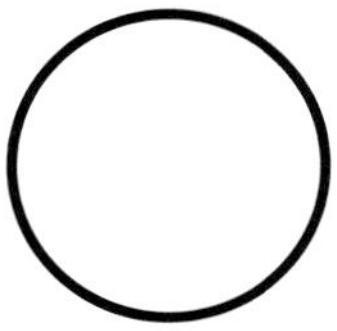 TEC43030	round with no corners TEC43030
square TEC43030	TEC43030	four corners and four equal sides TEC43030
rectangle TEC43030	 TEC43030	four corners, four sides, and two of its sides may be longer than the other two TEC43030
triangle TEC43030	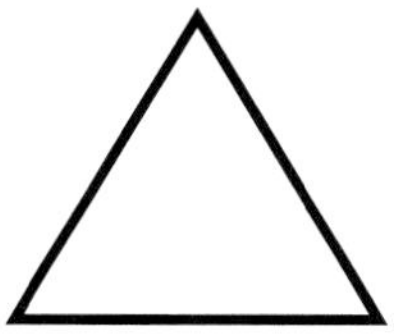 TEC43030	three corners and three sides TEC43030
trapezoid TEC43030	 TEC43030	four corners and four sides, two sides are parallel TEC43030
hexagon TEC43030	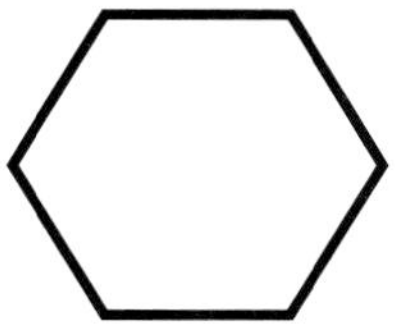 TEC43030	six corners and six sides TEC43030
octagon TEC43030	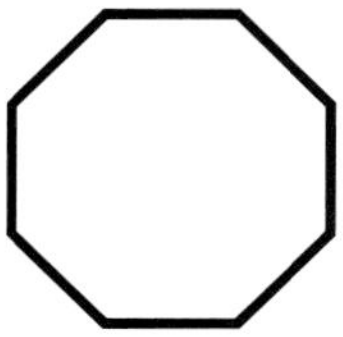 TEC43030	eight corners and eight sides TEC43030
parallelogram TEC43030	 TEC43030	four corners and four sides and its opposite sides are parallel TEC43030

Name____

Drawing Up Plans

Draw the shape that matches the movement.

A.

slide

B.

flip

C.

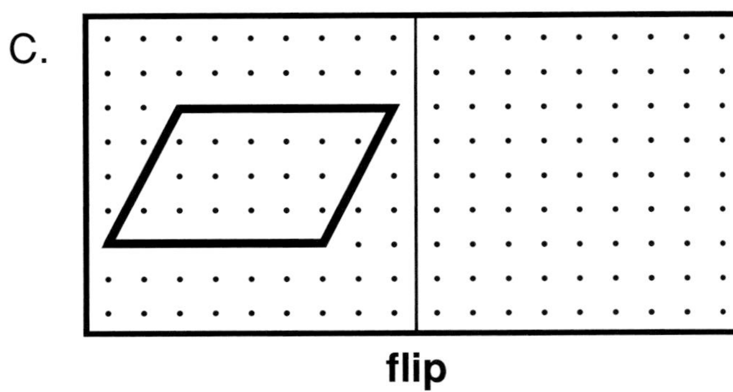

flip

D.

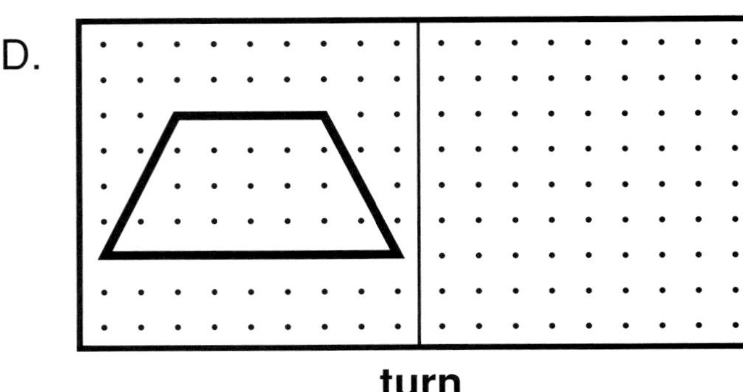

turn

E.

F.

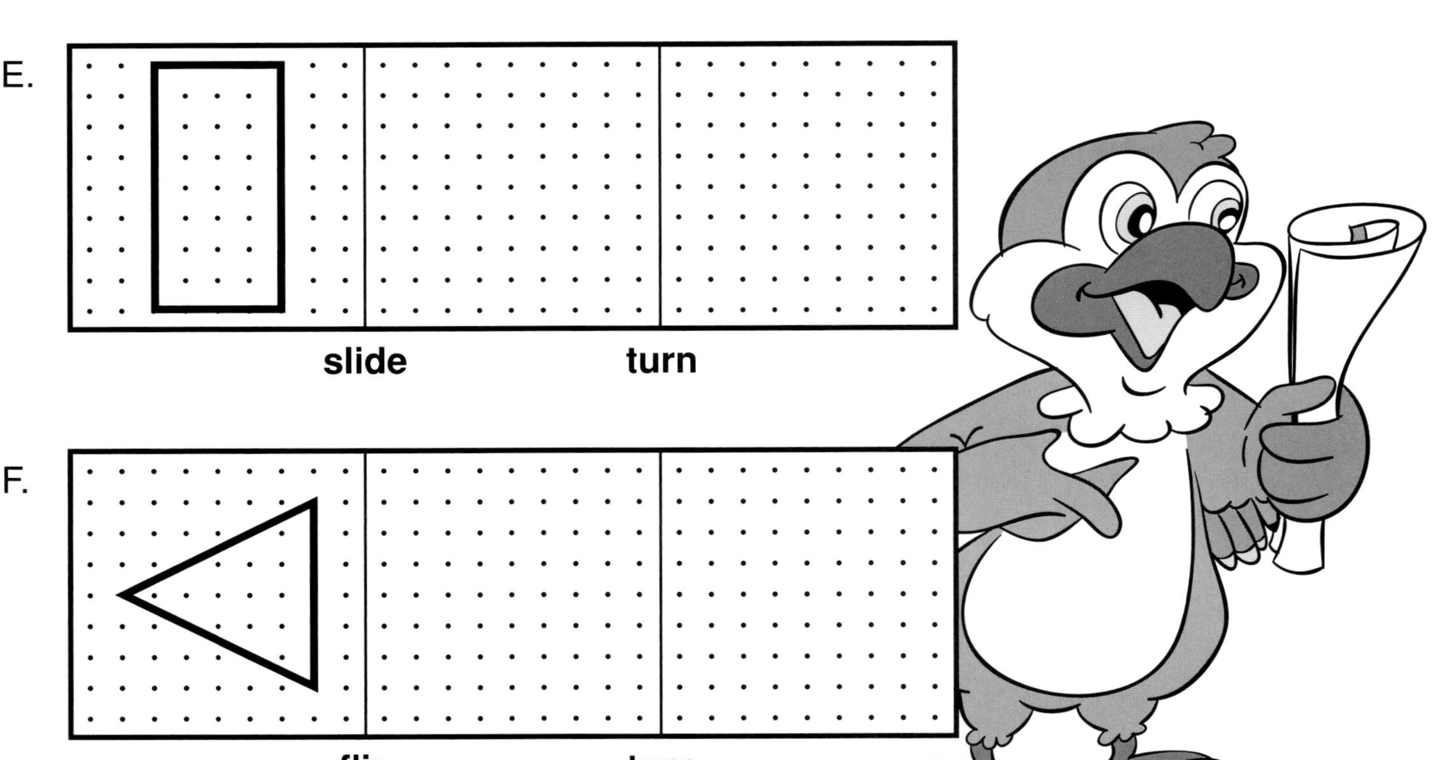

It's Showtime

Problem Solving

GIVE THEM A HAND
Solving word problems

Reinforce problem-solving skills with this self-checking activity. Copy the problem-solving cards on page 237, laminate the copies for durability, and cut them out. Put the word problem cards in one envelope and the answer cards in another envelope. Place the envelopes at a center along with a supply of paper. A child reads each problem and solves it on his paper. Then he locates the matching card for each problem and places the two pieces together. If the cards do not make a complete puzzle, he reviews his work to determine the correct answer. He continues in this manner until all the correct matches have been made.

Jennifer Cripe, James Bilbray Elementary
Las Vegas, NV

Word problems take center stage with this collection of easy-to-execute ideas.

IN THE ACT
Acting out a word problem

Provide a little entertainment while modeling word problems with this fun idea! First, fill a basket with math manipulatives, such as Unifix cubes, tiles, and plastic bags. Then place the basket near the front of the room. Next, select student volunteers to serve as the characters in a desired story problem. Read the problem aloud, pausing to allow time for the students to complete each action named, using the manipulatives as props. After the entire problem has been read, call on a student in the audience to give the answer and explain her thinking.

Karen Peterson, Mircovich Elementary, Ingleside, TX

Name William — Multiplying with 0–4 as factors / Draw a picture

Catch of the Day!

Opie Octopus fries fish for parties. Many groups have called in take-out orders. **Your job is to find out how many fish he needs to fry for each group.** Draw a picture to help you solve each problem.

Order Forms	Pictures and Multiplication Sentence
Group Name: Card Sharks Number of Members: 3 Number of Fish per Member: 4 Total Number of Fish: 12	3 x 4 = 12
Group Name: Whaley Blues Singers Number of Members: 6 Number of Fish per Member: 2 Total Number of Fish: 12	6 x 2 = 12
Group Name: Sea Turtle Racers Number of Members: 3 Number of Fish per Member: 5 Total Number of Fish: 15	3 x 5 = 15
Group Name: Lucky Lobsters Number of Members: 5 Number of Fish per Member: 4 Total Number of Fish: 20	5 x 4 = 20

MAKE A MARK
Drawing a picture

This idea makes problem solving a snap! Give each student access to a stamp marker or a mini rubber stamp and ink pad. Tell him to use the stamp to represent the objects in his word problems. When he is ready to solve by drawing a picture, he simply stamps the shape on his paper rather than drawing the object. If desired, place the stamp markers with problem-solving reproducibles at a center.

Julie Lewis, J.O. Davis Elementary, Irving, TX

IN GOOD SPIRITS
Following problem-solving steps

Make problem solving something to cheer about! Copy the chant shown onto a piece of poster board and display it. Then, before each problem-solving lesson, have students recite the chant while acting out the motions. Students will know just what they need to do to tackle their word problems!

Carol Cash, Green Valley Elementary, Schertz, TX

Read the problem, *Hold hands up as if reading a book.*
Underline the question, *Draw a horizontal line in the air.*
Circle the important stuff, *Draw a large circle in the air.*
Cross out the extra stuff, *Draw an X in the air.*
Look for the clue words, *Put hand over eyes as if searching.*
And solve it! You solve it! *Raise hands in air triumphantly.*

Problem-Solving Cards

Use with "Give Them a Hand" on page 235.

A. Each year the sea animals put on a talent show. This year there are twice as many acts as last year. There were 13 acts last year. How many acts are there this year?

TEC43031

26

TEC43031

B. There are 8 starfish, 2 crabs, and 13 fish backstage. Of these animals, 6 get cold feet and leave the area. How many animals stay to perform?

TEC43031

17

TEC43031

C. There are 48 costumes hanging backstage. The costumes are placed in groups of 6. How many groups of costumes are there?

TEC43031

8

TEC43031

D. Sherman Shark has hosted 36 shows this year. He has hosted 8 more night shows than daytime shows. How many night shows has he hosted?

TEC43031

22

TEC43031

E. Sherman has 5 special suits. Each suit has 7 buttons on it. How many buttons are there altogether?

TEC43031

35

TEC43031

F. Before the day of the show, 95 tickets were sold through presale orders. On the day of the show, 113 more tickets were sold. How many tickets were sold in all?

TEC43031

208

TEC43031

Name ____________________

Now Performing

Read.
Write a guess.
Solve to check.
Color a starfish with each final answer.

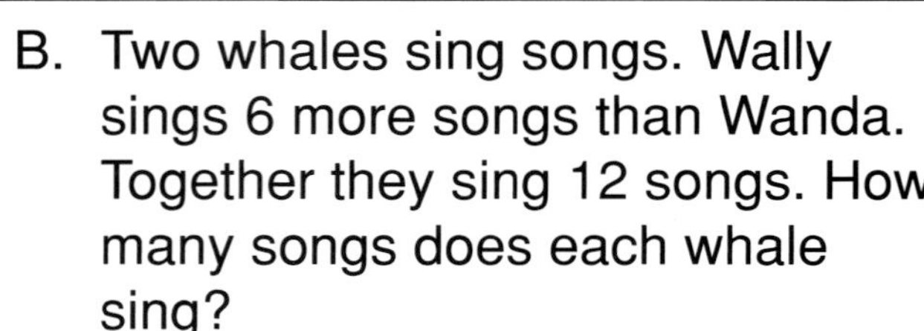

A. On Sunday, 25 starfish go to the talent show. There are 3 more girls than boys at the show. How many boys and how many girls are at the talent show?

Guess: girls ____ boys ____

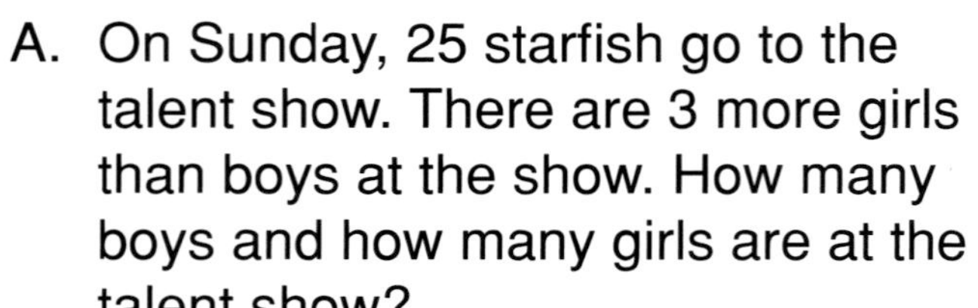

girls ____
boys ____

B. Two whales sing songs. Wally sings 6 more songs than Wanda. Together they sing 12 songs. How many songs does each whale sing?

Guess: Wally ____ Wanda ____

Wally ____
Wanda ____

C. The sea horses show off 20 of their best tricks. Sandy does 4 more tricks than Seth. How many tricks does each sea horse do?

Guess: Sandy ____ Seth ____

Sandy ____
Seth ____

D. At the talent show, the crab twins tell jokes. Together they tell 16 jokes. Chris tells 2 more jokes than Cam. How many jokes does each crab tell?

Guess: Chris ____ Cam ____

Chris ____
Cam ____

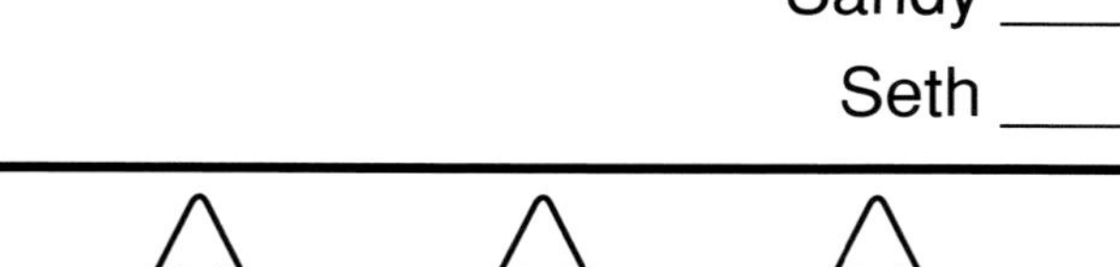

3 3 7
8 9 9 10
11 12 14

E. The turtles end the show with their tap dancing routines. They dance 13 routines in all. Tony dances 7 more routines than Ted. How many routines does each turtle dance?

Guess: Tony ____ Ted ____

Tony ____
Ted ____

SCIENCE AND SOCIAL STUDIES

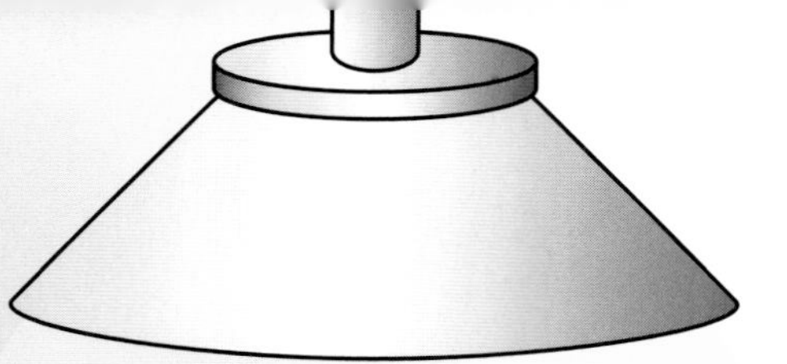

Super States

Experimenting With Solids, Liquids, and Gases

COLORFUL CHANGES

States of matter, physical changes

Have you ever wondered what to do with all of those broken crayons? Use them to explore states of matter! In advance, gather a supply of crayons and a muffin tin. Begin by having students sort the crayons by color, remove any paper coverings, and break them into small pieces. Next, discuss the properties of the crayons and ask students whether they are solids, liquids, or gases. Then place several same-colored crayon pieces in one section of a muffin tin, filling the section about halfway. Repeat the process until each section contains crayons. Show the tin to students, and have them predict what will happen to the crayons if they are placed in a warm oven. Put the tin in a 250 degree oven for about 20 to 30 minutes, checking it every few minutes. After the crayons are completely melted, remove the tin and allow students to observe it. Have them note the change in state from solids to liquids. Allow the crayons to cool completely and then remove them. Invite students to examine the crayons and use them. Ask the class to describe the changes that occurred in the experiment. Guide students to see that the crayons changed physically (from solids to liquids to solids) but not chemically because they are still crayons.

Julie Lewis, J. O. Davis Elementary, Irving, TX

Exploring the states of matter is simple with these ideas!

with ideas by Julie Hamilton, Renaissance Academy, Colorado Springs, CO

THREE IN ONE

Properties of solids, liquids, and gases

Before starting the activity, gather two effervescent tablets, a water bottle filled a quarter full with water, and a 12-inch balloon. Also make a class supply of the recording sheet on page 242. Start the lesson by allowing students to examine the two tablets. Discuss with the class the tablets' properties and mention that they are solids. Have students record their thoughts on the reproducible. Repeat the process with the water. Next, have students observe as you break the tablets into small pieces and put them inside the balloon. Place the balloon over the mouth of the bottle as shown, taking care that the tablets do not fall in the water. After securing the balloon, have students record their predictions. Then drop the tablets in the water. Ask students to identify what filled the balloon. *(A gas.)* Finish the experiment by discussing the properties of gases, the third state of matter in the demonstration.

MATTER SONG

Properties of solids, liquids, and gases

This tune helps students learn about the three states of matter!

Matter Song

(sung to the tune of "Three Blind Mice")

Solids, liquids, gases,
These are states of matter.
Solids, liquids, gases,
Our world is made of matter.
A solid has a definite shape.
A solid can always be seen.
A solid's volume is definite.
An ice cube is a solid.
A book is a solid.

Solids, liquids, gases,
These are states of matter.
Solids, liquids, gases,
Our world is made of matter.
A liquid has no definite shape.
But has a definite volume.
It almost always can be seen.
Water is a liquid.
Soup is a liquid.

Solids, liquids, gases,
These are states of matter.
Solids, liquids, gases,
Our world is made of matter.
A gas has no definite shape.
It has no definite volume.
It often is invisible.
Steam is a gas.
Air is a gas.

Robin Atlee, Hidenwood Elementary, Newport News, VA

Name

Solid, Liquid, Gas

The tablets are ______________________________

____

The water is ______________________________

____

What do you think will happen when the tablets drop in the water? ______________________________

____

Why? ______________________________

____

What state of matter was created? ______________________________

What are its properties? ______________________________

Draw and label each state of matter that was shown during the experiment.

____________	____________	____________

 Note to the teacher: Use with "Three in One" page 241.

Name ____________________

It's a Matter of Fact

Cut.
Match each word to its meaning.
Glue.

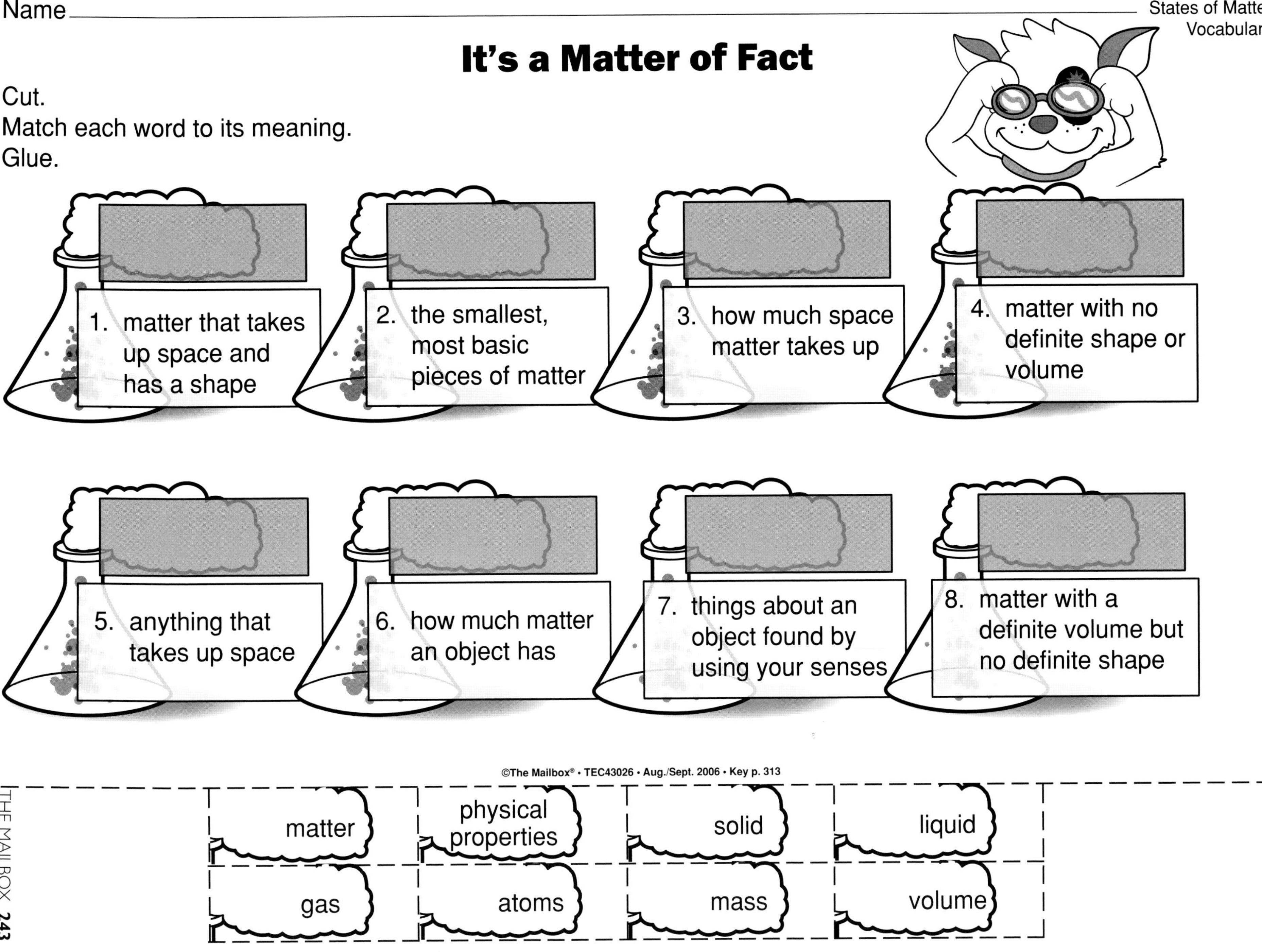

We the **People**

Saluting the Constitution

PICTURING THE PREAMBLE

Understanding a part of the U.S. Constitution

In advance, obtain a copy of *We the Kids: The Preamble to the Constitution of the United States* by David Catrow. Also make a copy of the strips on page 246. Cut the strips apart and store them in a paper bag. Begin by telling students that the preamble is the first part of the U. S. Constitution. It explains why the Constitution was written. Next, read the book aloud to the class. Point out the definitions at the beginning of the book and the illustrations on each page. Afterward, divide the class into eight groups and give each group a sheet of 9" x 12" white construction paper. The group draws a strip from the bag and glues it to the paper. Then the members work together to illustrate the phrase on it, referring to the book as needed. After each group finishes its page, bind the completed pages into a class book titled "Picturing the Preamble."

Build a better understanding of the constitution and its importance!

with ideas by Laura Johnson, South Decatur Elementary School, Greensburg, IN

CLASS BILL OF RIGHTS

Understanding personal rights

Start by reviewing with students the purpose of the U. S. Constitution. Remind the class that the Constitution explains how the government is supposed to work. It also tells the rights that every citizen has. Then explain that your classroom rules are similar to the Constitution because they tell how your classroom should work and the rights students have. Next, ask students what rights they have in the classroom and list their responses on the board. Then give each child a copy of page 247 and have him complete it. Invite students to discuss the classroom rights they think are the most important and the reasons why. After each child has had a chance to share his thoughts, give him three sticky notes and invite him to place a note by each of the three rights that he thinks are the most important. Tally the votes; then record the ten rights that received the most votes on a sheet of chart paper titled "Our Class Bill of Rights."

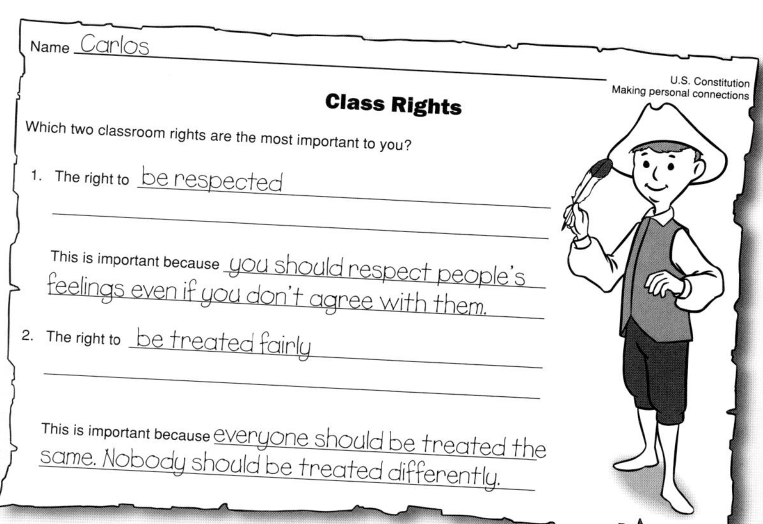

Name Carlos

U.S. Constitution
Making personal connections

Class Rights

Which two classroom rights are the most important to you?

1. The right to be respected

This is important because you should respect people's feelings even if you don't agree with them.

2. The right to be treated fairly

This is important because everyone should be treated the same. Nobody should be treated differently.

PERSONAL SCROLLS

Relating the Bill of Rights to students' lives

To create a personal copy of your classroom's bill of rights, each child first cuts around two sheets of light brown construction paper to form a parchment shape as shown. Next, she uses a black marker or pen to copy the class bill of rights on the first page. Then she glues the pages end to end, as shown, placing the blank page at the bottom. After each child has constructed her scroll, arrange the scolls side by side on a table or other flat surface. During the day, invite one student at a time to visit the area and sign each scroll. After all of the scrolls have been signed, have each child roll hers up and secure it with a piece of curling ribbon.

Preamble Strips

Use with "Picturing the Preamble" on page 244.

We the people of the United States,

TEC43026

in order to form a more perfect union,

TEC43026

establish justice,

TEC43026

insure domestic tranquility,

TEC43026

provide for the common defense,

TEC43026

promote the general welfare,

TEC43026

and secure the blessings of liberty to ourselves and our posterity,

TEC43026

do ordain and establish this Constitution for the United States of America.

TEC43026

Name ______________________

U.S. Constitution
Making personal connections

Class Rights

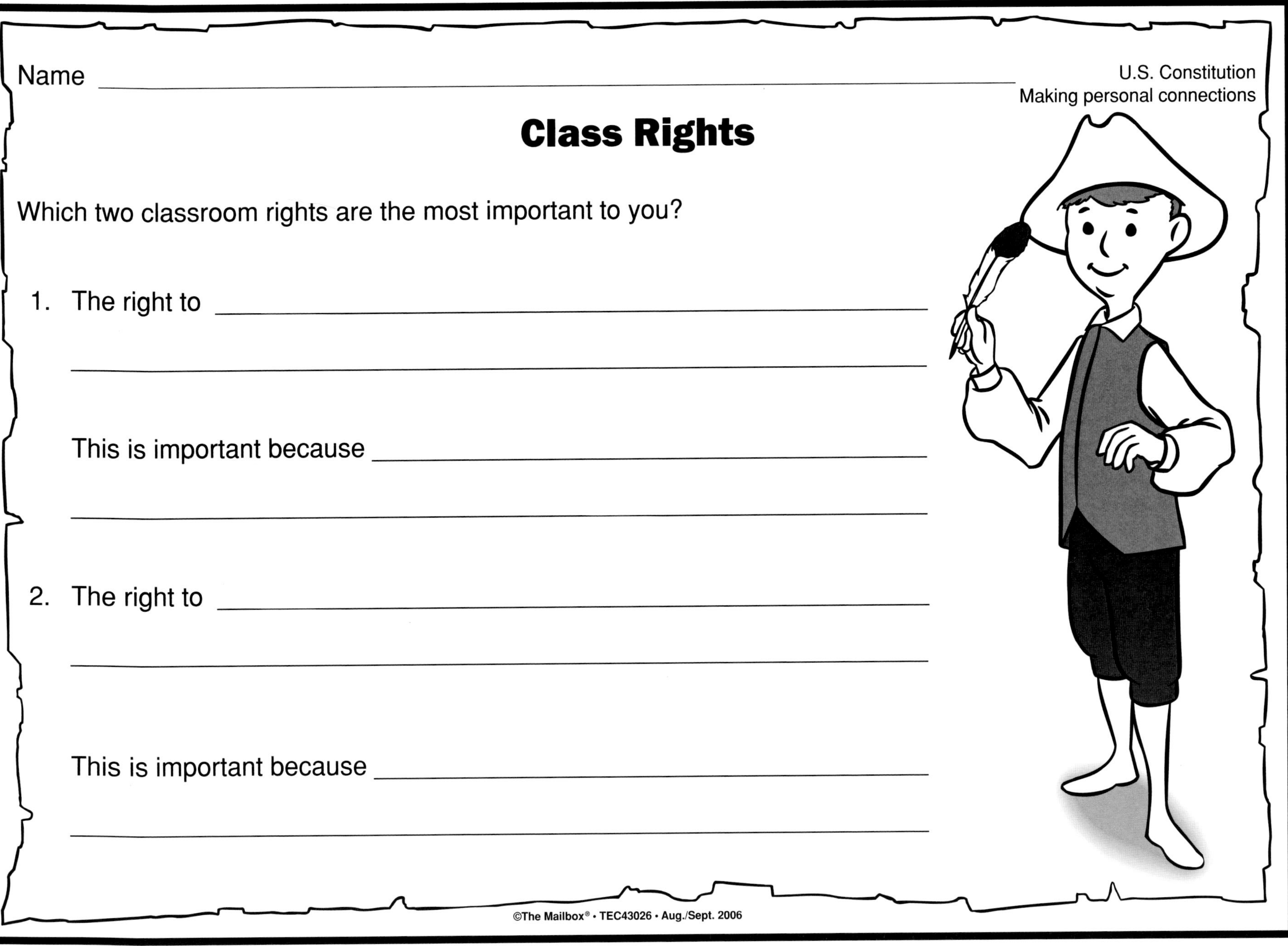

Which two classroom rights are the most important to you?

1. The right to ______________________
____

   This is important because ______________________
____

2. The right to ______________________
____

   This is important because ______________________
____

Note to the teacher: Use with “Class Bill of Rights” on page 245.

Home Turf

Getting Cozy With Communities

BLAST FROM THE PAST

Changes over time

Chronicle your school's past and present characteristics! Gather research about your school's history at the local library or school district office. Locate photos as well as facts; then share your findings with the class. Have students reflect on what the school was like in the past and how it is today; record their responses on the board. To make the project, give each child a construction paper copy of page 250 and have him label the time machine with the school's name. Then he writes a few facts on each square, telling what the school was like in the past and what it is like now. He cuts out the time machine and scores three lines along the dashed lines on each square. Next, he applies glue to the back edges of his paper and mounts it on a piece of white construction paper. Then he adds a matching illustration behind each flap. He trims off the excess construction paper and colors the time machine if desired.

Kick up your heels and rest easy! **This collection of activities is just what your students need to understand communities!**

with ideas by Bonnie Gaynor, Franklin Elementary, Franklin, NJ

A COMMUNITY CHART

Rural and urban

This T chart helps students sort their ideas about communities. To start, review the difference between rural and urban communities. Give each child a sticky note and have him write a sight, smell, or sound found in a community. Then post a T chart like the one shown and have each student place her sticky note in the appropriate column. If her idea belongs to both communities, give her another sticky note and have her label it with the same response. Discuss the results and keep the chart posted as a visual reference. To extend the lesson, periodically refer to a note on the chart. Ask students to explain how the corresponding environment lends itself to the idea. For example, ask, "Why would you find tall skyscrapers in an urban area?"

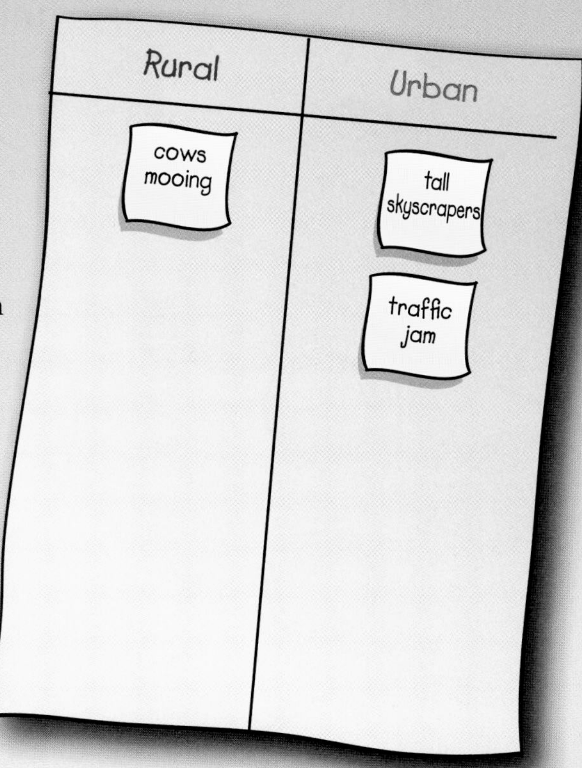

MORE THAN ONE

Distinguishing communities

Reveal the many layers of communities students live in with this two-part activity. Give each child a sheet of white paper and have him draw four circles of different sizes. He labels the circles as follows: "my house," "my town/city," "my state," and "my country." Then he includes an example of each community from his own life as shown. Next, he draws a small picture of his home on the smallest circle before he lightly shades each circle a different color. Then he cuts out the circles, stacks them from largest to smallest, and glues them together. Finally, he refers to his completed project as he sings "Where We Live" with the class.

Diana Aliberti, Helen B. Duffield School, Ronkonkoma, NY

Time Machine Pattern

Use with “Blast From the Past” on page 248.

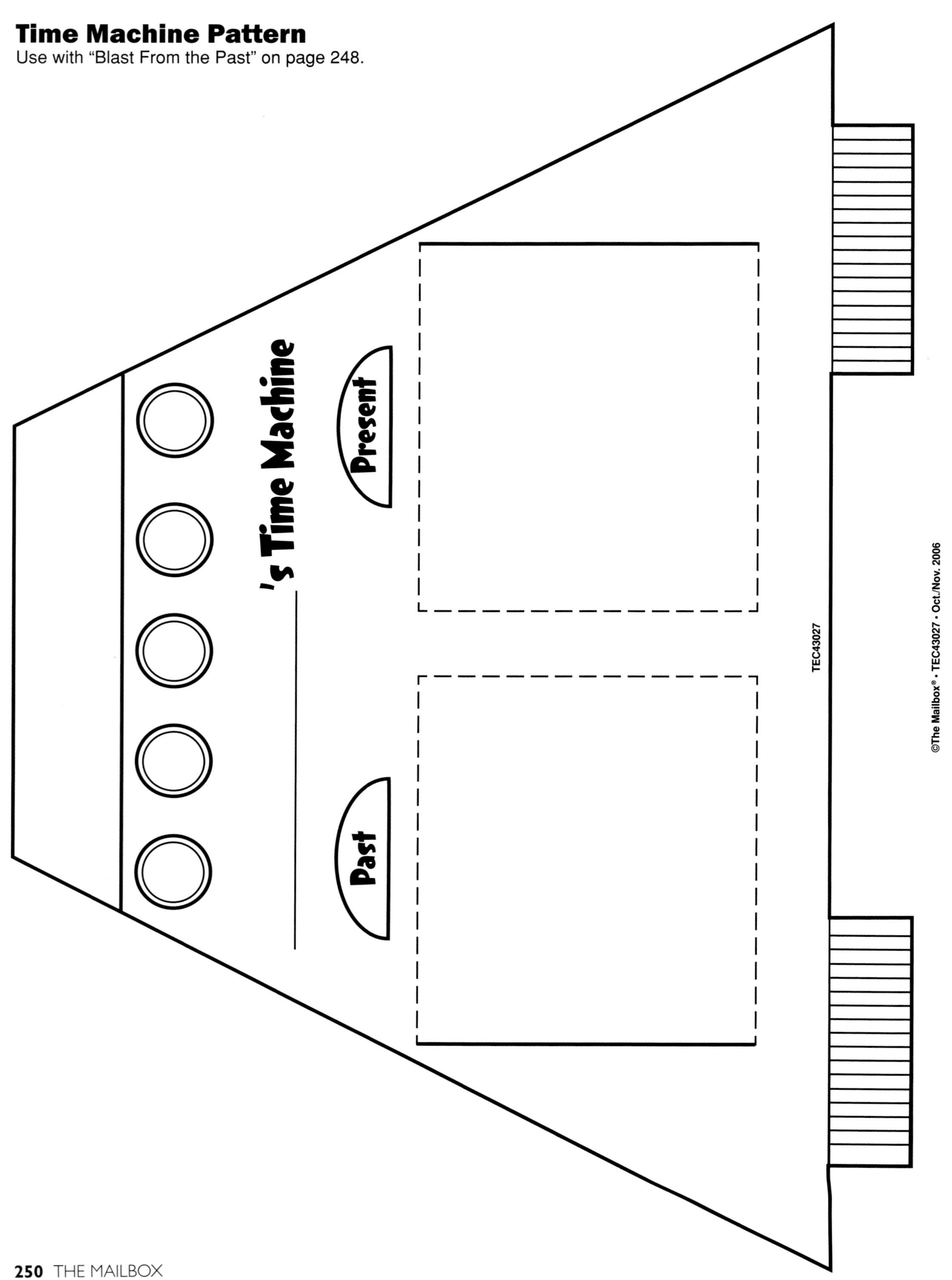

What a **Hoot!**

Getting Wise About the Weather

EASY ANEMOMETERS

Measuring wind speed

To make an anemometer, each child will need one-fourth of a large paper plate, a small balloon, a straw, and length of thread. Begin by having the child fold the plate in half twice, creating four equal sections. He labels each section, as shown, with a black marker and then lightly colors each section a different color. Next, he tapes the pattern to the straw as shown. He lightly inflates the balloon and ties the length of thread around its base. He ties the other end of the thread to the upper end of the straw, reinforcing it with tape. To use the anemometer, the child holds it in the wind, watching where the balloon rises on the tool. The higher it rises, the greater the wind speed.

Whoooo knows all about the weather? Your students will with help from these activities!

with ideas by Laura Wagner, Raleigh, NC

BALLOON BAROMETERS

Observing changes in weather

To make a barometer, gather the materials listed below. Pair students and have them follow the steps shown. To measure air pressure, the twosome places its barometer outside each morning and records the pressure on the tagboard, marking the date and time as shown. Afterward, the pair shares its observations with the class. As a class, discuss any discrepancies in students' results. Guide students to understand that when the air pressure is high, it pushes the balloon down and causes the straw to rise. If the air pressure drops, the balloon rises and the straw moves down.

Materials for each pair:
empty water or soda bottle
balloon piece large enough to stretch over bottle's mouth
small straw, such as a coffee stirrer
tape
rubber band
10" x 13" piece of poster board

Steps:
1. Stretch the balloon piece over the bottle. Secure it with the rubber band.
2. Tape the straw to the top of the balloon piece as shown.
3. Fold the poster board in half. Label it as shown.
4. Tape the folded side of the poster board to the back of the barometer.
5. Take the barometer outside. Draw a line on the posterboard to show the straw's position. Label the line with the date and the time.

To make a weather vane, see page 254!

TOOLS OF THE TRADE

Identifying weather instruments and their uses

After students have made and used the weather instruments in the unit, review the instruments as a class. Also review other weather instruments in your classroom, such as a rain gauge and a thermometer. Discuss how each instrument works and what it measures. Next, give each child several copies of the booklet pages on page 253. The student cuts the pages apart and labels each with a different weather instrument. Then she completes the pages with information about each tool. She staples the completed pages between two construction paper covers. Finally, the child writes her name and the book's title on the front cover.

Booklet Pages

Use with "Tools of the Trade" on page 252.

Tool: ______________________________

Measures: ______________________________

How it works: ______________________________

____

____

How it looks:

Tool: ______________________________

Measures: ______________________________

How it works: ______________________________

____

____

How it looks:

Weather Vane Patterns and Directions

1. Cut out a copy of the patterns. Trace them on poster board and cut them out.
2. Score two small lines on the center of the arrow. Also score the *X* in the center of the direction circle.
3. Slide a pencil through the scored lines on the arrow.
4. Slide the direction circle on the pencil below the arrow, aligning the *N* to the north.
5. Find the wind direction by observing the direction the arrow is pointing.

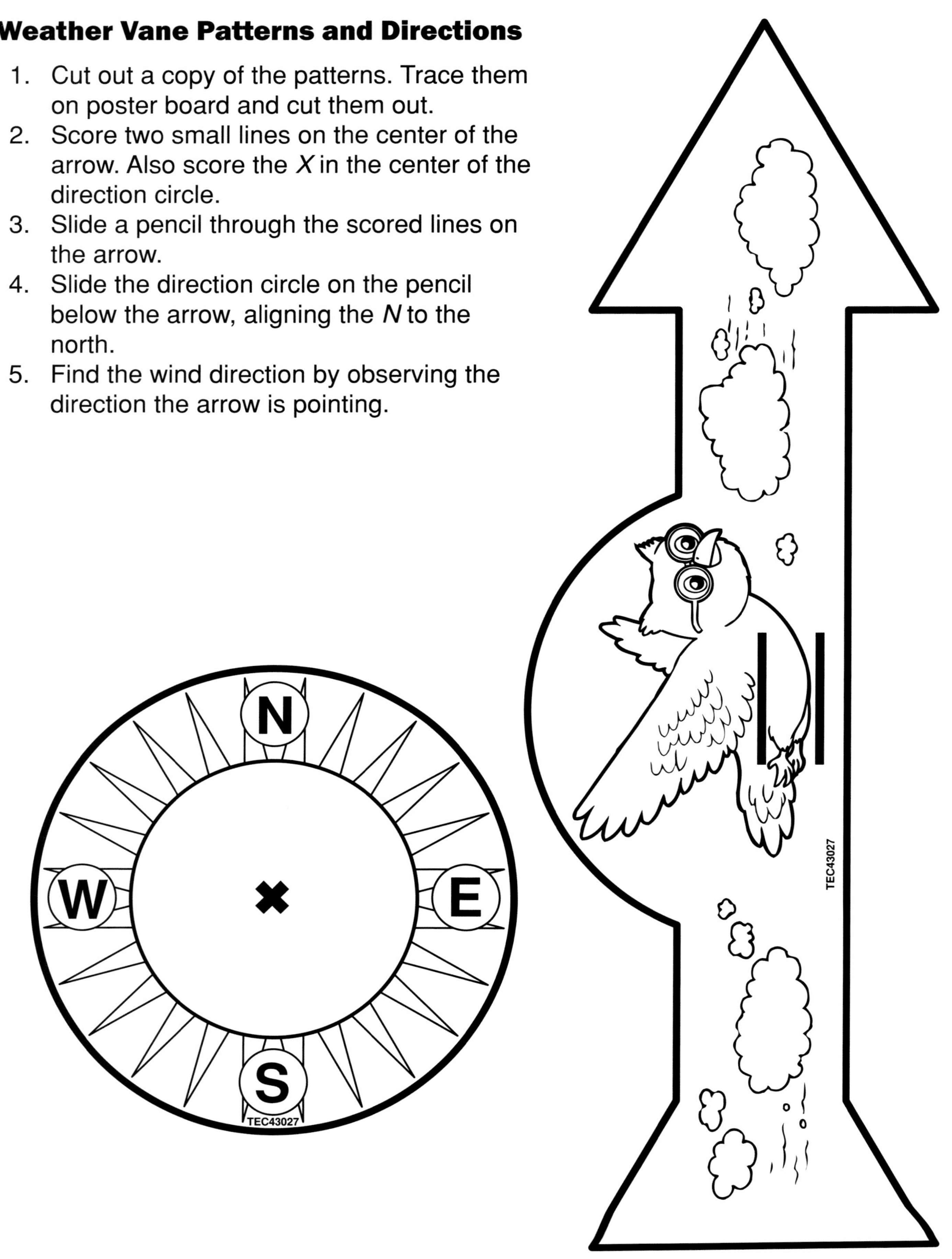

Staying **Alive**

Animal Adaptation Activities

ANIMAL CHOMPERS

Structural adaptations

Sink your teeth into this tasty activity! Share with students that animals' teeth are designed to help them eat. Herbivores eat plants, so they have flat teeth to help them grind; carnivores eat meat, so they have pointed teeth to help them tear. Next, give each student a few white dinner mints to represent flat teeth and a few Bugles snacks to represent pointed teeth. Then name an animal and the foods it eats. Have each student hold up the matching "tooth" snack. Continue the activity by naming other animals and their foods. Then give students time to munch on the snacks.

The diagnosis is excellent! These hands-on activities are just what your students need to have a better understanding of how animals survive.

with ideas by Mederise Burke, Courthouse Road Elementary, Spotsy, VA

TIME TO WINTERIZE

Adapting to the environment

Students share how animals prepare for winter with this easy-to-make pamphlet. Assign an animal to each small group and have the students list preparations that the animal must make for winter. Encourage students to consider whether the animal hibernates, migrates, or changes its coat. Or, if desired, have groups list preparations for a variety of animals instead. Next, give each student a sheet of construction paper and have her fold the paper into thirds. She titles the top flap and draws a picture of her assigned animal. Then she labels the inside flap as shown before unfolding the paper. She refers to her group's list and writes a sentence or two on each section that names a winter preparation activity. Then she draws a matching picture in each section. Display the completed pamphlets around the room.

HELPING HANDS

Structural adaptations

To begin this compare-and-contrast activity, discuss with students how people use their hands. Write students' responses on the board. Also discuss how various animals use their paws, and record these ideas. Then have each student fold a sheet of construction paper in half. On the left side, he traces his hand and writes a sentence telling how he uses his hands. On the right side, he draws the paw of a chosen animal and tells how the animal uses its paws. If desired, have him outline or color both shapes. Finally, bind the completed pages in a class book titled "That's Handy!" and place it at your science center.

Name ____________________

Who's Who?

Write the name of each animal below its matching description.

1. This animal lives in arctic regions. Its fur and fat keep it warm in cold weather. Its white color also helps it hide when hunting.

   ____

2. This animal lives in the rain forest. It has long arms. Its fingers and toes are shaped like hooks. This helps it swing from tree to tree.

   ____

3. This animal lives in the grasslands. It has a long neck. This helps it reach tree leaves way up high.

   ____

4. This animal lives in the desert. It has long eyelashes to keep out sand. It can go for days without drinking water.

   ____

5. This animal lives in the ocean. It has a stripe that runs over its eye called an *eyeband.* This helps it hide in the coral reefs.

   ____

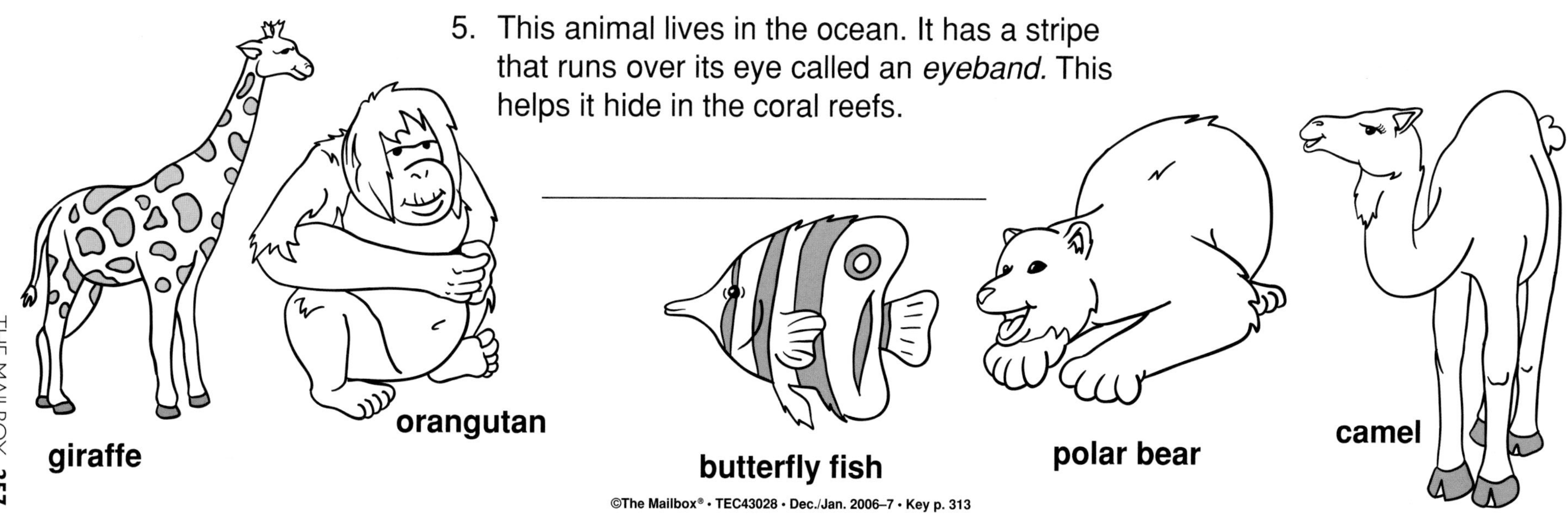

Can You Dig It?

Unearthing the Scientific Process

COMPARING NOTES

Making observations

Build background knowledge and practice observation skills with this hands-on project. Give each student samples of two kinds of soil. Have him use his senses to make observations of each; then have him wash his hands. Next, give each child a 4½" x 12" piece of construction paper and eight sticky notes. He labels two sticky notes with each sense (excluding taste) and records his observations for each soil. Then he writes the name of one soil on each side of the paper. To complete his project, he staples the matching sticky notes under the soil names as shown.

From observations to sharing results, students will plow through the scientific method with these simple soil activities.

DIG IN
Conducting an experiment, recording observations

Put students' observations to use as they conduct this small-group activity. To prepare for each small group, cut the tops off two matching plastic bottles. Remove the caps, invert the tops, and place one top in each bottle. Insert a small coffee filter into each bottle top, as shown, making sure to cover the hole. Next, measure equal amounts of the soils used in "Comparing Notes" on page 258 and place them in separate cups. Then fill two cups with equal amounts of water. Give each student a copy of page 260 and each small group a set of supplies. Encourage students to use their earlier observations as they work together to follow the directions on the page, complete each step, and record their findings.

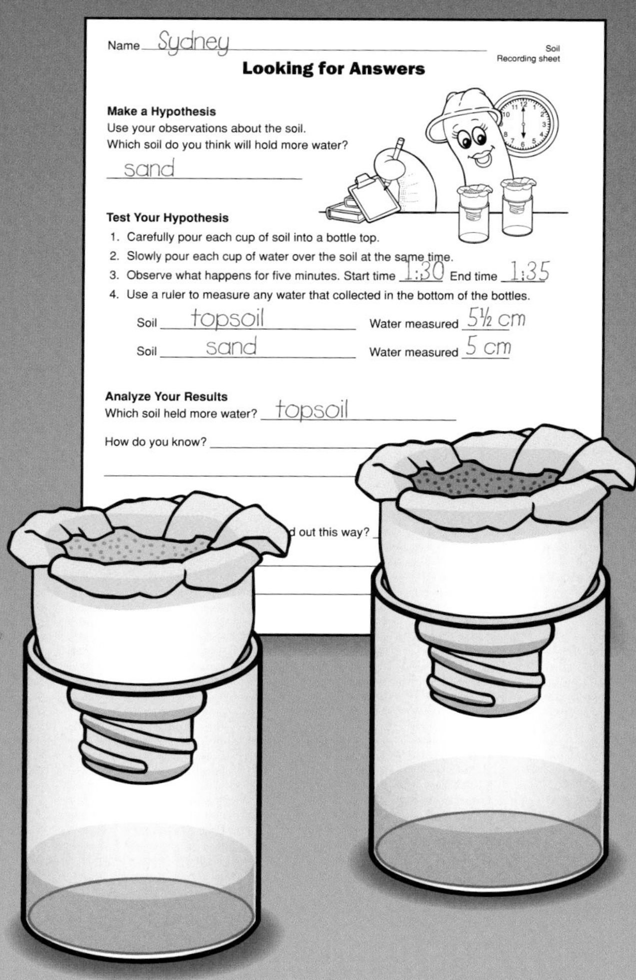
Name Sydney
Soil
Recording sheet

Looking for Answers

Make a Hypothesis
Use your observations about the soil.
Which soil do you think will hold more water?
sand

Test Your Hypothesis
1. Carefully pour each cup of soil into a bottle top.
2. Slowly pour each cup of water over the soil at the same time.
3. Observe what happens for five minutes. Start time 1:30 End time 1:35
4. Use a ruler to measure any water that collected in the bottom of the bottles.

Soil topsoil Water measured 5½ cm
Soil sand Water measured 5 cm

Analyze Your Results
Which soil held more water? topsoil
How do you know?

d out this way?

SOIL SUMMIT
Sharing scientific data

Invite students to share their findings with this whole-class activity. After student groups have completed "Dig In" (above) and filled out their recording sheets, provide time for students to review what they've learned. Next, explain to students that a summit is a meeting about an important topic and that your class will be hosting one about soil. Then have individuals or small groups give brief presentations of their findings to the rest of the class. If desired, keep track of students' results on the board or overhead projector. Use student responses to engage the class in a discussion about soil and the scientific process.

Name ____

Looking for Answers

Make a Hypothesis

Use your observations about the soil.
Which soil do you think will hold more water?

____

Test Your Hypothesis

1. Carefully pour each cup of soil into a bottle top.
2. Slowly pour each cup of water over the soil at the same time.
3. Observe what happens for five minutes. Start time ___:___ End time ___:___
4. Use a ruler to measure any water that collected in the bottom of the bottles.

Soil ______________________________ Water measured _______

Soil ______________________________ Water measured _______

Analyze Your Results

Which soil held more water? ______________________________

How do you know? ____

____

Make a Conclusion

Why do you think the activity turned out this way? ______________________________

____

____

 Note to the teacher: Use with "Dig In" on page 259.

Caregiver

Harriet Tubman

HATS OFF TO HARRIET

Identifying contributions of a historical figure

Recognize Harriet Tubman's lifetime of hard work with this informative display. Explain to students that "a person who wears many hats" is an expression for someone who has many jobs. Next, guide students in a discussion of the many jobs Harriet Tubman had throughout her life and list the jobs on the board. Then have each child choose a job and design a hat that might be suitable for it. To make a hat, each child folds a sheet of construction paper in half. With the fold at the top, he draws the hat shape and cuts it out, being sure to leave as much of the fold intact as possible. Next, he traces the shape onto a piece of notebook paper and cuts it out. He writes a short paragraph describing Harriet's role in the job the hat represents. He lifts the top layer of the hat and glues the paragraph inside. Finally, he completes the hat by writing the job title on the top flap and decorating it to his liking. Post the completed hats atop a construction paper head of Harriet Tubman as shown.

Introduce your students to the life and works of Harriett Tubman.

with ideas by Bonnie Gaynor, Franklin Elementary, Franklin, NJ

SETTING THE SCENES

Creating a timeline

This handy booklet serves double duty as a timeline! Give each child a copy of page 263 and have her read the event named on each card. She illustrates and cuts out each card. Next, she folds a sheet of 11" x 18" construction paper in half three times to make eight equal sections as shown. She cuts the paper lengthwise through the middle; then she overlaps an end section from each piece and glues them together to make one long strip. She accordion-folds the strip to resemble a booklet and writes a title on the top section. Then she turns the top section back like a book and adds a small portrait of Harriet Tubman on the other side. Finally, she arranges the cards in chronological order and glues each card to its corresponding section to complete her booklet.

MAKING NEWS

Identifying contributions of a historical figure

Freedom Times

Date March 12, 2007

Harriet the Heroine

by Austin

Harriet Tubman was a heroine to many people during her lifetime. She was a heroine because she was brave. Harriet helped hundreds of slaves get to freedom even though she could have gone to jail for it. Ms. Tubman was also a heroine because she was kind. When she was older, she set up a home for poor, older people so they would have a safe place to stay. Heroine is the right word for Harriet Tubman.

The Harriet Tubman Home was set up for people who were poor.

Report the facts about Harriet Tubman's accomplishments with this newsworthy activity. In advance, make a class supply of page 264 and gather a variety of books and resources about Harriet Tubman. Share with students current newspaper articles about people who have done heroic deeds. Then discuss with students the qualities that make a hero or heroine, such as bravery, helpfulness, and caring. Next, have students use research materials to name events that show how Harriet Tubman was a heroine. Then give each student a copy of page 264 and have him write a brief summary of Harriet Tubman's heroic actions. Also have him draw a picture of and write a caption about Harriet Tubman. Bind the completed pages in a class book titled "A Heroine Named Harriet."

Timeline Cards

Use with "Setting the Scenes" on page 262.

1820 Araminta Ross was born a slave. As a child, she took on her mom's name, Harriet.	1844 Harriet married John Tubman.	1849 Harriet escaped her slave life. She moved north and began helping other slaves find freedom.
1861–1865 Harriet worked as a nurse, cook, and spy during the Civil War.	1908 Harriet set up a home for the poor.	1913 Harriet Tubman died.

Freedom Times

Date ______________________________

Harriet the Heroine

by ____

 Note to the teacher: Use with “Making News” on page 262.

Hall of Fame

Studying Historic Figures

IN THE MONEY

Identifying historical figures' contributions

For this project, assign each student an important person from a current unit of study. Next, provide access to research materials and give each child a copy of the bottom half of page 266. Guide students to find and record the answer to each question on the page. Then give each child a copy of page 267 and help him follow the diagram on the page to report his research and create currency that honors his subject. When each child finishes, have him cut out his currency; then display students' work on a bulletin board titled "Mint-Condition Research."

Jean Erickson, Grace Christian School, West Allis, WI

Help students learn more about the people who have influenced our country's history with these clever research projects.

MONUMENTAL FIGURES

Understanding how individuals influence communities

Here's a project for the ages! Have each student research an individual other than George Washington, Thomas Jefferson, Theodore Roosevelt, or Abraham Lincoln who has influenced your community, state, or nation. Guide the child to find biographical details about the person as well as information about his or her historical impact. If desired, have the child use the bottom half of this page to guide her research. Next, give each student a copy of page 268 and have her add her subject to Mount Rushmore by drawing her subject's face in the space provided. Then have the child write a paragraph on the page that explains why this influential person should be added to the monument.

Lisa Buchholz, Abraham Lincoln School, Glen Ellyn, IL

Name Amy

Set in Stone Research

Mount Rushmore: Sandra Day O'Connor, George Washington, Thomas Jefferson, Theodore Roosevelt, and Abraham Lincoln

Sandra Day O'Connor was the first woman ever to be on the U.S. Supreme Court. She was a Supreme Court justice for 25 years. She is a good role model for girls. Ms. O'Connor was born in 1930 and she is still alive.

Name ______________ Research

Ready to Research

Find and record the answer to each question.

______________ person's name

When did this person live? ______________

Where did this person work? ______________

Why is this person famous? ______________

How does this person's work help us today? ______________

Note to the teacher: Use with "In the Money" on page 265.

Name_______________________________________

Report It!

Look at the diagram and follow the directions to complete the picture below.

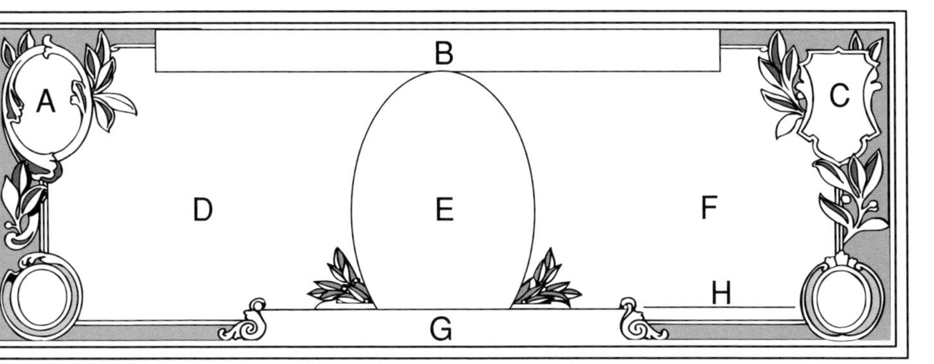

A. Write the person's birth year.
B. Tell why the person is famous.
C. Write the year the person died.
D. Draw a picture of where the person worked.
E. Draw a picture of the person.
F. Draw a picture showing how the person's work helps us today.
G. Write the person's name.
H. Sign your name.

TEC43030

Note to the teacher: Use with "In the Money" on page 265.

Name ____ Research

Set In Stone

Mount Rushmore: ______________________________, George Washington, Thomas Jefferson, Theodore Roosevelt, and Abraham Lincoln

____

____

____

____

____

____

____

____

 Note to the teacher: Use with "Monumental Figures" on page 266.

Make a Splash

Interdependence in a Pond Ecosystem

POP-UP POND

Plant and animal interdependence

To start, have each small group make a list of plants and animals found in a pond. Next, have each student choose a plant or animal from the list, making sure to keep a balance of both within the group. Provide research materials and have each student find information about his life-form's role in the pond. Once he has the needed information, the student folds a piece of white paper in half and draws the shape of his plant or animal on it so that some part of the shape runs along the fold. Then he cuts through both layers of the paper, keeping the fold intact. He colors, labels, and writes his name on his illustration; then he flips the top piece up and writes a description of the life-form and its role in the pond. To make a group poster, the students draw a pond and its surrounding land on a large sheet of paper. Have each child glue his plant or animal in an appropriate spot on the poster. Post the completed projects around the room; then provide time for students to visit each one.

Dive into these student-centered science ideas!

CLUED IN
Classifying

Draw on students' prior knowledge to introduce pond life. In advance, write a pond plant or animal name on each of a supply of index cards. Place the cards face-down in a stack. Choose a student to select a card and have her give clues by drawing the animal or plant and/or writing descriptive words about it on the board (if she is unfamiliar with the term she may choose another card). Call on students to try to name the plant or animal. When it is correctly identified, tape the card to the board. After all the cards have been posted, ask students to determine what all the words have in common. Then keep the words posted as a reference throughout your study of pond life, adding other words as they are introduced.

Suggestions for Directions

Make a food chain with three links.
Make a food chain with four links.
Make a food chain that includes a tadpole.
Make a food chain that ends with a heron.

LINKS TO LEARNING
Food chains

Provide food chain practice with this partner activity. After reading aloud a book about pond life, give each duo a sheet of construction paper and a copy of the cards on page 271. To make a tent, the pair folds the construction paper in half vertically and then makes a one-inch fold across the bottom. The students turn one bottom fold back and then score the folds with a pair of scissors. Next, the students stand up the tent and cut apart the cards. To complete the activity, the twosome uses the cards to create a food chain according to your directions (see suggestions shown). After making the chain the duo turns the tent around to reveal their work. If desired, call on volunteers to share their combinations aloud. Continue with different directions for as long as desired.

adapted from an idea by Laura Johnson
South Decatur Elementary, Greensburg, IN

Pond Cards

Use with "Links to Learning" on page 270.

sun TEC43030	algae TEC43030	water lily TEC43030	duckweed TEC43030
mosquito larva TEC43030	water flea TEC43030	dragonfly TEC43030	beetle TEC43030
tadpole TEC43030	newt TEC43030	perch TEC43030	turtle TEC43030
snail TEC43030	duck TEC43030	crayfish TEC43030	heron TEC43030

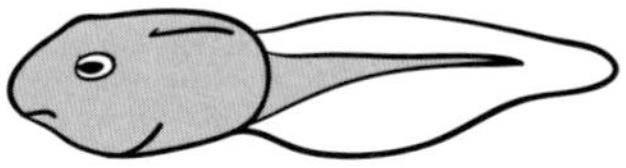

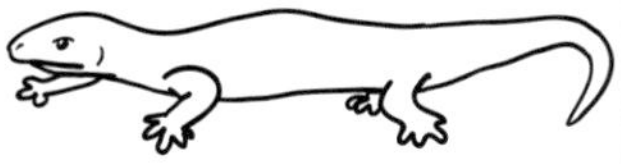

Name ______________________________

Pond Plant

When you think of a pond, do you see a lily pad? That's the leaf of a water lily. A water lily is a kind of plant found in ponds. Its leaves and flower float on top of the water. A thick underwater stem connects the leaves and flower to the roots. The roots grow in the soil at the bottom of the pond.

Water lilies help the animals in the pond. Muskrats eat their leaves and roots. Birds eat their seeds. Water lilies give frogs and fish a place to hide. Animals also help the water lilies. Beetles and bees pollinate the water lilies' flowers.

This pretty plant can cause problems in the pond too. It grows fast and tends to grow in large groups. When water lilies cover the water, they keep air and sunlight out. That can hurt the animals and other plants living in the pond.

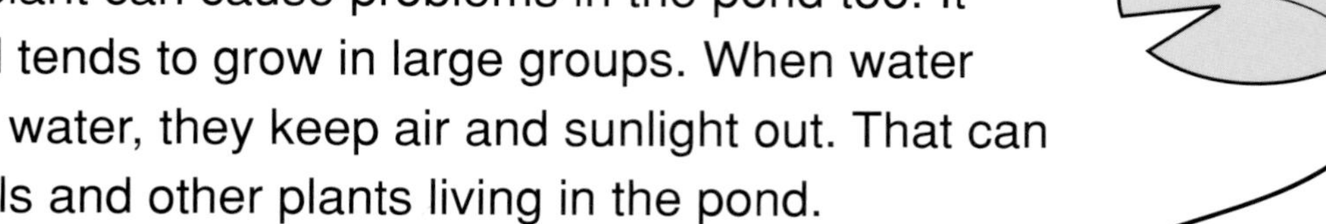

Answer each question.
Use the passage to help you.

1. What is a water lily? ______________________________

2. How do water lilies help pond animals? ______________________________

3. How do animals help water lilies? ______________________________

4. How can water lilies hurt other life-forms in the pond? ______________________________

Super Star

The Sun

ALL IN A DAY'S WORK

Understanding day and night

To begin, find your location on a globe and demonstrate how the earth completes a rotation on its axis every 24 hours. Explain to students that as it rotates, part of the earth faces the sun's light and part does not, causing day and night. Next, give each child a copy of the day and night patterns on page 275. To make a day and night manipulative, a child colors the sun and the sky on the top strip. After cutting out the strip, he removes the "day" half of the circle as shown. Next, he cuts out the project backing and the northern hemisphere pattern. He pokes a brad through the center dot on the earth; then he inserts the brad where indicated on the project backing. After opening the brad, he applies glue to the labeled areas on the backing and places the top strip on it. Finally, he turns the earth, identifying for which northern continents it is day and for which it is night.

Fuel your students with information about the earth's closest star.

with ideas by Bonnie Gaynor, Franklin, NJ

HOORAY FOR THE SUN

Identifying ways the sun helps the earth

Have each small group of up to four students make a list of ways that the sun helps the earth. Next, ask a group representative from each group to share an idea from her group's list. Write the ideas on the board. After all of the groups have shared, record any remaining ideas. Then give each child a copy of a sun pattern on page 276. Each group member chooses a different idea from the class list. She writes in the speech bubble, as shown, one or two sentences about a way the sun helps the earth; then she illustrates her writing in the remaining space. When all the group members are finished, have them glue their work to a piece of construction paper. Display the resulting posters around the room.

STELLAR STATEMENTS

Sharing prior knowledge and post-unit knowledge

To prepare these graphic organizers, trim a piece of yellow bulletin board paper into two large circles. Label each resulting chart as shown and post the one marked "What We Know About the Sun" on the board. Also label each of four index cards with a different season. To begin the activity, pair students and give them a short period of time to discuss what they know about the sun. When time is up, have each student write one statement about the sun on a sticky note. Next, arrange student chairs in a circle (chair backs facing the middle of the circle) and tape an index card to each of four chairs.

Explain to students that they will walk with their sticky notes around the chairs as music is played. When the music stops, each student sits in a chair. A student who sits in a chair displaying an index card reads his statement aloud, places his sticky note on the posted chart, and then returns to the circle. Restart the music and continue the process until each child has shared his statement. Repeat the activity when your unit of study is complete, posting the other chart, to determine what students have learned about the sun.

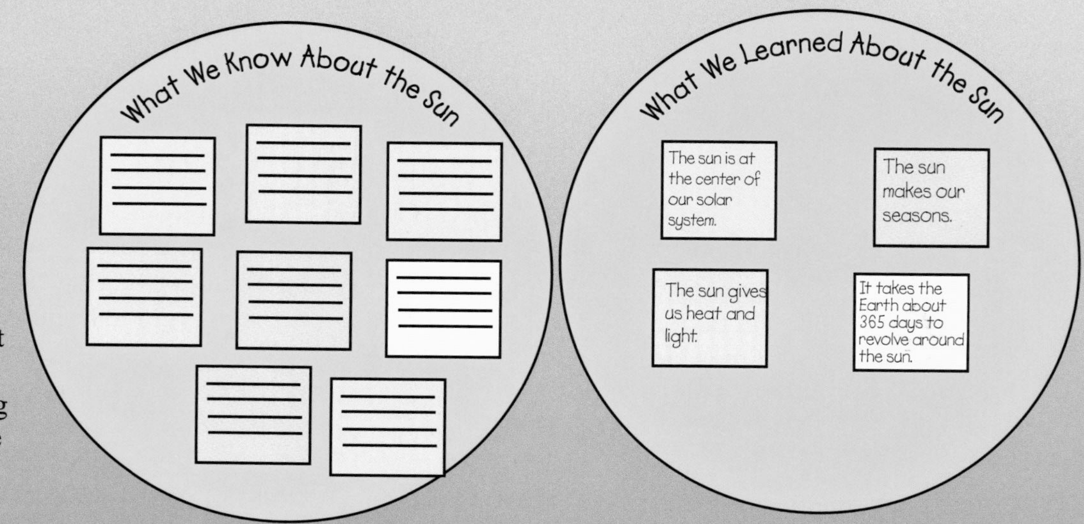

Day and Night Patterns

Use with "All in a Day's Work" on page 273.

Top Strip

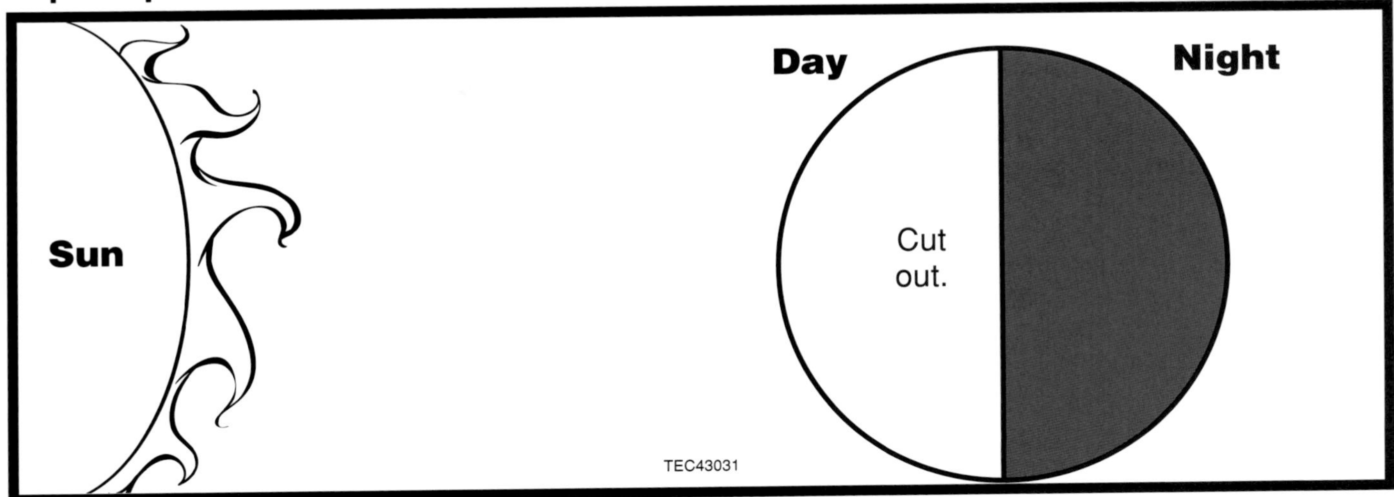

Backing

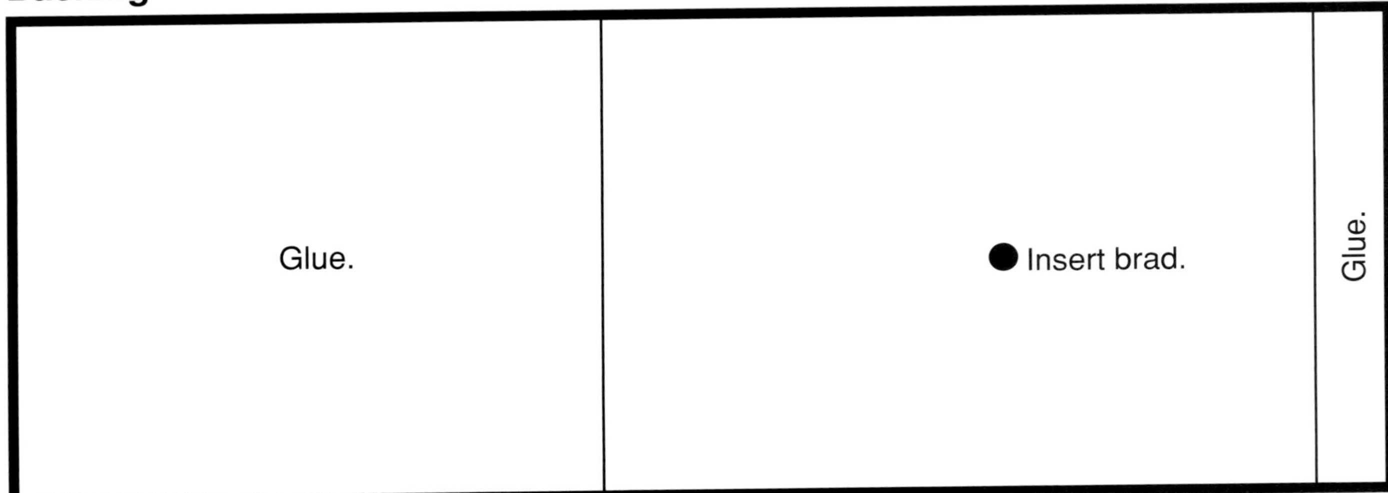

Northern Hemisphere

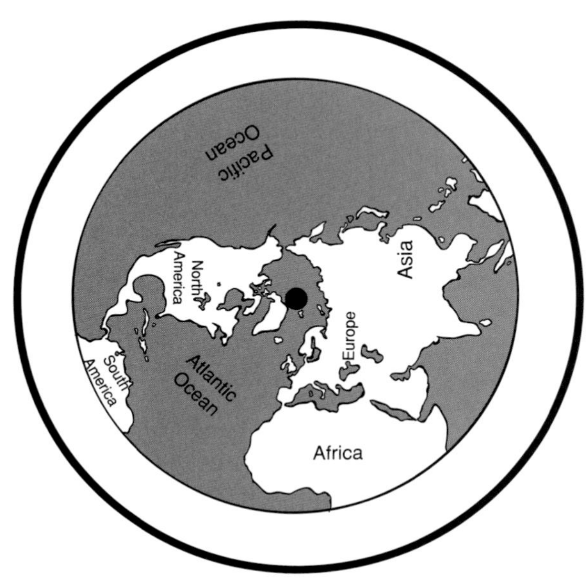

Sun Patterns

Use with "Hooray for the Sun" on page 274.

TEC43031

TEC43031

Cross Curricular & Seasonal Units

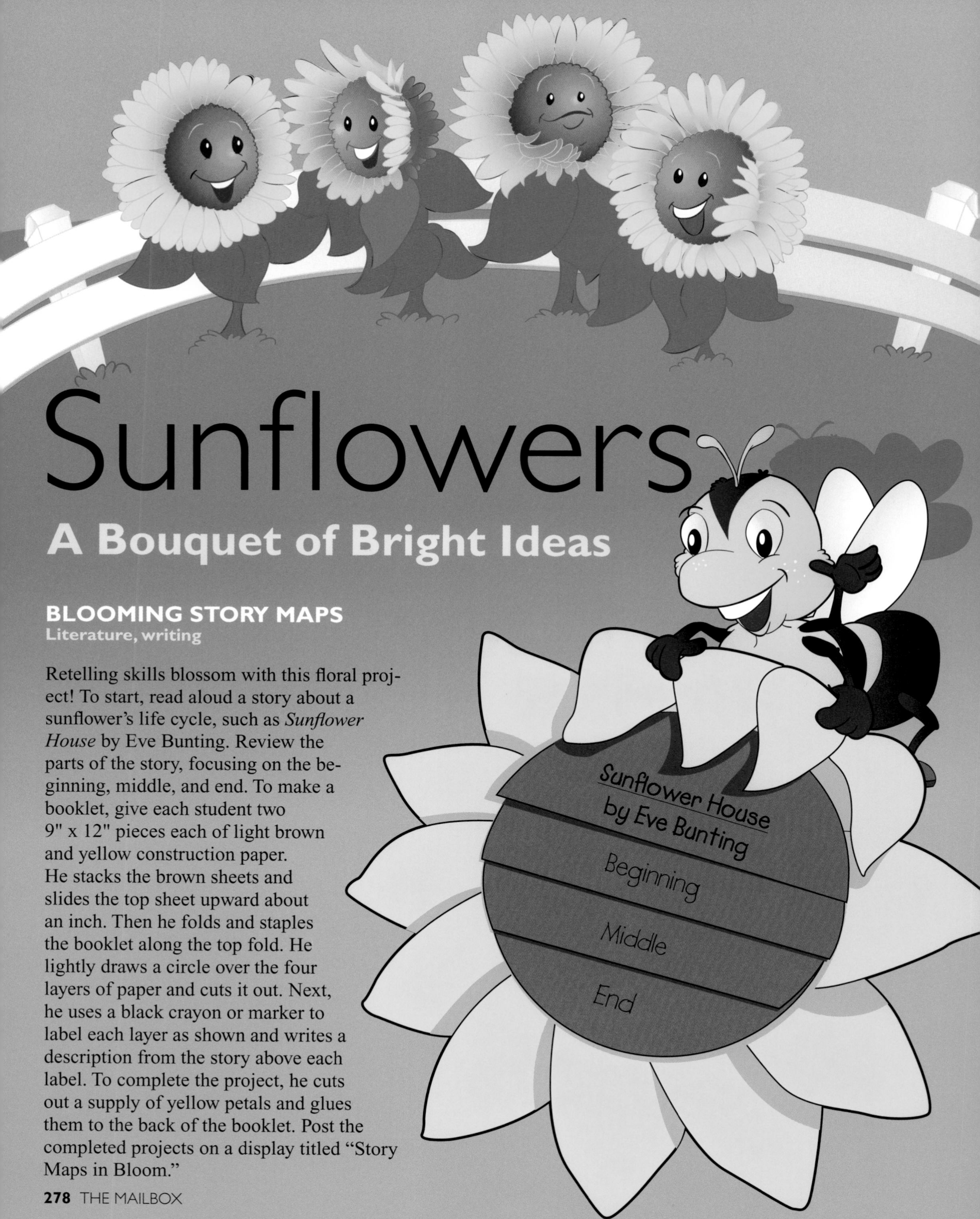

Sunflowers

A Bouquet of Bright Ideas

BLOOMING STORY MAPS

Literature, writing

Retelling skills blossom with this floral project! To start, read aloud a story about a sunflower's life cycle, such as *Sunflower House* by Eve Bunting. Review the parts of the story, focusing on the beginning, middle, and end. To make a booklet, give each student two 9" x 12" pieces each of light brown and yellow construction paper. He stacks the brown sheets and slides the top sheet upward about an inch. Then he folds and staples the booklet along the top fold. He lightly draws a circle over the four layers of paper and cuts it out. Next, he uses a black crayon or marker to label each layer as shown and writes a description from the story above each label. To complete the project, he cuts out a supply of yellow petals and glues them to the back of the booklet. Post the completed projects on a display titled "Story Maps in Bloom."

Watch students' skills flourish with this collection of head-turning ideas.

with ideas by Bonnie Gaynor, Franklin Elementary, Franklin, NJ

GROUPS OF SEEDS
Math

Cultivate fact family knowledge with this small-group activity! Give each child a half sheet of construction paper, a sheet of notebook paper, and some sunflower seeds. She draws a line dividing the paper in half and glues the seeds on each side to resemble a domino. Next, she draws the domino on her notebook paper and writes the resulting fact family. Then she rotates around her group, drawing each group member's domino and recording the matching fact family.

PUNCTUATION POTS
Mechanics

Punctuation skills take root at this center! To begin, copy a supply of the sunflower cards from page 280 on tagboard. Cut them out and write a question, a statement, or an exclamatory sentence on each stem, leaving off the end mark. If desired, lightly color each flower card. To make the cards self-checking, write the missing punctuation on the back of each card. Also program three plastic flowerpots as shown. Put the flower cards in a basket and place it at a center with the pots. A child places each sentence in its matching punctuation pot and then turns the cards over to check his work.

HOW MANY?
Science, math

This investigation helps students estimate and measure with nonstandard units. In advance, place a length of masking tape equal to the height of a sunflower (between three and ten feet) on the floor. Begin by giving each student a piece of drawing paper and an index card. She draws a sunflower on the paper and cuts it out. Next, she estimates how many times she would need to stack her sunflower end to end to equal the length of the tape (or the height of a real sunflower) and writes her estimate on the card. Then she tests her estimate and records the actual number on the card. Have each student tape her index card to the board; then use the data to lead a class discussion of the results.

Sunflower Cards

Use with "Punctuation Pots" on page 279.

Stock Up!

Skill-Based Activities on Turkeys

GUIDEBOOK
Language Arts

This easy reference booklet leads students to a better understanding of punctuation! To start, give each child a copy of page 283. He cuts out the booklet pieces and then glues them together. Next, he cuts out sentences from old magazines or newspapers and glues each under the appropriate heading. Finally, he accordion-folds the booklet and colors the cover. He refers to his completed booklet for punctuation examples as needed during writing activities.

Students will gobble up this inventory of seasonal treats!

with ideas by Mederise Burke, Courthouse Road Elementary, Spotsy, VA

FANCY FEATHERS
Math

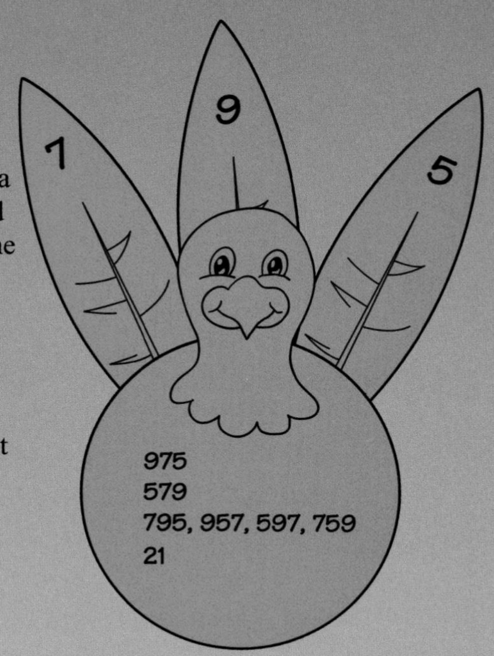

Put place-value practice on display with this simple math manipulative! Make a class supply of the patterns on page 284. Each student cuts out the patterns and writes an assigned number at the top of three feathers. Then she manipulates the feathers to determine the following:

- the largest number she can make with the digits
- the smallest number she can make with the digits
- all other possible numbers she can make with the digits
- the sum of the digits

She writes her answers on the turkey's body. Repeat the activity with a different set of numbers by writing the new digits on the backs of the existing feathers.

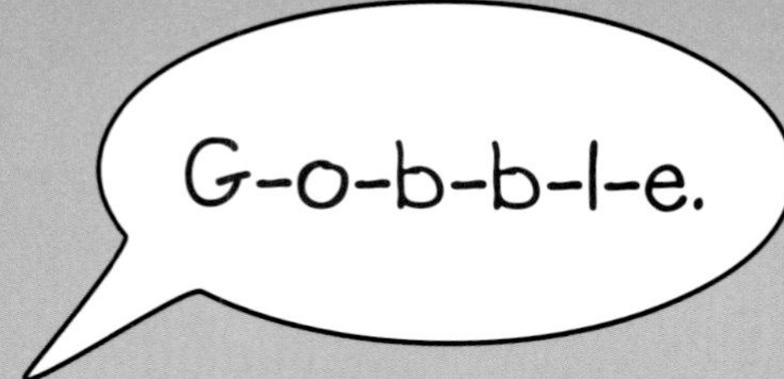

TALKING TURKEY
Spelling

To create this partner game, make two copies of the turkey body pattern on page 284, laminate them, and cut them out. Also make a supply of laminated feather cutouts using the patterns on page 284. (If desired, use craft feathers instead of paper ones.) Then write each spelling word on an index card and place the cards at a center with the cutouts. To begin, Player 1 shuffles the index cards and places them facedown. He selects a card and reads it to his partner. Player 2 spells the word aloud. If he spells it correctly, he places a feather behind his turkey; if incorrect, he places the card at the bottom of the deck and does not choose a feather. Player 2 then repeats the process. Play continues in this manner until all the words have been spelled. The player with more feathers wins.

STRUTTING THEIR STUFF
Positive Reinforcement

Show off your flock's best behavior with this decorative incentive idea! Make an enlarged copy of page 284 on colored paper and cut out the patterns. Program the back of each feather with a different reward, such as extra free time or a special snack. Also label the turkey's body with a behavior you wish the class to demonstrate. Post the turkey's body and place the feathers nearby. Each time students demonstrate the desired behavior, secure a feather to the turkey. When they achieve a predetermined number of feathers, have a student turn one over to reveal the class reward.

Booklet Cover and Pages

Use with "Guidebook" on page 281.

Gobbling Up Punctuation!

Name ____________________

.

A **period** is used at the end of a telling sentence.

?

A **question mark** is used at the end of an asking sentence.

!

An **exclamation point** is used at the end of an exciting sentence.

Glue.

Turkey Body and Feather Patterns

Use with "Fancy Feathers," "Talking Turkey," and "Strutting Their Stuff" on page 282.

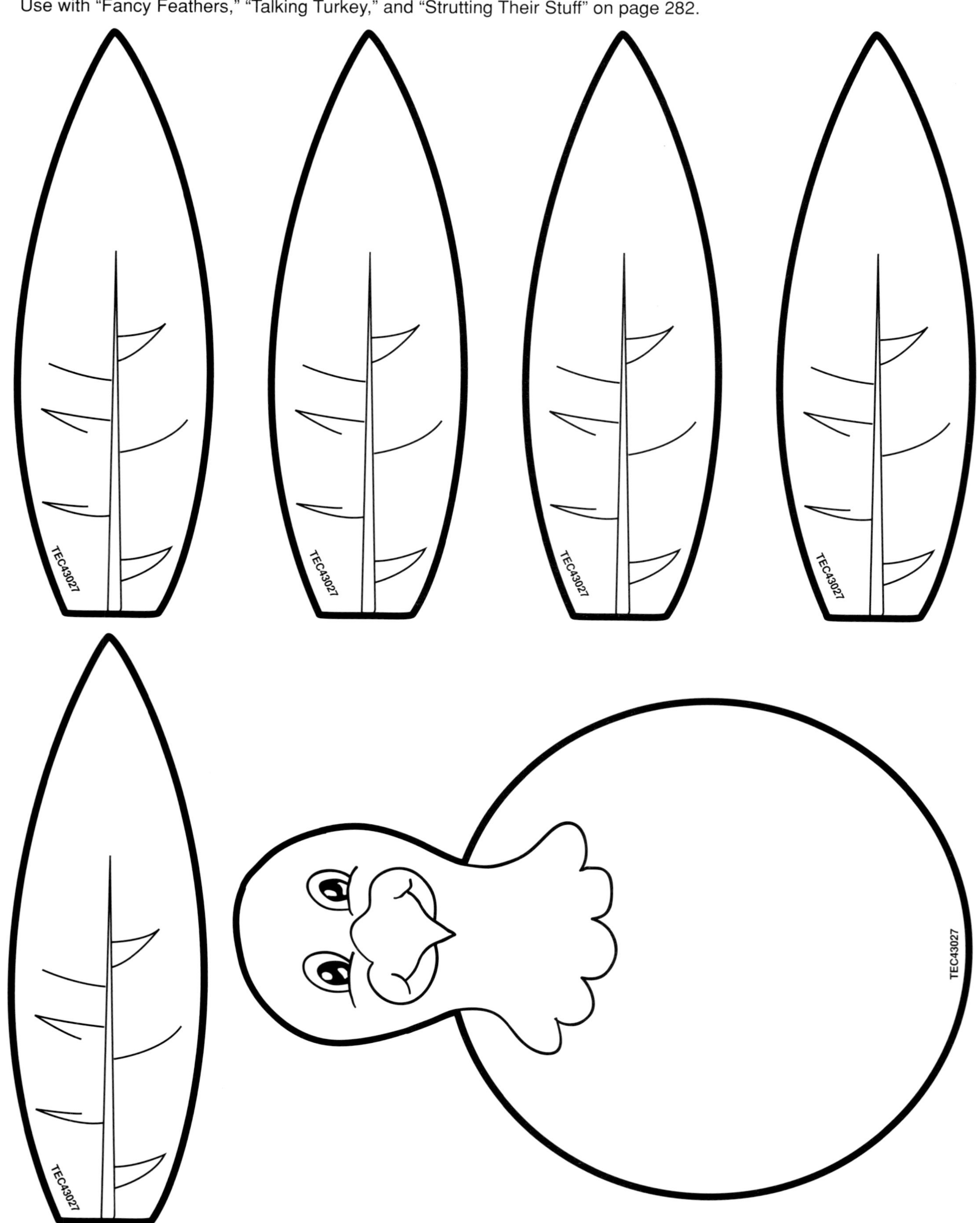

In the Trees

Branching Out With Skill-Based Activities

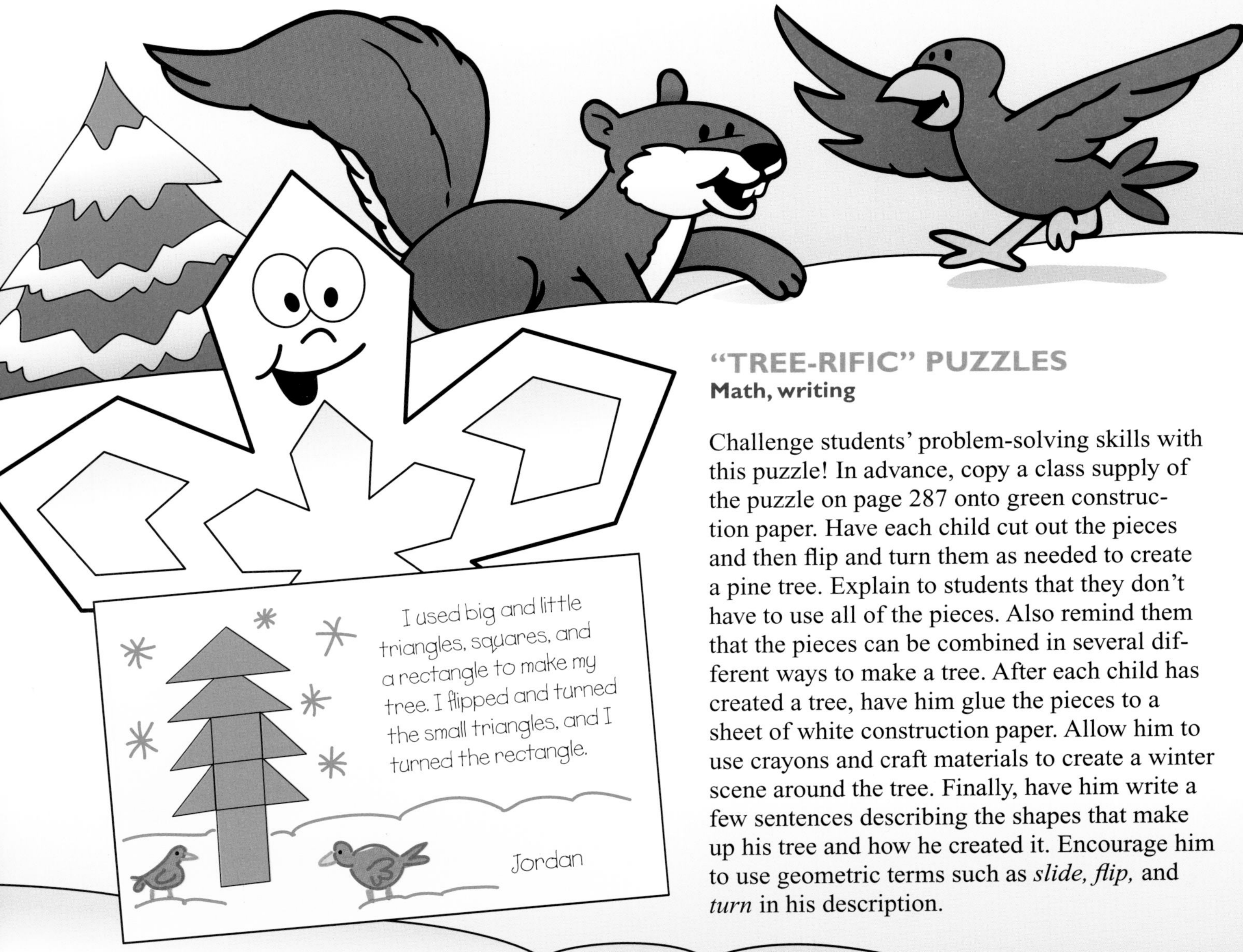

"TREE-RIFIC" PUZZLES

Math, writing

Challenge students' problem-solving skills with this puzzle! In advance, copy a class supply of the puzzle on page 287 onto green construction paper. Have each child cut out the pieces and then flip and turn them as needed to create a pine tree. Explain to students that they don't have to use all of the pieces. Also remind them that the pieces can be combined in several different ways to make a tree. After each child has created a tree, have him glue the pieces to a sheet of white construction paper. Allow him to use crayons and craft materials to create a winter scene around the tree. Finally, have him write a few sentences describing the shapes that make up his tree and how he created it. Encourage him to use geometric terms such as *slide, flip,* and *turn* in his description.

Students will be pining for these activities!

with ideas by Stacie Stone Davis, Lima, NY

FRACTION TREES

Parts of a set

Prepare this center activity by gathering the following items: a class supply of sugar cones, several cans of vanilla frosting tinted green, and a supply of chocolate candies or gumdrops. Also make a class supply of the recording sheet at the bottom of page 287. Place the items at a center along with a plastic knife. To make a fraction tree, a student visits the center and selects a cone. She positions it point side up and uses the knife to cover it with frosting. Then she selects ten candies and gently presses them into the icing. After finishing her tree, she writes on the recording sheet fractions to show the number of same-colored candies. Display the trees on several cookie sheets, and place the matching recording sheet in front of each tree.

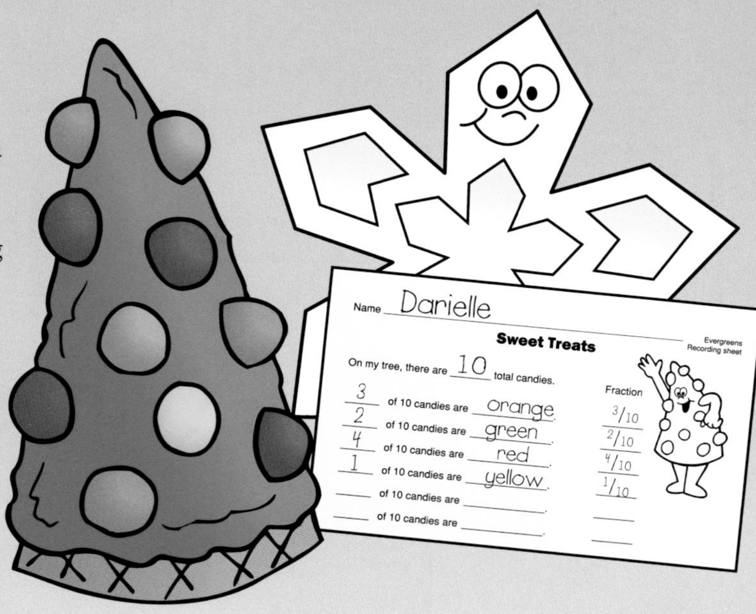

SAME OR DIFFERENT?

Vocabulary

Provide practice with synonyms and antonyms! Make a copy of page 288; then mount the sorting mat and cards on construction paper. Cut out the mat and cards; then program the back of each card for self-checking. A child decides whether each card contains an antonym or a synonym pair and places it on the corresponding space on the mat. After sorting all the cards, he turns them over to check his work.

PICK A PINE

Writing

Strengthen students' persuasive-writing skills with this simple activity! Discuss with students which type of evergreen tree they prefer: real or artificial. Invite them to share their reasons why they prefer one tree over the other. Then have each child write a persuasive paragraph about the type of tree she likes better. Remind her to include three reasons her chosen tree type is better than the other. After editing her paragraph, she copies it onto an evergreen-shaped cutout. Post the paragraphs on a display titled "Pick a Pine."

I like real evergreen trees better than artificial ones. The real trees smell really good. The fake trees smell like plastic. I also like real trees better because each year my family goes together to buy one. My sister and I get to pick it out. My last reason for liking real evergreens is that when Christmas is over, we get to plant our tree in the yard so that we can keep on enjoying it. That's why I like real trees.

Meredith

Puzzle Pieces

Use with "'Tree-rific' Puzzles" on page 285.

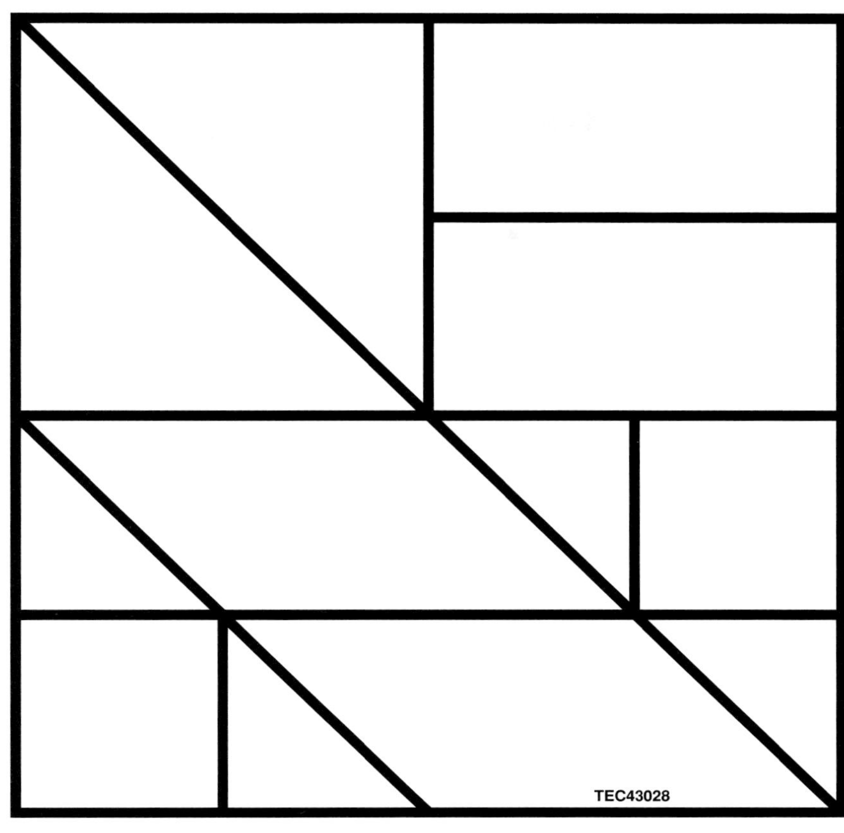

Name ______________________

Evergreens
Recording sheet

Sweet Treats

On my tree, there are ________ total candies.

Fraction

______ of 10 candies are ______________. ________

______ of 10 candies are ______________. ________

______ of 10 candies are ______________. ________

______ of 10 candies are ______________. ________

______ of 10 candies are ______________. ________

______ of 10 candies are ______________. ________

Note to the teacher: Use with "Fraction Trees" on page 286.

Sorting Mat and Cards

Use with "Same or Different?" on page 286.

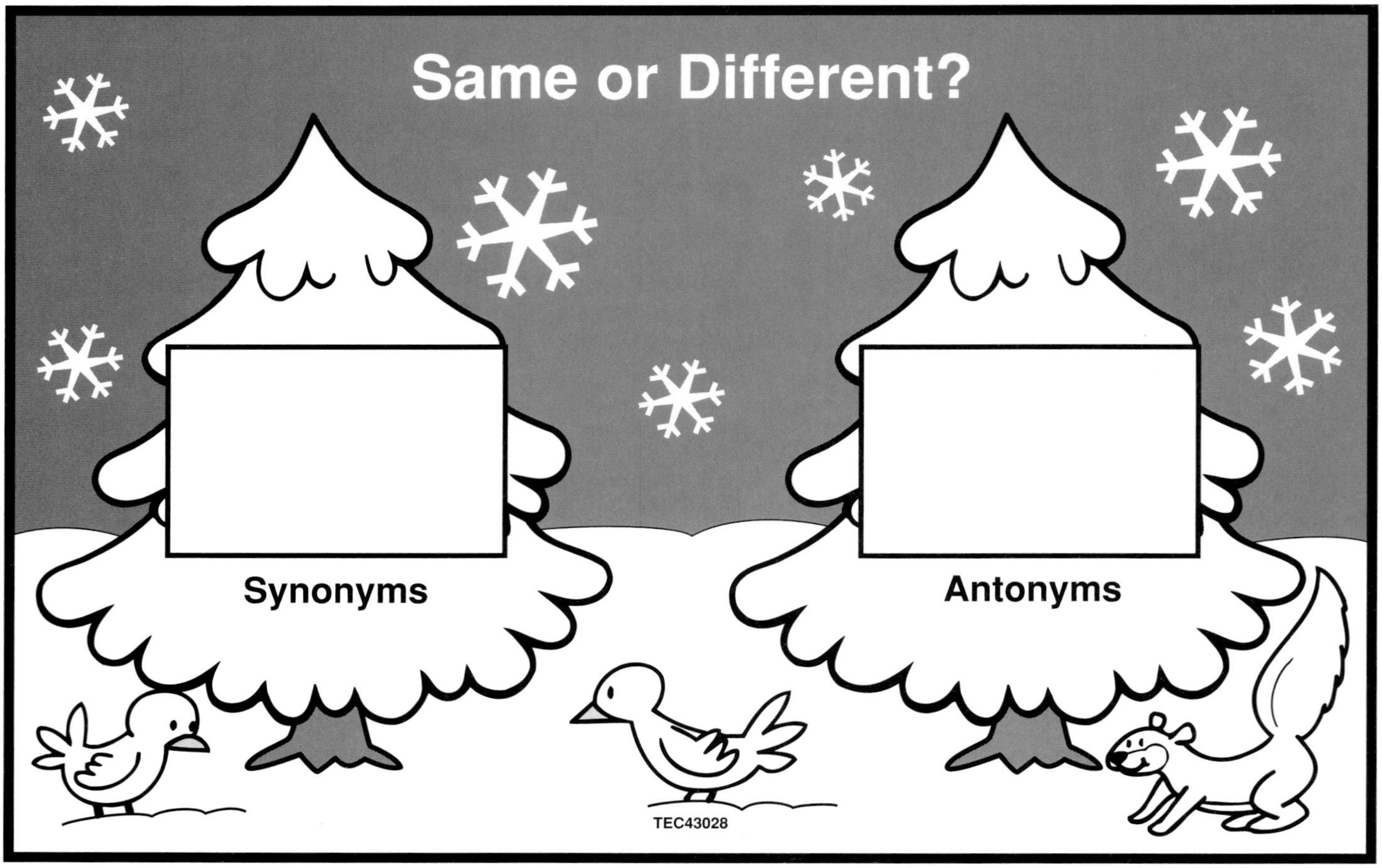

Same or Different?

Synonyms

Antonyms

TEC43028

hot cold TEC43028	open close TEC43028	big large TEC43028	laugh chuckle TEC43028
light dark TEC43028	stop go TEC43028	jump leap TEC43028	angry mad TEC43028
tiny huge TEC43028	front back TEC43028	yell shout TEC43028	alike same TEC43028
before after TEC43028	loud silent TEC43028	happy glad TEC43028	friend pal TEC43028

Name ____________________

Triangle Trees

Write a different digit from 0 to 9 in each circle.
The sum of the three digits should equal the number on the tree.

A. 8

B. 12

C. 17

D. 15

E. 13

F. 10

G. 19

H. 21

All Lit Up

Bright Ideas for Winter Holidays

COLORING PAGES

Holiday characteristics, vocabulary

Combine students' artistic and writing talents with their holiday knowledge. After reviewing characteristics of holidays such as Las Posadas, Hanukkah, and Kwanzaa, divide students into three groups (or groups equal to the number of holidays studied) and assign each group a holiday. Next, give each child a sheet of drawing paper and have him write a short paragraph about his assigned holiday, leaving blanks for key words. If desired, have him make his paper self-checking by writing the missing words on the back. Then he draws the outline of a matching picture like the one shown and traces it with a black marker. When each page is complete, have each child swap papers with a student in another group. Have him read the paragraph, fill in the blanks, and color his partner's paper. Bind the completed pages in a class book.

There are nine candles in a menorah. One candle is called a shammash. It is used to light the other candles. One candle is lit each night for eight nights.

Darius

Students will be all aglow with these curriculum-based activities!

EVERYONE'S INVITED
Writing

Get students in a festive mood with this fun project. After studying winter holidays, have each child choose one and list what she knows about that holiday on a piece of paper. She uses that information to create a party invitation, naming the holiday celebrated, where and when the celebration will occur, and important background information about the celebration. After reviewing her rough draft, she writes the final copy on colored construction paper or holiday-themed stationery. Post the completed invitations on a display titled "Be My Guest..."

Las Posadas | Hanukkah | Kwanzaa

This holiday is held from December 26 to January 1.
A candle is lit each night. There are seven candles.
Children get gifts of books and items that show their backgrounds.
Ron

Kwanzaa

HOLIDAY HELPERS
Research, writing

Put together a seasonal center with the help of your students! In advance, create a sorting mat by dividing a large sheet of construction paper into thirds, as shown, and labeling each section with a holiday name. Next, have each student choose one of the winter holidays listed on the paper sorting mat. Provide access to reference materials and have him research facts about his chosen holiday. Then he uses the facts to write a series of clues about the holiday on an index card. To make the card self-checking, he writes the holiday's name on the back. Place the completed clue cards with the sorting mat at a center. A child reads each clue card and places it below the matching holiday. When all of the cards are sorted, he turns them over to check his work.

WHAT'S THE WORD?
Vocabulary

Review vocabulary terms and their meanings with this easy-to-make game! When your study of winter holidays is complete, have students name words related to a holiday and list them on the board. If desired, list words related to all of the holidays studied. Next, have each child make a grid like the one shown, writing a different word from the board in each box. Then give each student a supply of game markers. To play, state the definition for one of the words on the board. A child looks for the matching word and, if she has it on her paper, covers the word with a marker. Continue in this manner, keeping a list of the words whose definitions you've stated. When a child has three covered words in a row horizontally, vertically, or diagonally, she responds with the name of the holiday or says, "Holidays." After checking her answers with your list, have the students clear their boards and play another round.

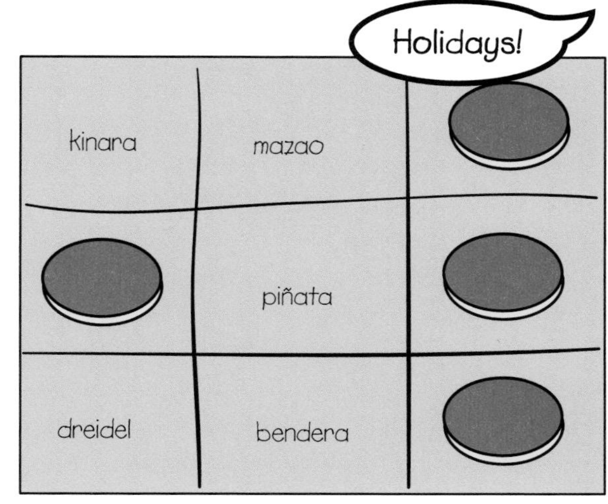

Name ______________________________

Celebrating With Candles

Complete the Venn diagram.
Use the paragraphs to help you.

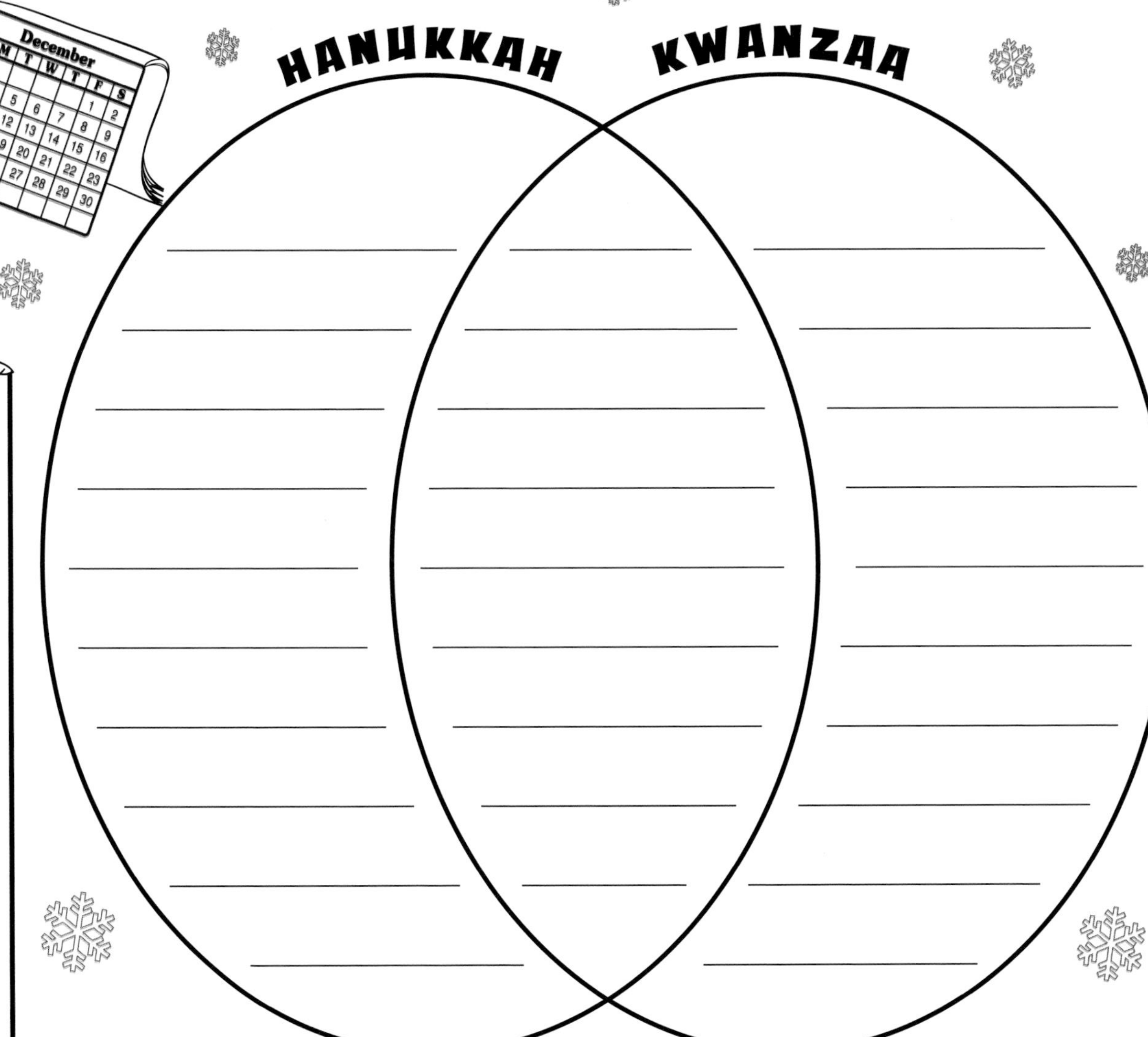

Hanukkah and Kwanzaa are winter holidays. Hanukkah often falls in December. Sometimes it happens in November or January. Hanukkah lasts for eight days. Each night a candle is lit. The candles are held in a menorah.

Kwanzaa starts on December 26 and ends on January 1. Kwanzaa lasts for seven days. A candle is lit each night during Kwanzaa. The candles are held in a kinara. There are three red candles, three green candles, and one black candle.

Jump to It

Cross-Curricular Ideas About Frogs

A LIFE LINE
Science

For this small-group game, give each group a copy of the gameboard on page 295 and a die. Also give each player a game marker and a copy of the sequence strip and game cards on page 296. To play, a student shuffles all the cards together and places them facedown on the gameboard. Player 1 rolls the die and moves his marker the appropriate number of spaces. If he lands on a space labeled "Card," he draws the card from the top of the stack and places it on the matching section of his strip. If he already has a card for that section, he returns the card to the bottom of the stack and his turn is over. Play continues in this manner until one player correctly completes his strip.

Carolyn Burant, St. John Vianney
Brookfield, WI

Move students’ skills forward with this collection of frog-related activities.

DAILY “HOP-PENINGS”

Writing

Have each student write “frog” or draw a small frog in the middle of a piece of paper. Next, have her draw four diagonal lines from the middle of the paper and label a circle by each one as shown. Then have her use her prior knowledge about frogs to complete the web. Provide time for each student to share her ideas with a partner. Then have her write a first-person account of a frog’s day, using realistic information from her web. Remind students to use an attention-grabbing introduction, realistic details, and a strong conclusion. Post the completed stories on a display titled “Daily ‘Hop-penings.’”

Catherine Jones, John Glenn Elementary, San Antonio, TX

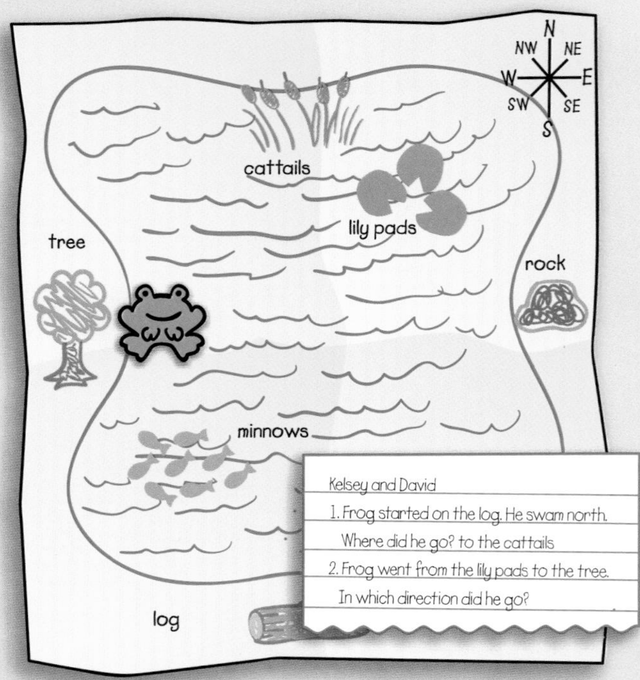

GOING PLACES

Social studies

Explore cardinal and intermediate directions with this easy-to-make map. Begin by having students name parts of a frog’s habitat (log, lily pad, cattail, rock, pond, river, tree) and list their ideas on the board. To make a map, each child folds a piece of drawing paper into fourths, unfolds it, and then draws and labels a habitat site on each crease as shown. Then he draws two more sites in any open area on the paper and adds a compass rose to a corner. Next, the student writes on another sheet of paper four sets of directions, similar to the ones shown and writes the answers on the back. Then he cuts out a paper frog and clips it to the map. Finally, he trades papers with a partner and moves the frog on her map according to the directions. He records his answers on her paper and then turns the paper over to check his work.

adapted from an idea by Carolyn Burant, St. John Vianney, Brookfield, WI

FROGGY FUN

Language arts

To review parts of speech, have each student write a frog-related noun, verb, or adjective on an index card. Also have her write the matching part of speech in parentheses. Collect the cards; then have students stand behind their seats. Read a card aloud without naming the part of speech. Have students croak like a frog if the word is a noun, hop up and down if the word is a verb, or stick out their tongues if the word is an adjective. Choose another card and repeat. Continue as long as desired or until all of the cards have been read. As an alternative, have each student write a frog fact or a frog opinion on an index card. Read a card aloud and have students hop if the statement is a fact or croak if it is an opinion.

adapted from an idea by Amanda Loveland, Stenwood Elementary, Vienna, VA

Check out the computation reproducible on page 296.

Note to the teacher: Use with "A Life Line" on page 293.

Frog Sequence Strip and Game Cards

Use with "A Life Line" on page 293.

5. The gills disappear and the frog moves to land.

TEC43030

4. Then the tadpole grows front legs.

TEC43030

3. The tadpole grows back legs.

TEC43030

2. A tadpole hatches from each egg.

TEC43030

1. Eggs are laid in a big group.

TEC43030

Name ______________________________ Frogs Computation

Fact Finding

Solve the problem to complete each sentence.

1. Frogs usually don't live longer than about six to ________ years in the wild.
   (16 – 8)

2. Many kinds of frogs can jump ________ times their body length.
   (5 x 4)

3. The goliath frog is about _________ inches long and weighs around ________ pounds.
   (6 x 2) (2 + 3 + 2)

4. The tomato frog's tadpoles take about ______ days to change into frogs.
   (100 – 55)

5. A dwarf puddle frog can eat as many as _____________ bugs in one night.
   (25 + 25 + 25 + 25)

Showing Off!

Cross-Curricular Ideas on Dolphins

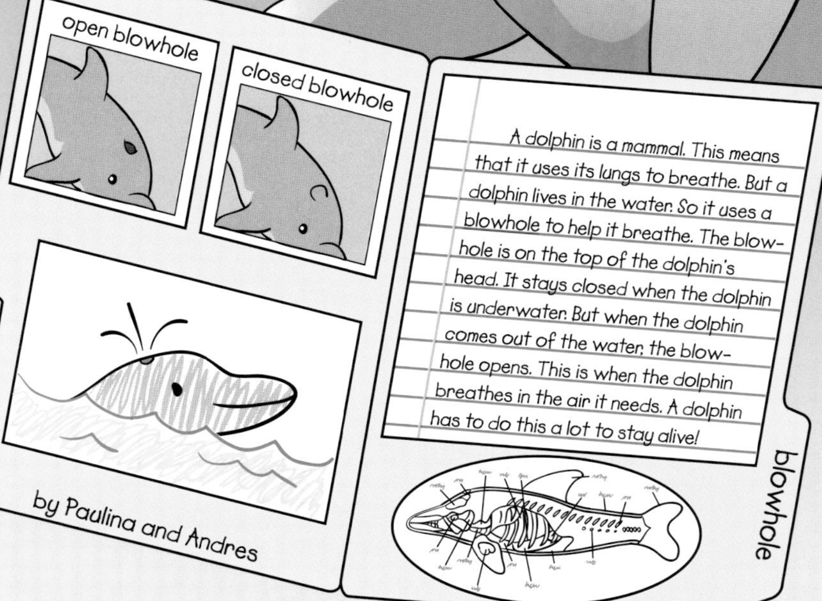

A TERM FOR TWO

Reading, writing, science

Build a better understanding of science vocabulary. Assign each student pair a dolphin-related word. After reviewing research materials, each twosome writes a short report about the meaning of its assigned word and how the word relates to a dolphin. Next, the students write the word on the tab of a file folder and glue the report to one half of the open folder. The partners then glue other related information, such as pictures or diagrams, in the remaining space. After student pairs share their research aloud, place the completed file folders at a science center for independent reading practice.

Make a splash with these integrated ideas!

SUPERSIZE
Math

Just how big is a dolphin? To find out, put your students' multiplication skills to work! Give each student a copy of page 299, a piece of 4½" x 12" construction paper, and a ruler. She cuts out the booklet pages and stacks them in order. Next, she folds the construction paper in half and staples the pages inside to make a booklet. For each booklet page, she measures the dolphin, writes its length in inches, and uses the provided scale to write a multiplication sentence. Then she solves the problem to determine the dolphin's actual length.

After each student has completed her booklet, take the class outside to a flat surface. Put students into small groups and assign each group a different dolphin from the booklet. Have the students work together to measure the dolphin's actual length in feet, marking the length with chalk and labeling the line with the dolphin's name. Provide time for students to visit each measurement to see just how big a dolphin can be!

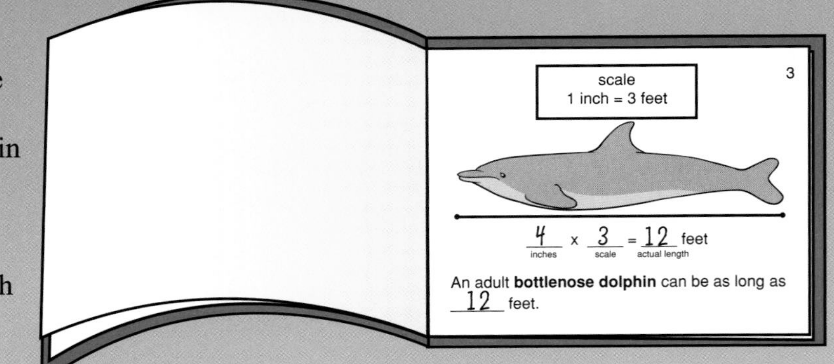

Jean Erickson, Grace Christian Academy, West Allis, WI

June 5, 2007

Dear Dolphin,

Hi! I hope that you are having a fun time swimming in a river or ocean. I bet it is fun to have so much freedom!

I am writing to tell you to stay away from noisy motorboats. Even though they go fast and look interesting, they are dangerous. If you get too close to a boat, you could get really hurt. That would make me sad. So watch out for those motorboats!

Your friend,
Daniel

ON THE LOOKOUT
Science, writing

Show students a can of tuna labeled as dolphin safe. Tell students that fishermen sometimes trap dolphins in their nets while fishing for tuna. Next, lead students in a discussion about other human behaviors that affect the lives of dolphins, such as pollution and boating. Then have each student use what they learned from the discussion to write a letter to a dolphin, telling the dolphin how to stay safe.

Tammy Geiger, Old Bridge Elementary, Woodbridge, VA

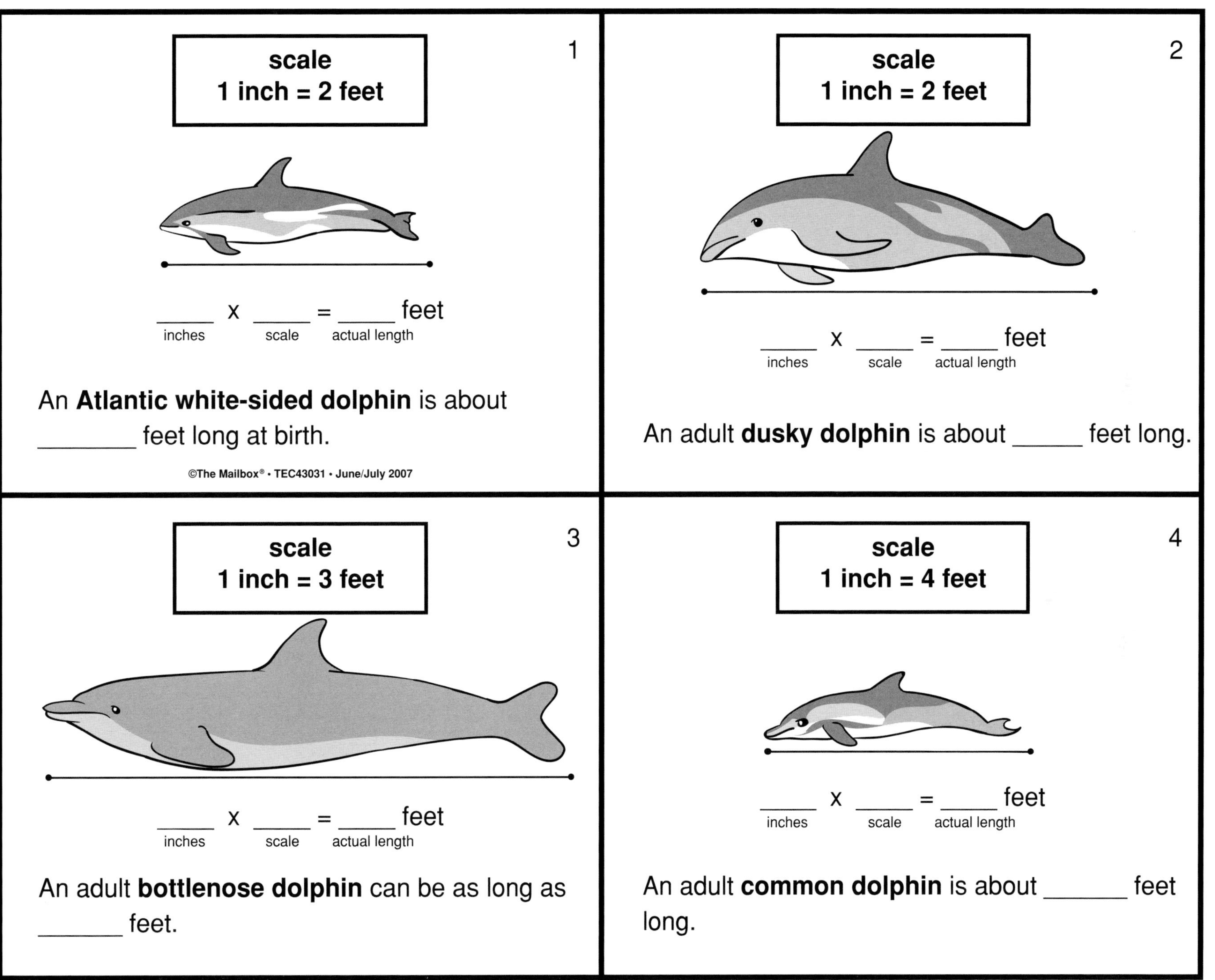
1
scale
1 inch = 2 feet
___ inches X ___ scale = ___ actual length feet
An **Atlantic white-sided dolphin** is about ___ feet long at birth.
©The Mailbox® • TEC43031 • June/July 2007
2
scale
1 inch = 2 feet
___ inches X ___ scale = ___ actual length feet
An adult **dusky dolphin** is about ___ feet long.
3
scale
1 inch = 3 feet
___ inches X ___ scale = ___ actual length feet
An adult **bottlenose dolphin** can be as long as ___ feet.
4
scale
1 inch = 4 feet
___ inches X ___ scale = ___ actual length feet
An adult **common dolphin** is about ___ feet long.

Name ______________________________

Dolphins and People

A dolphin is an animal that lives in rivers or oceans. It has flippers and a blowhole. A dolphin can't smell. But did you know that dolphins and people have a lot in common?

Dolphins and people are both mammals. This means that like us, dolphins have lungs. They are **warm-blooded.** Their bodies stay at about the same temperature whether the water around them is hot or cold. Young dolphins feed on their mothers' milk too.

A dolphin is a mammal, not a fish. It breathes air.

People can talk to each other. Dolphins talk too, but not in the same way. They do not use words. They use a set of sounds called **phonations.** The dolphins' phonations include whistles and clicks.

People live in groups called families. Dolphins live in groups too. Dolphin groups are called **pods.** Some pods might only have 12 dolphins while other pods join together to form herds with as many as 1,000 dolphins!

Follow the directions.

1. Underline the title.
2. Circle the caption.
3. Draw a box around each boldfaced word.

Answer the questions.

4. What text feature does the caption describe? ______________________________
5. What are pods? ______________________________

____

Bonus Box: Use the back of this paper to describe three ways that dolphins and people are alike.

Teacher Resource Units

Just in Time!

Ideas to Support English Language Learners

INTRODUCING…

Use this simple tip to **welcome ELL students and expose them to high-frequency words!** Give each child in your classroom a copy of page 303 and have him complete each sentence starter. Also have the student attach a photo of himself to the page. Each time an ELL student joins your class, make a copy of each page. Bind the copied pages into a book (keep the originals as a master copy), and present the book to the child. As he reads it, he will begin to associate names with faces. He'll also begin to recognize the high-frequency words that appear on each page.

Gina Bittner, Hoff Elementary, Keenesburg, CO

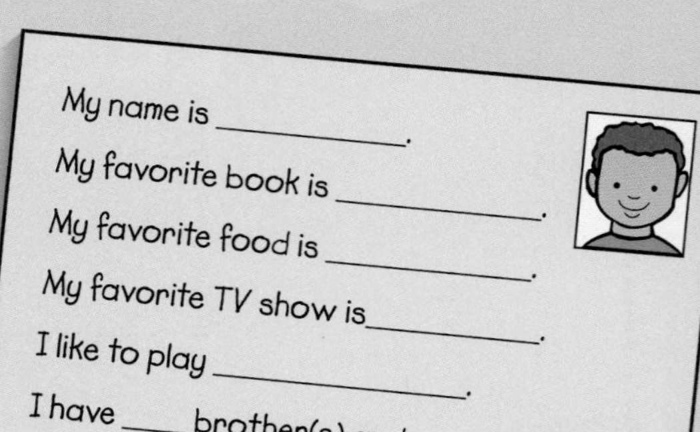

PERSONAL REFERENCE BOOKS

Have your ELL students make their own **picture dictionaries!** Start by giving each child several sheets of blank paper and a stack of magazines. The student labels the first page with a universal topic, such as favorite foods or hobbies. Next, she finds and cuts out several magazine pictures that match that topic. She glues the pictures to the page, leaving space between them as shown. Then she labels each picture with its name in English, asking for help or using a dictionary as needed. Punch holes in each page with a three-hole puncher, and store the pages in a three-ring binder. Have the student create other pages with frequently used topics such as school supplies, sports, household items, and clothing.

adapted from an idea by Carol Ubosi, Oak View Elementary, Burtonsville, MD

MAGIC PHONES

Help ELL students improve their **pronunciation and oral language skills!** Purchase a plastic J-trap (found in hardware stores) for each ELL student, and label it with the child's name and the words *Magic Phone.* Give each student his phone and have him use it whenever he is reading aloud or practicing new vocabulary words. He can hear himself clearly by speaking in just a whisper.

Keri Jackson, Brevard Academy, Brevard, NC

Use with "Introducing..." on page 302.

My name is ________________.

My favorite book is ____________.

My favorite food is ______________.

My favorite TV show is _________________.

I like to play ________________.

I have ______ brother(s) and _______ sister(s).

My name is ________________.

My favorite book is ____________.

My favorite food is ______________.

My favorite TV show is _________________.

I like to play ________________.

I have ______ brother(s) and _______ sister(s).

©The Mailbox • August/September 2006

To the Rescue

Tips for Managing Centers

FLAG YOU DOWN

To **avoid running out of commonly used center reproducibles,** try this easy trick! Place a sticky note like the one shown at the top of a reproducible and secure it with a paper clip. When a student reaches the flagged paper, have her bring it to you. After making more copies, return the marked paper to the bottom of the stack.

adapted from an idea by Jean Gentile, Mechanics Grove School, Mundelein, IL

PERSONAL PASSPORT

Guide students through their learning centers journey with these simple organizers. To start, have each child fold a piece of 12" x 18" blue construction paper in half and label the front as shown. If desired, also have the student glue a photo of himself inside the folder. Laminate the folder for durability. Next, make a copy of page 305 and program it with your current center activities. Then make a class set of the page and have each child put a copy in his folder. After completing each center, he stamps the box next to the center's name and places his work in the folder.

Melanie Land, Glenn Schoenhals Elementary, Southfield, MI

PICTURE-PERFECT ORGANIZATION

Keeping track of students during center time is a snap with this eye-catching chart! To begin, mount a photograph of each child on an index card and laminate it. Also, write each center name on a sentence strip. Display each center label with a small group of photos in a pocket chart. Rotate the cards each day to vary attendance at your centers. Now you, your students, or even a substitute teacher will only need a quick glance to know where each student belongs at center time.

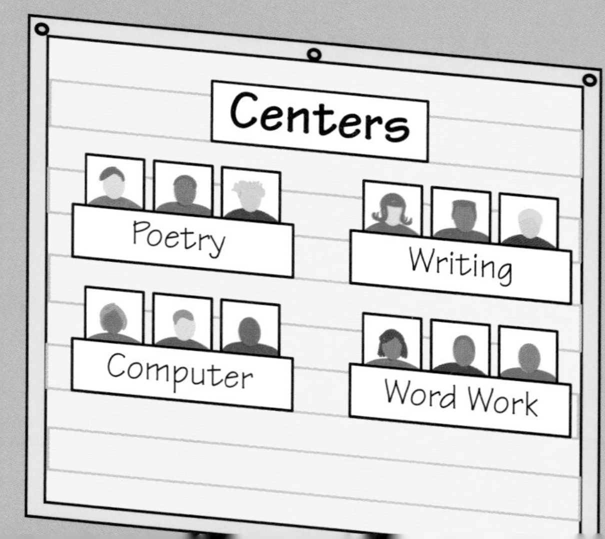

______________________'s Personal Passport

Places to Go

Note to the teacher: Use with "Personal Passport" on page 304.

Bon **Voyage**

Super Student Send-offs

REFRESHING PRESENT

Make a class supply of the water bottle labels on page 308. Sign the labels and cut them apart. Then tape each label around an eight-ounce bottle of water and use a length of ribbon to attach an individual packet of presweetened drink mix. On the last day of school, give a bottle to each student along with a wish for a great vacation!

Leann Schwartz, Ossian Elementary, Ossian, IN

Celebrate another great school year with these creative ideas!

ROUND UP!

For this memorable twist on the game of Hot Potato, have students sit in a circle. Turn on music and give one student a ball. Have the child pass the ball to her left. Have students continue passing the ball around the circle until you stop the music. When the music stops, the child holding the ball shares a memory of the school year. When you turn the music back on, the child passes the ball to her left. Continue playing until every child has shared a special memory!

I remember when we planted trees on the hiking trail. I'm going to go to the trail this summer and see how they are growing.

Denise Knox, New Temple Elementary, South El Monte, CA

AN UNFORGETTABLE YEAR

To remind students of your year together, arrange to have a picture taken with each child. Next, copy onto cardstock a bookmark from page 308 for each student. Then trim each photo so that it fits the space on a bookmark. After gluing each photo in place, sign the bookmark and punch a hole at the top. Finally, tie a ribbon through the hole to make a memento a child will treasure.

Jennifer Cripe, James Bilbray Elementary, Las Vegas, NV

IT'S ALMOST SUMMER!

For these beach-themed activities, have each child bring in a large towel. When you have time to spare during the last few days of school, move the desks aside and have students spread out their towels. Then pick and choose from any of these beachy ideas.

- While each student enjoys a snack of fish-shaped crackers on his beach towel, read aloud books about the ocean or underwater creatures, such as *The Magic School Bus on the Ocean Floor* by Joanna Cole, *Way Down Deep: Strange Ocean Creatures* by Patricia Demuth, and *In the Swim* by Douglas Florian.
- Provide each group of four students with a deck of cards and have the group play Go Fish.
- Toss a plastic beach ball toward students. Then challenge the student who catches the ball to spell a word from one of the year's spelling lists. Have the student toss the ball back to you and repeat as time allows.
- Toss a plastic beach ball toward students. Challenge students to recall addition, subtraction, or multiplication facts as they catch the ball and toss it back to you.
- Have each child decorate a copy of the shell pattern on page 309 to make his own pet seashell. Next, have the student write a story about his seashell. Then have each child share his pet and a story with a small group.

Lauren Levine, Clementon Elementary, Clementon, NJ

Water Bottle Labels

Use with “Refreshing Present” on page 306.

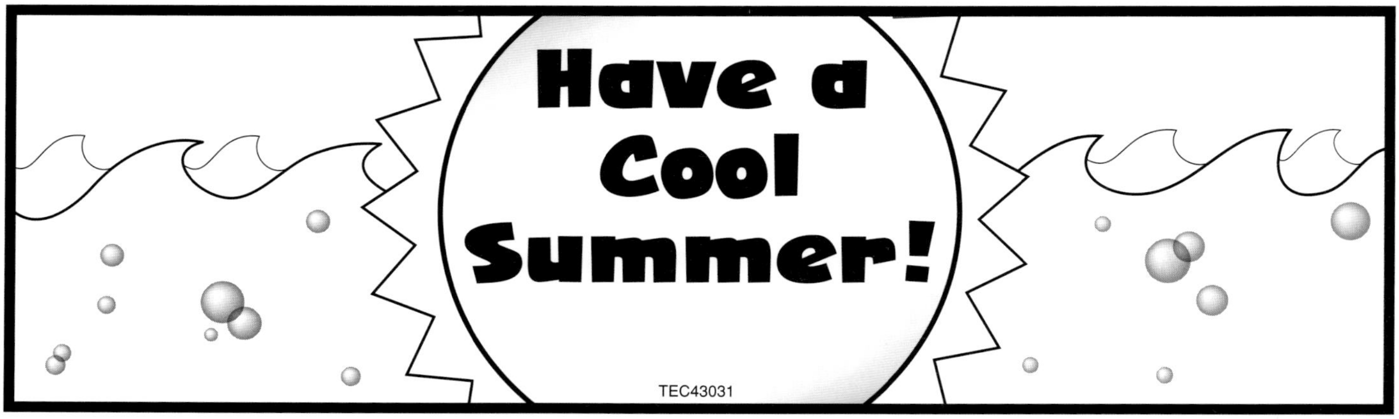

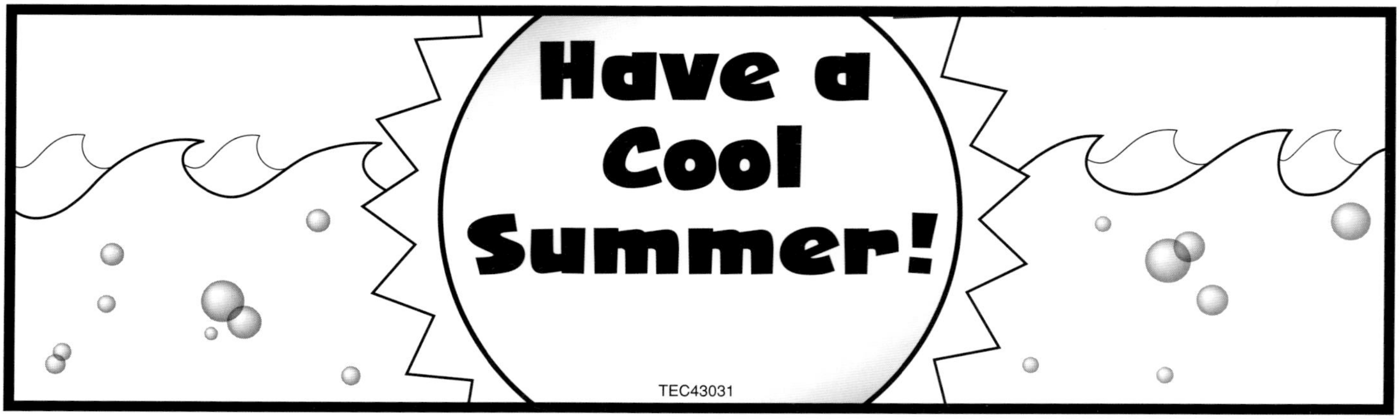

Have a Cool Summer!

TEC43031

Have a Cool Summer!

TEC43031

Bookmarks

Use with “An Unforgettable Year” on page 307.

WHEREVER YOU GO,
WHATEVER YOU DO,
BELIEVE IN YOURSELF!

Your teacher,

TEC43031

WHEREVER YOU GO,
WHATEVER YOU DO,
BELIEVE IN YOURSELF!

Your teacher,

TEC43031

Seashell Pattern

Use with "It's Almost Summer!" on page 307.

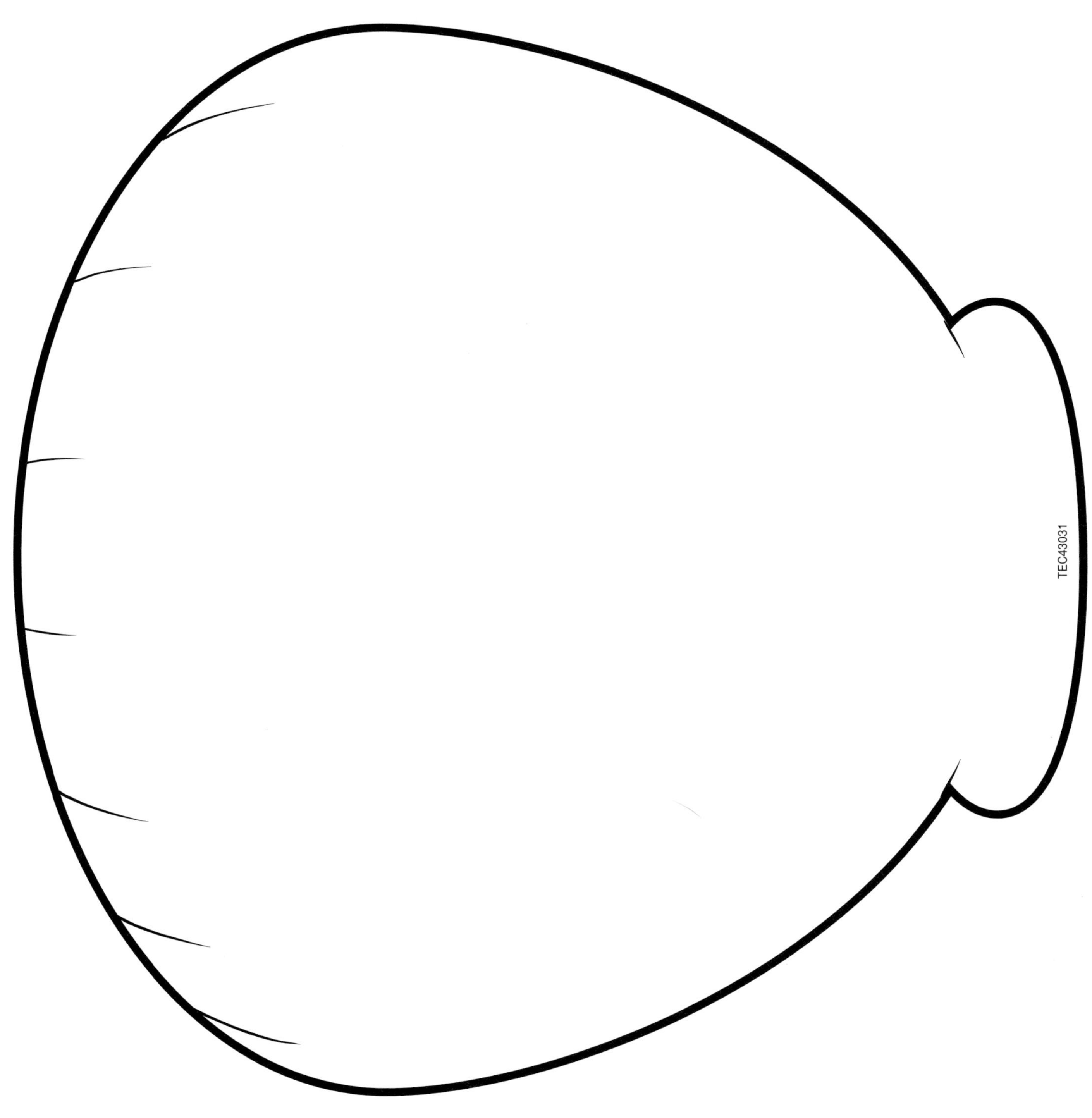

Answer Keys

Page 87

A. 50
B. 90
C. 10
D. 90
E. 40
F. 20
G. 70
H. 60
I. 70
J. 50

Page 94

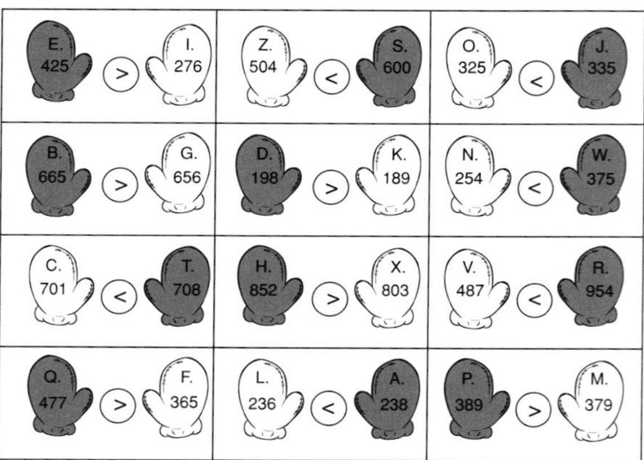

Because his PAWS WERE "BEAR"!

Page 95

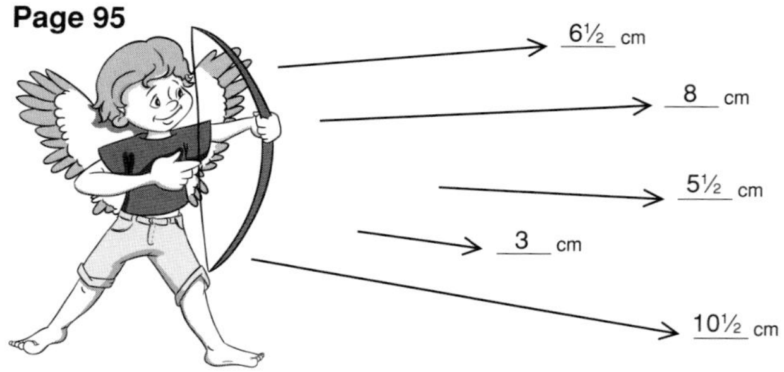

Page 96

	10 lb.	100 lb.	110 lb.	111 lb.	1,000 lb.
Lamar	X	X	X	✓	X
Leon	X	✓	X	X	X
Liam	X	X	✓	X	X
Louie	✓	X	X	X	X
Luke	X	X	X	X	✓

Page 97

A. less than
B. equal to
C. greater than
D. greater than
E. less than
F. less than
G. equal to
H. greater than
I. less than

Page 98

1. 81°F
2. 88°F
3. 91°F
4. 82°F

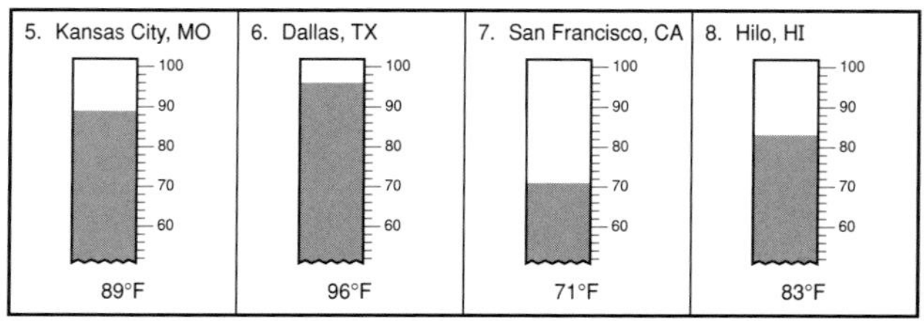

Page 145

Students' reasons will vary.

1. at the beach
2. at school
3. at a roller rink
4. fishing
5. playing basketball
6. putting money in his piggy bank

Page 157

Beginning of Sentences
I
That
While
My

Special Places
Westport
Seaside
Oregon
Pacific
Oceanside

Page 160

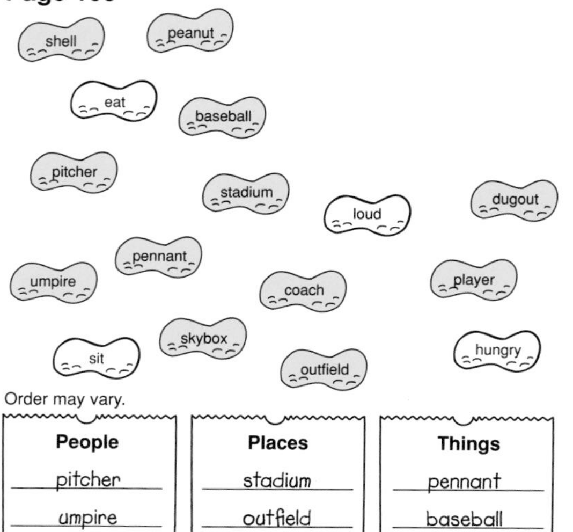

People	Places	Things
pitcher	stadium	pennant
umpire	outfield	baseball
coach	dugout	peanut
player	skybox	shell

Page 162

		Singular	Plural
1.	Tonight's <u>game</u> starts at 7:00.	Ⓝ	B
2.	The two best <u>teams</u> are playing.	M	Ⓔ
3.	The <u>fans</u> are excited.	S	Ⓟ
4.	Some are eating <u>hot dogs</u>.	A	Ⓞ
5.	Others are reading their <u>programs</u>.	F	Ⓝ
6.	The <u>batboy</u> is getting ready.	Ⓔ	K
7.	The <u>mascot</u> is dancing around.	Ⓝ	L
8.	The <u>players</u> are warming up.	P	Ⓔ
9.	A <u>coach</u> is talking.	Ⓗ	C
10.	Some <u>umpires</u> are stretching.	I	Ⓞ
11.	Is everyone in his or her <u>seat</u>?	Ⓐ	Y
12.	Let's play <u>ball</u>!	Ⓛ	D

<u>ON AN "ELEPHONE"</u>!

Page 166

<u>dis</u> agree	bright <u>ness</u>
<u>un</u> happy	care <u>ful</u>
<u>mis or re</u> write	snow <u>y</u>
<u>mis</u> understand	peace <u>ful or able</u>
<u>un</u> sure	enjoy <u>able</u>

Page 180

1. marches
2. terrific
3. strike
4. hopes
5. shouts
6. giant
7. swings
8. crack
9. whacks
10. fly

Abby hits a home run.

Page 184

A. 20, 7, 4, 100
B. 500, 30, 1, 90
C. 200, 800, 600, 8
D. 60, 700, 40, 300

Page 187

A. 3,129
B. 6,704
C. 7,292
D. 5,040
E. 3,790
F. 4,968
G. 5,345
H. 7,770
I. 9,030
J. 1,881

Page 190

A. +, +, –, +
B. –, +, +, +
C. –, –, +, +
D. –, –, +, +
E. –, +, –, –

Page 191

A. 2 + [8] = 10; 3 + [9] = 12; [6] + 3 = 9; [4] + 1 = 5; 8 + [3] = 11; 7 + [6] = 13

B. 9 + [6] = 15; [6] + 6 = 12; [0] + 7 = 7; 3 + [2] = 5; 9 + [1] = 10

C. 2 + [4] = 6; [5] + 8 = 13; [6] + 1 = 7; 8 + [9] = 17; 4 + [4] = 8

D. 3 + [0] = 3; [1] + 7 = 8; [4] + 9 = 13; 8 + [8] = 16

Page 192

	12 − 4 = 8	10 − 5 = 5	8 − 6 = 2	9 − 5 = 4
11 − 7 = 4	4 − 3 = 1	14 − 6 = 8	6 − 4 = 2	3 − 1 = 2
7 − 4 = 3	15 − 8 = 7	11 − 3 = 8	5 − 2 = 3	8 − 7 = 1
13 − 9 = 4	7 − 1 = 6	10 − 8 = 2	12 − 9 = 3	Police Station Precinct 253
8 − 4 = 4	12 − 5 = 7	18 − 9 = 9	9 − 2 = 7	

Page 195

T. 73
A. 996 U. 97 R. 114
M. 318 G. 881 E. 96 O. 199
H. 48 K. 84 N. 168 I. 423 D. 891 E. 102

Because <u>HE</u> couldn't <u>GO UNDER IT</u>!

Page 196

26 − 13 = 13	48 − 29 = 19	276 − 38 = 238	196 − 107 = 89
36 − 19 = 17	55 − 24 = 31	302 − 111 = 191	78 − 26 = 52
296 − 135 = 161	556 − 448 = 108	823 − 351 = 472	87 − 32 = 55
943 − 796 = 147	290 − 188 = 102	77 − 29 = 48	346 − 137 = 209

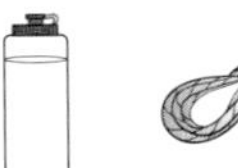
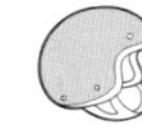
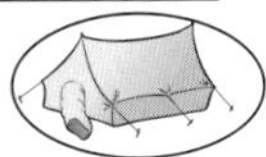

Page 201

R. 41 + 37 = 78	L. 69 − 15 = 54	I. 22 + 65 = 87	
U. 99 − 76 = 23	D. 34 + 43 = 77	P. 52 + 36 = 88	A. 87 − 22 = 65
A. 75 + 14 = 89	E. 83 − 72 = 11	N. 66 − 31 = 35	R. 41 + 11 = 52
E. 12 + 4 = 16	Y. 60 + 36 = 96	A. 96 − 22 = 74	G. 78 − 37 = 41

DURING A LEAP YEAR.

Page 202

Kalani: 17 + 3[2] = [4]9

Kalil: 45 + [2]1 = 6[6]

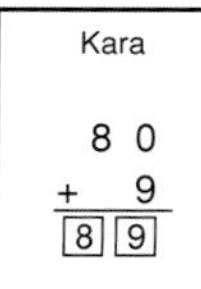

Karl: 24 + 6[4] = [8]8

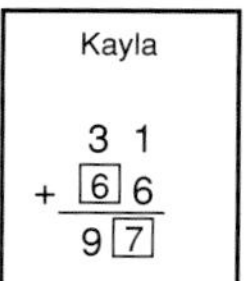

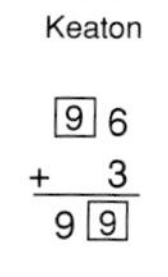

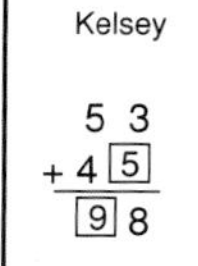

Kevin: 72 + [2]3 = 9[5]

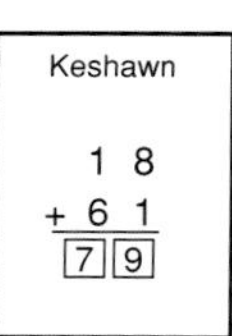

Kyle: 34 + 1[2] = [4]6

Keaton
Kyle

Page 207

A. 2 + 2 + 2 = 6
3 x 2 = 6

B. 3 + 3 + 3 + 3 = 12
4 x 3 = 12

C. 1 + 1 + 1 + 1 + 1 = 5
5 x 1 = 5

D. 4 + 4 = 8
2 x 4 = 8

E. 3 + 3 = 6
2 x 3 = 6

F. 5 + 5 + 5 = 15
3 x 5 = 15

Page 211

A. 44	B. 34
C. 50	D. 99
E. 15	F. 40
G. 67	H. 41
I. 55	J. 68
K. 39	L. 95

Page 212

A. 3	B. 6	C. 7	D. 5
E. 7	F. 9	G. 8	H. 1
I. 2	J. 4	K. 3	L. 8
M. 9	N. 9	O. 8	P. 9
Q. 2	R. 4		
S. 5			
T. 6			

Page 217

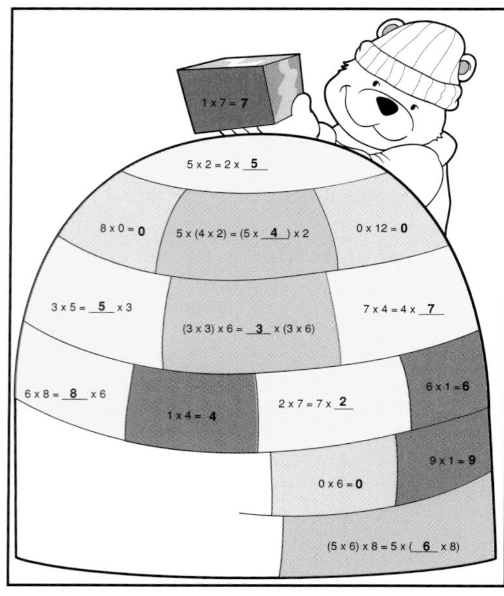

Page 220

Number of Farm Animals	
Cows	◫◫
Horses	◫◫◫◫◫◫◫◫◫◫
Pigs	◫◫◫◫◫◫◫▯
Sheep	◫◫◫◫
Goats	◫◫◫◫◫▯

Key ◫ = 2 animals

1. 15
2. 8
3. goats, 3
4. 4
5. 24
6. 58

Page 221

1. 3 pounds
2. 14 pounds
3. b
4. 7 pounds
5. a sheep and a goat
6. 10 pounds

Page 225

	Bonus Box:
A. 55¢	A. $0.55
B. 26¢	B. $0.26
C. 31¢	C. $0.31
D. 47¢	D. $0.47
E. 18¢	E. $0.18
F. 93¢	F. $0.93
G. 52¢	G. $0.52
H. 70¢	H. $0.70

Page 229

A.

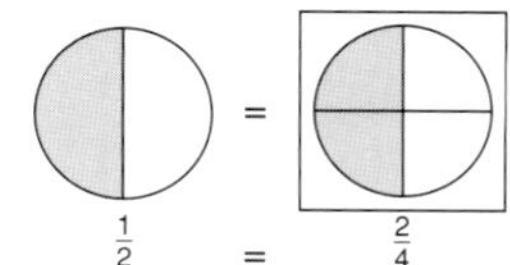

$\frac{1}{2} = \frac{2}{4}$

B.

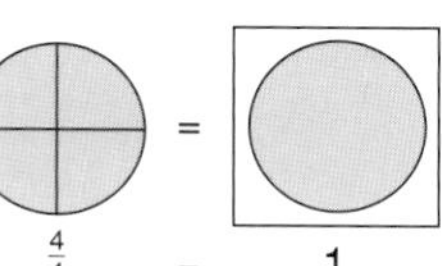

$\frac{4}{4} = 1$

C.

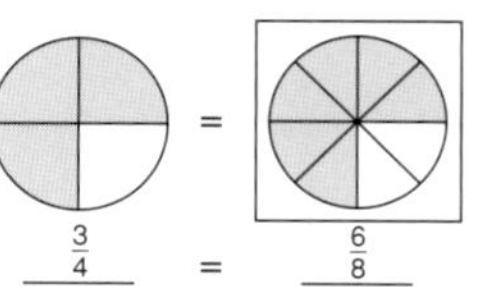

$\frac{3}{4} = \frac{6}{8}$

D.

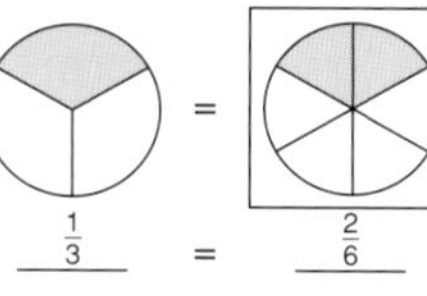

$\frac{1}{3} = \frac{2}{6}$

E.

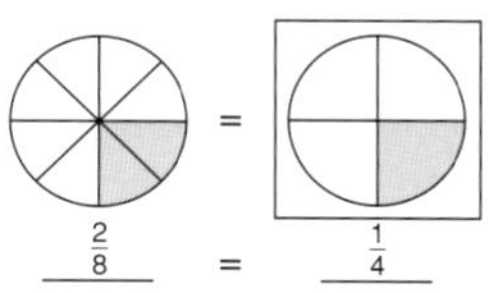

$\frac{2}{8} = \frac{1}{4}$

F.

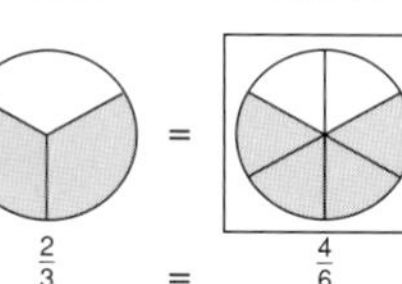

$\frac{2}{3} = \frac{4}{6}$

Page 230

A. $\frac{2}{3}$ = sprinkles
$\frac{1}{3}$ = no sprinkles

B. $\frac{5}{6}$ = sprinkles
$\frac{1}{6}$ = no sprinkles

C. $\frac{1}{4}$ = icing
$\frac{3}{4}$ = no icing

D. $\frac{6}{8}$ = icing
$\frac{2}{8}$ = no icing

E. $\frac{3}{5}$ = sprinkles
$\frac{2}{5}$ = no sprinkles

F. $\frac{10}{10}$ = icing
$\frac{0}{10}$ = no icing

Page 234

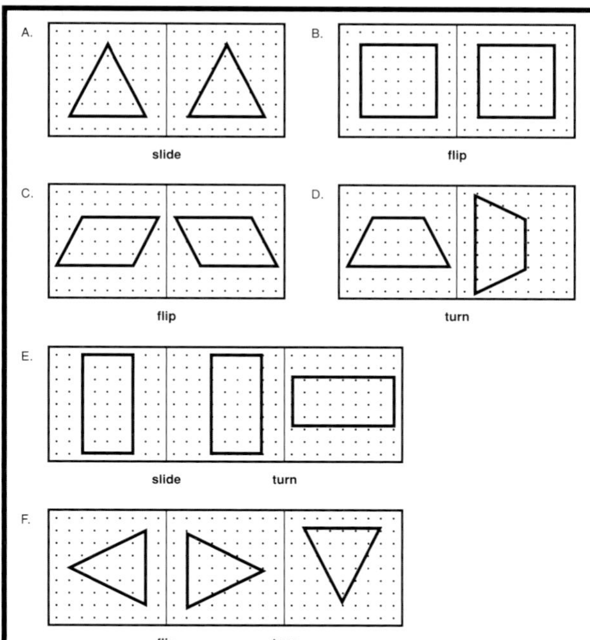

Page 238

A. girls 14, boys 11
B. Wally 9, Wanda 3
C. Sandy 12, Seth 8
D. Chris 9, Cam 7
E. Tony 10, Ted 3

Page 243

1. solid
2. atoms
3. volume
4. gas
5. matter
6. mass
7. physical properties
8. liquid

Page 257

1. polar bear
2. orangutan
3. giraffe
4. camel
5. butterfly fish

Page 272

Answers may vary.

1. It's a plant found in ponds. Its leaves and flowers float on the water. Its stem and roots are underwater.
2. They provide animals with food and places to hide.
3. They pollinate the flowers.
4. When too many water lilies grow, they block sunlight and air from reaching underwater pond life.

Page 289

Answers will vary. Possible answers are shown.

A. 1, 2, 5; 1, 3, 4
B. 1, 9, 2; 1, 3, 8; 1, 4, 7; 1, 5, 6; 2, 4, 6; 2, 3, 7; 3, 4, 5
C. 1, 9, 7; 2, 7, 8; 2, 9, 6; 3, 6, 8; 4, 6, 7; 4, 8, 5; 5, 3, 9
D. 1, 6, 8; 1, 5, 9; 2, 9, 4; 2, 8, 5; 2, 6, 7; 3, 4, 8; 3, 5, 7; 4, 6, 5
E. 1, 3, 9; 1, 4, 8; 1, 5, 7; 2, 3, 8; 2, 4, 7; 2, 5, 6; 3, 4, 6
F. 1, 2, 7; 1, 3, 6; 1, 4, 5; 2, 3, 5
G. 2, 8, 9; 3, 7, 9; 4, 7, 8; 4, 6, 9; 5, 6, 8
H. 4, 9, 8; 5, 9, 7; 4, 8, 9

Page 292

Answers may vary.

Hanukkah

It can be in November, December, or January. It lasts for eight days. The candles are held in a menorah.

Both are holidays. Both use candles. A candle is lit each night.

Kwanzaa

It always lasts from December 26 to January 1. It lasts for seven days. The candles are held in a kinara.

Page 296

1. 8
2. 20
3. 12, 7
4. 45
5. 100

Page 298

1. 2 x 2 = 4
2. 3 x 2 = 6
3. 4 x 3 = 12
4. 2 x 4 = 8

Page 300

Dolphins and People

A dolphin is an animal that lives in rivers or oceans. It has flippers and a blowhole. A dolphin can't smell. But did you know that dolphins and people have a lot in common?

Dolphins and people are both mammals. This means that like us, dolphins have lungs. They are **warm-blooded**. Their bodies stay at about the same temperature whether the water around them is hot or cold. Young dolphins feed on their mothers' milk too.

People can talk to each other. Dolphins talk too, but not in the same way. They do not use words. They use a set of sounds called **phonations**. The dolphins' phonations include whistles and clicks.

People live in groups called families. Dolphins live in groups too. Dolphin groups are called **pods**. Some pods might only have 12 dolphins while other pods join together to form herds with as many as 1,000 dolphins!

4. the picture
5. dolphin groups

Bonus Box: Answers will vary. Possible answers include the following: Both dolphins and people are mammals. Both dolphins and people have ways to talk. Both dolphins and people live in groups.

INDEX

ISBN-13: 978-156234815-1
ISBN-10: 156234815-9